DISCARD

The Making of India

A
Historical
Survey

Ranbir Vohra

Second Edition

M.E. Sharpe

Armonk, New York
London, England

Library of Congress Cataloging-in-Publication Data

Vohra, Ranbir.
  The making of India : a historical survey / Ranbir Vohra—2nd ed.
    p. cm.
  Includes bibliographical references and index.
  ISBN 0-7656-0711-5 (cloth: alk. paper)
  ISBN 0-7656-0712-3 (paper: alk. paper)
  1. India—History. I. Title

DS436.V6 2001
954—dc21   00-044657
                                                             CIP

Printed in the United States of America

The paper used in this publication meets the minimum requirements of
American National Standard for Information Sciences
Permanence of Paper for Printed Library Materials,
ANSI Z 39.48-1984.

BM (c)   10   9   8   7   6   5   4   3   2   1
BM (p)   10   9   8   7   6   5   4   3   2   1

This book is dedicated to my maternal grandfather, Chintram Thapar, who spent years in British jails as a pacifist Gandhian fighting for India's freedom; and to my maternal uncle, Sukhdev, who, at the age of twenty-four, was hanged to death by the British as a militant nationalist revolutionary also fighting for India's freedom; and to my family, who has served independent India with honesty and devotion.

Contents

Preface to the Second Edition

As I mentioned in the Preface to the first edition, this book had been written to explain India, a bewilderingly complex country, to nonspecialist students and educated lay readers in America. It is gratifying to note that the work has been so well-received that there is a call for a second edition.

At the time when the first edition appeared, Indian politics were in serious disarray: the rapid decline of the grand old Congress Party—that had ruled independent India for forty-five of its first fifty years—had made the national political system alarmingly unstable. As a result of this instability, several governments fell in quick succession, and the nation had to bear the burden of a number of unscheduled parliamentary elections. The possibility that the newly emerging Hindu nationalist Bharatiya Janata Party (BJP) might come to fill the void created by the failing Congress Party was very disturbing to Western and Westernized Indian analysts who viewed the BJP as an undemocratic, communal party out to destroy Indian democracy. To add to the fears of these liberal intellectuals, the Mandalization* of Indian politics had brought the backward—mostly illiterate—castes and classes into the mainstream of Indian politics. The phenomenon of low-caste-based parties and their leaders wresting power from the upper castes in the states was appalling because it obviously distorted Westminster-style democracy. Regardless of the critics, this ingenious variant in the Indian politics was there to stay; it had given the backward classes (that formed over half the population) a voice, and they wanted it to be heard at the national level, too.

The second edition takes the story of India to 2000. The years that lapsed between the two volumes are pivotal because it was during this period that Indian polity shifted course. Only time will tell whether the Congress will revitalize itself

---

*Mandal was the chairman of a commission that added reservation quotas for Other Backward Castes to those already enjoyed by the Scheduled Castes and the Scheduled Tribes. Mandal's recommendations came into force in 1993 and raised the reservation quotas to 50 percent in education institutions, government offices, and legislative bodies (see Chapter 9).

and reemerge as a major player on the national scene. Even if it does, the days of the Congress's dominance of the political scene are over. More importantly, despite the fears of the Westernized critics, the BJP *has* emerged as the leading party in the country, and this makes it necessary to reexamine the nature of *secularism* and *communalism* in the purely Indian context. Similarly, the *casteism* condemned by theorists of liberal democracy has acquired a new significance in the political scene and, therefore, also needs to be viewed afresh against the backdrop of the current paradigmatic shift.

The BJP's role in these developments has been critical. As of this writing (January 2000), the BJP has brought back stability to central politics and, by collaborating with the new local and parochial parties, given a novel orientation to political discourse. The BJP had, indeed, exploited Hindu sentiment to establish itself as a political party, but the apprehension—expressed mostly by analysts using Western theories of democracy—that the BJP was a "fundamentalist" party that had the potential to demolish Indian democracy was misplaced. This viewpoint was, perhaps, best expressed in the United States by the well-known India expert A.M. Rosenthal, who, writing for the *New York Times*, said that the "real power" of the BJP was in the hands of "killers and pro-Nazis."*

I had suggested in the first edition that if the BJP-connected developments were viewed in the context of the multifaceted interaction between the Indian tradition and the forces of change and modernity, the critics would be proven wrong. And so it actually turned out to be. The BJP government in 1996 (when the first edition went to press) had lasted a mere thirteen days and its future looked bleak. But, contrary to the projections of Westernized analysts, the BJP went on to gain greater and greater political strength and respectability: It formed a minority government in 1998 that was in power for thirteen months, and then, in the 1999 general elections, the BJP-led National Democratic Alliance (NDA) won a resounding victory that has given it a mandate to rule for a full five-year term.

To appreciate the true character of the BJP success, two things have to be kept in mind: One, that the 1996, 1998, and 1999 general elections were among the most fair and peaceful elections held since 1947, and that the BJP had been elected democratically by a people who were not driven by hysteria—it does not seem quite equitable to dub the BJP an undemocratic, fascist, communal party. Two, that many of the regional caste-based parties, having tried and failed to form a national government, came to the conclusion that, until they could mobilize the strength needed to achieve that goal, they could project themselves at the center by allying with the BJP; the BJP captured the spirit of this new political mood and established the NDA. Instead of being looked upon as a destroyer of democracy, the BJP's actions can be considered to have made Indian democracy more mass-based and creatively vibrant.

These developments of the last few years raise several questions: Why did the

---

*A.M. Rosenthal, "Facing India's Danger," *New York Times Op-Ed*, May 17, 1996.

so-called secular Congress Party—that had long been considered the sole articulator of the "common people's" aspirations—decline so precipitously? How did the BJP, a self-declared Hindu party, manage to gain the trust of the nation and of so many "secular" political parties that it could form the NDA government? Does the emergence of the lower castes into the mainstream of Indian politics represent a diminution of democracy or is it leading the country to a new, unifying national identity? What are the weaknesses in the new Indian democracy? In which direction will it take India's economic development?

This edition concludes with an examination of these, and other, issues to provide a sharper understanding of the perplexing religion-based and caste-based politics that are currently in the process of changing the nature of India's polity.

Ranbir Vohra
January 2000

Preface

I came from India to the United States in 1964 and have been associated with the American academe ever since. After gaining my doctorate in East Asian history at Harvard, I have had the privilege of teaching at various prestigious institutions of higher learning, including Harvard University, Amherst College, and Trinity College. My working life in America has been rewarding, and my contacts with my colleagues inside and outside my field of specialization have enriched my understanding of the world we live in. But one thing that has never failed to surprise me is my American colleagues' limited understanding of Indian affairs. The general public, of course, is even less informed.

Unfortunately, since the subject is neglected in the American school system, much of what Americans know about India comes from the media, which tend to report only the eye-catching negative events. As a result, while most Americans have heard of wife burning, the Hindu-Muslim communal riots over the Ayodhya Temple-Mosque issue, insurgency in Kashmir (an American kidnapped by a terrorist Kashmiri group made headlines in America), and so on, few have a meaningful understanding of topics such as the working of the Indian democratic system, the political parties, or even the reasons for the tensions in Indo–U.S. relations. Since 1991, when India launched its economic reform program and opened its doors to foreign investment and joint ventures, American interest in the country has increased noticeably. I hope this will lead to a demand for better sources of information on India.

Many of my colleagues from various disciplines, who share my keen interest in India and with whom I have spent hours discussing developments in that country, agreed with me that there was an acute need for a good, single-volume work on India that would provide the educated generalist and students with a readable overview of Indian history—a work that conveyed the complexity of India's civilization and an integrated view of her political, cultural, and economic development without making the subject abstruse. These colleagues persuaded me to undertake this difficult project, and I must thank them for their constant encouragement. I would especially like to thank Professors Clinton Bailey (Tel Aviv University), Fred Drake (University of Massachusetts, Amherst), Ellison Findly (Trinity College), and Meera Vishwanathan (Brown University) for reading my manuscript and offering invaluable comments and suggestions.

I would also like to express my profound gratitude to my brother, Dharam Bir Vohra, recipient of a national award for his book, *History of the Indian Freedom Movement,* for spending so much of his valuable time in going through the manuscript with such loving care. My wife, Meena, who hardly saw me for days on end even though I worked at home, may have lost her patience on occasion but never her enthusiasm for the project. She and our daughter, Carin, were the most critical of all those who read the manuscript; they put themselves in the position of an uninformed American and found so many passages that needed rewriting that I was often driven to despair. I am obliged to them, too.

Lastly, a word of thanks to Stephen Dalphin, Executive Editor at M.E. Sharpe. No one can ask for a more sympathetic and understanding editor.

Ranbir Vohra
August 1996
Trinity College
Hartford, Connecticut

Part I
Pre-Modern India
From Pre-History to 1857

1

Traditional India

An Overview

Indian civilization is noted for its historical continuity and for the fact that elements of Indian tradition are so firmly embedded in the country's culture that they persist in influencing contemporary social and political behavior. One of the best ways to comprehend the distinctive nature of the Indian traditional culture is to make a brief* comparison between the great traditions of India and China[†] and their historical development. Although the two countries have equally long and continuous civilizations, the Chinese civilization offers a sharp contrast to that of the subcontinent—a contrast that accentuates and illuminates the uniqueness of India's traditional culture.

The Chinese traditional ideology, popularly associated with Confucianism, is *sociopolitical* in nature, and it contributed to the making of a powerful, unified state and a self-confident, homogeneous society.[‡] The vitality of the Indian tradition, on the other hand, lies in the *socioreligious* developments identified with ideas and practices connected with Hinduism.[§] India, unlike China, never developed a

---

*Brevity, by its very nature, implies that the coverage is not comprehensive and that large chunks of information have been reduced to broad generalizations. The development of Hinduism is discussed in greater detail in the next chapter.

[†]When we refer to China we mean China proper—the area that does not include the homelands of the non-Chinese (technically, non-Han) peoples, such as Tibet, Mongolia, and Xinjiang.

[‡]Although *homogeneous* is a relative term, it is worth noting that 94 percent of the Chinese belong to the Han race and are unified not only by their common ideology but by a single written language. In our context, the term *Chinese* will refer only to the Han people.

[§]*Hinduism* is in many ways a confusing and a nebulous term (see discussion later in the chapter) and is being used here in its popular concept, which relates it to the manner in which Vedic-Brahmanical values have influenced Indian society and the caste system.

strong sense of political and social unity, and Indians are not a homogeneous people, but Hinduism contributed to the making of a social system that was held together by the strength of its religious philosophy and its unique caste structure. The difference between the two "unities" is that today there is no Chinese who does not consider himself as belonging to a single state; even Chinese in Taiwan do not look upon themselves as a separate entity (most of them are, indeed, looking forward to being reunited with the motherland). In India, on the other hand, separatist tendencies are widely manifested in demands by several sections of the population for independent homelands.

Chinese philosophy is society-centered, or *this-world*-centered, and directs man to find fulfillment through sociopolitical activities, whereas Indian philosophy looks upon the world as fleeting, transitory, and "unreal," and encourages human beings to seek spiritual realization of the Absolute (the Ultimate Reality, God) so that they can destroy their bondage to the chain of transmigration of the soul (which brings them back again and again into this world of sorrow). This liberation can only follow the annihilation of ego, which binds man to his finite individuality, enslaves him to the material world, and keeps him from achieving divine consciousness.

Civilization in India rose even before the Chinese Shang dynasty (c. 1600–c. 1100 B.C.E.) and it was even more advanced than the Shang. But, unlike China, the highly urbanized Indus Valley civilization (c. 2500–c. 1700 B.C.E.), which was first brought to light through archaeological findings in the twentieth century, did not even leave a historical memory behind. It is only in the last few decades that these archaeological findings have helped scholars to deduce that the Indus Valley civilization made an important contribution to the formation of Hinduism. The script used by the Indus Valley people (which has yet to be deciphered) was lost along with the disappearance of the Indus Valley civilization.

The collapse of the Indus Valley civilization synchronized with the invasion of northern India by pastoral Aryan tribes that settled in small territorial units and gradually extended their control over the Indo-Gangetic plain; much later their influence spread to south India. In China, too, the Zhou people, who lived beyond the pale, invaded Shang China and replaced the Shang (Zhou dynasty lasted from c. 1100–256 B.C.E.), but unlike the Aryans, they accepted the higher Shang civilization, the Shang writing system (which developed into the modern Chinese script), and the Shang notion that there could be only one ruler of China; the Zhou laid the foundation for the future development of the Chinese ideal of a humanistic, unitary imperial state. The Aryans, who had their own well-developed language and culture, felt no compulsion to emulate the advanced Indus Valley civilization, to borrow its script or language, or to adopt any of its sociopolitical institutions.

From the sixth century B.C.E. onward, China provides us with an increasing number of documents, written in the beginning on bamboo slats and silk cloth, and it is significant that most of these documents reflect a pervasive concern for political and worldly affairs. The Chinese veneration for the written word, and their penchant for history writing (helped by the invention of paper in the Han dynasty, c. 200 B.C.E.–c. 200 C.E.) has furnished the world an extraordinary volume of written materials: archival records pertaining to governmental activities (e.g., taxes, legal cases, famines), court debates, imperial edicts, district gazetteers, dynastic histories, histories of important families, memoirs, and works of literary writers and philosophers.

In India, it took 1,000 years after the Aryan arrival before an urban civilization reemerged and Sanskrit, the language of the Aryans, came to be written down. Archaeologically a void, this period in Indian history yields knowledge that can be gleaned only from the oral literature embodied in the Vedic hymns, prayers, and philosophical speculation, and from the epics, the *Ramayana* and the *Mahabharata* (which are much less dependable because of later accretions). Though archaeological, epigraphic, and numismatic sources begin to provide more firsthand information of life in India from the sixth century B.C.E., even that evidence is extremely fragmentary, and political history, until the thirteenth century, has to be recreated from various indirect sources, which leave many gaps and uncertainties in our understanding of historical developments. India, however, did develop a strong oral tradition, and many of the writings from 1500 B.C.E. to the Middle Ages, memorized by succeeding generations, were passed on through the centuries, though not always without interpolations. Significantly, these texts are mostly religious in nature, and though this may not prove that the Indians have "no sense of history," it does indicate that Indians were more preoccupied with religion than with current affairs. The first historical chronicle, *Rajatarangini* (River of Kings) was composed by the Kashmiri poet Kalhana in the twelfth century C.E., but it, too, concentrates primarily on the history of Kashmir. It is with the coming of the Muslims that history writing in India gained respectability.

In the middle of the first millennium B.C.E., when India and China were plagued by internal wars, both countries witnessed a great flowering of intellectual and philosophic thought. But, whereas the majority of the thinkers in China (Confucius was one of them) concerned themselves with theories of kingship and the nature of government, and prepared the country to replace feudalism with a unitary state and laid the foundations of a benevolent government and an egalitarian society, the Indian philosophers (Buddha and Mahavira being the outstanding ones) were grappling with the problem of transmigration of souls and underplaying the importance of life in *this* world. Religion, not politics, came to dominate Indian social life.

For different reasons, which we need not go into here, the wars and political chaos in both countries culminated in the emergence of universal empires: the Han (c. 200 B.C.E.–c. 200 C.E.) in China and the Mauryan empire (322–185 B.C.E.) in India. However, whereas the Chinese imperial system achieved permanence and stability because it adroitly combined the use of overwhelming military power with the sociopolitically oriented Confucian ideology of a unitary, humane government, the Indian empire lacked a strong unifying sociopolitical credo. The weak philosophic ideal of a centrally administered universal empire died with the collapse of the Mauryas. Not until the establishment of the British government was India to see an imperial system that extended over the entire subcontinent and had a direct structural relationship between the center and the villages. Ashoka, the greatest of the Mauryas, who had converted to Buddhism, did leave behind a legacy of religious toleration and the ideal that the duty of the king was to foster *dharma* (correct conduct based on religious values).

In spite of periodic invasions and a few eras of internal breakdown of government, the history of China from the Han to the nineteenth century saw the diffusion and strengthening of Chinese culture that helped to produce a relatively close-knit society. In India, the rise and fall of innumerable native and foreign dynasties from the Mauryas to the establishment of the British Empire, divided the country more than ever and facilitated the growth of regional culture areas, each with its own language. However, Hinduism, which had spread throughout the subcontinent, did provide the philosophic underpinnings for common religious and social attitudes, and for the caste system, which became an integral and enduring part of the social organization in village and nonvillage India. Thus, religion—not politics—became a unifier. Since caste itself is divisive, the "unity in diversity" achieved in the subcontinent is a distinctively Indian phenomenon. Even the Muslim and the British rulers could not destroy this basic structure of society.

Buddhism reached China by the end of the Han dynasty and, in the next few centuries, when China was in a state of political disunity, it spread through the entire country; indeed, by the seventh century A.D., it had become the state religion of China. However, Buddhist ethics and values were antithetical to Confucianism's "this world" ideology and so, soon after the empire had been reunified by the Tang (618–907) and Confucianism had made a comeback, Buddhism not only lost its high position but came to be viewed as an alien religion that had to be suppressed. Buddhism, officially controlled and regulated, did continue as a popular religion of the masses, but the mainstream of Chinese intellectual life shifted back to Confucian scholarship. The Confucian goals of a harmonious, hierarchical society, in which man could fulfill himself only through service to society and state, were once again affirmed. The strength of revived Confucian culture can be judged from the fact that when the "barbarian" Mongols conquered China in the thirteenth century, the Yuan dynasty they established there lasted a bare eighty-nine years (1279–1368), collapsing under the weight of a massive Chinese rebellion.

The Ming dynasty (1368–1644), which replaced the Mongol government, revived and strengthened the sense of Chinese identity and unity to such a degree that China can be said to have, at last, become a Confucian state par excellence. The highly centralized state, working through an elaborate hierarchy of central and provincial administrative offices, manned by officials recruited through the Confucian examination system, was so stable and orderly that, when the Ming fell and the government was seized by the "barbarian" Manchus (established Qing dynasty: 1644–1911), the invaders assiduously adopted and promoted Ming "culturalism" that ensured the continuity of the Confucian state.

If foreign invaders of China found it impossible to avoid being assimilated into the Chinese sociopolitical system, invaders of India, too, got absorbed into the Indian socioreligious system. The important political difference between the two countries was that in China the assimilation meant the continuity of a unified, centrally administered state, whereas in India it meant a proliferation of castes and independent kingdoms. Even the two attempts made by Hindu rulers (Guptas, 320–480; Harsha, 606–647) to repeat the Mauryan experiment resulted only in loose-knit empires limited to north India—the rulers exercised suzerainty over local dynasties and never established a Chinese-style centralized bureaucratic control system. Wars, fought primarily by military castes, led to an extension of overlordship but did not infringe on the entrenched socioreligious system or the lives of the population at large. The most significant development in the subcontinent, prior to the arrival of Muslims in the twelfth century, was the gradual replacement of Buddhism by Hinduism that had matured and become the primary religion of India, providing the country a unifying ethos.

Muslim invasions, and the subsequent establishment of Muslim kingdoms and the Mughal empire, introduced a radically new element into the subcontinent. Islam, a strong, militant religion, was wholly opposed to everything that Hinduism represented. It posited that there was only one true God, Allah, and it demanded that the true believers, who formed the casteless, egalitarian Islamic religious community, be ready to sacrifice themselves for the advancement of their religion as soldiers of Allah. The religious laws of Islam governed all aspects of the personal, social, and political life of its followers. Fortunately for the subcontinent, the conquerors, regardless of whether they were Arabs, Turks, Turko-Mongols, or Afghans, were few in number and therefore clearly unable to attempt the conversion of the vast local population to Islam. As a result, the Muslim rulers, and the Muslim ruling class, monopolized power at the center but had to allow local Hindu chieftains to continue as tributaries and the traditional Hindu socioreligious system to function in the countryside and the villages. Although later, under the Mughals, some attempt was made to reconcile the two communities, the Muslims, generally speaking, remained a colonial power that ruled the country through a feudal army-based bureaucracy; employed an alien language, Persian, as the court language; and hired Indian Muslims and Muslim migrants from Iran and Central Asia to man the upper levels of the bureaucracy.

Despite the tactical political alliances made by the Mughals with some of the Hindu rajas, there was no possibility of there ever being a true meeting of minds between Muslims and Hindus. The Muslims, who had accepted the fact that they could not convert the Hindus, allowed the Hindus to continue to live their orthodox caste lives undisturbed; and the Hindus, too, had reconciled themselves to the fact that they had to coexist with a people following an anti-Hindu religion. The Hindus, however, were never allowed to forget that they were second-class citizens of the empire; Aurangzeb (1658–1707), the last great Mughal ruler, reimposed the hated poll tax *(jizya)* on the Hindus and razed several Hindu temples and built mosques on their sites.

After Aurangzeb's death the Mughal power declined so rapidly that in a mere fifty years a British trading company, the East India Company, had overthrown the governor of Bengal (by far the richest province in India) and in another hundred years had established itself as the unchallenged ruler of the entire subcontinent. In China, on the other hand, British trading interests found the going much tougher. China was a powerful unitary state that did not allow foreigners to enter the country freely. In the eighteenth century, when the Qing dynasty had still not lost its vigor, the British had to agree to trade under severe constraints—they were denied even the right of permanent residence in Canton, the one and only port that was open to Western commerce. It was only in the mid-nineteenth century, when the Chinese state was on the decline, that it was forced to open its doors to Western penetration, and that, too, after being defeated in two major wars (1839 and 1860).

The modernization of India can be said to have begun around the mid-nineteenth century, when India became a crown colony of Britain. It is at this time that thoughtful Indian intellectuals and leaders of society, though still few in number, began the process of borrowing Western ideas with a view to re-energizing their society so that it could face the challenge of British occupation and fight for national independence. The fact that India was a colony of the British meant that the Indian response could take place only within a political framework imposed by the British who, from James Mill to Winston Churchill, were convinced that the immoral, corrupt, "benighted Hindoo" could only be saved by being introduced to Western civilization, and that, too, through the English language.

The task in China was qualitatively different. China has been called a "semicolony," which means that the Chinese, though exploited by Western imperialism, technically never lost their independence and, therefore, had to meet the foreign challenge by struggling to radically reorganize their traditional political culture and administration within the context of their *own* sociopolitical system. Nevertheless, it is worth noting that whereas practically all the Chinese reformers, openly, and harshly, denounced their traditional culture and sought substitute value systems from Western sources, the greatest of the Indian nationalist leaders, who were mostly Hindus, turned back to the foundations of Hinduism and used their religious ethos as a basis for modernization. Mahatma Gandhi, who is looked upon as the Father of Free India, declared that he made no "distinction between politics and religion," and he used the traditional Hindu idiom of *ahimsa* (nonviolence) to further the cause of nationalism and independence.

2

Indian Civilization

From Pre-History to the Eighteenth Century

India presents a picture of immense geographical and cultural diversity. The nearly-a-billion people of the country belong to several racial types, which are further divided into many mutually exclusive ethnic groups; they follow seven prominent religions (Hinduism, Islam, Buddhism, Sikhism, Christianity, Jainism, and Zoroastrianism) that are split by thousands of sects and castes; and they speak nearly two thousand dialects associated with fourteen well-established languages (each with its own script and literature). However, beneath this mind-boggling diversity lies a socioreligious culture that first emerged around 3000 B.C.E. and brought a sense of unity and continuity to the subcontinent. This chapter deals with the sources of pluralism in Indian culture, the main trends in the development of India's high tradition, and the major landmarks in Indian history from the time of the Indus Valley civilization to the eighteenth century, when the British first arrived on the scene.

Geographical Setting

The Three Zones

The Indian peninsula has conventionally been divided into three physical regions: the Himalayan mountain range in the north and its offshoots in the northwest and northeast, which separate the subcontinent from central Asia, Iran, and Burma, respectively; the Indo-Gangetic-Brahmaputra plains, which stretch from the Arabian Sea to the Bay of Bengal; and the Deccan plateau, which is separated from the great river plains by the Vindhya Mountains.

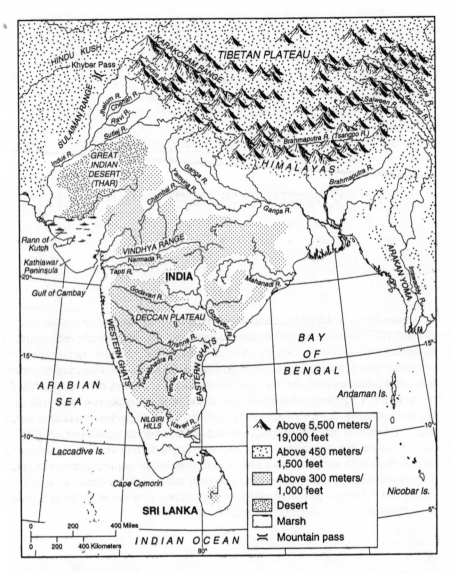

Physical Features

The lofty Himalayas are popularly considered to have provided protection from invaders. Actually, the passes in the northwest are so accessible that from time immemorial they have encouraged numerous invasions by central and western Asian peoples, from Aryans, Greeks, and Persians to Scythians, Huns, Turks, and Mongols. Other passes in the north and northeast have allowed for communication and movement between the sparsely populated Tibetan region and India.

The importance of the Himalayas is not that they kept invaders out, but that they keep the arctic winds from entering the subcontinent and the rain-bearing monsoons from leaving it, thus providing the country with a unique rain-oriented climatic feature.

One geographical factor that has had a decisive impact on South Asian history is the critical position of Afghanistan. Since the important overland routes between the subcontinent and western and central Asia pass through Afghanistan, this mountainous tract witnessed the greatest interaction between India and the non-Indian empires that rose in central and western Asia. Since Afghanistan lacked the physical features that could make it a natural barrier, an ascendant empire based in Persia or central Asia, which included Afghanistan within its fold, would invariably extend its borders into northern India, stopping if at all at the western side of the Indus River; conversely, an ascendant Indian power could protect its northern borders only by advancing into the central Asian plains beyond the Hindu Kush Mountains. To give some examples, Alexander's occupation of the Punjab and Sind may be viewed as a logical corollary to his subjugation of the Persian empire, which under Darius already stretched into the Punjab and Sind; the Mauryans reached into Persia to protect the Punjab; the eastern border of the caliphate (c. 750 C.E.) ran along the Indus River; the Mughal empire retained control of Afghanistan for almost a hundred years; and even the British tried to control Afghanistan to protect northwest India from Russian expansion.

Of the plains, the Brahmaputra Valley has historically remained rather isolated, but the Indo-Gangetic Valley has provided the country with the largest tract of rich agricultural land. It is no surprise that the Indo-Gangetic region became one of the most densely populated areas in India, and not only was the cradle of Indian civilization but witnessed the rise of India's early great empires. The Deccan, which lay south of the Vindhyas, got Sanskritized late, but eventually displaced the north as the center of civilization and saw the emergence of powerful kingdoms, some of which spread Hindu civilization into Southeast Asia.

Geography and Cultural Ecology

The division of India into three zones is, however, too simplistic and does not take into account the cultural ecology of the subcontinent. In fact, it is possible to delineate natural geographical areas that fostered regional cultures and that correspond, more or less, to linguistic states established in postindependence India:[1] the Himalayan uplands are divided into Kashmir, Nepal, Bhutan, and Sikkim. The Indo-Gangetic plain is divided into the western plain (further subdivided into the Punjab, Thar desert, and Sind), the Doab (the watershed between the Indus and the Ganges), the middle plain, Bengal, and Assam. The Aravalli and Vindhya central highlands constitute another such area bounded by Gujarat in the west and Orissa on the east. And the Deccan can be divided into several sections—the central plateau, the western and eastern coastal strips, and the Godavari, Krishna, and Kaveri river basins. It is the evolution of distinctly different cultural patterns in these areas that explains the bewildering diversity and complexity of Indian culture.

However, behind this diversity, the social and operational aspects of Hinduism, as well as its theology and ideology, did provide a unifying framework of remarkable persistency. When a historian like Vincent Smith emphasized the "underlying fundamental unity of India . . . [which] transcends the innumerable diversities of blood, color, language, dress, manners and sect,"[2] he was necessarily emphasizing the distinctive combination of abstract spirituality and well-defined, detailed social system that makes Hinduism what it is.

The Rise of Hindu Civilization

Hindu and Hinduism: A Question of Definition

Many Indians today, including Hindus, are troubled by the use of the terms *Hinduism* and *Hindu culture* to define traditional Indian culture. This is understandable because the history of the last decades of the British government in India were bloodied by animosity between Hindus and Muslims, and it was this communal hatred that finally resulted in the partitioning of the subcontinent. In a secular state, which independent India declares itself to be, there is a felt need to de-emphasize values associated with any particular religion and emphasize a common heritage that can unify all communities and provide a solid foundation on which India's future can be built. Continuing sectarian troubles in post-partition India show how religious sensitivities have sharpened and how not only the Muslims but other communities as well, such as the Sikhs, resent the dominant Hindu group and would like to ensure that their communities are recognized as belonging to distinctively separate nationalities.

One can, therefore, empathize with a nationalist leader like Jawaharlal Nehru for declaring that it was "incorrect and undesirable to use 'Hindu' or 'Hinduism' for Indian culture, even with reference to the distant past." Nehru suggested that "the correct word for 'Indian,' as applied to country or culture or the historical continuity of our varying traditions, is 'Hindi,' from 'Hind,' a shortened form of Hindustan [the land of the Hindus]."[3] Nehru's proposition did not receive an enthusiastic response because *Hindi* is a well-recognized term for one of the languages of India and is not popularly associated with the notion conveyed by the word *Indian*.

In contrast to Nehru, Radhakrishnan went to the other extreme when he said, "the term 'Hindu' had originally a territorial and not a creedal significance. It implied residence in a well-defined geographical area. Aboriginal tribes, savage and half-savage people, the cultured Dravidians and the Vedic Aryans were all Hindus as they were the sons of the same mother."[4] Radhakrishnan is correct, but only to a limited degree. The term *Hindu* is non-Indian in origin and was initially used by the Persians to denote the region of the Sindhu River (Sind); later the Persians, Greeks, and Arabs extended the region to include the whole of northern India. The term may even have referred to the people of the area, but after the entry of Islam into the subcontinent, it was distinctly used to distinguish the people who practiced Hinduism from the followers of Islam.

The pity is that it is practically impossible to find a neutral term, or coin an adequate new one, to replace Hinduism or Hindu culture. Unlike the Chinese, the early Indians, lacking a concept of a unitary political state, never devised a single name for the subcontinent. By the fourth or fifth century C.E., the term *Bharatvarsha* (homeland of the mythical Aryan king Bharata) may have been used to refer to the subcontinent,[5] but even if it did, it had a purely religiocultural connotation and denoted the Hindu culture area from the Himalayas to Kanyakumari (Cape Comorin). The word *Hindustan*, which became current during the Mughal period, technically applied to the northern Indo-Gangetic area and excluded Deccan. Although today the term India is commonly used outside the country, in English-language publications in the subcontinent, and by some of the elite when they speak in English, it remains a foreign word largely replaced by "*Bharat*" in common parlance.

The Constitution of independent India identifies the country in a most intriguing fashion: "India, that is Bharat." The statement goes to show how hard it was for the new leaders of free India to find an indigenous name for the politically unified country; if *Bharat* had been universally acceptable there would have been no need to continue with a foreign name. *Bharat,* derived from *Bharatvarsha,* was popularized by Hindu leaders and the Congress Party during the freedom movement in the term *Bharat-mata* (Mother India), at a time when, as Nehru informs us in *The Discovery of India,* most of his peasant audiences did not know what *Bharat-mata* stood for.[6] With the popularization of the term *Bharat,* one could talk of a "*Bharatiya* tradition," but this phrase would no doubt also be found unacceptable to non-Hindu communities, particularly Muslims, because it too has a close association with Hindu culture (witness its incorporation in the title of the Hindu fundamentalist party, Bharatiya Janata Dal). For our purposes, we will use the term Hinduism without attaching any value judgment to it but accepting it as a central and vital part of the great tradition of India. Hinduism, a relatively new term that first appeared in the nineteenth century, has come to define not only the religious values and ritual practices of the majority community but also the social relations and structures and the substance of traditional Indian polity.

The Evolution of Hinduism: India's Diversity and Cohesiveness

Unlike China, where the emergence of the Confucian sociopolitical order is so well documented, and where once established the system showed remarkable historical continuity, the evolution of the Hindu socioreligious system is so convoluted and undocumented that often we can only hypothesize as to how it arose. This, plus the fact that Hinduism continued to add new schools of philosophy, cults, and rituals through history, makes it necessary that we put Hinduism in its historical perspective.

Indus Valley Civilization

One of the early elements that went into the making of Hinduism is the synthesis that took place between the culture of the Indus Valley civilization and that of the Aryans; after all, it is reasonable to presume that although the Indus Valley civilization disappeared, the people belonging to this civilization continued to exist. Archaeological findings of the last few decades have established that the highly urbanized Indus Valley civilization was wholly indigenous and that it had spread all the way from the Indus Valley to the Ganga-Yamuna Doab (the plain lying between the Ganga and the Yamuna rivers) and down to Gujarat, and that the unified culture area, more vast than Mesopotamia and Egypt, was centrally administered. The larger cities, with broad avenues running north-south and east-west, excellent sewage systems, impressive buildings, public baths, and ventilated granaries—all built of standardized bricks—indicate advanced town planning and sanitary engineering. Weights and measures were uniform and based on the binary and decimal systems. Cotton cloth, India's contribution to the world, was extensively used and even exported; Indus Valley seals found in Mesopotamia provide evidence of a flourishing international trade.

Archaeological discoveries also reveal that some important elements that would later show up in Hindu civilization were already present. Though the script used on the Indus Valley seals remains undeciphered, and it is not known what language the people spoke, the absorption of Dravidian words into early Sanskrit indicates that there must have been Dravidian-speaking people living in the north, who were later pushed into the south.

The Indus Valley people loved gold and silver jewelry, and the women adorned themselves with necklaces, earrings, nose ornaments, combs, and bangles similar to the ones still used in the Punjab and Rajasthan. The bronze figurine of a nude dancing woman, apart from displaying a sophisticated sensitivity to form and movement, shows bangles worn all the way from the wrist to the upper left arm. One can see similar use of bangles in many parts of India, particularly among the Rajasthan peasants of today. Some of the other items linking the Indus civilization with the present are the bullock carts and boats still being used in some parts of northern India, house-building techniques, ritual bathing tanks, use (until recently) of a binary system for weights and measures, *kajal* (eye makeup), and dice.[7]

Far more important, from the beautiful carvings of human figures and animals on the many hundreds of seals discovered at some sites, it can be deduced that various popular cults connected with the worship of trees and animals (particularly the bull) and some kind of a Mother goddess, all of which later reemerged as a part of Hinduism, had flourished among the Indus Valley people. One of the seals has a figure of a three-faced man with an erect phallus, sitting in a yogic position of meditation, surrounded by various animals. This figure has been recognized as "proto-Shiva." Shiva, who was not one of the gods among the early Aryan pantheon but who subsequently surfaced as one of the three highest gods of Hinduism (the other two being Brahma and Vishnu), is called a *mahayogi* (great yogi) and *pashupati* (Lord of the animals); he is symbolized by the *lingam* (a polished stone phallus) and his mount is Nandi, the bull. Shiva is also connected with *shakti,* female power, the Mother goddess, represented in its many forms as Parvati (Shiva's consort), Durga, and Kali. We have every reason, therefore, to call the Indus Valley civilization people "Indians."

The Aryan Invasion

The entry of the Aryans increased the Caucasoid content in the country that was already inhabited by Caucasoid, Mongoloid, and Proto-Australoid racial groups. In spite of the considerable mixing of the races, the Caucasoid types are largely located in the north, the Mongoloid types are concentrated along the Himalayan foothills and in the northeast; and the Proto-Australoid strain is found in many tribes in central and south India. We do not have sufficient information as to where the Aryans came from, but it is conjectured that they moved eastward from western Asia and crossed into India through Afghanistan and Iran. They spoke Sanskrit, a language which has the same roots as Greek, Latin, Celtic, Slavic, and Persian.

As noted earlier, about the time the Aryans entered India, there was a major change in China, too, when the relatively "barbaric" Zhou overthrew the Shang dynasty (c. 1200 B.C.E.), but whereas the Zhou accepted the higher civilization of the Shang and built on it, the Aryans, a pastoral people who counted their wealth in terms of heads of cattle, destroyed the literate and urban Indus Valley culture. Furthermore, unlike the Zhou people, who were united under one ruler, the Aryans represented many tribes that not only fought the Indian natives but delighted in fighting each other.

By the time of the epics, the *Mahabharata* and the *Ramayana,* which give us a picture of life in India from c. 1000 to c. 500 B.C.E., Aryan social and political organizations had become more sophisticated, and small tribal groups administered by tribal assemblies *(sabhas* or *samitis)* gave way to larger territorial units under kings *(rajas)* who exercised state power through permanent government offices that administered justice and collected taxes—that is, the ruler's share of the surplus produce.* The person of the king came to be invested with divinity and elaborate

---

*The term *taxes,* though technically incorrect because it has a modern connotation, is being used here as an expedience.

ceremonies and sacrifices were performed for the consecration of the ruler. Though many of the early kings were elected, the institution finally became hereditary.

Aryan society was divided into four classes *(varnas):* the Brahmin priests were the most important; the aristocratic Kshatriya warriors came next, followed by the Vaishya commoners; and at the bottom of the scale were the Shudras, who were mostly of indigenous extraction and considered fit only for menial tasks. There was also a fifth, though unrecognized, class entrusted with the lowliest and most loathsome duties such as scavenging and handling of dead bodies; these unfortunates, the so-called Untouchables, were not only obliged to live under the most wretched conditions away from the village but were also not allowed to draw water from the village well or enter a Hindu temple. (In spite of the legal strictures imposed by the Indian Constitution, many at the lower end of society even today suffer from these caste taboos.)

Only those belonging to the first three classes were entitled to be initiated into the Vedic ritual (therefore called the "twice born," first physically and then spiritually at the time of initiation) and gain an education through the study of Vedic texts; the Shudras and Untouchables were denied this right. Unlike Confucian China, where theoretically the peasant masses were not barred from education, Hindu India kept over 50 percent of its population illiterate by design. It has been suggested that the class system may have its roots in the Indus Valley civilization[8] and that the Aryans only used it to perpetuate their superior position. Since the term *varna* also means color, the class system may indicate the arrogance of "white" Aryans and their contempt for the darker-skinned natives. When the Brahmin Sonadanda was asked by Buddha to describe the characteristics of the true Brahmin, he replied that a Brahmin, among other things, must have "great beauty of complexion [and be] fair in color."[9] Indeed, until today, Indians are among the most color-conscious people in the world. Parents in India invariably try to find brides for their sons who are "fair complexioned" and, failing that, "wheatish complexioned." And God pity the parents whose daughters are dark-skinned!

With the emergence of kingship, the role of the Brahmins became even more important because only the Brahmin could perform the rituals and sacrifices connected with the consecration of the ruler and other state functions. The Brahmins represented Divinity, but more important, Divinity was supposed to descend into their person when they were performing sacrificial rites. "India is probably the only country in the world where a particular class of men are given a position higher than that assigned to the gods."[10] The Brahmins became the preservers of Vedic religion and, thereby, of all "relevant" knowledge; they could never be displaced from their high status in society, even though theoretically they held no secular power. Peoples of all *varnas,* of course, continued to depend on the Brahmins to perform the ceremonies associated with birth, marriage, and death.

The Caste System

By the end of the fourth century B.C.E., divisions based on occupation, lineage, and so on, arose within the *varna,* and these divisions *(jati)* are the ones that can truly be described as castes.*

The origin of castes is extremely complex, and we still do not know enough about how all of them evolved. Briefly speaking, *jatis* were (and are) endogamous groups representing functional distinctions within a *varna* (e.g., barbers, carpenters, and weavers in the Shudra class). New *jatis* were formed when members of different *varnas* intermarried, when a group was degraded within a *varna* for not performing the religious rites expected of it, when a local or a foreign tribe was absorbed into the Hindu fold, or when members of a caste moved away from their original habitat or changed their profession.[11] In brief, while the four *varnas* provided a broad class division of society, it is the over 3,000[12] hereditary, endogamous, craft-exclusive *jatis,* or castes, each with its own name and norms of conduct that came to govern everyday family life in traditional India.

Modern India, because of many new developments—such as the spread of modern education among men and women, the emergence of a caste-blind work environment in the modern industrial, commercial, and bureaucratic sectors; and the increase in the numbers of nuclear families and working women—is witnessing, particularly in the urban areas, a certain modification in the pattern of social relations. Since our intention here is to understand the caste system and not the changes brought to it by the modernization process, we will continue to present a generalized view of the system without regard to the changes.

Every Hindu belongs to a group of families that share a common lineage *(gotra)* that traces its descent from a mythical ancestor. A *jati* incorporates several lineages that, sometimes, are referred to as subcastes. One of the most rigid rules in the caste system is that a person must marry within his or her *jati* (caste) but not within his or her lineage (subcaste). Once married, the bride, for all practical purposes, loses her lineage and becomes a member of her husband's lineage. Marital alliances are negotiated by the parents of the bridegroom and the bride without consulting the boy and girl involved. The girl's family, which traditionally initiates the negotiations, usually looks for a boy who will be a good provider and whose family has a somewhat higher status in the *jati;* the boy's family customarily seeks a good-looking girl with fair skin and genial demeanor, and one whose family is of equal status and wealthy enough to afford a big dowry. Although intercaste marriages are strongly discouraged, it is more acceptable that a man marry a woman from a

---

*The term *caste,* which is derived from the Portuguese word for race, has been popularly used to describe the four *varnas;* in recent years, the word, as will be seen in the explanation given in the text, has been more appropriately applied to the subgroups *(jatis)* that exist within the *varna.*

lower caste (the children of such a union retain their father's caste) than a woman marry below her caste (the children of this marriage are considered as outcaste).

Social relations are further regulated by the rigid concepts of purity and pollution. The *varnas* are associated with various categories of occupations that range from the very pure (that of the Brahmins) to the most polluting (that of the Untouchables). The system allows for an efficient exchange of services and commodities in the marketplace, but forbids social interaction at the personal level. For instance, one can only eat food prepared by a member of one's own caste or by a Brahmin; food touched by someone in a lower caste or an unclean caste (outcastes, Muslims, and other foreigners are included in this category) becomes polluted and has to be thrown away.

There are, of course, several rules of ritual purity that apply to all Hindus regardless of their caste affiliations. Within the extended family, to take a few examples, a woman during her menstrual period is not allowed into the kitchen to cook or to perform other chores in the house that can pollute those around her; a widow, besides having to perpetually wear mourning colors, can neither participate in religious ceremonies nor seek remarriage.

At the personal level, a good Hindu starts the day by brushing his teeth and having a bath. Before eating he has to wash his hands and feet (some have a bath) and bare his waist (some remove all clothes except the loin cloth). He eats facing east or west, not south if his father is still living, and never north or toward a corner in the room. Only the right hand can be used for transferring food to the mouth (since the left is used for washing one's self after defecating and, therefore, is polluted), and one never eats standing, walking, inside a transport, or in a "polluted" area like the cremation grounds.

The orthodox Hindu is told what fruits, vegetables, and meats he can eat on which day of the week or month; in what posture he should lie down; what he should not look at and which direction he should face while defecating; on what days and at what time of the day he can have intercourse with his wife; and so on. "Over-punctilious conformity to rules which [is] a dominant feature of Hindu psychology [is] largely inspired by the concept of purity and impurity[;] the purpose of the rules being usually preservation of purity."[13]

Although the majority of Indians are nonvegetarian, the great tradition frowns on the eating of meat, particularly beef (the cow is held sacred by the Hindus). This has had an interesting ramification for intercaste attitudes: "Thus among nonvegetarians, fish-eaters regard themselves as superior to the consumers of flesh of sheep and goats, while the latter look down upon the consumers of fowl and pig who, in turn, regard beef-eaters with great contempt."[14]

Since, in pre-modern India, the various castes living together in a village were more interdependent than they are today (the weaver and not the city mills provided cloth; the cobbler and not factories provided the shoes), the deeply ingrained concepts of pollution and purity contributed both to the segregation of the castes and to the definition of their interrelationship. The lower castes were *needed,* their functions were specific and complemented the functions of the higher castes, and, therefore, they were more accepted than they are today, even if they were no doubt held in contempt. It is to fight this degradation of the lower castes, which came in the wake of modernization, that Mahatma Gandhi tried to revive village handicrafts at the expense of modern industries.

The caste system, by delineating the occupation and daily life of an individual and his behavior pattern within the larger community in the village, provided stability and continuity to the social system. Each caste was free to pursue its own lifestyle without fear of interference. The caste system in the narrower framework of the village thus became a world unto itself and politics was largely irrelevant. As long as a village paid its share of the surplus produce to the power holders, the people within the village could carry on their activities as they had done for centuries. The rise and fall of empires and kingdoms did have an impact, but this was primarily on the authority and status of the dominant local castes, the local power holders. For the common villager a political disturbance could have a deleterious impact if warring armies marched through his fields or taxes were raised; on the other hand, it could prove beneficial if taxes were reduced and the new rulers made larger contributions to the building of irrigation canals and water tanks.

One of the positive attributes of the caste system was that it allowed for the coexistence of people with many levels of culture within the country, and also for the peaceful absorption of many racial groups that entered India prior to the coming of the Muslims. The alternative would have been, as history has shown in other parts of the world, mutual extermination or enslavement. Indeed, many of the famous Rajput clans have descended from the central Asian tribes who invaded India in the early centuries of the first millennium C.E.

However, the strength, creativeness, and flexibility of Hinduism began to decline in the second half of the first millennium C.E. and, after the entry of Islam, Hindu society withdrew itself into a shell and, in an effort to preserve itself, made caste regulations more strict and harsh. Yet it would be a mistake to conclude that the caste system became an obstacle to progress and change. Indeed, the deadening immobilization of the caste system did not come until after the British takeover and as a result of the British colonial policies.

Since the castes were autonomous bodies, with their own rules and regulations, and more important, with their own idiosyncratic religious beliefs and practices, it is pertinent to ask how they fitted into the larger Hindu order. The question may also be raised as to why the inherently unjust caste system survived at all? The answer is to be found in the doctrine of *sansara* (the transmigration of souls) and the associated doctrine of *karma* (the effect of deeds or actions performed in one life on the conditions under which one was born in the next).

The Basic Doctrines of Hinduism

As Hinduism evolved in the late Vedic period, the simple, polytheistic, nature-worshipping sacrificial Aryan religion underwent a major change and gave way to the mysticism of the Upanishads and to complex speculative thought. Ideas of *sansara* and *karma,* which had no place in early Vedic religion, now rose and spread rapidly, eventually becoming the basic tenets of Hinduism. It has been suggested that these doctrines could have been derived from beliefs held by the non-Aryan indigenous peoples.

Hindu religious thought came to be structured on the view that all sentient beings have an immortal soul that passes through a succession of lives in this material world of suffering and pain until it achieves liberation *(moksha, mukti);* that the moral quality of actions *(karma)* performed in one life determines the conditions under which one is born in the next (this logically leads to a certain amount of fatalism); that one's previous *karma* determines the caste into which one is born (one is, thereby, forced to unquestioningly accept one's place in society and not be envious of anyone enjoying a more comfortable status). Though this philosophy strengthened the inequality of the caste system, it also offered hope to the humble and the poor, albeit in the next life. The ultimate aim of the Hindu was, of course, to gain *moksha.* Good deeds and righteous practices commanded by one's *dharma* (duties as enjoined by religion and caste) could improve one's status in one's next birth, but *moksha* could be achieved only by gaining an insight into the cosmic mystery and becoming one with the cosmic principle. This could be done in several ways. But whatever the path chosen, it meant that the importance of the material world had to be de-emphasized.

One means of achieving *moksha,* which had gained popularity as early as the sixth century B.C.E., was through asceticism, which meant retiring into a forest, torturing the body (the source of desires) into submission, and engaging in the single-minded pursuit of transcendental knowledge, often with the help of Yogic exercises. Once an ascetic had risen above the joys and sorrows of the material world, he was supposed to become one with the Absolute, acquiring supernatural powers in the process. In contemporary India, there are several nationally recognized godmen (like the Sai Baba, who is known to produce diamond rings out of thin air for selected devotees) who are considered to be in possession of such powers. The surprising thing is that not only do millions of common people worship them blindly but leading politicians, high government officials, and businessmen come to seek their blessings and guidance.

Buddhism and Jainism, which rose in the sixth century B.C.E., were independent schools of thought that left a deep imprint on Hinduism. The founders of these religions—Gautama Buddha and Mahavira—rejected the world of wealth and power into which they were born and experimented with asceticism before gaining enlightenment and proclaiming their doctrines. Both religions were originally atheistic and spurned the role of gods and deities, however both accepted the existing concepts of *karma* and *sansara,* though in a slightly modified form. Both religions denied the possibility of an individual gaining any help from a divine entity, and in their early form, both made the individual responsible for his or her own salvation. And in both religions only the monks could reach perfection, though the laymen could gain merit through righteous action.

In emphasizing ethical actions, Jainism laid particular stress on *ahimsa* (non-violence) and prohibited the destruction of any life form. This aspect of Jain philosophy made a lasting impression on Hindu thought. In the twentieth century, Mahatma Gandhi, the universally venerated leader of the Indian nationalist movement, used *ahimsa* as a positive force in his nonviolent campaigns against the British.

Buddhism also propagated nonviolence, but the thrust of its philosophy was the pessimistic view that all life entails suffering and that suffering arises from craving, which can be eliminated only by destroying the ego. It taught that through right thinking, right speech, and right conduct, one could accumulate good *karma* and ensure reincarnation at a higher level. However, the bliss of *nirvana* (escape from bondage to *sansara*) could be achieved only through an intuitive understanding of the true nature of the cosmic reality through meditation. These notions found their way into Hinduism, and by the fifth century C.E., when Vishnu and Shiva had emerged as major Hindu gods, Buddha gained entry into the Hindu pantheon as an incarnation of Vishnu.

Vishnu was originally a minor Aryan divinity, and Shiva, a fertility god, was popular among the indigenous people and, as noted earlier, possibly inherited from the Indus Valley civilization. Local non-Aryan deities were gradually assimilated to these two gods and the doctrine of *avatars,* reincarnations of Vishnu, formulated; according to this doctrine, *avatars* of Vishnu, taking on a human or an animal form (the popular Hindu gods Rama and Krishna were both avatars), periodically descended to this world to save the people from impending destruction. This development allowed for devotion to a personal deity, such as Krishna, and had a great impact on the development of Hinduism in later history, because *bhakti-marga* (the path of absolute faith and devotion) also came to be accepted as a legitimate path to *mukti,* or permanent salvation.

The Bhagavad Gita, a section of the great epic *Mahabharata,* which deals with Lord Krishna's views of *sansara* and *karma,* codifies most of these ideas. Krishna, who may have been a historical figure, came to be looked upon as the most important incarnation of Vishnu, and the Bhagavad Gita came to be accepted as the most revered and popular scripture of Hinduism. It has influenced every great thinker in the last thousand years, from the philosopher Ramanuja (twelfth century C.E.) to political leaders of this century like Tilak, Radhakrishnan, Vivekananda, and Mahatma Gandhi, many of whom wrote commentaries on the Gita. Even the avowed atheist Jawaharlal Nehru kept a copy of the Gita at his bedside.

The Bhagavad Gita elaborates in detail three paths to the liberation of the soul: the way of transcendental knowledge *(jnana-marga)*, the way of action *(karma-marga)*, and the way of devotion *(bhakti-marga)*. The Gita plays down the importance of asceticism as the only approach to the renunciation of the material world. However, while insisting that man be active in this life, it qualifies the quality of action that will bring spiritual salvation. "Perform your prescribed duty, for action is better than inaction," says Krishna, but adds that it must be "disinterested" action, action performed as a "sacrifice . . . otherwise, work binds one to this material world."[15] What man has to renounce is the desire to gratify his senses through action, or for material rewards. The Gita also strengthens the cult of Krishna and encourages a devotional attachment to him: "For one who worships Me, giving up all his activities unto Me and being devoted to Me without deviation, engaged in devotional service and always meditating upon Me, who has fixed his mind upon Me . . . for him I am a swift deliverer from the ocean of birth and death."[16] Comparing *bhakti-marga* to asceticism, Lord Krishna says that "of the two, work in devotional service is better than renunciation of work."[17]

The rise in the popularity of local deities and personal gods led to iconolatry and the building of temples, which became a well-established part of Hindu religion by the Gupta period (320–480 C.E.). These deities, as mentioned earlier, were associated with Vishnu or Shiva, and "from the beginning of the Christian era, if not before, most educated Hindus have been either Vaisnavites (followers of the Vishnu cult) or Saivites (followers of Shiva)."[18] However, the sects were not rigidly exclusive and each accepted the other's god as another manifestation of the divine. The worship of female divinities (Mother goddess in various forms under various names) was established by the seventh century and added another dimension to the existing pantheon of deities. We may also mention, in passing, that at the popular level there were many cults that believed in earth-spirits and genie, and held certain trees and animals and reptiles (e.g., snakes) to be sacred.

From the ninth century through the Muslim period (thirteenth to the eighteenth century), *bhakti* movements spread throughout India, and Lord Rama, the hero king in the epic *Ramayana*, also became the focus of devotional cults. Simple faith and belief in a personal god, expressed through passionately devotional songs and dances, provided not only an emotional release but a relatively less rigorous and exacting path to *moksha*. After all, did not Krishna say in the Bhagavad Gita: "Even if a person of extremely vile conduct worships Me being devoted to none else, he is to be reckoned as righteous for he has engaged himself in action in the right spirit."[19] And, "For those . . . who take refuge in Me, even though they be lowly born, women, vaishyas, as also shudras—even they attain to the highest goal."[20]

Hinduism thus came to be such a complex composite of disparate beliefs that it belies easy definition. Hinduism is not a religion of revelation. It has no church or hierarchy of priests that can make authoritative pronouncements on doctrinal disputes. It has no set doctrines. It is not congregational. And it does not aspire to establish a theocratic state. What makes Hinduism the most tolerant of religions is its syncretic nature and its acceptance of the fact that there are many paths that lead to God (all "gods" are subsumed in the Absolute Reality, the Supreme Spirit, which we may, for convenience, call God), and that God accepts all of them. In the words of Lord Krishna, "And even those also who worship other gods with a firm faith in doing so, involuntarily worship me, too."[21]

To sum up, Hinduism attempts to be all things to all people. It makes provision for speculative thought, mystical experience, devotional fervor, self-discipline and compassion. In an otherwise rigid caste system, it gives freedom to an individual to establish a personal relation with God and even to seek salvation by breaking with society. Though some elements of Aryan thought, as expressed in Vedic literature, have remained at the heart of Hindu philosophy and some Aryan rituals, such as the ones connected with marriage and death, are used even today, it is the vast number of pre- and post-Aryan deities, religious ideas, and practices that have contributed to the formless form of Hinduism. Thus, most of the 33,000 gods (a figure used by Indians to convey not the actual number but the idea of innumerable gods) in Hinduism are non-Aryan. Because of this absorptive power of Hinduism even well-defined heterodox sects, such as Buddhism and Jainism, got fitted into the Hindu order and their members came to form separate castes. In conclusion it may be said that though India did not develop political unity, it did, in the larger sense, create a countrywide umbrella of socioreligious cohesiveness under which the diversity of caste practices could coexist without fear of being persecuted on orthodox religious grounds. The fact that the system allowed neither a state-enforced nor a religion-enforced orthodoxy made India the most liberal of countries until the entry of Islam into the subcontinent.

Unfortunately, this liberalism of Hinduism was based on the ghettoization of society. Intercaste communication was limited to business dealings and there was no intercaste socializing. In a manner of speaking, each caste lived in a ghetto, separated from other caste groups by invisible but impassable walls. In such a social system it was not difficult to coexist with non-Hindu foreigners like the Muslims as long as they, too, lived in self-contained and isolated enclaves. After the terrible Deccan earthquake of 1993, which killed tens of thousands, the government of Maharashtra built a model township to house the displaced peasants and decided that the new houses would be allotted by the drawing of lots. To the dismay of many progressive officials, the earthquake may have wiped out families irrespective of caste, but the surviving peasants rejected the official allotment procedure because upper-caste families refused to live next to lower-caste ones. Faizullah, a Muslim survivor, agreed with the caste-Hindus saying, "The system [of allotment] is not at all suited to our social structure, and certainly we will oppose it."[22]

The Hindu Tradition of Political Thought

The three most important factors that influenced the making of Hindu political thought and system were (1) a relatively undisturbed period of 1,000 years that allowed the Aryans to penetrate the subcontinent and evolve from seminomadic tribes to principalities and kingdoms; (2) the *varna* system, which separated class status from political authority; and (3) the caste system. Unlike China, which already had a comparatively well-defined view of a unitary state when the Zhou dynasty was established, the early Aryan age was one of constant fighting among tribes anxious to acquire pasture and agricultural land in the Indo-Gangetic plains. As a result, mutually antagonistic, small tribal settlements established numerous minor principalities *(janapada)*. By the late seventh century B.C.E., these gradually gave way to a dozen or so larger units *(mahajanapada)* with powerful armies and impressive capital cities. When one of these *mahajanapadas,* Magadha, established hegemony over the others, it prepared the groundwork for the first empire in Indian history, the Mauryan empire, which rose in 320 B.C.E. and lasted until 185 B.C.E.

The Mauryan empire, which at its height stretched from Afghanistan in the north to the Mysore plateau in the south (leaving only the Tamilnad area out of its control), and from Kandahar and Sind in the west to the Brahmaputra Valley in the east, was an impressive achievement, but it lacked the ingredients that could make it a lasting one. The first Chinese empire, which came into existence around 200 B.C.E., was so centralized that it had no reason to adopt a hegemonic approach. The Mauryan empire, on the other hand, in spite of its elaborate administrative structure, depended heavily on local rulers, who were converted into hereditary governors of their own territories. More important, the Chinese government not only established uniform regulations and laws that bound the remotest hamlet to the center but propagated a sociopolitical philosophy that put politics in absolute command. Based on the theory that a utopian state had existed in early Zhou, the Chinese made the reestablishment of that ideal state their historical goal; they looked upon history as the touchstone of their achievements and produced a political and social philosophy that could guide man's life on earth. In India, the major indigenous religions asserted that the material world was impermanent and transitory, and that human history was not significant.

It is believed that the rise to power of the Mauryas was engineered by Kautilya, the author of the tremendously influential manual on statecraft entitled *Arthashastra* and the chief political adviser of the first Maurya. According to Kautilya, the state striving for victory *(vijigsu)* would find itself to be at the center of a circle *(mandala)* of states that would be its neighbors and natural enemies. However, the next circle of states, neighbors of the enemies, would be the victor's natural friends or allies. Kautilya gives elaborate instructions as to how the aspiring state should strengthen itself internally and the means it should employ to systematically weaken its enemies. His main recommendations were that the ruler should (1) use *danda* (punitive authority) to ensure that the Hindu class system is rigorously observed (being the built-in guarantee of social order), and (2) treat all neighbors as potential enemies. In this connection the following extracts from *Arthashastra* are of interest:

> The observance of one's own duty leads one to *svarga* [heaven] and infinite bliss. When it is violated, the world will come to an end owing to confusion of castes and duties.
>
> Hence the king shall never allow people to swerve from their duties; for whoever upholds his own duty, ever adhering to the customs of the Aryas, and follow the rules of caste and divisions of religious life, will surely be happy both here and hereafter.[23]

> Whoever is inferior to another shall make peace with him; whoever is superior in power shall wage war; whoever thinks, "No enemy can hurt me, nor am I strong enough to destroy my enemy," shall observe neutrality; whoever is possessed of necessary means shall march against his enemy; whoever is devoid of necessary strength to defend himself shall seek the protection of another; whoever thinks that help is necessary to work out an end shall make peace with one and wage war with another.[24]

In retrospect, the Mauryan state, which appeared to have destroyed the pattern of the *rajamandala* (circles of enemies and friends) and come to dominate the "national" political scene, was an aberration. In Basham's words, "The inspiration of the Mauryas was soon almost forgotten. . . . All later Hindu imperialism was of a quasi-feudal type, loose and unstable. . . . Aggressive war again became the sport of kings, and was looked upon by theorists as a normal activity of the state . . . and the political, though not the cultural, unity of India was lost for nearly two thousand years."[25] After the Mauryas, the country as a whole saw little unity and the warring kingdoms seldom found it possible, or considered it necessary, to unite even when faced with a foreign invader. Even the limited territorial unity established by later regional empires, with the exception of the Gupta empire (320–480 C.E.), "was surface unity."[26]

It seems, however, that Ashoka, the greatest of the Mauryan emperors, did make a conscious attempt to provide a unifying principle for his sprawling empire. Though he became a Buddhist, he did not betray any overwhelming partiality for his adopted religion and went no further than declare himself to be the protector of *dharma* (or *dhamma,* the Prakriti equivalent used by the Buddhists); he appointed *dhamma-mahamatras* (supervisors of morality) to ensure that his officials discharged their duties with humane even-handedness. He was also anxious to be seen as a father figure and a just ruler by all his subjects, regardless of their caste or creed. In his rock edicts, Ashoka declares that all citizens "are my children" (Kalinga Edict), that "all sects may dwell everywhere" (Rock Edict VII), and that "all the sects have been honored by me with honors of various kinds" (Pillar Edict VI).[27] The edicts also, repeatedly, enjoin his subjects to show equal generosity to the *sramanas* (Buddhist monks) and Brahmins.[28]

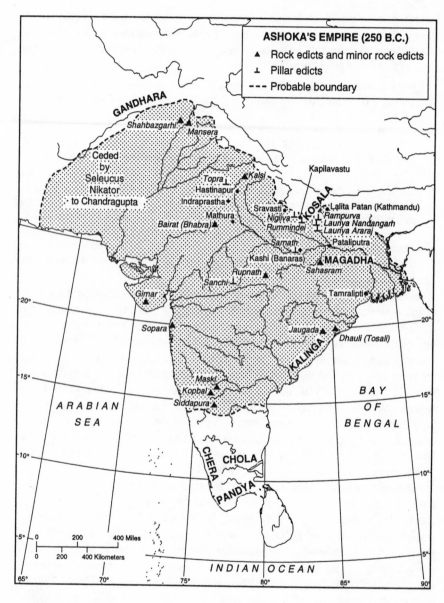

ASHOKA'S EMPIRE (250 B.C.)
▲ Rock edicts and minor rock edicts
⊥ Pillar edicts
--- Probable boundary

Ashoka's Empire

Although Ashoka's *dhamma* did not contribute to the establishment of a cohesive, long-lasting empire, the example he set in holding all religions in equal esteem had an enduring impact. Later rulers of Hindu India made it a point to make equally liberal donations to Hindu, Buddhist, and Jain shrines. In conclu-

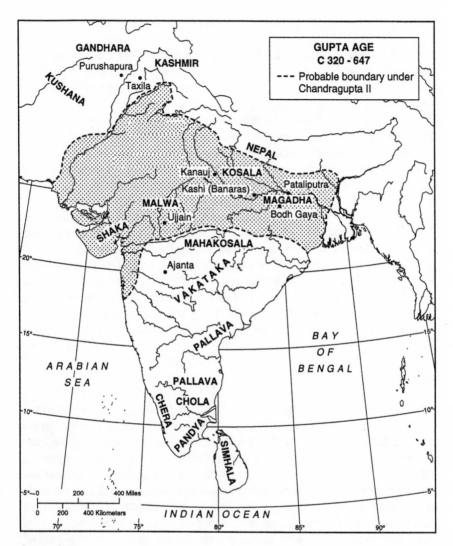

Gupta Age

sion, one can generalize that traditional Indian political thought produced no political ideology that could unify the country politically, or encourage the rulers to identify with the subcontinent as a whole. Though the Mauryan empire practically reached the geographical boundaries of the subcontinent, the concept of a state as an entity transcending the person of the ruler and his government was never formulated. Romila Thapar's interpretation is most apt: "With the development of political ideas in [Mauryan] India, the loyalty which in most other cultures is given to the state was given to the social order. As long as the social structure remained intact, the idea of the overall state failed to draw either recognition or support."[29]

The Hindu political tradition did not recognize the need for the government to look upon men as being equal and help ameliorate the condition of those at the bottom of society; on the contrary, it subordinated polity to the exigencies of an hierarchical social structure. By accepting the idea that various social groups (castes, guilds, etc.) should be autonomous and could use their own discrete system of regulations and laws, the traditional state failed to develop a common legal system or a universal social philosophy.

Since Hinduism lacked a national organization, the result was that neither the state nor the church could initiate social reform. Also, the political, social, and religious emphasis on caste made it unnecessary for an individual to look beyond caste for personal fulfillment or demand a participatory role in a government far removed from his orbit of activities; an individual's loyalty to caste was more fundamental than his loyalty to any abstract political unit called the state.

Although throughout pre-British Indian history the villages, both in the north and in the south, remained largely autonomous and self-governing, there was no extension of the village political life into a larger territorial unit—the district, the province, or the kingdom as a whole. The village communities, even if they are called "little republics" by some, provide no foundation for modern-style democracy.[30]

Islam in India

For over four centuries (c. 180 B.C.E.–c. 200 C.E.), following the collapse of the Mauryan empire, northern India was overrun by a series of successive foreign invasions led by Greeks, Sakas (Scythians), Parthians, and Kushans. Though the resulting foreign dynasties, particularly the Greek, had some impact on Indian culture in the realm of art and astronomy, their overall influence was minimal. On the contrary, the foreigners got Indianized and were absorbed into the caste system, and some of the foreign rulers became great patrons of Indian thought and learning; under the Kushans, who also held extensive territory in central Asia, Buddhism and Indian art spread through Turkestan to China, Korea, and Japan. Following the disappearance of the Kushans from the historical scene, India, except for a few decades of intrusion by the Huns in early sixth century, remained free of foreign invasions for a period of about a thousand years. And except for 160 years of the imperial Gupta dynasty (320–480 C.E.) and 40 years of Harsha's empire (606–647), when practically the whole of northern India was unified, the history of this period is a story of incessant warfare among kingdoms in the north and the south.

Although our knowledge of the Gupta period is indirectly drawn from archaeology, coins, epigraphic sources, art, literature, and accounts written by Chinese travelers, there is every reason to believe that it marked the high point of classic

Hindu civilization. In fact, northern India was then, "perhaps the happiest and most civilized region of the world, for the effete Roman Empire was nearing its destruction, and China was passing through a time of troubles between the two great periods of the Hans and the T'angs (Tangs)."[31]

Among the many universities in India, the university at Nalanda, with its eight colleges and three libraries, was a unique institution. It was, no doubt, one of the greatest universities of the world, and it attracted students and scholars from as far away as China and Indonesia. The era saw a blossoming of Sanskrit literature at the hands of such outstanding playwrights as Kalidas; Hindu mathematics, among other things, contributed algebra, "Arabic numerals" (Hindu numerals transmitted to Europe by the Arabs), the zero, and the decimal system to the world, while Indian textiles, metal crafts, and spices found ready markets abroad.

Broadly speaking, after the Guptas, India began its long decline. There was a brief revival under Harsha in the north and the creative impulse continued, for some more time, to quicken Hindu civilization in the south, yet in the words of Jawaharlal Nehru, it had passed its creative "high noon."[32] The basic reason for this development is, no doubt, the growing rigidity of the Hindu social structure, which thwarted the spirit of enquiry, initiative, and innovation. Alberuni (973–1048), the famous scholar from Khiva who had studied Sanskrit and was an admirer of Indian philosophy and science, had this to say of the Hindus after his stay in Punjab in the early decades of the eleventh century: "The Hindus believe that there is no nation like theirs, no king like theirs, no religion like theirs, no science like theirs. They . . . withhold [knowledge] from men of another caste among their own people, still much more, of course, from any foreigner. Their haughtiness is such that if you tell them of any science or scholar in Khurasan or Persia, they will think you both an ignoramus and a liar. *If they travelled and mixed with other nations, they would soon change their mind, for their ancestors were not as narrow-minded as the present generation is*" (emphasis added).[33]

Alberuni could have added that the Hindu rulers had no sense of unity and would much rather see their local Hindu enemies destroyed by foreign Muslim armies even if it led to their own destruction later. It is under these circumstances that Turko-Afghan and central Asian Muslims entered the politically fragmented subcontinent, first as raiders who looted the wealth of Hindu kingdoms and temples in northern India and later as invaders who carved out successive empires in India that lasted from the thirteenth to the eighteenth century. The longest-lasting dynasty was that of the Mughals, which at one point controlled most of the subcontinent; the dynasty technically lasted from 1526 to 1857, but in actuality began to decay rapidly after about 1700.

Interestingly enough, China, too, came under foreign domination in the thirteenth century, but the Mongol "Yuan dynasty" lasted only eighty-nine years (1279–1368) and was overthrown by a countrywide Chinese rebellion. The invaders of India met with no such grand-scale resistance. Although some of the Rajput rulers in the north fought the invaders with great bravery and desperation, they were often also engaged in fratricidal wars at the same time. And imagine a war in which the ruling fighter castes could not mobilize the lower castes and fight shoulder-to-shoulder with them! Imagine, again, an army where meals had to be cooked separately for different castes—indeed, where individual warriors frequently cooked their own meals!

Islam was first introduced quite peacefully to India's west coast by Arab traders and even the Arabs who invaded Sind in 712 were not violently anti-Hindu. A much harsher version of Islam and a spirit of intolerance were brought to the subcontinent by the Turko-Afghans, recent converts to Islam who first made their presence felt around 1000 C.E. Almost every year between 1000 and 1027 Mahmud of Ghazni led massive raids into northern India aimed at plundering cities and temples and putting the infidel population to the sword. The destruction and killings were on such a massive scale that their memory scarred the Hindu psyche as nothing had ever done before. Somehow Mahmud did not seem interested in conquest, though he did annex northern Punjab (the area that constitutes Pakistan Punjab today). It is worth noting that the basic Islamic features he introduced there came to characterize all future Islamic rule in India: Persian as the official language, Sunni as the primary creed, and the Hanafi interpretation of Islamic law as the law of the country.

After nearly 170 years of relative peace, the first true Islamic empire in India was founded by Muhammad Ghuri (Ghori), whose armies subdued the whole of northern India and reached as far east as Bengal and Bihar. The Delhi sultanate established by Muhammad Ghuri was a wholly new political entity and had no roots in Hindu India. Later dynasties that took over the Delhi sultanate expanded Muslim rule to the Deccan and southern India. The expansion of the Delhi sultanate, however, weakened central control and local Muslim generals began to declare their independence. In the fourteenth century, independent sultanates had come into existence in Bengal, Kashmir, Gujarat, Deccan, Jaunpur, Khandesh, and Malwa, followed in the fifteenth century by Berar, Ahmadnagar, Bidar, and Bijapur; Golconda broke away in 1512.

This politically chaotic climate encouraged the emergence of Hindu principalities willing and able to assert their independence. The foremost among these was Vijayanagar. In 1370 the ruler of Vijayanagar, then a small principality, defeated the sultan of Madurai and eliminated the hold of the Muslims on what had been the Delhi sultanate's southernmost province. Thereafter, for over a century, the Vijayanagar rulers, apart from indulging in coups d'état and internecine struggles, carried on wars against the Bahmani sultans in the north and the Hindu Gajapati rulers of Orissa.

A high point was achieved by Vijayanagar when its ruler, Krishnadeva Raya (1509–1529) brought peace to the kingdom by defeating the combined armies of the Deccan sultans under Muhammad Shah Bahmani and vanquishing the

Gajapatis. But instead of expanding the empire, Krishnadeva reinstated the defeated Bahmani sultan and married a Gajapati princess. As a result of this policy (which reminds one of Kautilya's mandala doctrine) while the Muslim problem was not solved, Hindu Orissa was so weakened that it was soon taken over by Muslims from the north. So much for any sense of Hindu unity in the face of a common enemy! A conscious Hindu revival was yet to come. In fact, Vijayanagar did not hesitate to recruit Muslims into its army, some of whom were given very high rank. In 1565, when Vijayanagar was once again faced by the armies of the sultans, two of its Muslim generals sealed its fate by changing sides.

The era of the sultanates, in which the Muslim rulers had tried to Islamize the country and shown little consideration for the subject population, ended in 1526 with the invasion of India by Babur, who claimed descent from Timur and was the ruler of Kabul. Babur founded the Mughal empire (1526–1858) which, ultimately, brought northern and central India under unified central control.

Akbar: The First and Last Unifier of Indian Society

It was during the reign of the Mughal emperor Akbar (born 1542, ruled 1556–1606) that an attempt was made to reconcile the Hindus to Muslim rule. Akbar truly sought to be the ruler of all Indians and thereby strengthen the base of his empire. His liberal and conciliatory policies were aimed at winning over not only the Hindu ruling classes but also the Hindu masses.

What surprises one is that Akbar displayed such wisdom when he was still young and surrounded by orthodox advisers. He was only nineteen years old when he married a Rajput princess and appointed her nephew, Raja Man Singh, to a high post in the court. Within the next two years Akbar abolished the tax on Hindu pilgrims visiting holy places and the humiliating poll tax. Later he married other Rajput princesses, and though all his Hindu wives were formally converted to Islam, their family members brought on court service were not. Even the emperor's Hindu consorts continued Hindu practices and celebrated all the Hindu festivals, in which he himself took an active part. Akbar also patronized Hindu artists and writers and made endowments to Hindu temples, besides elevating a few Hindus to high office. One of his ablest administrators, and one who has left his mark on Indian history, was Raja Todar Mal, the Hindu finance minister, whose revenue assessment system, based on an accurate measurement and classification of agricultural land, came to be applied uniformly throughout the empire. And another Hindu, Raja Man Singh, was one of his best generals.

In his own unique way, Akbar was the only ruler in pre-modern India who came nearest to realizing that religions were creating a rift among the diverse peoples of the country and that unless the state was secularized there would be no peace or harmony. He tried to achieve this end by introducing, in 1581, a new religion called Din-i-Ilahi (Divine Faith) that was supposed to embody the best of *all* religions and whose basic features had taken shape during the debates Akbar had organized between Muslim theologians and learned exponents of Hinduism, Jainism, Zoroastrianism, and Christianity. As it turned out, except for a few sycophants, the religion made few converts and succeeded only in offending the Muslim *ulama,* who believed that Akbar was an un-Islamic ruler out to destroy Islam. The leaders of the reaction began to demand that Islamic injunctions be imposed with greater strictness and all concessions extended to the idolatrous Hindus, including the ban on cow killing, be withdrawn. And ultimately it seems to have dawned on Akbar that "the identification of Muslim orthodoxy and Muslim political power was too close and too real and [that] they would stand or fall together."[34] Din-i-Ilahi died a quiet death, but Akbar could not stem the ascendancy of orthodox nobles at the court; even the existing basis of harmony had been corroded.

The gulf between the Muslims and Hindus reached unbridgeable proportions under Aurangzeb (1658–1707), the last great Mughal ruler, a zealous Muslim who abolished the ban on cow killing, reimposed the poll tax, ordered the destruction of "unauthorized" Hindu temples, stopped Muslims from attending educational institutions run by Hindus, and removed all Hindus from high or independent office. The disintegration of the Mughal empire from 1707 to 1857 is discussed later in the chapter.

The Impact of Islam on India: An Overview

The fact that the Muslim invaders were few in number and the indigenous population vastly greater in size had several implications for India.* First, it meant, that since the entire subject population could not be forcibly converted, as in central Asia, Iran, and Afghanistan, the alien rulers had to maintain a huge army, out of proportion to their numerical strength. The army was the only means by which they could maintain control over the vast Indian territories they had conquered and also protect themselves from the constant threat of invasion by other central Asian powers.

Second, since a large army had to be maintained, it became necessary to squeeze as much surplus as was possible out of the land. During the period of the sultanates, increased revenues were also considered helpful in grinding down Hindu resistance. According to Sultan Alauddin Khalji's (1290–1316) injunctions: "The Hindu was to be so reduced as to be unable to keep a horse to ride

---

*Though reliable demographic figures are not available, it is estimated that in 1600, Muslims constituted 9.85 percent of the population (N. A. Siddiqui, *Population Geography of Muslims of India* [S. Chand & Co., 1976], p. 35). If we presume that 70 percent of these were converts from the lower Hindu castes and had no political standing, then the Muslim ruling class (foreign born or of foreign extraction) could not have counted for more than 3 percent of the total population.

on, to carry arms, to wear fine clothes, or to enjoy any of the luxuries of life. . . . The Hindus will never become submissive and obedient till they are reduced to poverty. I have, therefore, given orders that just sufficient shall be left to them from year to year, of corn, milk, and curds, but they shall not be allowed to accumulate hoards and property."[35]

Although Alauddin's draconian policy was not (and could not be) fully carried out, the trend toward squeezing the maximum out of the countryside was continued through the Muslim period. Centuries after Khalji, rural levies under the Mughals amounted to half, or over half, of the peasant's crop; the burden was further increased because payments had to be made in cash. "Since taxation tended to be raised to the total surplus . . . it was not only the lower strata that felt the brunt of the burden of taxation; the upper strata were also ruined. Thus inherent in the Mughal system was a tendency also to subvert superior cultivation."[36]

Third, as a small ruling class, the Muslims found it necessary to inject into their administrative structure a form of military feudalism by granting fiefs to their officials. The Mughal bureaucracy—civil and military—was based on a military ranking system (the *mansabdari* system), whereby all officials were expected to maintain a certain number of troops. The thirty-three grades of *mansab* ranks ranged from a command of 10 to a command of 10,000—the highest ranks were reserved for the princes and the nobility. The *mansabdars* were 85 percent Muslim officers (70 percent from outside India) and 15 percent Hindu loyalists.

Each *mansabdar* was allotted a *jagir* (a parcel of land, an estate), the taxes from which provided his income and funds for the maintenance of the troops. Since the officers could be promoted or transferred, they had no permanent lien on any fixed *jagir*. However, because they were foreigners to the land and had no long-term interest in its development, they tended to be oppressive and exploitative. Numbering about 7,500 (in 1646) and claiming nearly a third of the revenue, they exercised an inordinate authority over the country, completely out of proportion to their number. When *mansabdars* broke allegiance with the center, as often happened at the end of the Mughal empire, they became autonomous local rulers. The responsibility of collecting the land tax from the villagers remained with the hereditary Hindu officials called *zamindars* (landed overseers of land; *zamin* means "land"). The income of the *zamindars* came from a percentage of the tax collected; the *zamindar's* rights were transferable, but his role in his villages was governed by tradition of *dharma* and customary practices.

Fourth, the underlying Muslim contempt for the idol-worshipping Hindu, and the brutal, inhumane policies followed by many of the rulers, left an indelible mark on Hindu-Muslim relations. Hindu India had never witnessed any religious wars, but from the first raids by Mahmud of Ghazni, when the invaders displayed unbounded enthusiasm for destroying and plundering Hindu temples (Mahmud is reported to have collected a booty of 6.5 tons of gold from the Somnath temple alone), to the harsh and cruel religious policy of Aurangzeb, the subcontinent saw the rise of religious animosity and the hardening of feelings of mutual antagonism and suspicion between Muslims and Hindus.

Fifth, because of the humiliations they were subjected to and their virtual exclusion from government service, the Hindus were reduced to the status of second-class citizens. In response they not only invested their caste system with greater sanctity but refused to accord any form of social recognition to their political masters. In the words of Alberuni (as valid in the eighteenth century as in the eleventh century when they were written): "All their [Hindu] fanaticism is directed against those who do not belong to them—the foreigners. They call them *mlechchas* i.e. impure and forbid having any connection with them, be it by intermarriage or any other kind of relationship, or by sitting, eating and drinking with them, because, thereby, they think they would be polluted. They consider as impure anything that touches the fire and water of the foreigner. . . . They are not allowed to receive anybody who does not belong to them, even if he wished to, or was inclined to their religion. *This, too, renders any connection with them quite impossible, and constitutes the widest gulf between us and them*" (emphasis added).[37]

Sixth, at certain levels there was significant interaction between the two communities. Apart from the blending of the Hindu and Islamic art forms, and the development of a new common language, Urdu, in northern India, the Muslim converts carried over certain kinship structures from their Hindu background. Indeed, the Islamic ruling classes developed some caste patterns of their own with the Sayyids (descendants of the Prophet), the Mughals, and the Afghans forming the highest castes, in that order.

Many Hindus were, in their turn, influenced by the ideas of mysticism and brotherhood as practiced by the unorthodox Muslim Sufi order. The tombs of many Sufi "saints" became places of worship and pilgrimage for both communities. Kabir (early fifteenth century), a Muslim weaver by birth, wrote songs that are popular to this day, in which he preached a religion of love and called upon the people to recognize that there was only one God, and that "Allah and Rama were but different names" of God. Nanak (1469–1539), a Hindu by birth who attacked the caste system and idol worship, became the founder of a new religion —Sikhism—that initially attracted both Hindu and Muslim followers. (Because of post–Akbar Mughal oppression and intolerance, Sikhism became militarized by 1700 and, thereafter, lost its universalistic appeal for the Muslims.)

Seventh, a substantial number of Hindus were converted to Islam. It is generally accepted that, except for a few areas such as Kashmir, the Muslim rulers did not follow any well-defined or widespread policy of conversion by force. In certain parts of the country, like Bengal and Punjab, where post–Buddhist Hinduism had not struck deep enough roots, Islam was accepted by outcaste and low-caste communities as an escape from their social bondage, or because it brought them material benefits from the new rulers. Some upper-class Hindus, who had lost their caste status for one reason or another, also found it convenient to convert to Islam. However, it appears that a significant number accepted Islam because of the popularity of the Sufi "saints" mentioned earlier; Hindu revivalism brought an end to these conversions by the early seventeenth century.

In contrast to the urban Muslims, the Hindu converts in the countryside persevered in following their traditional rites, superstitions, and customs. Professor Mujeeb has given a colorful account of how in many rural areas the Muslim converts continued to worship local village deities, celebrate major Hindu religious festivals, follow Hindu marriage ceremonies, and practice casteism.[38] This meant not only that the diversity and regional variations that characterized the Hindu community were also reflected among the new converts but that the two communities could coexist in a less bitter environment than they did in the cities.

Eighth, Islamic criminal and civil law was introduced into India, but only the criminal part was applied to the subject population; on the civil side, Islamic law was confined to settling cases involving Muslims, and customary Hindu personal law (arbitrated by Brahmins, and caste and guild *panchayats**) was allowed to settle civil disputes between the Hindus. Though Hindu law codes (*dharma-shastras,* or treatises on righteous behavior) provided a basic system of personal law generally accepted by all Hindus, there were many discrete regional and caste variations in usage and interpretation. Traditional India never developed a universal law of the land.

Last, Muslim rulers, in a manner of speaking, drew India into the Islamic world order, and regardless of the degree to which the invaders were Indianized, they still had a greater sense of brotherhood with Muslims outside India than with the Hindus in India. Throughout the Muslim period practically any educated Muslim from abroad could saunter in and get a high post in India, while the native Hindus, however talented, were mostly employed in lower positions because there was no alternative.

Furthermore, in spite of the centuries of domicile in India and adaptation to Indian conditions, the Muslim rulers could never give up their concern to be seen as ruling the country according to the *shari'a* (the laws of Islam), which emphasized the view that there was an unbridgeable gap between the believer and the nonbeliever, and between Dar al-Islam (lands under the law of Islam) and Dar al-Harb (land of the infidels). Like Hinduism, Islam prescribes a clearly defined code of conduct for all believers; but unlike Hinduism, Islam also unites the religious and political functions of an egalitarian society; the Islamic community *is* a state with its own ethos and legal institutions.

The overwhelming pressure on modern Islamic states to declare themselves to be theocracies is, therefore, understandable. One reason for the demand of the Indian Muslims for the creation of Pakistan was that most of the educated and politically conscious Muslims, descendants of the Mughal ruling class, had come to look upon the alien British government as being neutral, and felt that it would be unbearable to

---

*A *panchayat* was composed of five *(panch)* locally accepted leaders of the community.

live in independent India, however democratic or secular, because politics would inevitably be dominated by the majority community, the infidel Hindus.

India on the Eve of Mughal Eclipse: An Overview

Politics

Politically, India under the Mughals had failed to evolve into a state as the Western countries had done over the same period: "The Mughal emperor was *Shah-an-Shah,* 'king of kings,' rather than king of India. He was the highest manifestation of sovereignty, the court of final appeal. . . . But many of the attributes of what we would call the state pertained not to the emperor or his lieutenants, but to the Hindu kings [rajas] of the localities. . . . [However] even the rajas, for all their importance as guardians of the caste order and sacrificers-in-chief of the Hindu religion were dependents in turn on the warrior farmers who controlled the villages [and] ultimately . . . were the real lords of men and resources in India."[39]

The eighteenth century saw the weakening of Mughal power and imperial hegemony. The north had been ravaged by the Persian invasion (1739) under Nadir Shah, who after massacring 30,000 in Delhi alone and looting the capital, returned home with jewels and bullion worth 30 million pounds sterling and Shah Jahan's famous Peacock Throne. By absorbing Afghanistan into his empire, Nadir Shah reduced northwest India more or less to the geographical limits it was to acquire under the British. Nadir Shah's exploits were repeated by the Afghan chief Ahmad Shah Abdali (Durrani) who, having overthrown the Persian rule, raided northern India four times between 1747 and 1757, sacked Delhi on his last incursion, and placed his own governor over Punjab.

The center of power in India was weakened to such an extent that regional power holders became virtually independent, and the Mughal emperors became puppets in the hands of whoever could claim hegemony. The Marathas, who had risen in revolt against the Mughals and founded a Hindu kingdom in Maharashtra, posed the most serious threat to the Mughal dynasty. By 1750, they had expanded their power eastward over central India and Orissa and northward to Gujarat and Delhi. Ahmad Shah Abdali, the only other viable contender, who considered the Mughal emperor to be his protégé, returned to confirm his hegemony over northern India. However, the costly battle of Panipat, in 1761, marked the end of Ahmad Shah Abdali's ambitions for an Indian empire and also decisively damaged the Maratha potential for an imperial takeover.

The power vacuum in the north was filled by the rise of anti-Mughal armed Sikh bands, who ultimately established an independent kingdom in Punjab by the end of the century. In the rest of India, apart from the practically independent *nawabs* (Mughal provincial governors) of the large and opulent provinces of Avadh and Bengal and the minor kingdoms of Rajput princes in Rajasthan, the major power holders were in the Deccan: the

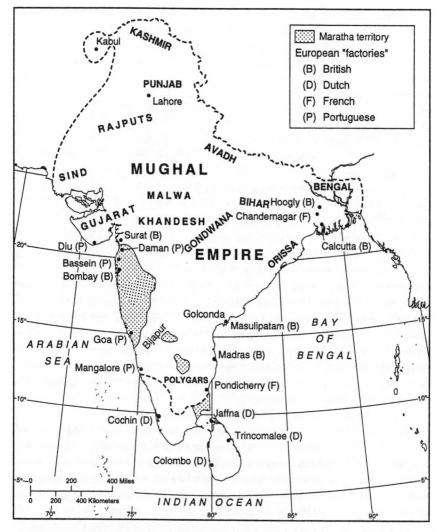

The Subcontinent around A.D. 1700

Marathas, the Nizam of Hyderabad, and after 1761, the sultan of Mysore. When the East India Company (EIC) got involved with local Indian politics in the 1750s, the country was divided among several hundred Hindu and Muslim kingdoms and chiefdoms, though most of them were petty in size and insignificant as far as the national scene was concerned. By 1765, the EIC, having defeated the *nawab* of Bengal and been appointed the *diwan* (revenue collector) of Bengal and Bihar by the puppet Mughal emperor, had become the de facto local ruler and, thereby, a serious though as yet unrecognized aspirant to the throne in Delhi.

Society

Socially, the country was even more divided than it was politically. Persian, the court language, may have made communication possible among the ruling classes, but it was a foreign language that disappeared from the scene soon after the British replaced the Mughals. Arabic, the language of Islam, continued to be taught in Muslim religious establishments, but it was not even understood by the common Muslim laity. Classical Sanskrit remained the language of scholarship among the Hindus and was also regularly used by Brahmin priests in performing Hindu rituals, but it was a dead language, incomprehensible to the people at large, who spoke one or the other of the hundreds of dialects associated with the fourteen major regional languages that had come to replace Sanskrit. While the northern languages had evolved from Sanskrit, the four southern languages, Tamil, Telugu, Malayalam, and Kannada, had descended from the pre-Aryan Dravidian language. One of the vernaculars, totally new to the subcontinent, was Urdu, which was an admixture of Persian and Hindi vocabulary; it used Hindi grammar but was written in the Persian script.

Apart from being divided linguistically, the people were also divided by religion. All the major religions of the world—Hinduism, Islam, Buddhism, Sikhism, Jainism, Zoroastrianism, Christianity, and Judaism (Christianity and Judaism both came to the subcontinent centuries before the arrival of the Portuguese and the British)—were represented in India. The majority of the population was Hindu, but that did not spell unity within that community either, because the Hindus were not only fragmented by language but also split by hundreds of different religious cults and atomized by thousands of mutually exclusive castes.

Once Muslim rulers had slowed down their drive to proselytize, the Hindus had no difficulty in living under Islam. Islam was the "other" that could be totally ignored; it posed no threat to the self-contained caste ghettos of the Hindus. The Muslims found themselves living in their own ghettos. Business contacts were maintained, but there was no social interaction; members of various caste groups did not invite each other to their homes or dine together, so it was no great departure from the norm for Hindus not to mix socially with the Muslims.

A word here about the village communities of India would not be inappropriate. Broadly speaking, these communities retained their autonomy and their contact with the state remained the headman, the *zamindar* or the *jagirdar,* who collected the taxes. As these officials, because of the disturbed nature of the state, began to acquire ownership over the lands under their control, the peasants can be said to have become renters or tenants. However, India lacked the Western perception of property, and what the emperor, the tax collector, the peasant, the village Brahmin, and the village artisans had were *interests* in the land and not *exclusive ownership* of the land. Land was held in common by a village community and the peasant's (or tenant's, if you will) interest in the land was protected by customary practices and usage. The landlords could transfer or sell their right to collect rents (taxes), but had no right to sell any of the village land; similarly, the peasants' rights to the land could be inherited, subdivided, or, in some areas, even sold, but never to an outsider who did not belong to the village community. "The relation of a zamindar to government and of a *ryot* [tenant farmer] to zamindar is neither that of a proprietor nor a vassal but a compound of both. The former performs acts of authority unconnected with property rights. The latter has rights without real property."[40] The internal government of the villages continued to be run by *panchayat* councils (mostly in the north) or village committees (in the south). The nonagricultural artisan and service castes were maintained by being provided a fixed share of the village produce and, sometimes, through allocation of small plots of land. The interdependent socio-economic organization in village India is known as the *jajmani* system.

Economic Condition

Recurrent wars and the huge increase in the military expenditures under Aurangzeb, who had doubled the size of the Mughal army without any parallel increase in revenues, led to a financial collapse of the empire. Aurangzeb also raised the number of *mansabdars* precipitously (to 14,500), despite being in no position to supply them with appropriate *jagirs*. This not only weakened the *mansabdari* system, because the military lords could not maintain the expected number of cavalry without a proper income, but also alienated the *mansabdars*. Sometimes the soldiers were not paid for years on end. As a result, the army was enfeebled, corruption in civil and military administration became rampant, local power holders began to declare their independence, and rebellions became ubiquitous. As the exactions from the peasantry became unbearably large, many peasants abandoned their villages. Famines became endemic, and in one famine alone, in 1702–1704, over 2 million persons died. François Bernier, who was in India from 1658 to 1664, made a penetrating analysis of the country's ills: "The country is ruined by the necessity of defraying the enormous charges required to maintain the splendour of a numerous court, and to pay a large army maintained for keeping the people in subjection. . . . The cudgel and the whip compel them to incessant labour for the benefit of others."[41]

By the eighteenth century, according to Professor Saiyid Nurul Hasan, "as the village handicrafts began to collapse, whatever 'prosperity' the village has—I am using prosperity . . . in a purely relative sense—begins to disappear more and more."[42] Overall, in both agriculture and manufacturing, Indian technology remained stagnant and was surpassed not only by Europe but also China. "In the use of wind and water power, metallurgy, printing, nautical instruments, and basic tools and precision instruments . . . India failed to produce proper cast iron . . . [to] use her coal despite the availability of surface deposits. . . . Nautical instruments like the compass [discovered by the Chinese and used by them for centuries] and the telescope were known but never used."[43]

The expansion of the British occupation of the subcontinent from 1765 to 1858, and its consequences to India, will be taken up in the next chapter, however it may be mentioned here that, like the Qing rulers of China, the Mughals kept their attention turned landward and did not become a naval power. This despite the fact that, unlike the Chinese, the Mughals had no reason or desire (nor the capability) to isolate the country from the outside world; indeed, the Mughals not only needed to have regular shipping that could assure passage for Haj pilgrims but they, from princes to *nawabs,* were investing heavily in commercial enterprises associated with lucrative maritime trade.

India had historically been at the heart of a thriving east-west (east as far as China, west as far as Arabia, Egypt, and Africa, and overland to Europe) trade. The kingdoms along the eastern and western seaboards of India had developed a maritime orientation through the centuries, exporting cotton and silk cloth, raw cotton and raw silk, rice, wheat, beans, pepper, indigo, and oil, and importing horses (used for cavalry but difficult to breed in India), ivory, and bullion. The balance of trade was favorable to India. However, by the middle of the eighteenth century, the political disintegration of the Mughal empire led to a veritable collapse of Indian shipping, and though trade continued, commodities were now carried in foreign—mostly English—bottoms. The old ports, such as Surat, Calicut, and Masulipatam, declined in importance and gave way to new ones developed by the British: Bombay (Mumbai), Madras, and Calcutta.

The bright spot in this otherwise dismal picture of the eighteenth century is the growth of domestic and foreign demand for manufactured and agricultural commodities and the monetization of the economy. Internal demand increased because of the rise of hundreds of large and petty rulers who needed not only weapons, uniforms, and cash to service their growing armies but also luxury articles that could lend glamour to their courts and establish their stature and importance. External demand grew with the expanding European market for Indian goods. This stimulated the trend toward area specialization in manufactures and the beginnings of an integrated national market. It also resulted in the rise of dynamic commercial classes who acquired political importance as the bankers to the new mid-level upstarts in the political arena (the new *nawabs* and *zamindars*) and who loaned money to the merchants and traders and provided advances to the artisans manufacturing textiles.

The sophistication and complexity of the commercial network and the significant increase in production of manufactured articles have given rise to the idea among some historians that, but for the British colonialists, India would have had an industrial revolution of its own. Revisionist historians, seeing parallel developments in late-traditional China, have also argued that possibilities of an industrial revolution in that country were similarly thwarted by imperialist penetration. There is no justification for such theses because both these societies were essentially traditional, self-sufficient, agrarian economies lacking the preconditions for a modern technological and capitalist revolution.

Notes

1. This topic has been taken up by a pioneering work by S. C. Malik, *Indian Civilization: The Formative Period* (Delhi: Motilal Banarsidass, 1987).

2. Vincent Smith, *Oxford History of India* (Oxford, UK: Oxford University Press, 1919), p. x.

3. Jawaharlal Nehru, *The Discovery of India* (New Delhi: Oxford University Press), 1985, pp. 75–76.

4. Sarvepalli Radhakrishnan, *The Hindu View of Life* (London: Unwin Books, 1927), p. 12.

5. *Vishnu Purana,* II.3.1.

6. Nehru, *The Discovery of India,* p. 60.

7. Malik, *Indian Civilization: The Formative Period,* pp. 122–123.

8. Ibid., pp. 106–107.

9. Trevor Ling, ed., *The Buddha's Philosophy of Man* (London: J.M. Dent and Sons, 1981), p. 43.

10. N. K. Dutt, *Origin and Growth of Caste in India* (Calcutta: Firma KLM, 1986), p. 57.

11. For a detailed discussion of this subject see Dutt, *Origin and Growth of Caste in India.*

12. Ibid., p. 2.

13. Subhaya Dasgupta, *Hindu Ethos and the Challenge of Change* (New Delhi: Arnold-Heinemann, 1977), p. 167.

14. M. N. Srinivas, *Social Change in Modern India* (Berkeley: University of California Press, 1966), p. 26.

15. A. C. Bhaktivedanta Swami Prabhupada, tr., *Bhagavad-gita: As It Is* (New York: Collier Books, 1974), pp. 169, 170.

16. Ibid., p. 602.

17. Ibid., p. 273.

18. A. L. Basham, *The Wonder That Was India* (New York: Grove Press, 1959), p. 309.

19. Quoted in Wm. Theodore De Barry, gen. ed., *Sources of Indian Tradition,* Vol. I (New York: Columbia University Press, 1964), p. 290.

20. Ibid.

21. William Q. Judge, tr., *The Bhagwad Gita* (Bombay: Theosophy Company, Ltd., 1942), p. 67.

22. See report by Milind Palnitkar, "Caste Impeding Rehabilitation," in *India Abroad,* October 29, 1993, p. 12.

23. Sarvepalli Radhakrishnan and Charles A. Moore, eds., *A Sourcebook in Indian Philosophy* (Princeton: Princeton University Press, 1957), p. 198.

24. Ibid., p. 209.

25. Basham, *The Wonder That Was India,* pp. 57–58.

26. A. R. Desai, *Social Background of Indian Nationalism* (Bombay: Oxford University Press, 1949), p. 15.

27. See Sachchidananda Bhattacharya, *Select Asokan Epigraphs* (Calcutta: Firma K.L. Mukhopadhyay, 1960).

28. For example, see 11th Major Rock Edict in ibid.

29. Romila Thapar, *Asoka and the Decline of the Mauryas* (Delhi: Oxford University Press, 1963), p. 210.

30. See Sir George E. Schuster and Guy Wint, *India and Democracy* (London: Macmillan and Co., 1941), and A. E. Punit, *Social Systems in Rural India* (New Delhi:

Sterling Press, 1978). Punit gives a positive view of traditional village self-government, and describes its decay and revival in modern India, but in no way proves that the traditional *panchayat* system provides any roots for democracy.

31. Basham, *The Wonder That Was India,* p. 66.

32. Nehru, *The Discovery of India,* p. 223.

33. Quoted in Hermann Kulke and Dietmar Rothermund, *A History of India* (Totowa, NJ: Barnes and Noble, 1986), p. 165.

34. M. Mujeeb, *Indian Muslims* (New Delhi: Munshiram Manoharlal Publishers, 1985), p. 264.

35. See translation of *Tarikh-i-Firuz-Shahi* in H. M. Elliot and J. Dowson, *The History of India as Told by its own Historians,* Vol. II (London: Trubner, 1867–77), pp. 179 ff.

36. Tapan Raychaudhuri and Irfan Habib, eds., *The Cambridge Economic History of India,* Vol. I (Cambridge: Cambridge University Press, 1982; reprinted by Orient Longman, India, 1984), p. 240.

37. Quoted in J. N. Sarkar, *Hindu-Muslim Relations in Medieval Bengal* (Delhi: Idarah-i-Adabiyat-i-Delhi, 1985), p. 11.

38. See Mujeeb, *Indian Muslims,* chap. 1.

39. C. A. Bayly, *Indian Society and the Making of the British Empire* (Cambridge: Cambridge University Press, 1988), pp. 11–12.

40. Quoted by Tapan Raychaudhuri, "The Mid-Eighteenth Century Background," in Dharma Kumar, ed., *The Cambridge Economic History of India,* Vol. II (Cambridge: Cambridge University Press, 1982; reprinted by Orient Longman, India, 1984), p. 13.

41. Quoted in Anil Chandra Banerjee, *The New History of Modern India* (Calcutta: K.P. Bagchi, 1983), p. 5.

42. Saiyid Nurul Hasan, *Thought on Agrarian Relations in Mughal India* (New Delhi: People's Publishing House, 1973), p. 37.

43. Kumar, *The Cambridge Economic History of India,* Vol. II, pp. 18–19.

3

India's Adjustment to British Aggression

1756–1857

As we enter the modern period it is necessary to reiterate that, though many of the Europe-centered points of view regarding Asian development which were popular until the end of World War II have been corrected, it will still take some time before the century-and-a-half-old Western self-image of cultural, moral, and intellectual superiority (paralleled by a contempt for non-Western peoples for lacking these high qualities) is wholly demolished.

The responses of non-Western peoples to Western domination, ranging from a rejection of their own cultural heritages and imitation of the West to a rediscovery of their past greatness and a condemnation of Western moral and cultural values, have also not yet produced a confident, well-defined sense of self-identity.

However, the process that will contribute to a more balanced approach to the evolution of the post–Industrial Revolution global order is well under way. The last four decades of the postimperialist era have given an opportunity to Western and non-Western historians to look more objectively at the interaction of the forces that resulted in the century of world dominance by Western imperialism. While the Westerners are coming to recognize the hollowness and arrogance of their earlier claims, the non-Western historians, too, have come to discard the simplistic notion that Western domination and imperialism were an unmitigated blight responsible for all the ills that afflict their countries.

Industrialization, Modernization, and Imperialism

It is now generally recognized that the roots of Western imperialism lay in the Industrial Revolution, which was a Western phenomenon. In a limited sense, the

Industrial Revolution implied changes in technology that allowed society to tap new energy sources (steam, electricity, petroleum) to run newly invented power machines (power looms, railway engines, steamships) that replaced the use of hand tools and human muscle power and, thereby, greatly increased production and surplus wealth. These changes fostered the streamlining of industrial production by division of labor and labor-saving devices and led to mass production and the "factory" system.

Thus, the use of machines and the application of science revolutionized traditional agriculture and reduced the amount of human labor needed to work the land. Peasants released from the land went off to the cities to find work in the new factories and become part of the new wage-earning working classes. Expanding industries and commerce demanded skilled workers, and this called for an expansion of the educational system. There was growth of a cash economy and wider distribution of wealth. Cities grew in size and so did the bourgeoisie, who demanded better services (sewerage, sanitation, health care, hospitals, medication, schools, colleges, libraries, street lighting, running water, and so on) and a greater voice in political decision making. Communications improved, banking grew, and service industries multiplied. On the psychological front, rationalism began to replace blind faith, the vision of unlimited progress began to grip the popular imagination, and nationalism began to acquire the lineaments of a religion.

These developments were the harbingers of modernization, which changed human life even more drastically than the Industrial Revolution itself. Among other things, the individual, not the family, became the basic unit of society; the rule of law replaced rule by fiat; all individuals gained equality in the eyes of the law; the church was separated from the state; all relationships came to be regarded as secular and justiciable; political power was vested in institutions rather than in individuals; and the communication media were allowed to freely report on all matters concerning the state so that the people were well informed and could exercise their judgment on political affairs. Since the industrialized and modernized West gained the wealth and power that allowed it to dominate the globe, a myth was created that there was something inherently superior about Western civilization. As a consequence, the purely exploitative element of imperialism came to be masked by the theory that the white man had a mission (his so-called burden) to civilize the colored natives by bringing to them the benefits of Western culture.

Speaking in 1895, Cecil Rhodes was brutally forthright in laying bare the real impetus behind British imperialism: "In order to [improve the standard of living of the British people and] save . . . the United Kingdom from a bloody civil war, our colonial statesmen must acquire new lands for settling the population of this country, to provide new markets for the goods produced in the factories and mines. The Empire as I have always said is a bread and butter question. If you want to avoid civil war, you must become imperialists."[1] Britain did just that and at the height of its imperialist expansion, it ruled over one quarter of the population of the world.

On the other hand, persons like Rudyard Kipling took a leading part in glamorizing the burden myth. In a poem, "The White Man's Burden," written in 1899, not long after Rhodes's speech, Kipling made the poignant appeal:

> Take up the White Man's burden-
> Send out the best ye breed-
> Go bind your sons to exile,
> To serve your captive's need:
>
> . . .
>
> Your new caught sullen peoples,
> Half devil and half child.

Several decades earlier, in 1833, Thomas Babington Macaulay, one of the most ardent advocates of Western education for Indians, had expressed the same sentiment in a somewhat different way: "Having become instructed in European knowledge, [Indians] may, in some future age, demand European institutions," and he hoped that that would create an "imperishable empire of our arts and our morals, our literature and our laws."[2]

The self-proclaimed superiority of the Europeans and their self-assumed role as saviors of souls and "civilizers" of the non-Western world had diverse ramifications for various countries. Although tribal Africa suffered the most and societies in the old civilizations of Asia were less overwhelmed, the impact of the European attitude toward progress in the colored societies made it difficult for non-Western peoples, as a whole, to separate the superficial aspects of Western culture from the essentials of modernization. In the words of Ashis Nandy, "The West is now everywhere, within the West and outside; in [our] structures and in [our] minds,"[3] causing intellectual and moral confusion among the once-subject peoples.

In contemporary parlance, the term *Westernization* as a path to modernity has acquired a pejorative connotation and is carefully avoided by both Western and Third World scholars, but the fact remains that there is an understandable tendency among developing peoples to consider the more "developed," the more "advanced," the more "modernized" states of the West as models.* If the whole world is inexorably moving toward a common universal culture of modernity, surely the West is nearer to the ideal than the Third World. So why not Westernize? The term is rejected by the Third World because Westernization is perceived as embodying a tainted culture that is unacceptable.

This fear of acculturation is graphically illustrated by the Chinese case: The very same Communist Chinese leaders who had opened the country twenty years ago to Western technology, science, and investment capital have now begun a

---

*Since the impression remains that Japan developed by borrowing from (if not aping) the West, Japan fails to qualify as a true model.

campaign against the seepage of Western culture into China because they fear that it will lead to "spiritual pollution." They are perplexed by the activities of young Chinese who associate modernization with the behavior of the youth in the United States and have taken to such things as the wearing of blue jeans and disco dancing. This trend may be dismissed as a trivial by-product of change, but it does reflect a larger historical truth that all relatively weak and underdeveloped nations of the world try to ape the "advanced" Western nations, even in matters that have no direct bearing on modernization. Psychologically, some things are considered more "modern," although they may not make one whit of a contribution to modernization. One has just to look around the cities of India to see how "Americanized" youth have become there.

The British Ascendancy in India: 1757–1857

The British conquest of India, a product of the expansionist activities of the East India Company (EIC), was completed in several phases between 1757 and 1848, and it resulted in the establishment of a mercantile precapitalist empire. This vast empire was technically ruled by the EIC (technically, because the British Parliament began to exercise increasing control over the company's administration after 1773) until 1858, when the colony was transferred to the British Crown and the Indian administration was placed directly under the control of the government of Britain. The establishment of India as a Crown Colony synchronized with the rise of Western imperialism, and during the remaining nine decades of British rule in India the country's development was affected both by theories and practices that supported imperialism and by those that attacked imperialism and inspired an Indian reaction to foreign rule.

The question that has often been asked and never satisfactorily answered is: Why did the British conquer India? Was it "in a fit of absence of mind," as Sir John Seeley told the students at Cambridge in 1883? Was it part of a grand imperialist design? Was it because of international rivalry between the European powers? Was it a by-product of the private interests of the greedy and predatory company's servants in India, who saw an opportunity to fill their bottomless pockets with ill-gotten wealth by using British military power? Was it because the company had to defend itself to protect its trade from the rapacity of local rulers? Or was the company sucked into the internal affairs of India because of the vacuum created by the breakdown of Mughal authority and had no recourse other than expansion and conquest?

The answer to all these questions is both yes and no. The mix of causes of the expansion of British power was different from stage to stage. In each stage several overlapping factors can be traced, though only one or two of them may appear to play a dominant role.

Many modern historians categorically deny that the beginning of the process of British expansion can be connected with the word *conquest,* maintaining that in 1756, neither the EIC, a chartered company of merchants, nor Britain, as a state and a government, had any grand design to conquer India.[4] Technically, this may be correct, but it would not be inappropriate to mention that (1) the EIC was not purely a mercantile body and that it had the solid backing of the British government represented by several men-of-war from the Royal Navy and by units of the royal army; (2) the EIC was as keen to protect its trading interests through conquest as the Portuguese and the Dutch had done before them, and had repeatedly made suggestions to that effect to its directors in London; (3) by 1756, the British were exercising the rights of sovereignty in Bombay Presidency (the territory was obtained from the Portuguese and not from the Mughals and this gave the EIC the right to mint coins and make war and peace) and had acquired the political authority to establish local municipal governments in Madras and Calcutta presidencies (so-called because their administration was headed by a president, sometimes referred to as "governor"); and (4) the EIC at the same time had already built up a sepoy army of considerable size and gained experience in successfully interfering in Indian internal politics. By the early decades of the eighteenth century, only the French and the British were the main European competitors for primacy in the Indian theater. The British had well-established and fortified factories at Bombay, Madras, and Calcutta; the French were entrenched in Pondicherry (near Madras) and Chandernagar (near Calcutta).

The three wars the British and French fought in the subcontinent between 1744 and 1763 were not really over trade; they were an expression of their rivalry for world domination and an extension of their conflict in Europe and North America. Though each side had its share of successes and failures in these hostilities, and even though after the 1763 treaty settlement (which ended the Seven Years' War in Europe), the French regained possession of Pondicherry and Chandernagar, the wars marked the end of French ambitions in India.

Nevertheless, the Anglo-French conflict had the effect of radically transforming the political scene in India. The process started when the visionary Joseph François Dupleix, governor of Pondicherry from 1724 to 1754, got the idea that the French could counter the naval superiority of the British by taking sides in the wars between local potentates and, thereby, establish a strong land base of their own. What Dupleix did was to raise companies of well-drilled, well-equipped, French-led Indian infantrymen (called sepoys from *sipahi,* the Urdu word for a trooper), and made them available to his protégés in the Deccan and the Carnatic (Karnataka). The extraordinary triumphs achieved by these companies enabled the French to rapidly expand their sphere of influence. In return for the service rendered, the victorious *nawabs* and *rajas* signed subsidiary alliances, which forced them to cede a number of districts to the French to subsidize the maintenance of the sepoy units placed at their disposal. Thus, the French, without any cost to themselves, acquired indirect control over Hyderabad and the Carnatic and direct (colonial) control over certain districts. As it turned out, however, this ingenious arrangement did not meet the approval of the French government and Dupleix was abruptly withdrawn. But the British were quick to appreciate the vast potential of the French formula and made it the bedrock of their future policy.

It is worth noting here that the advantage the British sepoy armies enjoyed over the armies of native rulers derived not so much from superior technology as from a superior drilling technique and a superior command structure. Although many Indian rulers later tried to imitate the British and raised infantry divisions of their own, often trained by Western mercenaries, they never managed to produce a unified, cohesive, disciplined army in which all parts acted in unison. There can be no doubting that Robert Clive's victory at Plassey in 1757, which made the British the de facto rulers of Bengal, was based as much on the excellence of his sepoy army as on the chicanery and bribery that had already softened up and demoralized the enemy's forces.

Possibility of Hindu Takeover

Until 1761, there were two main contenders for supremacy in the subcontinent: the Hindu Marathas, a purely indigenous power; and the Muslim Afghans, who were once part of the Mughal empire but were now independent. In view of the manner in which Ahmad Shah Abdali had repeatedly invaded India and ravished Punjab, one would be tempted to look upon him as an outsider, a non-Indian. But this was not quite so. Many Muslim noblemen and power holders in India were themselves from Afghanistan and had strong links with their "homeland." From the time of Aurangzeb, a strong movement among the orthodox *ulama* to cleanse Islam of the syncretic elements introduced by Akbar led many to believe that the answer to the Mughal problems lay in establishing a purer Islamic state. One such thinker was Shah Waliullah (c. 1702–1763), who could not tolerate the idea of Ghazi-ud-din, the *wazir* (prime minister) of the ruling Mughal emperor, allying himself with the Marathas against Ahmad Shah Abdali and he "appealed to the Afghans to 'save' Delhi from its 'Hindu Raj.' "[5]

Abdali, who may not have intended to attack Delhi, responded to the request of Waliullah and other Muslim nobles. Was Shah Waliullah an Indian? Hardly so, if we consider his admonition to his family that "it should express its gratitude to God for its Arab blood and speech [by retaining] as far as possible Arab habits and customs and not permit[ting] the intrusion of [non-Islamic] customs and the habits of the Hindus."[6] Percival Spear sees in this intellectual movement "the first seeds of the Pakistan of the future."[7] However, neither the anti-Hindu Muslim purists nor the anti-Muslim Hindu or Sikh revivalists could draw, at this stage of Indian history, any clear-cut lines of confrontation. Muslim and Hindu rulers, whatever their inner feelings, continued to make alliances and counteralliances with each other and depend on support from both Hindu and Muslim vassals.

Although the battle of Panipat (1761) neutralized both the Afghans and the Marathas, the Marathas soon recovered their fighting capacity but not their pre-

1761 potential for empire. The opportunity, if one ever existed, for the reunification of India by a purely Indian Hindu power was lost forever. The conclusion that one is forced to reach is that in the absence of any political ideal of a genuinely unified state—an ideal which Hinduism had failed to develop—the Marathas found it convenient to function within the military-feudal structure established by the Mughals and to continue to pay respect to the phantom central authority represented by the Mughal emperors. This gave them the freedom to act as they chose and then acquire legitimacy for their actions by getting them ratified by appropriate imperial edicts issued by a puppet Mughal emperor. Indeed, all the major players in the Indian political arena, such as the *nawabs* of Avadh and Bengal, the *nizam* of Hyderabad, and the EIC, sought to represent themselves as agents of the Great Mughal.

Therefore, the myth of a central power headed by the Great Mughal was carefully maintained, and even strengthened, in inverse proportion to the ruling emperors' actual authority. In return for a negotiated and often extremely limited tribute, the puppet emperors were always glad to exercise their "power" and honor a successful Hindu or Muslim aggressor with titles and offices legitimizing his newly acquired territories. In 1765, after the company had soundly defeated the "imperial" forces, the EIC received a *firman* (a royal decree) from Emperor Shah Alam granting it the *diwani* (the right to collect revenue) of Bengal, Bihar, and Orissa in perpetuity (originally the *diwan*, the financial head of the province, was appointed for a specific duration and the post was transferable) in return for 2.6 million rupees as annual tribute. As late as 1783, when the ruling emperor was hardly in control of his own palace, the Sikhs, who had consolidated their hold over Punjab, made a ceremonial offering to the throne. And in 1792, the brilliantly successful Maratha general Mahadaji Sindhia (Scindia), having extended his influence over Delhi and the titular emperor, got the emperor to appoint the *peshwa* (chief minister of the Marathas) as *Vakil-i-mutlak* (vice-regent). And the *peshwa* was invested with this office in Pune (Poona) at a grand ceremony!

This strange desire of the mighty warlords to remain vassals of a fictitious central authority makes sense only if we bear in mind that the hollow shell of feudalism was used by the dominant local rulers as a device to legitimize their territorial expansion and that it conceded them the right to become overlords of lesser *nawabs* and *rajas* and have vassals of their own. The Mughal military-feudal system, though modified, was the only style of politics that the new power holders could understand and follow. This style also reflects the traditional Hindu style of polity: "Like the relations of worship established in puja, the root political metaphor, political relations commence when a lesser king or noble offers service to a greater lord or king. They are 'established' once the service is recognized in the form of gifts made by the superior to the inferior. The gifts include titles, emblems, and honors, right to enjoy the usufruct of particular lands, and/or the privilege to rule on behalf of the superior over a particular area. . . . At the moments

of greatest separation, or independence [of the inferior], the continued maintenance of certain forms of connection is not a contradiction."[8]

As a result, the Marathas, who at one stage had the capability of replacing the
Muslims and establishing a consolidated Hindu empire—indeed Peshwa Baji
Rao (1720–1740) had talked enthusiastically of pursuing the ideal of a *Hindu-
pad-padshahi* (an empire under a supreme Hindu emperor)—not only failed to
do so but could not even found a unified state of their own. The predatory
character of the Maratha forces outside their homeland of Maharashtra, their
plundering and looting of non-Maratha Hindu communities such as the Rajputs,
lost them the respect of the Hindus and the right to lead the Hindus against the
Muslim rulers. The Bengali Hindus have left us a vivid picture of the behavior of
the Maratha raiders: "They shouted over and over again, 'Give us money,' and
when they got no money they filled the peoples' nostrils with water, and some
they seized and drowned in tanks. . . . In this way they did all manner of foul and
evil deeds."[9]

Thus, incipient Hindu nationalism, which first emerged with Shivaji, gave
way to Maratha imperialism and the Maratha state itself was turned into a feudal
"confederacy."

It is worth noting that Shivaji (1627–1680), who laid the foundation of the
Hindu Maratha empire and instilled a spirit of independence among his people,
was a low-caste Hindu who had to go all the way to Banaras to find a sympathetic Brahmin to recognize him (and his caste) as Kshatriya, and crown him
king in a Hindu ceremony (1674). Shivaji tried hard, and succeeded to a considerable degree, in unifying the Marathas and getting them to act as one people.
However, his descendants (kings of Satara) lost power to the Brahmin *peshwas*
(chief ministers). The post of *peshwa* became hereditary, and though its incum-
bents continued to receive their appointment from their king in Satara, they made
Pune, where they held court, the capital of the Maratha empire. The ascendancy
of the Brahmin *peshwas* provoked the jealousy of the most important non-Brah-
min military lords, who gradually began to exercise independent authority within
their fiefdoms that lay outside the Maratha homeland (Maharashtra), though the
peshwas were allowed to "appoint" the *diwans* to their estates (how similar to the
powerless emperor's appointment of the company as *diwan* of Bengal!). From
around 1770, not only did the *peshwa*'s primacy become nominal, but the Maratha military feudal lords began to make alliances with non-Marathas to fight
each other; the most important of these local rulers were the Scindia family in
Gwalior, the Gaekwad in Baroda, the Holkar in Indore, and the Bhonsle in
Nagpur.

Bengal: The Beginnings of the British Empire

Until the mid-eighteenth century, Bengal was the richest province in the Mughal
empire. It was a food surplus area and exported, among other items, rice, sugar,

and oil to many parts of northern, southern, and western India. Bengali raw silk was the main support for the Gujarat silk industry; it was also exported to the Middle East. Bengal cotton and silk textiles were not only available all over India but were exported in large quantities to Southeast Asia. After 1700, when trade in spices declined, the East India Company became one of the most important buyers of Bengal textiles. Bengal was also an importer of the specialized manufactures from other parts of India.

Merchants with diverse regional backgrounds, ranging from Central Asian Muslims, Iranian Armenians, Middle Eastern Jews, and Europeans, to Parsis and Gujaratis from western India and Marwaris and Jains from Rajasthan, flocked to Bengal to participate in its thriving trade. One banker from Rajasthan, who settled in Bengal in the early eighteenth century, was so rich that the Nawab of Bengal made him his treasurer and gave him the title of *jagat seth* (world banker) and the right to mint coins. This financial magnate had the capability of dispatching the entire revenue of the eastern provinces to Delhi with a *hundi* (a bill of exchange) drawn on his Delhi agent's establishment. Working closely with revenue farmers and indigenous merchants, the bankers in Bengal thus acquired tremendous political influence. By withholding loans or advances, or shifting their allegiance, they could undermine the authority of the *nawab.*

This is exactly what happened in 1757, when the *jagat seths,* angered by the harsh taxation introduced by the new *nawab,* Siraj-ud-daula (ruled 1756–1757), joined other alienated elements such as the local *zamindars* and the EIC and underwrote a conspiracy that aimed at overthrowing Siraj-ud-daula and replacing him with one of his key generals, Mir Jafar. The conspiracy cost the *jagat seths* and their malcontent partners 1,250,000 pounds sterling (over 20 million pounds sterling in 1988 currency) in bribes, most of the money going to the company and its servants.[10] The EIC was also "compensated" by the new *nawab* and other *zamindars,* and the "initial settlement resulted in some 4,000,000 [pounds sterling] being [moved] ... between India and Britain." Clive, alone, received 234,000 pounds sterling.[11] According to some calculations the total settlement was for about 18 million pounds sterling (about 360 million in 1988 currency) "probably exceeding all the movable property of Calcutta's inhabitants."[12]

This elaborate conspiracy notwithstanding, it was by no means certain that Clive's force numbering no more than 3,000 (including about 900 Europeans) could defeat an army of 50,000 infantry and 1,800 cavalry. Nobody, neither the nobles or *seths* of Bengal, nor the directors of the EIC, nor, for that matter the company officials in India—fully grasped the significance of the Battle of Plassey. Most of the Indians concerned, no doubt, expected a return to the pre-Plassey status quo. The company expected to add to its trading privileges and generally function in an environment of relatively greater freedom with less fear of the authorities. Plassey, however, introduced a revolutionary situation in Bengal that was to have a profound influence on the future history of the subcontinent.

One element in the story of Plassey that Indian historians have played down, and the contemporary revisionist Cambridge historians have a tendency to overlook, is the incident that became known as the Black Hole of Calcutta.[13] When Siraj-ud-daula took over as *nawab*, he had reason to be irritated by the company's behavior. Among other things, the EIC had refused to pay the customary gift of money demanded by the new *nawab*, had fortified Calcutta without permission, and had abused the privilege, granted earlier by the Mughal emperor, of not having to pay customs duties on their exports and imports by extending it to cover inland trade.

In June (the hottest month of the year) 1756, Siraj-ud-daula attacked Fort William (the company headquarters in Calcutta) and having reduced it, imprisoned 146 prisoners in the fort's jail, which happened to be a small chamber about 18 feet by 15 feet that soon came to be known as the "Black Hole of Calcutta." It was reported that 126 of the captives died overnight owing to suffocation and the heat. Recent research has proved that the number who died may have been much smaller and that, in any case, Siraj-ud-daula was not personally responsible for this act. These findings are, however, irrelevant to the fact that the incident was used to inflame public opinion in England and to justify a forward policy in India: the monstrous offenses against the British by an Oriental despot were wholly unpardonable and the despot needed to be taught a lesson. The "incident was made into the centerpiece of one of the first great atrocity campaigns of modern times."[14] And this, in turn, made it possible for Clive to think in terms of replacing Siraj-ud-daula with a more pliable *nawab* even after Clive had relieved Fort William and made an adequate treaty settlement with Siraj-ud-daula; the treaty compensated the company for its earlier losses, permitted it to refortify Calcutta and gave it the added privilege of minting coins.

After Plassey, the Bengal branch of the East India Company under Clive, who had gotten himself made governor of Calcutta in a most unorthodox manner, could no longer retain its purely foreign and commercial character and became an active participant in the internal politics of Bengal. Mir Jafar was a protégé of the company, as was symbolically made clear when Clive led Mir Jafar by the hand to his throne. Mir Jafar was not only financially in debt to the company (a debt he could never get rid of during his brief reign, 1757–1760) but wholly dependent on company armies for his security. To compensate the company, he had to allow it to collect revenue from specific districts (24 *parganas*) around Calcutta. In 1759, after Clive had defeated various armies (including that of the Mughal crown prince) that had invaded Bengal and Bihar, Mir Jafar got the emperor to award Clive the title of *omrah* (which put Clive in the category of the Mughal nobility) and the 24 *parganas* as his personal *jagir*. In 1759–60, Clive once again proved worthy of the trust accorded to him by defeating the invading imperial armies of emperor Shah Alam (the crown prince of the earlier war, who had ascended the throne after murdering his father). Of course, poor Mir Jafar had to pay dearly for every battle fought by the sepoy army. The *jagirdar* "nabob" Clive returned to England in 1760 as a highly honored and a very, very rich man.

After Clive's departure the bankrupt Mir Jafar could no longer satisfy the insatiable financial demands of the East India Company, and since he hesitated to dismember Bengal and hand over some of the richest districts to the company, the British discarded him in favor of his son-in-law, Mir Kasim (reigned 1760–1763). Mir Kasim paid the bribes (Governor Vansittart alone received 225,000 pounds sterling) and ceded the three districts demanded by the company, but that was only the beginning of his problems. Mir Kasim had inherited an empty treasury, he could not tax the company trade or the private trade carried on by the company's servants, and the company kept increasing its demands on him. In spite of his straitened circumstances, Mir Kasim tried to bring back some order to Bengal and extricate himself from the claws of the company. But his attempts at reform came to naught because he could not restrain the British merchants from monopolizing trade in many important commodities and even from dealing in commodities reserved for the state (e.g., salt). It was bad enough that the company did not pay any duties, but the situation became intolerable when the company's servants extended the company's privileges to their private trade and also began to sell certificates *(dastaks)* to Indian merchants so that they, too, could avoid paying customs levies. In the words of Panikkar, the British had "established a robber state where, without reference to the rights of the others, they freely plundered and looted under cover of their 'rights.' "[15]

To end this regime of reckless plunder Mir Kasim took a desperate step and declared all trade to be duty free (1763). However, for this act, which he had every right to mandate, the EIC declared war on Mir Kasim for a "breach of the company's privileges" and reinstated Mir Jafar on the throne! Mir Kasim formed a hasty alliance with Nawab Shuja-ud-daula of Avadh (the most powerful and important ruler in northern India) and Emperor Shah Alam, but the allied forces, numbering around 150,000, were totally defeated at Baksar (1764) by the company's army of about 40,000. The company's forces then occupied Avadh and made a prisoner of Shuja-ud-daula; Shah Alam had already sought shelter with the British. Clive, who was back as the company's governor of Bengal, arranged the terms of peace: Shuja-ud-daula was reinstated as *nawab* but had to cede the districts of Kora and Allahabad to the territory-less Shah Alam, pay an indemnity to the company, and allow it to trade duty free in Avadh. The emperor, whose nominal sovereignty was recognized by all the warlords, granted the company the *diwani* of Bengal, thus legitimizing the company's actual position, which it had arbitrarily secured through force of arms. Incidentally, it must have been intriguing to the emperor to be granting this office not to a person but to the "Company Bahadur" (literally "Brave *or* Honorable Company").

Mir Jafar's death in 1765 expedited the complete takeover of the government of Bengal by the company, which nevertheless, continued to appoint puppet *nawabs* in Bengal, who in return for a pension left the governing of Bengal,

Bihar, and Orissa to the EIC. As if this were not enough, the company showed far more concern for its responsibilities to the Court of Directors in London than to any Indian power or to the teeming population of Bengal. The Court of Directors ordered the company to "superintend" the revenues but allow the *nawab* and his ministers to administer Bengal. Clive's local solution was to appoint a deputy *diwan* and a deputy *subahdar* to administer the province on *behalf of the company and not on behalf of the* nawab, who was still, technically, the *subahdar* of emperor Shah Alam. Thus, the company used its power to squeeze all it could out of Bengal but never felt itself to be responsible for law and order or the welfare of the native population.

Unfortunately, it was the illegal activities of the EIC's servants that milked the province of its surplus, leaving much less for the company than the directors expected. The terrible famine in Bengal in 1770, which destroyed one-third of its population, underscored the degeneration of the administration of the province under the company's indirect rule. "In their blind rage for enrichment [the company's servants] took more from the Bengali peasants than those peasants could furnish and live. And the peasants duly died."[16] It is only after 1770 that the company felt it necessary to reform its administration and the British Parliament interjected itself into Indian affairs by passing the Regulating Act in 1773, which unified the government of the three presidencies of Bengal, Madras, and Bombay under a governor-general headquartered in Calcutta.

Achievement of Hegemony: The First Phase

The occupation of Bengal and the pacification of Avadh provided the company a dominion, but it also meant that the company now had frontiers that had to be defended. And the company was yet far from being invulnerable. It faced a serious threat from the two formidable expanding powers in the subcontinent: the Marathas, who had recovered from the setback they had suffered at the battle of Panipat (1761); and Haider Ali of Mysore. Haider Ali, a Muslim military commander in the service of the Hindu *raja* of Mysore, had usurped power (though not the throne; he made himself regent of the *raja*) in 1761 and in a very short time had practically subdued the whole of southern India.

The British also still feared the revival of French power in India, since many of the Indian rulers had hired French generals to train their troops; for example, Haider Ali had "750 good European troops commanded by General Lalley,"[17] and Mahadaji Scindia employed De Boigne in 1784 to raise several battalions of infantry. Incidentally, since the Marathas were proud of being horsemen and held the infantry in contempt, De Boigne had to recruit Rajputs and Muslims to handle the artillery. After Haider's death in 1782, his son and successor, Tipu Sultan (1783–1799), a great hater of the British, established an even greater rapport with the French, augmented his army with several French detachments, sent missions to the court of Louis XVI, and later, after the French Revolution, tried to get Napoleon to invade India. Tipu established a Jacobin Club and was hailed by the French in Mysore as "Citizen Tipu." Though he got little help from France, Tipu's activities naturally made him out to be an even greater threat in the eyes of the Franco-phobic British than he already was.

The EIC's success in Bengal did not immediately give it political ascendancy. Indeed, the Madras and Bombay armies suffered disastrous setbacks in 1778 and 1779 at the hands of the Marathas and Haider, and had it not been for the energy and diplomatic acumen of Governor-General Warren Hastings (1771: governor of Bengal; 1774–1785: governor-general of India), the EIC may have lost its position even in Bengal. In 1780, the Marathas, the *nizam* of Hyderabad, and Mysore joined forces and formed a formidable anti-British alliance that threatened the very existence of the British in India. However, of the three, only Haider Ali looked upon the British as the scourge that needed to be eradicated from the face of India; since the other two had divergent goals, the "grand alliance" lacked unity and harmony. Warren Hastings exploited the selfish and short-sighted aims of the *nizam* and the Marathas by returning some territory to the *nizam* to wean him from the alliance, and by weakening the Marathas by buying out Bhonsle with a huge bribe. Hastings then inflicted a humiliating defeat on Scindia, the strongest of the Maratha chiefs, and signed a treaty (1782) that ensured twenty years of peace between the Marathas and the British. The war in the south, which had been complicated by the arrival of a French naval force, was concluded by the Treaty of Mangalore (1784) on the basis of mutual restitution of conquests. This treaty in no way diminished the stature of Tipu Sultan, who now came to be seen by the EIC as the main threat.

Governor-General Lord Cornwallis (1786–1793), whose tenure is notable for administrative reforms within the EIC's establishment, rather than for any forward policies did, however, consider it necessary to reduce the irrepressible Tipu to size. Lord Cornwallis, in alliance with the Marathas and the *nizam,* defeated Tipu and forced him to cede half of his territories to the allies and hand over his sons as hostages until he paid the huge indemnity imposed on him. Tipu promptly increased the land revenue assessment and paid off the indemnity by 1794.

The nonintervention policy, prescribed by the Home Office and, but for some minor exceptions, assiduously followed by Cornwallis and his successor Sir John Shore (1793–1798), reduced the prestige of the EIC, whose territories, with the exclusion of Bengal, still constituted no more than the few districts around Madras and Bombay and were peripheral to the powerful states of Mysore and Hyderabad, and the mighty Maratha confederacy. British neutrality led to an increase of French influence in native courts. Not only was "Citizen Tipu" feverishly seeking help from the French, but the best infantry units of the Maratha chiefs and those of the *nizam* were now commanded by French officers. After

---

Tipu: A Patriot by Default?

When Tipu succeeded his father, he deposed the powerless *raja* of Mysore and made himself *padishah* (emperor). This act displeased many of the Hindu courtiers, and though they may or may not have actually conspired against him, Tipu, an orthodox Muslim, became suspicious of them and began to replace them with Muslim officers in whom he could repose more trust. Tipu also appears to have lost hope in getting the Marathas and the *nizam* to help him fulfill his mission of driving the British from the subcontinent. Showing a certain sense of world politics and faith in pan-Islamic cooperation (which never seems to have lost its fascination for Muslim rulers), Tipu turned to France for help and also made frantic appeals to the sultan of Turkey in 1784 and 1785, and to Zaman Shah, ruler of Afghanistan (1793–1799), to come to his aid as fellow Muslims. Although Turkey, embroiled in a war with Russia and desirous of getting British support, turned down Tipu's request, and though Zaman Shah, the grandson of Ahmad Shah Abdali, did not need any encouragement from Tipu to invade India, which he did several times but got no further than the Punjab, Tipu's pan-Islamic thinking is significant.

Tipu invited Zaman Shah to occupy Delhi because "The state of disorder and of anarchy in this Empire is more visible than daylight. Delhi, one of the seats of the Mahommedan Government, is reduced to such a state that the infidels predominate everywhere in it; but if [Zaman Shah] the Ornament of the Throne, the Conqueror of Empires, would agree to the plan I propose to him, he will contribute to the glory of the faith."[18] Another suggestion made by Tipu was that Zaman Shah, after occupying Delhi should establish a "confederation of the Mahommedan Princes and that he should take the lead for the achievement of the supreme object, viz., the triumph of the faith."[19] Tipu also tried to buttress his army with Muslim mercenaries recruited in Arabia and Africa.

Despite all this, Tipu is, today, looked upon as a great Indian patriot because of his abiding hatred of the British.

Napoleon's defeat, some of his generals were to find their way to the Punjab and help in Europeanizing Maharaja Ranjit Singh's forces. This situation was radically changed during the next few decades.

Achievement of Hegemony: The Second Phase

Anglo-French rivalry and fear of French ambitions in the East had as much to do with the new policies as had a new sense of imperialism. When revolutionary France extended its control over the Dutch Republic, the British seized the strategic Cape of Good Hope (1795) to keep it from falling into the hands of the French. For the same reason, Dutch Ceylon (Sri Lanka) was made a crown colony in 1798, the year the Marquis of Wellesley came to India as governor-general (he was governor-general from 1798 to 1805). Affairs in India now became part of British global strategies.

Wellesley, during his seven years in India, reversed the nonintervention policy and sought stability for the EIC's Indian dominions through conquest and subsidiary alliances (SAs). A subsidiary alliance, as discussed earlier, was an arrangement whereby a native state was made to relinquish territory in return for military aid. But the EIC refined it by posting a "resident" in the SA state to ensure that the state made no move that was inimical to the interests of the British. In practice this meant that the company took over the foreign relations of the state, while promising noninterference in the internal affairs of the state "as long as no other foreigners were employed by the ruler."

Before moving against Tipu, whose pro-French activities made him a dangerous enemy, Wellesley neutralized the *nizam* by getting him to sign a subsidiary alliance that compelled the *nizam* to replace his French detachments and the French officers commanding native troops with British equivalents, and which forbade the *nizam* from corresponding with the *peshwa* without British consent. Although the Marathas, torn by rivalries and factional infighting, were no threat to his designs against Tipu, Wellesley ensured their neutrality by promising them a share in the spoils of war. Only then did Wellesley turn to Tipu and demand his submission, knowing full well that Tipu would rather fight than submit. In the brief campaign that followed Tipu was thoroughly defeated and he died in battle (1799). Wellesley annexed half of Mysore and placed the rest under the client child-prince from the old Hindu dynasty that had been deposed by Tipu.

In 1802, even as the Scindia and the Holkar were fighting an internecine battle outside Pune over the control of the Peshwa Baji Rao II, the *peshwa* fled to the Bombay Presidency and voluntarily signed a treaty with the EIC, by which he entered into a subsidiary alliance in exchange for a British assurance that he would remain the *peshwa*. Wellesley declared the treaty to be binding on all Maratha chiefs, and since this was not acceptable to them, they opened hostilities against the British. However, even under these grim circumstances, the Maratha chiefs could not forge a united front. The British army defeated them one by one and Wellesley, by making subsidiary alliances with some of their vassals, succeeded in truncating the Maratha states. At the same time, the EIC made Avadh a protectorate and annexed Rohilkhand, which brought the lands between the Ganges and the Sutlej under its direct control. And last but not the least, the Great Mughal, Shah Alam II, was made a pensioner of the British. Though these gains were staggering, the war had been costly and London felt that Wellesley had gone much further in his military operations than was advisable. Also, there was the threat of an invasion of Britain by Napoleon. Wellesley was recalled in 1805. The final solution of India was postponed to the end of the Napoleonic wars (1815).

By 1816, Governor-General Lord Hastings (1813–1823; he came to India in 1813 as Lord Moira but gained the title of Marquis of Hastings in 1817), not to be confused with Warren Hastings, had drawn up a plan that would make "the British Government paramount in effect, if not declaredly so," and "vassals, in substance, though not in name,"[20] of all native states. In keeping with this plan Hastings got the Maratha chiefs, who posed the biggest threat to company supremacy, to sign subsidiary treaties: Bhonsle in 1816, *peshwa* and Scindia in 1817. The Gaekwads, who had remained loyal to the subsidiary alliance they had made in 1805, did not figure in the new arrangement, and the internal troubles among the Holkars kept Indore from reaching a decision. The treaty with the *peshwa* was most humiliating because it forced him to renounce suzerainty over the other Maratha chiefs and give up even his right to communicate with them.

Enraged by the restrictions imposed upon them, the *peshwa* and the Holkar and the Bhonsle chiefs made a last desperate effort to throw off the EIC's yoke, but the effort was totally futile. The 120,000-strong British army (which included 13,000 British troops), the largest the EIC had ever fielded in India, with its 300 cannons, won decisive victories in all the battles it fought. At the end of the war, which lasted only a few months (1817–1818), the British abolished the office and title of *peshwa,* the symbol of Maratha unity, and annexed the whole of Maharashtra (the *peshwa*'s territory and the Maratha homeland) to Bombay Presidency. The Rajputs, who had suffered so much at the hands of the Marathas, were happy to be freed from the Maratha bondage and become subsidiary allies of the British. In 1819, except for Punjab and Sind in the northwest and Assam in the northeast, the British found themselves masters of the entire subcontinent—an empire larger and more populous than any European state.

Achievement of Hegemony: The Last Phase

The British occupation of the subcontinent was completed in the third phase, which lasted from 1824 to 1849. Assam was the first to be acquired as a consequence of the First Burmese War (1824–1826). The rulers *(amirs)* of Sind (nominally a province of Afghanistan) had signed subsidiary alliances, but the British in a most callous fashion provoked the *amirs* into hostilities and took over Sind in 1843. Punjab, unified by the brilliant Sikh ruler Ranjit Singh (1799–1839), offered a much more formidable challenge, but the state fell into disunity after Ranjit Singh's death. The British took advantage of the situation and were helped by traitors in the Sikh camp, who deserted with their troops in mid-battle or kept ammunition and supplies from reaching them. The Sikh soldiers fought with unbelievable courage and steadfastness, but even if they had not been betrayed by their commanders, they could not have won the war against the power of the British Empire of India. Punjab was annexed in 1849.

One of the reasons for the annexation of Sind and Punjab was the growing British fear of the Russian expansion into central Asia. The strategic importance of Afghanistan for the subcontinent (discussed in the last chapter) led the British to try and forestall any extension of Russian influence in that area by sending a huge army in 1839 to remove the pro-Russian Dost Mohammed and install their protégé Shah Shuja in his place. The army marched through Sind and duly completed its assigned task, but Afghanistan proved difficult to pacify and the British had to withdraw in 1842. Of the 16,500 persons (700 Britons, 3,800 sepoys, and 12,000 camp followers) who began the retreat, only one (Surgeon William Brydon) made it to the safety of the British encampment at Jalalabad. In the next several years, the occupation of Sind and Punjab pushed British arms to the foothills of the western and northwestern mountain ranges and made Afghanistan a buffer zone between Russia and British India.

The Company's Success in Controlling India

That a trading company could establish an empire of this size in sixty years or so is a remarkable achievement by any standard. Rejecting the argument once made by Western chauvinists and imperialists that the Indians were inherently inferior and the British intrinsically superior, the reasons for the British success can be related partly to the conditions in India and partly to the manner in which British power evolved through the critical decades between 1750 and 1820.

First, since India had yet to develop the modern concepts of state and nationalism, the Indian rulers had no sense of any common danger. Except perhaps for Haider Ali and Tipu, the Indian princes did not look upon the EIC as presenting any greater threat than they, themselves, did to each other's ambitions. This narrow, parochial outlook prevented even the Maratha rulers, despite their ties of kinship and their common allegiance to the *peshwa,* from acting in unison against the British. By comparison, the British, regardless of sporadic infighting and clash of personalities, were a remarkably cohesive group. A strong feeling of nationalism and a strong belief in their manifest destiny to rule the globe provided them with a sense of purpose and a reason to die for "the cause."

Second, the sepoy armies of the EIC, as mentioned earlier, were better disciplined, better equipped, and led by better strategists than the native armies. Although many of the native army units were trained by Europeans, the native armies as a whole lacked that overarching and centralized command that the British had. The European officers in the native armies were known, on occasion, to refuse to accept the orders of their Indian commanders, and sometimes they refused to fight at all. It was also not uncommon that, unlike the British officers, the native commanders could be bribed not to fight; there was no sense of absolute loyalty to even one's own prince. Furthermore, the resources that the British commanded increased progressively after 1760 while those of Britain's enemies decreased. Also, being located in Bombay, Madras, and Calcutta, and equipped with a modern navy, the EIC had the strategic advantage of being able to move its troops rapidly and attack the heartland states from many directions.

Third, the British received ready help from Indians at all levels of Indian society. Lacking a sense of state and nationalism, and having experienced rule under a variety of foreigners (military adventurers from Afghanistan, Central Asia, and Persia were still making inroads in the eighteenth century), Indians (most of whom were Hindus because they formed the bulk of the population) did not find anything particularly repugnant in the "foreignness" of the British. Within the context of India's international commerce the British, much earlier, had already been domesticated into the Indian scene along with the Armenians, the Jews, the Persians, the Arabs, the French, and the Dutch. As traders, the British naturally developed close and mutually beneficial links with the Hindu mercantile capitalists, and it was the great *jagat seths* of Calcutta who drew the company into the political conspiracy that overthrew the governor of Bengal. Such collaborations became more common as the decades rolled by and the British became increasingly substantial power holders on the Indian scene. Equally significant was the eagerness with which the local Indian rulers (the "little kings") sought protection from the British or made alliances with them in order to be better able to fight off their enemies or further their expansionist designs. Finally, the Hindu administrative castes who had been working at the lower levels of the Mughal administration and had learned Persian and Arabic to serve alien rulers (whom they otherwise may have disliked for their anti-Hindu religious policies) found it psychologically easy to shift from one foreign language (Persian) to another (English) and shift their loyalty from the Muslims to the British.

The Impact of EIC Government's Economic Policies

From the very beginning of its rule in Bengal, the EIC had betrayed an unholy passion to squeeze as much as it could from its Indian possessions. It has been estimated that between 1757 and 1780, the equivalent of 760 million pounds sterling (at 1988 value) of unrequited wealth was sent out to Britain. This was quite apart from the loot pocketed by Clive and his countrymen. The terrible famine of 1770 that claimed millions of Bengali lives was one of the consequences of this heartless policy. Another consequence was the immense expansion of the company's Bengal Army, which by 1805 boasted a strength of 150,000.

To work out a revenue system that would guarantee a dependable annual income, the British, in 1793, converted the *zamindars* (who under the Mughals had been revenue collectors with rights to keep back a certain part of their collection) of Bengal into landlords in the British legal sense, and arrived at a permanent settlement with them that guaranteed the EIC a fixed annual revenue. In the process, the company abdicated its obligation to protect the peasant, who was now a mere tenant of the *zamindar* and whose possessions could be seized if he failed to pay his dues. "In the last resort social justice was of less concern to the company than the security of its revenues."[21]

The settlement (pitched at a shockingly high level attempted to squeeze more out of Bengal than the *nawabs* had ever done) must be seen in the context of the growing military expenditures of the company and the establishment of, in the words of Professor Bayly, British "military despotism outside Bengal."[22] The company, unlike the Mughals, made no adjustments for the vagaries of the weather, the floods, and the droughts that are commonplace in the subcontinent. In a year of crop failures, many *zamindars,* in spite of their harsh exploitation of the peasantry, could not afford to pay the fixed revenues and saw their lands auctioned off to businessmen from Calcutta. The new absentee landlords were even less interested in the condition of the peasantry. In the long run, however, as the land values began to rise, the delinking of tax from production did improve the situation somewhat. If the laws in England made property central to the concept of liberty, the application of these laws in India took away the customary rights of the peasants and, at least in the initial stage, impoverished them.

The success of the EIC's war against Tipu Sultan in the last decade of the eighteenth century rapidly expanded the territorial control of the Madras Presidency from a few small holdings to include most of southern India. At first the company was satisfied to continue the land system followed by Tipu, who, permanently in need of funds to fight his wars, had increased the land revenue assessment by removing many of the intermediaries between the government and the peasantry and replacing them with tax farmers. The only difference was that the company was even more ruthless in its exactions and imposed a monetary demand rather than a tax in kind.

Later, when the company regularized its revenue structure, it avoided the mistake made in Bengal and adopted the *raiyatwari** system whereby, instead of creating a body of artificial landlords, the company collected the revenue directly from the peasant tiller. The system also allowed the company to make periodic reassessments of land and increase the revenue demand. After the annexation of the *peshwa's* dominions, the *raiyatwari* system was extended to the Bombay Presidency. In the early decades of the nineteenth century, the condition of the heavily overassessed peasantry under the *raiyatwari* system was hardly any better than that of the tenant-tiller under the Permanent Settlement. The "wasteland," which was never taxed and which belonged to the village to be used as pastureland and as a hedge against drought, was now appropriated by the state and all peasants in a village were made jointly responsible for revenue shortfalls.[23] The *raiyatwari* system also undermined the corporate solidarity of the village communities, as did the British emphasis on laws and law courts that gradually began to subvert the traditional system of social security and justice provided by the caste and village *panchayats.*

A third system of land tenure known as *mahalwari* was introduced in north-

---

*Raiyat, sometimes spelled as *ryot*, means tax-paying peasant.

ern India in the 1820s and given its final form by the 1850s. It was the least harsh of the three systems, particularly as applied in Punjab, where the assessment was deliberately kept low. In the *mahalwari* system the settlement was made with the village community as a whole and the members of the community were jointly as well as severally responsible for the payment of the revenue. The village elders apportioned the amount to be paid by each member, but a careful record was maintained of the actual size of the land holdings. The system had the virtue of recognizing the subordinate right of the peasants who were entitled to permanent and heritable tenure if they could prove that they had worked on the land for twelve years.

The different land assessment systems that came to be formalized had one thing in common: the British tried to impose elements of their ideas of property rights and justice on the Indian rural scene, but lacking an adequate bureaucracy, had to work within the traditional Indian social framework. If their new system displaced the old local magnates, the British had to recruit new ones (whose loyalty to the British was not suspect) with the same class and caste standing because that alone ensured that they would have the necessary influence over the village community. The dilemma between an egalitarian approach and the pragmatic need to maintain stability in society by upholding the traditional structures of society was never fully resolved; it did produce tensions that would, over time, lead to some reorientation of social relations. The British, during the period under consideration, produced no social revolution at the grass-roots level and, by and large, their policies failed to promote agricultural output. Indeed, for some time agricultural production actually fell in many areas. In other economic spheres also, the extension of British dominion in India resulted in new tensions and a negative impact on many aspects of Indian economic life. The primary reason for this was that, in the words of Adam Smith, "the government of an exclusive company of merchants is perhaps the worst of all governments for any country whatever."[24]

If Bengal is taken as an example, when the British ceased to import bullion for their purchases in Bengal, there was a shortage of silver, and this created immense difficulties for the peasantry because taxes had to be paid in cash and the copper currency (the only one with which the peasant was familiar) got devalued. Bullion scarcity was further increased when the EIC exported Bengal silver to China for the trade in tea. The reduction of textile exports after 1800 impoverished the weavers and the population of textile-producing cities like Dhaka fell precipitously, the unemployed weavers having been forced to migrate in search of work. The company's monopolistic control over the textile, saltpeter, opium, and salt industries allowed it to keep the workers in debt and forced them to accept wages arbitrarily decided by the company that were so low the workers were reduced to the level of indentured labor. The prices paid to the weavers in the 1820s, for example, were often 80 percent less than what the open market would have paid them.[25] On top of this, the decline of the old nobility not only meant the disbandment of their armies and the reduction of the size of their entourage but the atrophying of the urban luxury industries. Many specialized professional castes, such as the producers of high-quality steel and iron, also began to disappear, some because of the decay in internal demand and some because of their incapacity to compete with cheaper imports.

By 1820, the EIC had not only come to monopolize Bengal's overseas trade but replaced Indian textiles with mill-made cloth from England. As a result, the artisanal industries in Bengal shrank and were reduced to supplying only the home market, and Bengal capital was curtailed to servicing petty commodity production. The company excluded Indians from large-scale commercial and fiscal enterprises. And the situation outside Bengal was not radically different. For example, the production of cotton, indigo, tea, and opium as cash crops for export tied the Indian economy to the world market, and India became a periodic victim of depressed international finance and commodity markets over which it had no control. But there was one relieving feature: the banking and merchant castes in southern and western India, especially the Parsis, began to take an active part in the new economy. Trade was also helped by the fact that the company-minted silver rupee became standard currency in British India after 1835 and replaced the large number of confusing currencies in circulation.

Through the last decades of the eighteenth century, and well into the nineteenth, the EIC established an interesting trade triangle between India, China, and Britain. Until its annexation of Bengal, one of the major criticisms the company had faced at home was that it was exporting bullion (an act condemned by economists) for the purchase of textiles in India and tea in China. The company resolved this dilemma by resorting to an underhanded but beautifully simple stratagem: private traders, most of them British, bought opium in India (a company monopoly) and smuggled it to China (where the drug was contraband but ravenously consumed by a growing population of Chinese addicts) and used the proceeds to buy Chinese teas and other commodities for export to Britain. Professor Tan Chung has summed up this triangular trade in the following words: "Indian opium for the Chinese, Chinese tea for the Britons, and British Raj for the Indians!"[26]

The East India Company's Sociopolitical Policies

During the first two phases of the EIC's expansion, its economic policies had begun to deviate from the norms that were current in Mughal India, but in the sociopolitical arena the company was still, more or less, an Indian-style game player. It is in the third phase that the company finally decided to make a major shift in its political and social policies that radically changed the nature of the company's presence in the subcontinent and created massive strains within Indian society that led to the Great Rebellion of 1857 (often referred to as "The Mutiny" by the British and as "The First War of Independence" by some Indian nationalist historians). The Great Rebellion forced the British government to take over the rulership from the hands of the company and make India a Crown Colony.

The EIC's policies from the 1770s to 1857, which led to these developments, can be divided into two phases.

Phase I: The Indianization of the Company

The nature of early British rule in India (that is, under the control of the East India Company) was influenced by the fact that British merchants, interested primarily in making profits for both themselves and the EIC, quickly caught on to the advantage of operating in league with the locals. The company man worked through *banians* (not to be confused with the Indian trading caste of *baniya*), middlemen and brokers who knew the local market and could assist the British official in various ways. The *banian* could help the official to get loans from Indian bankers, act as a link between him and the community of weavers who would be given an advance and the patterns of cloth to be produced, and then collect the finished product on behalf of the official. Both the British merchant and the *banian* thrived on this system and often accumulated fabulous riches. There was little racial intolerance at the upper level of the company's officials and quite a few Britons even regarded Indian culture favorably; they learned the local language, spent their leisure hours with their Indian friends, drinking and smoking the hookah, and even married into Indian families. As John Strachey records, "during the eighteenth and early nineteenth centuries two of my collateral ancestors . . . had married what the late nineteenth century British would, so offensively, have called native women. [They married] without exciting the least adverse comment or injuring their careers in any way."[27]

Clive's entire success can be explained by his ability to understand the Indian mind and work with native power holders. His personal venality, as well as the bribery and graft that flourished under his patronage, was initially of a piece with accepted Indian practice. The appointment of the company as revenue collectors for the Mughal emperor shows how far the company had come in being accepted as a part of the Indian scene. Regrettably, the British soon outdid their Indian mentors and set altogether new standards of corruption that, as mentioned earlier, brought so much misery and suffering to Bengal.

It was not until Warren Hastings became governor of Bengal in 1772 (he was governor-general 1774–1785) that the company took direct control of the civil administration of Bengal and appointed British district collectors and judges in law courts. Hastings, who had already spent many years in India and acquired proficiency in Bengali and Urdu and some knowledge of Persian, had genuine respect for Indian civilization and its values. He believed that "to rule effectively, one must love India; [and] to love India, one must communicate with her people."[28] Hastings, therefore, sought to get his officers to learn Indian languages and understand Indian culture so that they could work in harmony with their Indian counterparts.

Since Hastings saw no reason to try and reshape Indian society or culture, he made no efforts to substitute Hindu and Muslim law with English law. Instead, he encouraged his like-minded aides to translate Hindu and Muslim civil laws into English and codify them (so that the English judges could better administer the country), and to translate the company regulations into local languages (so that the native officials could better understand the new rulers). What is more, Hastings got Hindu pundits to translate Sanskrit classics into the vernacular and established colleges to teach Indian youth their own laws and past heritage. Hastings also made a very important contribution to the development of Bengali language and literature (Persian and Urdu, not Bengali, were the court languages of Bengal under the Mughals) and the growth of the Bengali press. At the same time, Hastings encouraged Indian intellectuals to study English as a means of understanding European civilization.

Another important achievement of Hastings was the establishment of the Asiatic Society of Bengal in 1784, whose researches and translations helped in the rediscovery of India's past civilization and "brought into being a new concept of the Hindu golden age as a legacy for the rising Indian intelligentsia."[29] Thanks to him, Calcutta became the center of a new cosmopolitan culture. Sir William Jones (1746–1794), the first president of the Asiatic Society, is internationally recognized as one of the greatest scholars of Sanskrit and the person who, by proving that Sanskrit and several European languages had a common origin, founded the science of Comparative Philology. His work stimulated other Western scholars, the Germans being outstanding among them, to study Sanskrit literature. These developments not only brought a tremendous sense of pride to Indian intellectuals in their own heritage but made them more sympathetic to Western concepts of rationalism and humanism.

Marquess Wellesley (governor-general, 1798–1805), who, as we have noted earlier, used the system of subsidiary alliances to firmly establish the British Empire of India, continued many Mughal political practices, suitably modifying them to ensure that the British paramountcy would remain unchallenged. The Indian Princely States, accounting for one-third of India, were allowed to continue in the traditional fashion, holding lavish *durbars,* patronizing the Brahmins (or the *ulema,* in the case of Muslim states), endowing temples and mosques with land and funds, and so on. In fact, the company itself, in the style of native rulers, became a patron of the native religions.

Wellesley carried forward Hastings's policies of "Indianizing" British administration by founding the College of Fort William in Calcutta (1800), where British administrators got training in Indian languages, history, and Indian laws. The development of Indian languages and the popularization of vernacular literature was greatly enhanced by the setting up of presses and the casting of fonts to print works in these languages. Interestingly enough, much of this work, including the translation of Hindu religious texts, was first undertaken by missionaries. The most important of the missionaries in this context was William Carey, "one of the creators of Bengali prose," who had become so Indianized that he could declare with pride that the language and customs of the "Hindoos" was so familiar to him, "as if I myself was a native."[30]

The British Orientalists, so-called because of their genuine respect for Indian culture and their pioneering efforts to rediscover the roots of Hindu civilization, contributed to what has often been called the Indian renaissance. Through their patient research, scholarly writings, and translations, the Orientalists not only introduced ancient and medieval Indian learning to Europe but recovered Sanskrit literature and reconstructed Hindu history that had been lost to the Indians. For example, James Prinsep deciphered the Brahmi script (which no Indian could read), in which the Ashokan inscriptions were written, and, in 1837, announced the rediscovery of Mauryan India.

In 1807, the Court of Directors in London decided that newly recruited civil servants should get their education in the European part of the curriculum in Hailebury, England, before proceeding to the College of Fort William. This did not reduce the influence of the Calcutta Orientalists because Wellesley's policy of recruiting only the best students from Fort William College to the highest administrative posts was continued by Lord Minto (governor-general, 1807–1813).

However, for reasons discussed below, time ran out for the Orientalists when the EIC changed its policies regarding the British administration in India. The College of Fort William was closed in 1830, and the new recruits to the civil service began to receive all their training at the hands of the Cambridge clergy.

Phase II: The Anglicization of India

The policies of Warren Hastings and Orientalists presumed that British interests would be best served by bringing peace and tranquillity to the subcontinent and allowing Indian society to continue to function within its traditional socio-religious framework. Not everyone agreed with this formulation. The British Evangelicals felt that they were being denied their God-given right to save the idolatrous, immoral, satanic Indians from the fires of hell. Then there were the Utilitarians, who believed equally strongly that they had a duty to bring the rationalism and enlightenment embodied in Western laws and civilization to the barbaric and superstitious natives. Both of these groups attacked such Indian practices as *sati* (the practice of burning a widow on her husband's funeral pyre) and slavery to strengthen their argument that such inhuman, cruel, and barbaric practices could be abolished only by bringing Western religion and Western civilization to India.

Anti-Hastings ideas had started infiltrating India even before the demise of the Orientalists. Governor-General Cornwallis (1786–1793), for example, came to

India with the idea of making "everything as English as possible in a country which resembles England in nothing."[31] His Permanent Settlement can be viewed as an attempt to produce a British-type landed elite (the gentry) in India, and his removal of all Indians (except for one judge) from all high posts is a bid to establish an efficient, impersonal administration of the British kind. Cornwallis also stopped the company's civil servants from engaging in trade and raised their salaries to make them financially secure. Though he allowed Hindu and Islamic laws to continue to operate in civil disputes, Cornwallis introduced English law to guide the courts in criminal cases and even made the government legally answerable for its actions. Law was coming to occupy the high place of honor given to it in the West, but which it had never been accorded in the East.

Cornwallis, unlike Hastings, had an extremely poor opinion of the Indians, every one of whom, he believed, was totally corrupt. The sense of European racial superiority that began to replace the Orientalists' respect for Asian cultures is best reflected in the Utilitarian James Mill's assessment of Indian and Chinese character in 1819; he found both peoples to be insincere, dissembling, treacherous, mendacious, cowardly, unfeeling, conceited, and "disgustingly unclean."[32] The Evangelists, who had otherwise little in common with the Utilitarians, expressed a similar sentiment: the Indians, according to Charles Grant's tract written in 1790, were a race of men "lamentably degenerate and base."[33]

The company's traditional policy had been to bar missionaries on the grounds that their activities created local strife, disturbed the peace, and engendered anti-foreign sentiment, thereby impeding trading activities. However, in 1813, the company's new charter, which took away its trading monopoly, also obliged it to establish the Church of England in India.

It was during the regime of Governor-General Lord William Cavendish Bentinck (last governor-general of Bengal 1828–1833 and the first governor-general of India 1833–1835) that the ascendancy of the Utilitarian-Evangelist combine first became apparent. Bentinck, neither a bigot nor an extremist in his thinking, did believe in the Utilitarian principle of the "maximum happiness of the maximum numbers," and followed policies of reform intended for the good of the Indian peoples. Bentinck's social and educational reforms are considered to truly represent Utilitarian and Evangelical philosophies. He abolished *sati* and put down the Thugs, who practiced ritual assassination and robbery. Though both these actions supposedly touched upon Hindu religion (*sati* being looked upon as a customary Hindu practice and the Thugs being followers of the goddess Kali), the reforms were supported by many educated Hindus.

On quite a different plane, Bentinck revealed his positively anti-Orientalist attitude when he decided to expand English education at the expense of traditional Indian education. One of the consequences of this decision was the closure of the College of Fort William and another was a drastically reduced level of financial aid to such institutions as the Asiatic Society and the Calcutta Sanscrit College.

But perhaps the most crucial of Bentinck's decisions was his acceptance of the view of Charles Trevelyan and Thomas Babington Macaulay, the ardent Westernizers, that English should be made the official language of India. Trevelyan ridiculed the Orientalists for trying to revive the "dead" Indian civilization, and Macaulay not only thought that the Indian people were "a race debased by three thousand years of despotism and priestcraft"[34] but also believed that "a single shelf of a good European Library was worth the whole native literature of Arabia and India."[35] The idea, in Macaulay's words, was to create, through English education, "a class of persons, Indian in blood and color, but English in taste, in opinions, in morals, and in intellect," who would be interpreters between the rulers and the ruled.[36]

If Macaulay's aim was to create a vast class of semieducated, low-paid, English-speaking subordinates who could facilitate the British administration of India and help promote British business interests, then the "reforms" were eminently successful. Furthermore, since British resources for education were limited, the new policies had the further negative effect of directing funds and attention away from mass literacy and mass education. However, it must be admitted that English-language education in higher institutes of learning did produce, in due course, a small Westernized elite who paved the way for a progressive evolution of nationalism and an anti-British revolution. But that is another story that will be dealt with in a later chapter. Our immediate concern is the Great Rebellion of 1857.

The Great Rebellion of 1857

The thirty-five-year-old Governor-General Lord Dalhousie, who came to India in 1848 (retired in 1856), was the most dedicated empire builder the country had so far seen. He completed the goals of both the imperialist Wellesley and the Anglicizer Bentinck, the former by using a trivial excuse to declare war against the Sikh kingdom and annexing it by force—thus at last extending the British Empire of India over the entire subcontinent—and the latter by extending the British administrative system to the limits that lasted until 1947.

Dalhousie's firm belief that British rule was more beneficial to the Indians than native rule led him to ruthlessly utilize the "doctrine of lapse" (which allowed the EIC to take over any subsidiary state whose ruler had no natural heir) to "peacefully" annex the states of Satara, Jaitpur, Sambalpur, Jhansi, Nagpur, Baghat, Udaipur, and Karauli. Though the last three were later restored to the adoptive heirs, Dalhousie's action had the effect of removing pockets of native rule that came in the way of establishing territorial contiguity in British India. Curiously, the inadmissibility of adoptive heirs was extended even to titular rulers such as the ex-*peshwa*, whose adopted son Nana Sahib was denied his father's pension.

One of the last acts of Dalhousie before he left India was the annexation of Avadh in 1856. Once a rich province of the Mughals, Avadh had become a highly exploited feudatory *nawabdom* under the EIC since 1801. The annexation of Avadh was carried out on the grounds that the current ("puppet") *nawab*'s irresponsible administration had brought "suffering to millions."

When a self-satisfied Dalhousie left India in 1856, he was oblivious to the undercurrent of popular apprehension that his policies had generated. It was left to his successor, Lord Canning (governor-general, 1856–1862) to face the massive native rebellion that followed in 1857. The rebellion started with a mutiny of some disgruntled sepoys, but it spread across northern and central India and came to include various segments of society, from dispossessed rulers to landlords and commoners.

The military part of the trouble can be said to have begun in May 1857, in Meerut, when the British officers court-martialed and imprisoned eighty-five Hindu and Muslim sepoys of the Bengal army who had refused to use the newly introduced greased cartridges; the sepoys, who had to bite off the tops of the cartridges before loading them into the rifles, regarded the action as defiling their religions because the grease came from the fat of cows (a good Hindu could not tolerate the killing of cows, let alone eating them) and pigs (looked upon as unclean animals by Muslims). On May 10, fellow sepoys, resenting the punishment meted out, rose against their British officers, shot them dead, and released the prisoners. Two days later the rebels had reached Delhi, captured it, and proclaimed the eighty-two-year-old Bahadur Shah II, puppet pensioner of the British (who had been surprised and bewildered by the uprising), the "Emperor of India."

The mutiny spread rapidly through the garrison towns of Lucknow, Bareilly, Kanpur, and Agra and the British administration in north-central India (from west Bengal to Delhi in the north to the Narbada in the south) collapsed with amazing suddenness. Many local princes, *zamindars,* and petty power holders joined the rebels; the most important of them, no doubt, was the valiant *rani* of Jhansi, who had been deposed by Dalhousie. The recently humiliated Nana Sahib, aspirant for the *peshwa* title, turned up near Kanpur where the brilliant Maratha general Tantia Topi had brought his Gwalior troops to fight the British. After some initial successes Tantia withdrew to central India, joined the *rani* of Jhansi, proclaimed Nana Sahib to be the *peshwa,* and tried to inspire other Maratha leaders to join the rebellion.

Although Delhi was recaptured in September 1857, Kanpur relieved in June, and Lucknow in November, the rebellion was finally put down only by July 1858. The memory of the wanton slaughter and butchery of the innocent perpetrated by both sides left bitter memories that cast a shadow over British-Indian relations for a long time. The upheaval ended the company's rule in India and the subcontinent was turned into a Crown Colony. The administration of India now became the direct responsibility of the government of England.

Causes of the Rebellion

There is a wide range of opinion on the great sociopolitical upheaval of 1857. On the one extreme, the British, immediately after the event, tended to dismiss it as a "sepoy mutiny," implying that, regardless of the butchery and horror involved, it was basically a military mutiny carried out by disgruntled sepoys. On the other extreme, a nationalist leader like V. D. Savarkar, looking back at 1857 from the perspective of the 1910s, viewed it as a national "revolutionary war" and published his interpretation in a book entitled *The First Indian War of Independence of 1857.* Though Savarkar is not quite correct in his assessment, because modern nationalism had yet to take several decades to emerge as a force of any significance, there were many more causes behind the rebellion than just the greased cartridges. The causes were military, religious, political, and social.

While the immediate cause of the rebellion is related to the story of the greased cartridges, the alienation of the Bengal army had far deeper roots. Most of the Hindus in the army were from high castes, many being Brahmins. To gain the whole-hearted cooperation of such troops, the British officers should have respected the religious susceptibilities of the sepoys. In the earlier days, after the occupation of Bengal, when the EIC's army was still small and the company's authority still not fully established, the officers had very good rapport with the sepoys. However, as the company territory, authority, and army expanded, an attitude of superiority and aloofness entered the officer corps. The old sense of intimacy between officers and men was replaced by distance and contempt. At the same time, the salary differential between the British noncommissioned officers and their Indian counterparts became so large that there was no possibility of any camaraderie between them. The ordinary sepoys were now often looked upon as menial servants and were often ill-treated.

The British should have known better. They should have remembered how, at the turn of the century, decades before 1857, sepoys in southern India had mutinied when ordered to remove their caste marks.[37] And Hindu sepoys in the Afghanistan campaign of 1838 had expressed unhappiness at not being able to bathe as often as their religion demanded and became restless when weather forced them to wear sheepskin jackets (such contact with leather is forbidden to upper-caste Hindus).[38]

As the company's area of operation expanded, sepoy units had to be sent to distant places in India, far from their home bases. Since they received field service pay for fighting "foreign wars," and since they mostly returned home after the campaigns were over, they usually accepted these military exigencies without fuss. But when the new territories were annexed and the sepoys were no longer qualified for field service pay, they resented being posted so far from their families.

It was worse when the sepoy units had to fight wars in foreign countries (Persia, Afghanistan, Burma, and China). Apart from the resentment caused by long stints of duty away from home, the expeditions were particularly offensive to Hindu sepoys because of religious taboos against travel overseas. During the First Burmese War (1824–1826), an entire regiment of the Bengal army had to be disbanded because it refused to go abroad; and in 1850, when the "foreign service allowance" was made inadmissible, several regiments in Punjab had mutinied.[39] Canning, the newcomer to India, showed his utter disregard for sepoy sentiment when, by the Act of 1856, he made new recruits swear an oath that they would go wherever required, inside or outside India.

Many in the Bengal army, both Muslims and Hindus, had been recruited in Avadh, and though they served the British, they still had a sense of loyalty to the ruling house of Avadh. As mentioned earlier, Dalhousie justified the annexation of Avadh on the grounds that the *nawab* was mismanaging the government. This may have been a good enough reason in the minds of the British, but it looked like a sneaky pretext in the eyes of the Indians. When the *nawab* of Avadh refused to sign the treaty surrendering his country "voluntarily," the British declared their takeover by proclamation.

There was a widespread feeling of shock, humiliation, and resentment that was shared by all, including the sepoys. The reaction of the Muslim sepoys, and the Muslim population, was particularly violent because the *nawab* was the last surviving symbol of Muslim supremacy. To add insult to injury, the company dismissed 65,000 of the *nawab*'s troops and forced them to join the ranks of the unemployed. And on top of all this came the backbreaking land taxes imposed on Avadh by the new company administration. Many of the distressed peasantry and the dismissed troopers belonged to the families of the sepoys in the company's Bengal forces.

The atrocities perpetrated by the company in Avadh were replicated, though not to the same degree, in other states that had been deprived of their Indian rulers. Hence, it was that the rebel leadership included such diverse figures as Hazrat Mahal, the Avadh *nawab*'s widow, the *rani* of Jhansi, Kunwar Singh of Bihar, and Nana Sahib, the ex-*peshwa*'s son.

Other causes, which are impossible to quantify, are associated with unpopular British policies that either had no roots in the Indian tradition or went contrary to that tradition, but in either case hurt popular sentiment and generated a widespread feeling of disaffection. The Religious Disabilities Act of 1856, for example, provided that a son who had changed his religion could not be debarred from inheriting property. This undermined Hindu inheritance laws and was viewed by many as a British attempt to create an environment that would foster conversions to Christianity. The apprehension was not totally baseless. It rose from the fervor of the Christian missionaries, the proselytizing zeal of some of the army officers (one, Colonel Wheler of the 34th Native Infantry, told the sepoys that "they must inevitably become Christians"[40]), and the periodic statements made by responsible British politicians. A chairman of the Court of Directors of the EIC, speaking in the House of Commons, put it most bluntly: "Providence has entrusted the extensive empire of Hindustan to England in order that the banner of Christ should wave triumphantly from one end of India to the other. Everyone must exert all his strength that there may be no dilatoriness on any account in continuing the grand work of making all Indians Christians."[41]

If this goal needed any governmental confirmation it was provided by Prime Minister Lord Palmerston himself when he said that he "firmly believed" that "God meant England to [Christianize] India" and that "Till India is leavened with Christianity she will be unfit for freedom."[42] Speaking, in 1855, at a dinner given in honor of the newly appointed Governor-General Lord Canning, Lord Palmerston reiterated his hope: "Perhaps it might be our lot to confer on the countless millions of India a higher and holier gift than any mere human knowledge."[43] Why would the sepoys, or other citizens of India, not have believed that the cartridges were a part of a scheme to further the cause of Christianity by making the sepoys outcasts from Islam and Hinduism?

We began this section with a rejection of the interpretation that the rebellion was a war of national independence. However, we can conclude it with the observation that, in the larger context, if one reflects on the fact that vast numbers of non-British civilian and military elements, of their own volition, joined the rebels, the rebellion—however limited in extent—did possess a pseudo-national flavor. It was the first time in the history of India that so many disparate elements, from many diverse regions, although guided by conflicting aims and lacking a unified organization or program, made a foreign power the common target for attack.

Causes of the Failure of the Rebellion

After a little over a year of military action, accompanied by indiscriminate slaughter and butchery of the innocent, in which each side outdid the other, the rebellion was suppressed. The reasons for British success are easy to delineate. In the late eighteenth- and early nineteenth centuries, many Indian princes and rulers were alarmed by the British encroachment—some, like the Marathas and Tipu Sultan, had even tried to crush the rising British power—but once the native rulers had been drawn into the system of subsidiary alliances (SA) they had been rendered totally ineffective. As a result, the uprising was wholly localized: Punjab in the northwest, Rajputana and Sind in the west, Bombay Presidency in the southwest, the *nizam* of Hyderabad in the Deccan, Madras Presidency in the south, and most of Bengal and Bihar in the east remained largely undisturbed. Not only did the Bombay and Madras Presidency armies remain loyal, but even the native SA princes helped the British suppress the revolt. By expeditiously disarming the disaffected sepoy regiments outside Avadh, the British kept the rebellion from spreading beyond the Doab and central India.

Surprisingly enough, it was the Sikh regiments raised in the newly conquered Punjab who provided the most valuable aid. The Sikhs, it must be remembered, had no loyalty to the Mughal emperor; besides, they wanted to avenge their defeat at the hands of the Bengal army.

The British control of the high seas and of "loyal" India also meant that the

EIC could quite quickly raise new regiments and import troops from abroad. As soon as they had recovered from the initial shock, the company, whose troops soon outnumbered the armed rebels, met the challenge on a war footing, and using telegraphic communications to coordinate their campaigns, entered the rebel heartland from various directions and gradually stamped out the rebellion.

The rebels, on the other hand, had no unified organization or cause, and lacking good communications, could only fight uncoordinated local skirmishes. Even though they won several battles, their victories were nothing more than local triumphs that counted for little in the overall context. The biggest handicap of the rebels was that they lacked a proper command structure. Initially, the sepoys, both Hindus and Muslims, had looked vainly for leadership from the last Mughal emperor, but very soon their loyalties were split. After the recapture of Delhi by the British in September 1857, the symbolic unifying value of the emperor (he and three Mughal princes were taken prisoner by Captain Hodson, who shot the princes in cold blood) was lost. In 1858, Tantia Topi, by declaring Nana Sahib to be the *peshwa,* factionalized the movement even further by giving the impression that the goal of the rebellion was the revival of Hindu Maratha power.

Mutual jealousies and intrigues, and lack of common ideals, destroyed all possibilities of the rebellion developing into any kind of true national movement. As the area of trouble spread, dozens of local Hindu and Muslim leaders emerged, who, to gain momentary glory or profit, often ended up fighting each other rather than the British. As a matter of record, the few Westernized Indians who were around in 1857, and who may have already developed some notions of nationalism, kept themselves conspicuously aloof from the troublesome developments.

The termination of the rebellion brought to a close the EIC's rule in India, and on November 1, 1858, the British Crown assumed direct authority over the land. Queen Victoria's proclamation promised that Britain would "respect the rights, dignity, and honor of native princes as our own," and declared that the Crown felt "bound to the natives of our Indian territories by the same obligations of duty which bind us to all our other subjects." In the long run, the second part of this grand and eloquent statement of intent proved hollow and inconsequential, but even before Her Majesty's Indian subjects could come to that realization, they got a taste of the exploitative nature of the new imperial order. The 1857–1858 war had been very costly to the British, but as the secretary of state for India proudly declared, unlike other wars fought by Britain, "no part of the cost of suppressing [the Indian Mutiny] was allowed to fall on the Imperial Exchequer; the whole of it was . . . defrayed by the Indian Taxpayer."[44]

Notes

1. Quoted in John Strachey, *The End of Empire* (New York: Praeger, 1964), p. 146.
2. Quoted in M. E. Chamberlain, *Decolonization: The Fall of the European Empires* (Oxford: Basil Blackwell, 1985), p. 5.

3. Ashis Nandy, *The Intimate Enemy: Loss and Recovery of Self Under Colonialism* (Delhi: Oxford University Press, 1983), p. xi.

4. See, for example, Vol. II.1 of *The New Cambridge History of India* (Cambridge: Cambridge University Press, 1988); and Judith M. Brown, *Modern India: The Origins of an Asian Democracy* (New York: Oxford University Press, 1985).

5. Stanley Wolpert, *A New History of India* (New York: Oxford University Press, 1977), p. 182.

6. Mujeeb, *Indian Muslims*, p. 282.

7. Spear, *A History of India*, pp. 56–57.

8. Nicholas B. Dirks, *The Hollow Crown; Ethnohistory of an Indian Kingdom* (Cambridge: Cambridge University Press, 1987), pp. 47–48.

9. Excerpt from the *Maharashtra Purana*, quoted in P. J. Marshall, *Bengal: The British Bridgehead/ Eastern India 1740–1828*, Vol. II.2. *The New Cambridge History of India* (Cambridge: Cambridge University Press, 1987), p. 72.

10. Marshall, *Bengal: The British Bridgehead*, p. 77.

11. See P. J. Marshall, *East Indian Fortunes: The British in Bengal in the Eighteenth Century* (Oxford: Oxford University Press, 1976), pp. 164–165, and Strachey, *The End of Empire*, p. 33.

12. K. Antonova et al., *A History of India: Book 2* (Moscow: Progress Publishers, 1978), p. 23.

13. Both C. A. Bayly, *Indian Society and the Making of the British Empire* (Cambridge: Cambridge University Press, 1988); and Marshall, *Bengal: The British Bridgehead*, in their *New Cambridge History of India* volumes have not even mentioned the incident.

14. Strachey, *The End of Empire*, p. 21.

15. K. M. Panikkar, *Asia and Western Dominance* (London: Allen and Unwin, 1953), p. 118.

16. Strachey, *The End of Empire*, p. 41.

17. Par J. Michaud, tr. from the French by V. K. Raman Menon, *Michaud's History of Mysore* (New Delhi: Asian Educational Services, 1985), p. 26.

18. Ibid., p. 104.

19. Ibid., p. 105.

20. Quoted in Anil Chandra Banerjee, *The New History of Modern India* (Calcutta: K.P. Bagchi, 1983), p. 231.

21. Marshall, *Bengal: The British Bridgehead*, p. 125.

22. Bayly, *Indian Society and the Making of the British Empire*, p. 86.

23. Burton Stein, "Idiom and Ideology in Early Nineteenth Century South India," in Peter Robb, ed., *Rural India: Land, Power And Society Under British Rule* (London: Curzon Press, 1983), p. 44.

24. Quoted in *The Cambridge Economic History of India*, II, p. 289.

25. Ibid., p. 288.

26. Tan Chung, "The Britain-China-India Trade Triangle 1771–1840," in S. Bhattacharya, ed., *Essays in Modern Indian Economic History* (Delhi: Munshiram Manoharlal Publishers, 1987), p. 129.

27. Strachey, *The End of Empire*, p. 55.

28. David Kopf, *British Orientalism and the Bengal Renaissance: The Dynamics of Indian Modernization, 1773–1835* (Berkeley: University of California Press, 1969), p. 21.

29. Ibid., p. 31.

30. Ibid., p. 80.

31. Quoted in A. Aspinall, *Cornwallis in Bengal* (Manchester: University of Manchester Press, 1931), p. 173.

32. James Mill, *History of British India,* Vol. II (London: James Madden and Co., 1840), p. 135.

33. Quoted in Geoffrey Moorhouse, *India Britannica* (London: Paladin Grafton Books, 1986), p. 67.

34. See Reginald Reynolds, *The White Sahibs in India* (Westport, CT: Greenwood Press, 1970), p. 275.

35. Stephen Hay and I. H. Qureshi, eds., *Sources of Indian Tradition,* Vol. II (New York: Columbia University Press, 1964), p. 45.

36. Ibid., p. 49.

37. Brian Gardner, *The East India Company* (New York: Dorset Press, 1990), p. 252.

38. Ibid., p. 249.

39. Boris Mollo, *The Indian Army* (Poole, Dorset: New Orchard Editions, 1981), pp. 51–52, 87.

40. See Sir Penderel Moon, *The British Conquest and Dominion of India* (London: Gerald Duckworth, 1989), p. 679.

41. Gardner, *The East India Company,* p. 251.

42. Reynolds, *The White Sahibs,* p. 88.

43. Moon, *The British Conquest,* p. 676.

44. Quoted in Reynolds, *The White Sahibs,* p. 97.

Part II

India Under the British, 1858–1947

The Establishment of a Nonsecular Polity

4

The British Record

An Overview

"Supposing that one hundred years hence the Native character becomes ele-vated from constant intercourse with Europeans and the acquirement of gen-eral and political knowledge as well as modern arts and sciences, is it possible that they will not have the spirit as well as the inclination to resist effectually any unjust and oppressive measures serving to degrade them in the scale of society?"[1]

—Raja Rammohan Roy (1772–1833)

"It is no pleasure to me to dwell on the wretched, heart-rending, blood-boiling condition of India. . . . The sum total of all is, that without such intention or wish, and with every desire for the good of India, England has in reality been the most disastrous and destructive foreign invader of India."[2]

—Dadabhai Naoroji (1825–1917)

"And why do I regard the British rule as a curse? It has impoverished the dumb millions by a system of progressive exploitation. . . . It has reduced us politically to serfdom. It has sapped the foundations of our culture. . . . It has degraded us spiritually."[3]

—Mahatma Gandhi (1869–1948)

Long before the British departed from India, English popular opinion was firmly convinced that the British rule had been an unquestionable blessing for the Indians because, among other things, it had brought political unity and law and order to the subcontinent; introduced modern education and the ideals of free speech, free press, democracy, and participatory government; made English the lingua franca of a linguistically divided country and, thereby, contributed to the emer-gence of a class of national leaders; unified the subcontinent with the steel structure of the Indian Civil Service; established railroads and a post and tele-graph system; and improved the living standards of the people by promoting hygiene, building irrigation canals, and so on.

In fact, this view was more than just popular opinion. From the days of the East India Company, long before India became a Crown Colony, British officials at the highest levels of government were convinced that they were involved in the noble mission of bringing civilization to backward, heathen India. We have seen in the last chapter how, at the turn of the nineteenth century, persons like Macaulay and Bentinck had hoped that the British, through a diffusion of West-ern knowledge, could dispel the darkness that enveloped India. A hundred years later, Lord Curzon (viceroy from 1900 to 1905) reiterated the sentiment: "To me the message is carved in granite, it is hewn out of the rock of doom—that our work is righteous and that it shall endure."[4] And Sir Winston Churchill, speaking in the House of Commons in the mid-1930s, when perceptive minds could see that the end of empire was near, thundered that "Our Government . . . is incom-parably the best government that India has ever seen or ever will see."[5]

The sharp division in the perceptions of the British and the Indians is under-standable because an alien ruler's viewpoint can hardly be expected to coincide with that of the suppressed natives. Without getting into a debate as to which side is in the right, it can be safely concluded that many modern elements, such as railroads and the telegraph, would have made an appearance in India even if the British had never conquered the country. Similarly, modern ideas and values would have entered the subcontinent, one way or the other.

On the other hand, it is difficult to conceive of the possibility of a native power unifying the country politically and administratively, introducing a univer-sal legal system and the principle of electoral politics. It is the British occupation that was responsible for these changes, though one must hastily add that the new institutions were not without flaws. "Unity" under the British not only allowed for hundreds of autonomous princely states but culminated in the partitioning of the country. The legal system was not uniform because it avoided interfering with personal law. The Indian Civil Service (ICS) was manned by arrogant bureaucrats who looked upon themselves as the rulers, not the servants, of the people. The introduction of English as the official language and the medium for higher instruction produced an Anglicized Indian elite who tended to acquire many of the negative attributes of the British ruling class. The electoral process, when inaugurated, was undemocratic because it was based on communal repre-sentation. And the British hardly made a dent in the poverty and illiteracy from which the country suffered.

Regardless of the pros and cons of British rule in India, one fact is undeni-able: the process of political transformation that has made India the country it is today unfolded during British rule, and the alien basis of this transformation has been quietly accepted by independent India's leaders. Why then was the British period of rule—1858 to 1947—marred by so much antagonism and bitterness?

And why did it end in bloodshed and the destruction of India's unity?

One reason is that, unlike previous foreign powers that had occupied India, been absorbed by it, and become a part of it, the British did not identify with India and considered it no more than one of their many colonies, albeit the most important one. Their loyalty lay elsewhere, and they looked upon their Indian possession as a source of profit for the people and the government of Britain. When, after World War I, profits began to dwindle and the empire became a financial burden, the British began to lose interest in India, although psychologically they were still unprepared to give up the "jewel in the crown." Practically until the very end, the British monopolized all posts of power and authority and maintained an attitude of superiority over the people they ruled.

The second reason is even more important. In their view of the future of Anglo-Indian relations, the British had always envisaged the possibility of civilized (modernized, in our terminology) India regaining independence. This vision was clearly enunciated by pre-1858 reformers such as Charles Trevelyan, Mountstuart Elphinstone, and Thomas Babington Macaulay. Macaulay, who is otherwise condemned for his arrogant dismissal of Indian learning, made the famous speech in the House of Commons in 1833, in which he spoke rapturously of the "proudest day in English history" when Indians, "having become instructed in European knowledge . . . [will] demand European institutions."[6] During the imperialist period that followed the takeover of India by the Crown, this vision became blurred and the prospect of India's becoming independent appeared too remote to be taken seriously. As a result, the British, on the one hand, hesitatingly introduced elements of representative government, and on the other, unhesitatingly suppressed or thwarted the efforts of nationalist Indians who sought quicker action. The reluctance to part with power also led the British to seek succor from divide-and-rule policies and policies of physical repression.

In the ultimate analysis, it was the emergence of a new, "modern," English-educated, Indian intelligentsia, which the British had themselves originally fostered, that led to the rise of Indian nationalism and initially to the demand for a modicum of Indian participation in administration and policy making. This was the very elite that Macaulay had hoped for. Ideally speaking, the British should have welcomed this development and led the way to self-government. But instead of gracefully acceding to the minimal demands of the nationalist elite who had established an all-India organization, the Indian National Congress (1885), the British, who equated loyalty to abject submissiveness, viewed even the moderate goals of the Congress as seditious and Congressmen as troublemakers. Within three years of the founding of the Congress, Viceroy Lord Dufferin, in 1888, spoke contemptuously of the Congress as "a microscopic minority" whose contention that "it represents the people of India" was wholly groundless.[7]

As the Indian National Congress grew in strength, and yet failed to be taken seriously, the nationalist sentiment began to turn anti-British. Some extremists in the Congress, having lost faith in the sincerity of the British claim that they were

the Congress, having lost faith in the sincerity of the British claim that they were guiding India toward self-government, discarded the politics of collaboration and replaced it with that of confrontation. This confirmed the British view that the Congress had to be weakened and its claim to represent the Indian "nation" to be undermined. Taking advantage of the fact that many Muslim leaders had kept aloof from the Congress (in which Muslims *were* underrepresented) and were antagonistic to Congress-style politics, the British, in 1906, officially encouraged them to set up their own organization, the Muslim League. Forty-one years later, the Muslim League was instrumental in the division of the country and the establishment of the separate Muslim state of Pakistan.

The British not only kept harping on the need to look after the interests of the Muslims, but in due course, they extended this "protective" approach to other minority communities, such as the Sikhs and the Scheduled Castes. The leaders of these communities, having come to the conclusion that they, too, could make greater political gains by working outside the Congress, began to reject the claim of the Congress that it represented all segments of the population and that it was the only party that was both secular and national.

Unfortunately, in the early decades of the twentieth century, some of the Hindu leaders of the Congress thought it fit to exploit Hindu religious sentiments for political purposes. Coincidentally, the countrywide Hindu religious movements, aimed at revitalizing Hindu society and reviving the glory of ancient Hindu India, also carried a strain of anti-Muslim sentiment. Since the Congress leadership happened to be largely Hindu, the notion grew that the Congress was a Hindu communal party, even though many Congress leaders were genuinely committed to secularism. There were other reasons, too, for the Muslims to be suspicious of the Congress. Having been tardy in accepting Western education, they were perturbed to see Hindus rise to positions of prominence in the fields of education, journalism, and law, as well as in the British administrative and judicial services.

As a result, the Muslim leaders concluded that elective self-government was not in their interest because it would, inevitably, put power in the hands of the Hindus, the majority community. An incipient idea that the Muslims and Hindus were two separate nations that could not coexist gradually began to evolve into a full-fledged theory. Under these circumstances it was not difficult for the British to use divide-and-rule tactics to further widen the gulfs between various Indian communities, primarily between the Muslims and the Hindus. It can be said that the British inaugurated the era of communal* politics in the constitutional re-

---

*The term *communal* has a unique meaning in India, and communalism is a uniquely Indian development. Broadly speaking, communal groups are defined by their religion and not by their ethnicity, language, or region. An Indian newspaper, reporting a "communal riot" gives the religion of the parties involved and the location of the riot, but provides no details of the caste, language, or ethnic identity of the participants (unless that has a special significance).

this one act the British laid the groundwork for Muslims to detach themselves from the unified nationalist movement. The Muslim interest no longer coincided with any abstract notion of national interest.

Up until the First World War, the British had managed to reconcile their imperial aims with limited appeasement of the so-called nationalist aspirations. The war changed the equation radically. Indians, who had provided massive support to the Allies to fight a war to "save democracy and freedom" and, according to President Wilson, establish a new world order where all subject peoples would gain the right of self-determination, demanded that Britain declare its intentions regarding India. The Congress Party, at its 1916 session, moved a resolution formally asking Britain to proclaim that it would give India self-government at an early date. The Muslim League, not yet wholly alienated from the Congress, supported this demand.

But Britain, once again, disappointed India, and the postwar Government of India Act of 1919, while increasing the size of the legislatures and allowing Indians to take charge of some of the provincial ministries, kept real power firmly in the hands of the British viceroy, the British provincial governors, and their British ministers in control of key ministries. The act perpetuated the principle of communal representation and enlarged it to include not only Muslims but also Sikhs in Punjab, non-Brahmins in Madras, Marathas (a low-caste community) in Bombay, Europeans, Anglo-Indians, and Indian Christians. In the same year, the British displayed the ruthlessness of their morally bankrupt regime by shooting 379 innocent people—men, women, and children—who had gathered peacefully in the city of Amritsar to celebrate an annual fair. General Dyer, who considered the gathering as defying the official ban on meetings, placed his machine guns in the only exit of the fairgrounds (called Jallianwala Bagh) and fired indiscriminately into the crowd.

The Jallianwala Bagh massacre marked the end of the moderates in the Congress, which now came under the leadership of Mahatma Gandhi, who totally reshaped the nature of Indian politics. Gandhi turned the Congress into a mass party with branches at the provincial and district levels. The membership of the Congress was open to anybody over twenty-one who agreed with the Congress goal of *swaraj* (independence). And Gandhi transformed the highly Westernized elite Congress leaders into leaders of the masses. The leaders discarded their three-piece suits for hand-spun garments of the type worn by ordinary people, and they toured the countryside speaking to the peasants in their own language. Gandhi also introduced his unique political doctrine of *satyagraha* (truth-force, explained in the next chapter) that encouraged the people to defy the unjust laws of the government but in a nonviolent, passive manner. Gandhi's passive civil disobedience movements in 1920 and 1930 shook the very foundations of the government. However, Gandhi failed to unite the Hindus and the Muslims. Although he did have many loyal and dedicated Muslim followers, the Muslim League took the line that Gandhi's saintliness was embedded in Hindu culture and that his political goals, such as the achievement of *Ramraj* (or *Ramrajya,* the just society that had supposedly existed under Lord Ram) were shaped by Hindu ideology.

Meanwhile, the British moved slowly on to provide India a new constitution through the Government of India Act of 1935. The 1935 act had a section dealing with a federal center and another with the provinces; the provinces were made more autonomous, and though the governors still had considerable powers, the franchise was extended and the provincial ministers made wholly responsible to elected legislatures. The system of separate communal electorates was made more elaborate by adding the Backward Tribes to the earlier list of Muslims, Sikhs, Indian Christians, Europeans, Labor, the universities, landholders, commerce and industry, and an electorate termed "general population," which was essentially Hindu.

Both the Congress and the Muslim League rejected the federal part of the act because it brought no devolution of power at the center and reluctantly agreed to give a trial to the provincial part. In the 1937 elections, the first under the 1935 act, the Congress, which had consistently maintained that it was a secular body, proved itself to be so by taking all but three of the eleven provinces. The Muslim League, chastened by its failure, appealed to the Congress to form coalition ministries, but the Congress rejected the overtures with an unwise show of arrogance. Muhammad Ali Jinnah, the absolute leader of the Muslim League, convinced that there was no future in trying to work with the Congress, decided that the only goal of the Muslim League should be the demand for a separate Muslim homeland, Pakistan. The goal was officially announced in 1940.

The Second World War placed the government of India in a dilemma. It needed the support of the Indian leaders to push its war efforts, but it was not ready to concede the Congress demand that it declare India "to be an independent nation." In 1942, a British proposal for postwar reform was found so unacceptable that the Congress launched the Quit India movement that called on the British to withdraw from India immediately. The mass movement incited the biggest wave of civil disobedience the country had ever witnessed, and all the Congress leaders, along with 60,000 followers, were thrown into jails across the country. Significantly, the day the Congress ministries had resigned was celebrated by the Muslim League as Thanksgiving Day.

By the time the war was over and the Congress prisoners had been released, the British were, indeed, ready to quit India but had no formula that could satisfy both the Muslim League and the Congress. In the 1945/46 elections, the second under the 1935 act, the Muslim League won all the Muslim seats for the Central Legislative Assembly and 439 of the 494 Muslim-electorate seats reserved for Muslims in the provincial assemblies, thus proving that it was now in a position to speak for the Muslims. The Congress was universally successful in the general electorates, but not so in the Muslim electorates. Thus, the Muslim League had no longer any reason to compromise with the Congress or the government.

no longer any reason to compromise with the Congress or the government.

In 1946, a cabinet mission visited India and put forward a proposal for a federal system that made an attempt at satisfying the demands of the Muslim League and yet saving the union. The Muslim League and the Congress accepted the proposal, but later, when Jinnah was persuaded that the Congress would not abide by the proposal after independence was gained, he rejected the proposal and called for "direct action" by the Muslims on August 6, 1946. This Direct Action Day unleashed communal violence that took 4,700 lives in Calcutta and 12,000 in the whole of India.

When it became apparent that there was no way to get the Congress and the Muslim League to agree with one another, Prime Minister Attlee announced on February 20, 1947, that, come what may, the British would leave India in June 1948. The new viceroy, Lord Mountbatten, instructed to work out any proposal that would ensure Britain's withdrawal, brought forward that date to August 1947. The lines of the partition were demarcated in a hurry, and apart from the Muslim-majority provinces of North West Frontier Province and Sind, Pakistan was given Muslim-majority districts in Punjab and Bengal. This last act of the British—that of relinquishing their responsibilities without thought to the consequences—brought the most appalling communal carnage to the subcontinent. Nearly a million Hindus, Sikhs, and Muslims were slaughtered, 5 million Muslims fled to Pakistan, and an equal number of Hindus and Sikhs crossed over to what now constituted India, and more than 12 million were made homeless.

The partition did not end the story of India's communal troubles. The heightening of religious hostility and the trauma resulting from the bloodshed still cast a heavy shadow over the subcontinent. First, the formation of Pakistan did not solve the Muslim issue. The number of Muslims that migrated from India to Pakistan was a fraction of the Muslim population that remained behind. Today, the 120 million plus Muslim citizens of India—practically equal to the entire population of Pakistan—constitute nearly 12 percent of India's population. Since most of these Muslims had voted for the Muslim League, they were naturally looked upon with suspicion by the Hindus. Acceptance of these Muslims as citizens of a secular republic has been a long time coming.

Second, the introduction of a secular constitution in India has yet to completely destroy the notion, confirmed by the formation of Pakistan, that a religious-ethnic community can struggle for and gain a separate homeland. As a result, to name just a few of such conflicts, post-1947 India has witnessed the violent struggle for an independent Khalistan by the Sikhs, an independent Nagaland by the Naga tribes, and an independent Kashmir by the Kashmiri Muslims. The post-partition history of India begs the question: Has the dialectics of communalism got so strongly rooted in India's political system that it has come to undermine, if not to replace, the notions of secularism and democ-

Notes

1. See Stephen Hay, ed., *Sources of Indian Tradition, Vol 2: Modern India and Pakistan* (New York: Columbia University Press, 1988), p. 33.
2. R. P. Masani, *Dadabhai Naoroji* (Delhi: Publications Division, 1960), p. 75.
3. Martin Green, ed., *Gandhi in India: In His Own Words* (Hanover and London: Published for Tufts University by the University Press of New England, 1987), p. 114.
4. Mark Bence-Jones, *The Viceroys of India* (New York: St. Martin's Press, 1982), p. 178.
5. Quoted in Nemai Sadhan Bose, *Indian National Movement: An Outline,* 3rd ed. (Calcutta: Firma KLM Press, 1982), p. 137.
6. Quoted in R. C. Majumdar, gen. ed., *British Paramountcy and Indian Renaissance,* Part II, 2nd ed. (Bombay: Bharatya Vidya Bhavan, 1981), p. 383.
7. Quoted in Majumdar, *British Paramountcy,* pp. 557–558.

5

The Making of a Communal Polity

1858–1908

The elimination of the Mughal emperor and the assumption of direct authority over India by the Crown of Great Britain in 1858 introduced British-style despotism to the subcontinent. The idea that the conquered people should have a say in the government of their country did not arise. The British reconciled the ideas of democracy and liberalism, which they were so proud of in England, with authoritarianism in India by projecting the notion that they were bringing civilization to a barbarous people and, thereby, preparing them to govern themselves at some future date.

Such thinking had guided the actions of many of the Orientalist and the Utilitarian officials in the East India Company government in India. For example, Governor-General Lord Hastings, writing in his private journal in 1818, looked forward to the day when England, "having used her sovereignty towards enlightening her temporary subjects," would be proud to relinquish her domination over India.[1] About the same time, Elphinstone, the governor of Bombay, drew the conclusion that "it is for our interest to have an early separation from a civilized people, rather than a violent rupture with a barbarous nation."[2] This theme was, perhaps, best expressed by Thomas Babington Macaulay in his speech to the House of Commons in 1833, referred to, in passing, in the last chapter: "It may be that the public mind of India may expand under our system till it has outgrown that system; that by good government we may educate our subjects into a capacity for better government; that, having become instructed in European knowledge, they may, in some future age, demand European institutions. . . . Whenever it comes, it will be the proudest day in English history."[3]

Unfortunately, this positive, optimistic approach, though never wholly discarded, lost much of its value after 1858. As a colonial power, Britain was now much more interested in establishing a strong government that could control the vast country, keep it pacified, and make it a valuable part of the empire than in guiding the natives toward democracy. Policies for India, viewed as an appendage of Britain, were made in London and debated, if at all, in Parliament; Indians had no place in this arrangement. As the decades rolled by, educated Indians did begin to voice their complaints about the wrongs being done to India, but London's views had hardened to the extent that Lord Salisbury (1830–1903; twice secretary of state for India and thrice prime minister) could dare to remark that "the Hindus know that they are governed by a 'superior race.' When a man has a black, red, or yellow skin, and I should add when he has the 'Providential' chance of being governed by whites, he ought not to have, he has not in fact, an opinion. It is enough to bow down and utter thanks."[4]

In a similar vein, Lord Hamilton, then secretary of state, sent a forceful message to the viceroy in India (April 14, 1899): "We cannot give the Natives what they want: representative institutions or the diminution of the existing establishment of Europeans is impossible."[5] And this was on the eve of the twentieth century. We can conclude the fifty-year period under consideration with a quote from a speech by Viceroy Lord Curzon in 1904, in which he emphasized certain principles governing public appointments: "The highest ranks of civil employment in India . . . must . . . as a general rule, be held by Englishmen, for the reason that they possess, partly by heredity, partly by upbringing, and partly by education, the knowledge of the principles of Government, the habits of mind, and the vigour of character, which are essential for the task, and that, the rule of India being a British rule, and any other rule being in the circumstances of the case impossible, the tone and standard should be set by those who have created and are responsible for it."[6]

Curzon had the greatest contempt for the Indians, whom he viewed as a congenitally inefficient race. When it was suggested to him that he nominate a prominent Indian to the Executive Council, he replied categorically: "In the whole continent there is not one Indian fit for the post."[7] As the fiftieth anniversary of Queen Victoria's Proclamation of 1858, which had announced the assumption of the government of India by the Crown, drew near, many British officials at the highest levels of the government in London and Calcutta were sorely embarrassed by the clause in the proclamation that had recognized the equality of races. ("Our subjects of whatever race or creed, shall be freely and impartially admitted to offices in our service.") Curzon went so far as to call it "one of the greatest mistakes" made by Britain. Under these circumstances, in 1908, it was unrealistic to even think of the possibility of India becoming independent in the foreseeable future.

But much had changed in the last fifty years. A new generation of Indians, most of them born at the time of the Great Rebellion or soon thereafter, furnished modern India with some of its greatest thinkers and leaders—persons who shaped the fate of the country. These highly educated and often highly Westernized leaders could not accept the arrogant British imperialist attitude toward Indians and began to agitate for the right of Indians for a greater representation in the administration of the country. When their initial, hesitatingly made, very limited demands went unheeded, they launched an organized movement that, by 1908, had practically assumed the dimensions of a national struggle for independence.

Several factors, dealt with below, contributed to the rise of national consciousness and the uniquely divisive profile that nationalism acquired in the subcontinent. Two important factors were connected with the British government: the nature of British economic exploitation of India and the exclusiveness of the Indian Civil Service. Other factors had more to do with internal developments involving the Indian peoples.

Economic Imperialism

We have noted in an earlier chapter how the EIC employees squeezed huge profits through private (monopoly) trade and how the company's high officials retired with unbelievably liberal pensions (the Marquis of Hastings, not counting his salary, received 60,000 pounds sterling as a lump sum). After 1833, when the EIC was stripped of its trading functions, the stockholders of the company were assured a 10 percent dividend regardless of any fluctuations in the market. These moneys, extorted from poor peasants and handicraft workers, can no doubt be considered as exploitative and an economic drain on the country. The stockholders continued to receive their 10 percent dividend for sixteen years after 1858, at which time the company's "stock," capital and interest, was redeemed for the sum of 37.2 million pounds sterling. This sum was added to India's debt and ultimately paid by the Indian taxpayer.

Another, even more important drain on Indian resources was related to the British government's ability to dip into the revenues of India. Even before 1858, London had periodically ordered the East India Company to participate in wars outside India—wars that had no concern with India but that were charged against revenues collected in India. As Sir George Wingate, who had served for many years in the Bombay Presidency administration, pointed out in 1859, "most of our Asiatic Wars with countries beyond the limits of our Empire have been carried on by means of the military and monetary resources of the Government of India, though the object of these wars were, in some instances, purely British, and in others but remotely connected with the interests of India. . . . [India] has never in any instance been paid a full equivalent for the assistance thus rendered which furnishes irrefragable [undeniable] proof of the one-sided and selfish character of our Indian Policy."[8] The cost to India of the First Afghan War was 15 million pounds sterling; of the first two Burmese Wars, 14 million pounds sterling; and of the expeditions to Persia and China, 6 million pounds sterling. We have already mentioned the fact that 40 million pounds sterling spent on suppressing the Great Rebellion were charged to India. Even the cost of transporting British troops to India, in British ships, was not borne by the British Exchequer!

One of the significant aspects of post-1858 economic imperialism is related to the construction of railroads in India. By 1900, the Indian railway network was the fifth largest in the world, but its development, while helping the British industrialists, only added to India's debt. Strange as it may seem, British industrialists who had fought and won the battle for free trade suddenly became monopolists and protectionists when it came to investments in India. The British Government of India provided free land to the "guaranteed companies" that invested capital in the building of railways; if the railway showed a loss, the government paid the company a guaranteed, fixed, minimum interest at a rate that was higher than the prevailing market rates. These moneys came out of Indian revenues and increased the public debt; by 1900, the payment involved was more than 50 million pounds sterling. This strange system of "speculation" was without any risk to the speculator because it amounted to private investment at public risk. The guarantee system not only did *not* place constraints on the companies to avoid wasteful construction or inefficient operations (lines constructed by the government cost less than half of those constructed by the companies) but in the words of Sir Richard Strachey, it also created "a very valuable property at the expense of the taxpayers of India."[9]

One would have expected that, regardless of the uniquely exploitative nature of the railway system, the establishment of the railways would have contributed to the growth of ancillary Indian industries, such as the manufacture of locomotives and rolling stock. The British policies, which brazenly favored British industrialists, kept this development from taking place. It is shocking to learn that by 1947, when India gained independence, the country had produced only 700 locomotives indigenously.

From the early decades of the nineteenth century, when the Industrial Revolution was rapidly developing in England, the traditional Indian manufacturing industries lost ground to the machine-made wares of Britain. At the same time, however, Indian exports of indigo, cotton, jute, tea, oilseeds, linseed oil, and hides increased. In 1882, the tariff rate on imports, which was already extremely moderate, was abolished and India became a free trade country. Only in 1894, after Indian public opinion had begun to criticize British policies, was a duty of 5 to 15 percent imposed on imported goods; thereafter, British goods except for cotton textiles (the only important modern industry in India) no longer enjoyed preferential treatment. In any case, the overall effect of fifty years of British rule was to transform India "from a country of combined agriculture and handicrafts into a purely agricultural colony of British industry, resulting in the severe over-pressure on agriculture which has remained one of the most critical problems of India."[10]

In 1895, a commission commonly known as the Welby Commission was set up to look into Indian expenditures. The Welby Commission's report, published in 1900, revealed a number of cases where excessive or unjust payments had been made by the Indian government. The most glaring one was that of the Red Sea and India Telegraph Company. The company was formed in 1858 and invested 11 million pounds sterling. Although the company's operations collapsed after a few days when the telegraph line broke down, it continued to receive the guaranteed 4½ percent return on its capital for fifty years. As the Welby Commission report noted, "in 1861 an act was passed declaring that the guarantee was not conditional upon the telegraph being in working order."[11]

The expenses of the office of the secretary of state for India and the upkeep of the India Office were also charged against the Indian Exchequer because the secretary of state was supposedly working to protect Indian interests. In reality, operating as he was from London with limited knowledge of India, he could hardly be expected to resist the pressures from indigenous British merchants and capitalists.

While the Indian public debt in 1900 stood at 234 million pounds sterling, the annual drain of 16 million pounds sterling constituted 25 percent of the total revenue of India. R. C. Dutt, who, at the turn of the century, published the first authoritative and scholarly exposé of the economic exploitation of India, calculated that in the year 1900–1901, these "Home Charges" were equal to the total land revenue for that year.

Apologists who have tried to criticize the "drain theory" as an exaggeration appear to forget that during the first fifty years of British rule, India was the largest single market for British manufactured goods and a recipient of nearly one-tenth of British overseas investment capital. Whichever way one views it, the uniquely immoral economic policies of Britain kept the incipient Indian industries from developing and its economy from modernizing. As Judith Brown has analyzed it, "the British connection with India . . . enabled Britain to perform as an economy with a world-wide balance of payment surplus when her own trading position had declined [in the opening decades of the twentieth century]."[12]

The Indian Civil Service: British Monopoly of High Office

Disregarding the promise that Queen Victoria had made that Indians should be "impartially and freely admitted to office in our service," the post-1858 British rulers made it a policy that all high offices in the Indian Civil Service (ICS) were to be monopolized by Britishers, whose main function was to govern efficiently but remain aloof from the populace they governed. This, among other things, meant that Indians could not contribute to the making of public policies and that the government got estranged from the governed.

A side result of the British policy was the glamorization of the Indian Civil Service. In his private correspondence, Lord Curzon used terms such as "torpor," "crassness," "indifferent," and "incompetent" to describe ICS officers, who he said "had no taste for [their] work" and who "dislike the country and the people" and "had no interest in India as India, and in the Indian people as our fellow subjects whom we are called upon to rule."[13] This "truth" is sharply contradicted by the public assessment of the service by Lord Dufferin (governor-general, 1884–1888): "For ingenuity, courage, right judgement, disinterested devotion to duty, endurance, open-heartedness, and, at the same time, loyalty to one another and their chiefs, [the ICS officers] are to my knowledge, superior to any other class of Englishmen."[14]

There were two basic reasons for the state of affairs that led Curzon to make the comments he did. First, in the latter half of the nineteenth century, and increasingly so in the twentieth, there was a certain disdain in England for those who served in India. Eminent professional lawyers, like Sir Fitzjames, who served as legal member of the Viceroy's Executive Council from 1869 to 1872, came back to England to find that they had lost their opportunity for advancement. This led Sir Fitzjames to remark, "It seems to me that a country which treats Indian service in that spirit hardly deserves to have an empire."[15] If this was the image of Indian service at the highest level, one can imagine how the comparatively lowly ICS officers were looked upon. Why would anyone with education and talent be attracted to join the ICS?

Another reason was the progressive lowering of the age limit for the ICS examination in the hope of luring young men into the service before they graduated from the university and became eligible for other jobs. Though the age limit was lowered from twenty-three to twenty-two in 1859, and again to twenty-one in 1866, university students did not come forward in substantial numbers. By 1874, 43 percent of the ICS recruits had not attended a university, and the number that came from Oxbridge fell from a high of 43 percent in 1861 to a low of 18 percent in 1871.

In 1876, having decided to give the successful candidates two years of university education before sending them to India, the age limit was further reduced to nineteen. This move did little to improve the quality of the candidates, but had the effect of creating the suspicion in India that the real motive was to keep Indians out of the ICS. A strongly worded memorial, protesting the action, was sent by the Indian Association in Calcutta to Parliament; the agitation sparked a "spirit of unity and solidarity among the people of India."[16] Partly as a concession to Indian candidates, but primarily because opinion in England had reversed and it was felt that a higher age limit would attract better candidates, the age limit was raised to twenty-three in 1889. This, too, proved ineffective; while the number of candidates fell from 226 in 1899 to 166 in 1906, the number of vacancies rose from 56 to 61.

As far as the Indian candidates were concerned, raising the age limit can be considered a concession because few Indians could be ready for the competition by the age of nineteen, even if they could afford to go to England to study (the examination was based on English school education and held only in England). As a consequence, out of the 939 members of the ICS in 1892, only 21 were

Indians. There was some debate over the issue of holding the examination simultaneously in England and India, but the Government of India persistently opposed such a move because it would have inevitably brought more Indians into the service, and Indians, however talented and well qualified, were considered to lack the character (which the British, obviously, were endowed with) required of rulers of men. The Indian members of the ICS, however few they were, never met their British counterparts except at rare official dinners or ceremonies; they were never allowed to step into the British clubs.

The basic administrative unit in British India was the district (it remains so even today), with an average population of 1.5 million. The appointment after training of a British officer in his mid-twenties, as a district officer made him the linchpin of the administrative system. He supervised the collection of land revenues, was responsible for law and order and for the arrest and then the punishment of evildoers, and was expected to oversee the general welfare of "his" people (education, medical relief, public health). The district officer embodied the authority and power of the British government. And he was still in his twenties!

Internal Developments and the Emergence of Indian Nationalism

As noted earlier, the researches and writings of the Orientalists had rediscovered India's great past and ancient glory and, thereby, infused into the emerging Indian elite a sense of self-respect and pride in their history. The subsequent attacks by the Utilitarians on the so-called bankruptcy of Indian civilization only hurt these feeling of self-esteem and strengthened the elite's identification with their heritage. This first stirring of what is commonly termed "Indian nationalism" needs to be examined carefully because in the Indian context, the word *nationalism* came to have a somewhat special connotation.

Broadly speaking, the definition of national identity is related to the concept of nation-state, where a nation, bound by the myth of a common historical heritage and common culture, is located within the physically defined boundaries of a state. It is the function of the regime to reflect national identity in its policies. In a state composed of one major culture group and several smaller ones that do not identify with the culture and history of the major group, national identity must maintain its validity by focusing on genuinely secular national symbols that reflect universal principles transcending sectarian identities. The Indian context distorted the development of nationalism, for several reasons discussed below.

The Making of Nationalism and Communalism

The Role of English Education

The Emergence of Hindu Leadership. The introduction by the British of English as the official language of India and as the medium of higher instruction has had a major impact on the development of Indian nationalism and Indian politics. Even today, English retains its importance as the link-language of India because the country—with 179 languages, 544 major dialects, and thousands of minor dialects—has not yet been able to establish a national language.

Even before India entered the nineteenth century, and before political circumstances forced Indians to learn English to gain EIC jobs, Hindu intellectuals, like the great Bengali *savant,* Raja Ram Mohan Roy (1772–1833), became enthusiastic students of Western literature and philosophy. Roy was a renaissance figure who by an early age had mastered Arabic, Persian, Sanskrit, English, and, of course, his mother tongue, Bengali. He became a prolific essayist and wrote with facility in Persian, English, and Bengali. In 1816, a group of Bengali Hindus inspired by Roy raised ½ lakh (or lac = 100,000) rupees to establish Hindu College in Calcutta, the first private institution of modern higher learning in India.

Not counting the missionaries, these Bengali intellectuals, most of them Brahmins, were the pioneers of English education in India. By 1835, there were twenty-five schools such as the Hindu College. Their aim, succinctly expressed by Raja Ram Mohan Roy in a letter he wrote in 1823, was to "promote a more liberal and enlightened system of instruction, embracing Mathematics, Natural Philosophy, Chemistry, Anatomy, with other useful sciences."

This development is significant because it came despite the deadening inertia that marked EIC's educational policies from 1813 to 1835. The Charter Act of 1813 had provided 1 lakh of rupees a year for the advancement of education in India, but the EIC was frozen into inaction by the controversy raging between the Orientalists and the Utilitarians—one wanting to promote vernacular education and the other demanding that the funds be used for Western education. In 1835, the issue was resolved once and for all when it was decided that the moneys would be spent "on English education alone."

In 1844 the company gave further impetus to the study of English by declaring that preference for administrative jobs would be given to English-educated candidates. A decade later, in 1854, the future structure of the Indian educational system was carefully defined: a director general of education, assisted by Departments of Public Instruction in every province, would oversee the national educational system, where vernacular primary schools were to be followed by Anglo-vernacular high schools, and topped off by universities modeled on the London University, where the medium of instruction would be English (universities were established in Calcutta, Madras, and Bombay in 1857); other than these government-funded and government-run institutions, grants were also to be made to private institutions observing religious neutrality. Since funds for primary education remained extremely meager, the system became top-heavy, which it remains till today.

By 1901, there were 140 English Arts colleges in the country: 32 government run; 55 private but government aided; and 53 wholly privately run; the total enrollment figure was 17,148. In the same year, the number of students in the 3,097 English secondary schools was 422,187.

The development of education in India was marked by three special features. The first was that, in numbers of higher institutions of learning, Bengal, Madras, and Bombay led the rest of the country by a wide margin. In the academic year 1891–92, there were seventy-eight colleges in these three presidencies and only twenty-one in the rest of India. The second was that Hindu students (including a very high proportion of Brahmins) constituted an overwhelming majority in all these institutions while the percentage of Muslim students was far below the Muslim representation in the population of each presidency. The third was that, relative to their population, the Parsis were far ahead of even the Hindus. To give a few examples, (1) in Bengal, more than half the population was Muslim, but between 1836 and 1886, only 5.2 percent of the students who passed examinations at Calcutta University were Muslims (85.3 percent were Hindus); (2) in Madras Presidency, since 91.4 percent of the population was Hindu and only 6.2 percent Muslim, it is more readily understandable why the number of Muslim students in the colleges would be small—in 1881–82, Muslim students were 1.8 percent of the total, while Hindu students were 90 percent; and (3) in Bombay Presidency, Muslims formed 18.4 percent of the population and the Hindus, 73.4 percent, but here, too, of the successful candidates in university examinations between 1876 and 1886, only 1.3 percent were Muslim, whereas Hindus constituted 72.6 percent. Surprisingly, the Parsis who formed only 0.4 percent of the population contributed 26.1 percent of the successful candidates.

There were several important long-term consequence of these developments:

1. The first Western-educated leaders of Indian public opinion emerged in Calcutta, Madras, and Bombay; their mother tongues were totally different, but these leaders could readily communicate with each other in English. It is they who, having imbibed Western knowledge, came to idealize freedom and democracy and to use the conqueror's own political ideology as a weapon to force the conqueror to make concessions. And thus they gave a new meaning to the words *India* and *Indians*.

2. These leaders were mostly Hindus, and generally Brahmins. While they encouraged the advancement of education that was rational and scientific, they also got involved with religious reform movements that would revitalize and revive a moribund society. Thus, politics and religion got intertwined.

3. The introduction of vernacular primary education and the rise of the vernacular press (thanks to the introduction of printing in the early nineteenth century) were the harbingers of a dynamic literary renaissance in regional languages. The growing sense of nationalism found ready expression in this new medium. Once again, Hindu writers dominated the arena of the modern press and modern literary writing, with Bengal taking the lead. A poem written by Bankim Chandra Chatterjee (1838–1894), "Bande Matram," was accepted as the national anthem of pre-1947 India.

4. Despite their insignificantly small population, the Parsis assumed an important role in all aspects of Indian national development.
5. The Muslims were largely left out of the mainstream leadership that came to guide political change.

The Slow Response of the Muslims. Whereas Hindus had accepted secular Western education with enthusiasm, Muslims reacted very differently. The Muslim elite, conscious of their erstwhile status as the rulers of India, for the longest time maintained a rejectionist attitude toward all things British, and turned their attention inward to revive and purify Islamic spirituality by getting rid of Hindu practices that had infiltrated Indian Islam. One important Islamic revivalist, Sayyid Ahmad of Rai Bareli (1786–1831), went so far as to reject the country of the pagans, notwithstanding that it was the land of his birth, and move to the northwest frontier to establish an Islamic state. He died waging a *jihad* (holy war) against the Sikhs.

Even after 1857, when it was clear that the British were there to stay and that Mughal India had met its demise, Muslim leaders still could not reconcile their Islamic fundamentalism with Western secular education. In 1867, the Deoband school of *ulama* (Islamic scholars) developed a more rigid form of scriptural Islam. By 1900, forty schools connected with Deoband had been established to spread this strictly orthodox form of Islam throughout India.

Another school of thought that attracted Indian Muslims was that of the Iranian thinker Jamal-ud-din al-Afghani (1838–1897), who sought to resist the West by consolidating the world of Islam under the spiritual leadership of the Ottoman caliph. Jamal-ud-din visited India several times and his influence culminated in the 1919 pan-Islamic Khilafat movement.

It is said that the British attitude toward the Muslims was also a factor in keeping the Muslims away from modern education. The British did, indeed, feel that Muslims were more responsible than Hindus in creating the upheaval of 1857, and since Muslim loyalty and allegiance were suspect, the British favored the recruitment of Hindus into the administrative services. Also by this time Hindus, having already accepted Western education, were well prepared to participate in the new scheme of things. A liberal Muslim leader, R. M. Sayani, speaking at the Calcutta session of the Indian National Congress in 1896, perhaps summed up the situation nicely:

> When the Musalmans were rulers of the country . . . the Hindus stood in awe of them. . . . By a stroke of misfortune, the Musalmans had to abdicate their position and descend to the level of their Hindu fellow-countrymen. The Hindus who had before stood in awe of their Musalman masters were thus raised a step by the fall of their said masters, and with their former awe dropped their courtesy also. The Musalmans, who are a very sensitive *race,* naturally resented the treatment *and would have nothing to do either with their* [new] *rulers or with their fellow subjects.* . . . The learning of [English] an entirely

unknown and foreign language, of course, required hard application and industry. The Hindus were accustomed to this, as even under the Musalman rule, they had practically to master a foreign tongue, and so easily took to the new education. *But the Musalman had not yet become accustomed to this sort of thing, and were, moreover, not then in a mood to learn, much less to learn anything that required hard work and application, especially as they had to work harder than their former subjects, the Hindus. Moreover they resented competing with the Hindus, whom they had till recently regarded as their inferiors.* . . . Ignorance and apathy seized hold of [the Muslims] while the fall of their former greatness rankled in their hearts (emphasis added).[17]

Be that as it may, by the 1870s the British recognized the backwardness of the Muslims and the need to take measures to help spread Western education among them. In 1882—by which time the British administrators had begun to feel uneasy with Hindu agitators demanding reforms—concrete proposals such as the allotment of tuition-free seats to Muslim students in government schools and the award of scholarships for higher education were made to encourage Muslim education.

It is also around this time that a great Muslim leader, Syed (later Sir Syed) Ahmad Khan (1817–1898), who had been an employee of the EIC and had supported the British during the 1857 revolt and been honored by them for his loyalty, emerged to rehabilitate his community in the eyes of the government and help it adjust to the Westernized "modern" world growing around them. Sir Syed, often referred to as the Father of Muslim India and the Father of Modern Muslim India, was not known as a religious thinker, but he realized that he could succeed only by arguing that there was no conflict between modernism and Islam. The gist of his teaching was that an attitude that failed to allow "the Muslims to progress as a people . . . to make provision for education in those worldly sciences which are beneficial and useful, to ensure economic security, to open avenues of honest employment, to remove the blemishes in social life" could not be "justified in the eyes of God."[18]

In 1864, Sir Syed organized the Translation Society, later renamed the Aligarh Scientific Society, which translated English works on history and political science into Urdu, the language of the Muslim elite. In 1877, he established the Mohammadan Anglo-Oriental College (popularly known as M.A.O. College, or as the Aligarh College), in which students received instruction in Arabic and Islamic studies along with modern Western subjects. Sir Syed dismissed Deoband-style schools as going against "the spirit of the times." At the inauguration ceremony of Aligarh College, the guest-of-honor Viceroy Lord Lytton was presented an address in which the founders declared that "the British Rule in India is the most wonderful phenomenon the world has ever seen."[19] The founders stated that the aim of the college was "to make the Muslims of India worthy and useful subjects of the British Crown; to inspire them with loyalty which flows . . . from a sincere appreciation of the benevolence of a good govern-

flows . . . from a sincere appreciation of the benevolence of a good government."[20] Unfortunately, Aligarh College did not achieve great success in expanding Western education among the Muslims; from 1898 to 1902, twenty years after it was founded, the college produced only 220 Muslim graduates.

Until 1880, or there about, Sir Syed still considered Hindus and Muslims as "belonging to the same nation," but in 1883, when the British government began to discuss the possibility of conceding to Indian demands for elected local governments, Sir Syed expressed his fear that "the system of representation by election means the representation of the views and interests of the majority of the population . . . [which] would totally override the interests of the smaller community."[21] It was for this reason that Sir Syed turned against the Indian National Congress soon after it was established in 1885 and in 1888 founded an organization of his own, the United Indian Patriotic Association, which aimed at preserving "peace in India and strengthen the British rule; and to remove those bad feelings from the hearts of the Indian people, which the supporters of the Congress are stirring up throughout the country and by which great dissatisfaction is being raised among the people against the British government."[22]

Although the Congress demand that university degrees and competitive examinations be required for various offices, and that the ICS examination be held simultaneously in England and India, was objected to by many Hindus in the interior (they felt that this would give an edge to the more highly educated Bengalis), it posed a special threat to Muslims in general. In the same vein that he had condemned the elective principle, Sir Syed, in 1887, declared that "our country is not fit for the competitive examinations."[23] He, therefore, campaigned against competitive examinations and pushed the concept of "loyalty to the British" as a basis for job quotas and nominations to office. Speaking before the Public Services Commission (which sat from 1886 to 1887), the twenty-four-year-old British principal of Aligarh College, reflecting Sir Syed's views, threatened that if the government "shut to [Muslims] the door by which they may hope to gain legitimate influence, it will give a dangerous impetus to those with whom the idea of *jihad* is not yet dead."[24]

It was the fear that Hindus would dominate Indian administration and politics if, and when, the British left the country that drove Sir Syed to change his view (expressed in 1883) that "India is like a bride which [*sic*] has got two beautiful and lustrous eyes—Hindus and Mussulmans," to the totally contradictory ones he expressed in 1888, when he said that the "*two nations,*"* the Muslims and the Hindus, could not sit "on the same throne and remain equal in power." If, however, the Muslims could not capture power, "then our Mussalman brothers, the Pathans, would come out as a swarm of locusts from their mountain valleys, and *make rivers of blood to flow from their frontier in the north to the extreme*

---

*Syed used the Urdu term *qawm,* which can be translated as "community" or "nation."

conquerors—would rest on the will of God. *But until one nation had conquered the other and made it obedient, peace cannot reign in the land*" (emphasis added).[25]

Sir Syed also propounded the theory that the "blue-blooded" rulers (the British and the Muslims, one presumes) should not mix with the "commoners" thrown up by the elective and educational systems. No Muslim, he remarked in 1887, would "like [it] that commoners, even if they possess B.A. or M.A. degrees, should ... exercise authority" over them, adding that such lowly born officials could never be invited by the viceroy to dine with dukes and earls.[26] And as for the ICS, it was all right for a Britisher, whatever his family background, to be in it, because "we do not know at this distance from which class they come," but "how can noble classes of Indians [Muslims] tolerate petty commoners [Hindus] whose origins they know very well, as administrators."[27]

Sir Syed's Aligarh faction continued to influence Muslim opinion long after he had died. As Maulana Azad (1888–1958), a highly respected Muslim nationalist leader, put it, "[as late as 1912] the leadership of Muslim politics ... was in the hands of the Aligarh party. Its members regarded themselves as trustees of Sir Syed Ahmad's policies. *Their basic tenet was that Muslims must be loyal to the British Crown and remain aloof from the freedom movement* (emphasis added).[28] Before we leave the subject, it is worth noting that, at one stage in his life, Sir Syed, like his namesake Sayyid Ahmad of Rai Bareli, had thought of leaving India altogether and settling down in Egypt!

The Role of the Press

During the period 1858–1908, the rapid growth of a free, modern press, in English and the vernacular, made an unquestionable contribution to strengthening the newly awakened consciousness of nationalism. By the turn of the century there were more than 500 newspapers in the country. Though a few of them were run by Britishers (not all of whom were unsympathetic to the Indian cause), the bulk were managed and published by Indians, most of whom were Hindu entrepreneurs; surprisingly, even the majority of the Urdu newspapers and journals in the 1860s were edited by Hindus. Some of the nationalist associations and leaders established their own newspapers; a good example of the former is the Calcutta-based Indian Association's *The Hindu Patriot;* and of the latter, Bal Gangadhar Tilak's *Kesari** (Lion). The vernacular press was particularly outspoken in its criticism of the government.

From the 1860s the press became more fearless in expressing the view that the interests of the rulers and the ruled could not be reconciled without greater participation by Indians in the government's policy-making bodies and its ad-

---

*Tilak (1857–1920), the Father of Indian Unrest, was one of the top leaders of the Indian National Congress and perhaps the most outstanding spokesman for militant nationalism in the early decades of the twentieth century.

ministrative organs. The government was caught in a dilemma: should it limit the freedom of the press in the interest of its own stability, or grant it full freedom to gain the confidence of the people?

After the famines of 1876–78, when over 6 million lives were lost, the vernacular press was so critical of the government that Governor-General Lord Lytton personally prepared a memorandum that became the basis of the Vernacular Press Act of 1878. The act, dubbed the "Gagging Act" by the Indians, sought "to furnish the Government with more effective means than the existing law for the purpose of punishing and suppressing seditious writing which were calculated to produce disaffection towards the Government in the minds of the ignorant population."[29] The act brought such a strong censorial control over the vernacular press that the best-known Bengali language newspaper, the *Amrita Bazaar Patrika,* transformed itself overnight into an English paper (the act did not cover the English-language press). So bitter and widespread was the reaction to the act that it was repealed in 1881. The act had only helped to whip up the nationalist sentiment.

From this time on the press and the national movement grew in tandem. Thus, Surendranath Banerjee, an outstanding secular nationalist leader, was imprisoned for using the columns of his paper, *Bengalee,* to condemn a British judge for indulging in the sacrilege of hauling into his court a holy stone deity *(saligram)* as evidence. This imprisonment resulted in sympathy meetings being held in several cities of India, leading Banerjee to jubilantly remark that the incident had "operated as a unifying force."[30]

Unfortunately such "unity" was sectarian, as a stone idol was far from holy in the eyes of the iconoclastic Muslim. The Hindu outcry in 1891 over the Age of Consent Bill (which raised the age of marriage for a woman from ten to twelve) led to assertions of the superiority of Hindu religion and to statements such as: "The *Sanatana* religion is pure gold; be it Aurangzeb or . . . Lansdowne . . . , whoever may burn it, only the dross will be burnt, the gold will come out all the brighter."[31] Tilak added his voice to the storm of protest, saying that a foreign government had no right to interfere in the social reform of the Hindus.

Tilak had made a name for himself by using his paper, *Kesri,* to rouse nationalistic sentiments among the Marathas by exploiting the memory of historical figures such as Shivaji. The articles he wrote on the occasion of the Shivaji festival, 1896–98 (which he had helped to organize), raised such passions that he was prosecuted for sedition and sentenced to a year and a half's rigorous imprisonment. This action of the British Government of India only made a martyr of Tilak and raised his and his paper's standing in the eyes of the populace. Parenthetically, it should be mentioned that Shivaji, the founder of the Maratha empire which had contributed significantly to the collapse of the Mughal dynasty, was, of course, no hero in the eyes of the Muslims.

In 1905, Viceroy Curzon's decision to partition Bengal into a Muslim-majority province and a Hindu-majority province was seen by Indian leaders as a sinister move to perpetuate divide-and-rule policies by creating a split between two Bengali communities that shared a common language and culture. This became an all-India issue, and despite official repression, the press played an important role in spreading anti-British sentiment and creating a revolutionary situation. It was the press that first suggested a new form of attack on the British: boycott British goods and buy native, *swadeshi* products. The *swadeshi* movement led to the public burning of English textiles, and, therefore, to clashes with the police. Soon the agitators began to call for *swaraj* (independence). The Bengali press was naturally inflamed, but the temper of the times can be gauged by the fact that Tilak, on the other side of the subcontinent, wrote such forceful articles in support of the *swadeshi* movement that he was again prosecuted (1908) and sentenced to six years' internal exile.

In 1908, the government passed the Newspapers (Incitement to Offence) Act, which empowered the local district magistrate to confiscate a printing press if it printed any matter that was likely to provoke violence. As a result many important newspapers had to cease publication. A more detailed act, The Indian Press Act of 1910, made it obligatory for owners of printing presses and publishers of newspapers to deposit a sum of money as security, which was liable to be forfeited if a newspaper violated the act. The act gave the local government—that is, *the executive*—wide-ranging and unfettered discretionary powers to punish the press for "objectionable" and "seditious material." The terms were so broadly defined that any legitimate publication could be suppressed without explanation. The act was not repealed until 1922.

Thus, in the period when there was as yet no formally organized opposition party, the press—in particular, the vernacular press—rendered an important national service as a critic of the government, as a disseminator of nationalistic* ideas, as an educator, and as a formulator of public opinion.

Hindu Revivalism and Nationalism

Brahma Samaj

As early as the last decade of the eighteenth century, Raja Rammohan Roy, when he was only sixteen or seventeen years old, had begun to attack the idolatrous practices of the Hindus, which according to Roy contradicted the monotheism of the Vedanta. After several years of writing about the issue of idolatry, and discussing it with orthodox Hindu leaders (who naturally condemned his approach), Roy not only became the first Indian Unitarian but established the Vedanta College in 1825 and the Brahma Samaj (Divine Society, or One God

---

*Nationalistic, rather than *national*, because the local press advanced the cause of parochial nationalism: Bengal nationalism, Maratha nationalism and so on.

Society) in 1828. The object of Brahma Samaj was to reform Hinduism by ridding it of idol worship, caste, and discrimination against women. The Brahma Samaj movement stood for monotheism on a nonsectarian basis.

The Brahma Samaj, under attack from orthodox Hindus, had not yet established firm roots when Roy passed away in 1833. After a decade of decline, the fortunes of the Samaj improved when Devendranath Tagore joined the society in 1843. Brahma Samaj "missionaries" became active and founded branches of the society in the countryside. A school was established to provide religious instruction to young men. The more youthful members of the Brahma Samaj began to advocate female education and widow remarriage, while denouncing intemperance and polygamy. Under the direction of Keshab Chandra Sen (1838–1884), the message of Brahmaism was spread throughout Bengal and even carried to other parts of India.

Though the Brahma Samaj movement subsequently lost much of its vigor, and though it never did manage to persuade Hindu society to give up idol worship, it did help to renovate Hindu society by softening caste rigidity and promoting the emancipation of women. But its recognition of Christ and Mohammad as great religious teachers did not find favor with the majority of the Hindus.

Ramakrishna and Swami Vivekananda

One of the great spiritual leaders of Hinduism in the late nineteenth century was Ramakrishna Paramahamsa (1836–1886), who through meditation and prayer attained such a divine personality that he came to be looked upon as an incarnation of God. His one great message was that the inherent truth in all religions was the same and that the gods of all religions were the same Great God who is one and many, with and without form, and who may be conceived either as a universal spirit or through symbols. He also taught that the development of character was more important than the gaining of knowledge, and that one could serve God by serving one's fellow human beings selflessly.

Ramakrishna's vision and doctrine were given concrete shape by his favorite disciple, Swami Vivekananda (1863–1902), who established the Ramakrishna Order (1887) and later the Ramakrishna Mission (1897). In 1893, Vivekananda became an international celebrity when he gave his spellbinding speeches (in English) at the World Congress of Religions, held in Chicago; on his return to India in 1897, he was received as a hero by his grateful countrymen because Vivekananda had raised India's prestige in the eyes of the world.

Besides being a powerful exponent of Vedantic Hinduism, Vivekananda was a very patriotic Indian, acutely aware of the poverty and backwardness of the Indian masses. "The poor, the ignorant, the illiterate, the afflicted," he preached, "let these be your God: know that service to these is the highest religion."[32] He believed that while the West would suffer for its excessive devotion to materialism, India would suffer if it continued to ignore mundane affairs and remained mired in misery. "This is why he thought that the freedom of India and her material prosperity were needed for the salvation of the world."[33] By restoring the self-confidence of Hindus in their religion and culture, and quickening their sense of national pride and patriotism, Vivekananda combined politics with ethical values, just as Mahatma Gandhi would do later. This, of course, reinforced the forces of *Hindu nationalism* rather than nationalism.

Arya Samaj

Although Bengal had taken the lead in launching movements for the reform of Hinduism, similar movements soon emerged in other parts of India. A profoundly learned Sanskrit scholar from Gujarat, Swami Dayanand Saraswati (1824–1883), fulminated against the evils that had crept into Hinduism ever since it moved away from the Vedas. "Go Back to the Vedas" was his call and he vigorously attacked idolatry, caste, child marriage, discrimination against women, and superstitions such as the ban on travel overseas and faith in horoscopes.

In 1875, Dayanand established the Arya Samaj (Society of the Aryas), which took root in Punjab and western Uttar Pradesh and did excellent work in the fields of education and women's emancipation. Though Dayanand himself was an out-and-out Sanskritist, he used Hindi for the propagation of his faith and recognized the utility of Western education. Dayanand founded schools and colleges (D.A.V.—Dayanand Anglo-Vedic—schools and colleges), some of which were meant solely for girls. Besides achieving excellent academic standards, the D.A.V. schools and colleges imparted a strong sense of nationalism and pride in the Hindu heritage to its students. Needless to say, Dayanand was strongly anti-British. "At present what little there is, is foreign-trodden," he said, adding that "however good others may be, self-government is the best government."[34] Having denounced caste and Brahmin superiority, Dayanand made education, not birth, the determinant of social status. Arya Samaj was also the first purely Indian organization that founded orphanages and widows' homes.

At another level, Dayanand turned Arya Samaj into a missionary body by redefining the concept of *shuddhi* (ritual purification of erring Hindus) to encourage the reconversion of Hindus who had embraced some other faith because they had been thrown out of the caste system for having broken a Hindu taboo. And perhaps to underscore the desirability of bringing Muslim converts back into the Hindu fold, he made intemperate references to Islam; for example, he called the Quranic paradise "a grove of prostitutes."[35] He and his successors combed the history of Islam in India to discover evidence of Muslim atrocities against the Hindus. Dayanand proved to be a great force in the promotion of Hindu nationalism. Unfortunately, it is equally true that the Arya Samaj movement alienated the Sikhs, but more important, it widened the gulf between the Hindus and the Muslims.

Political Associations

Patriotic Associations

As in so many other developments, it was Bengal that took the lead in establishing organizations that, however limited their goals and however mild their approach in the initial stages, were the first to express Indian grievances against British policies.

The first such organization was neither purely religious nor wholly political; it combined religion and politics in a manner that foreshadows later development of nationalism in India. In 1866, Rajnarayan Basu* (1826–1899), a Hindu reformer who had studied at Hindu College and been exposed to Western thought and Christianity, founded the Society for the Promotion of National Feeling among the Educated Natives of Bengal. The society's goal, according to its prospectus published in the *National Paper* (started 1865), was to promote ancient India's "enlightened customs . . . such as female education, personal liberty of females, marriage by election of bride, marriage at adult age, widow re-marriage, inter-marriage, and travel to distant countries,"[36] and to revive respect for Indian medicine, arts, music, physical exercises, and native languages. The society also aimed to "introduce such foreign customs as have a tendency to *infuse national feelings into the minds of its members*" (emphasis added).[37]

A follower of Basu instituted the annual Hindu Mela (Fair) to promote national feelings and a sense of unity and patriotism. An association called the National Society was established (1870) to help organize the Melas and propagate its message. The Mela was held fourteen times up until 1880 (when other organizations took over its work), and it made a significant contribution to the development of arts and crafts, and to the political and national movements in Bengal. The patriotic poems sung at the Mela are still part of Bengal's living heritage.

At one point a reader wrote to the *National Paper,* criticizing the term *national* in National Society, saying that since the society was exclusively Hindu, the word was incorrectly used. The *National Paper* replied: "We do not understand why our correspondent takes exception to the Hindus who certainly form a nation by themselves, and as such a society established by them can very properly be called National Society."[38] On another occasion, the editor contended that, just as love of country promoted nationalism among the Greeks and the Mosaic law among the Jews, the basis of national unity in India was Hinduism. "Hindu nationality," he said, "embraces all of Hindu name and Hindu faith throughout the length and breadth of Hindustan. . . . *The Hindus are destined to be a Hindu nation*" (emphasis added).[39]

Shifting our attention to the development of purely secular political estab-

---

*Sometimes referred to as Rajnarayan Bose.

lishments, it is worth noting how deeply a section of the emerging intelligentsia had been influenced by ideas of Western liberalism; they were familiar with the political philosophies of Burke and Rousseau and the liberation movements inspired by Parnell in Ireland, Mazzini in Italy, and Bismarck in Germany. As early as 1851, an exclusively Indian organization, the British Indian Association, was formed by the leading Hindu *zamindars* of Bengal. Technically, the association lasted until the establishment of the Indian National Congress (1885), but in reality the importance of its activities had already been overshadowed in the 1870s, when more aggressive and vigorous political organizations appeared on the scene. Despite the fact that the British Indian Association was not nationalistic and represented only a narrow section of the population, its humbly written memorials to the viceroy, the home government in London, and the British Parliament did raise some of the issues that later became the rallying cry of the nationalists. Thus, for example, the association suggested that Indians be appointed to the legislature and higher levels of the judiciary, that the Civil Service examination be held in India, that the government not use revenues to maintain the Christian ecclesiastical establishment, and that the government inquire into the hardships caused by the salt tax and the exploitation of the cultivators by the British indigo plantation owners.

Associations similar to the British Indian Association were also established in Madras and Bombay, but they had even less impact on British policies, and despite their declared intentions, the associations of the three presidencies never managed to coordinate their activities and present a united front to the British government. It took another twenty-five years for a national-level organization to make its appearance. This was the Indian Association, headquartered in Calcutta and founded in 1876, by Surendranath Banerjee (1848–1925, knighted in 1921), who had been dismissed from the ICS (1869) on frivolous grounds.

The objectives of the Association were:

1. The unification of the Indian races and peoples on the basis of common political interest and aspirations
2. The promotion of friendly relations between Hindus and Muslims
3. The education of the masses and their involvement in public movements, and the creation of a strong body of public opinion.

Although the executive committee of the Indian Association was composed entirely of Hindus, Surendranath Banerjee never tired of exhorting the people to unite in their nationalistic endeavors: "In the name . . . of a common country, let us all, Hindus, Muslims, Christians, Parsees, members of the great Indian Community, throw the pall of oblivion over the jealousies and dissensions of bygone times and, embracing one another in fraternal love and affection, live and work for the benefit of a beloved fatherland."[40]

Shortly after the association was established, two actions of the British government provided issues that transcended race and religion and on which national attention could be focused. The first was the lowering of the age limit for the ICS examination from twenty-one to nineteen, the second was the passing of the Vernacular Press Act. Surendranath organized massive protest meetings nationwide and almost overnight became a national figure. As already noted, the Vernacular Press Act was repealed in 1882; on the age limit question, however, the government refused to budge for seven more years. Regardless, the association had been successful in rousing nationalistic sentiment.

In 1879 and 1880, the Indian Association in its annual meetings discussed the question of self-government and came to the conclusion that local self-government must precede national self-government. To prepare the people for the first step, the association increased its activities in the district towns, encouraging them to send petitions to the government to introduce the elective system in the municipalities. When the Local Self-Government Act came into force in 1884, the association urged the people to participate in the elections and try to get nonofficials to be presidents of the local bodies. But the act offered very little independence to these local bodies, and "once Indian opinion realized that reform of the [Legislative] Councils was not to be the corollary, they lost interest."[41]

However, the second big boost to all-India nationalism had come a year earlier, in 1883. In that year, Lord Ripon, the liberal viceroy, introduced a measure, the Ilbert Bill, that upheld the principle of equality before the law by allowing Indian judges to try Europeans (the Indian judges being of the same rank as the British judges who could try the Europeans), something that had not been permitted so far. The handful of Britishers in India reacted so strongly to the bill that it had to be toned down. Implicit in this reversal was reconfirmation of the notion that Indians were an inferior race, unworthy of being treated as equals. Many Indian leaders and newspaper editors reacted by adopting a sterner tone in their criticism of the government.

In 1883, Surendranath Banerjee, who by now was recognized as the primary Indian spokesmen for the nationalist movement, organized an "all-India" Indian National Conference in Calcutta, with representatives from all parts of India. This was the first nationwide political congress, and it marked a new stage in the history of nationalism in India. The conference was not sectional or regional, but truly national; among the more than 100 delegates there were Hindus and Muslims representing over twenty urban areas, including Bombay, Madras, Delhi, Lahore, and Ahmedabad. In its discussions, the conference took up such subjects as employment of Indians in the administration, elective government, and the separation of the judicial, the legislative, and the executive organs of the government.

In 1884, the Indian Union was formed in Calcutta by a coterie of lawyers, mainly Hindus but also a few Muslims, to provide a base for political activities in Bengal. In the same year, with the establishment of the Madras Mahajana Sabha, whose aims were similar to those of the National Conference of 1883, the

Madras Presidency ended its era of isolation and moved on to the national stage. In January 1885, the Bombay Presidency Association (BPA) was founded and its promoters declared that it would be a "well-organized and truly national organization" that would work in close harmony with similar organizations in the rest of the country. In September, the BPA, in collaboration with the Indian Association and the Madras Mahajana Sabha, sent a delegation to England to support the pro-Indian Liberals in the forthcoming parliamentary elections.

The year 1885 was a year of extraordinary political activity; it ended with the establishment of the Indian National Congress, which held its first session (in Bombay) that year.

Indian National Congress 1885–1908

By 1885, when the Indian National Congress (hereafter referred to as "the Congress") was established, the Indian political environment was ready for a well-defined national assemblage to replace the provincial associations and unify political action. As Subrahmania Aiyar, moving the first resolution at the first session of the Congress, put it: "From today forward we can with greater propriety than heretofore speak of an Indian nation, of national opinion and national aspirations."[42]

There is an ongoing debate as to who first thought of the idea for such an organization, but the credit for convening the Congress must go to Allan Octavian Hume (1829–1912). Hume was a high-ranking ICS officer who had retired to Shimla in 1882 after thirty-three years of service, and his liberal views and sympathies for Indian aspirations were well known. Hume was the general secretary of the Congress for twenty-two years, from its inception to 1908. Because of Hume, the inauguration of the Congress also received the indirect support of Viceroy Lord Dufferin, who possibly believed that such a body of Indian politicians could function as a loyal opposition and a safety valve, and help the government to keep in touch with public opinion.

The Congress was not conceived as a political party. It was more like a club where the leaders of the country met once a year with the intention of coming to know each other better, "to promote personal friendship and intimacy." This friendly intercourse was meant to help eradicate religious, racial, and regional prejudices and aid in consolidating sentiments of national unity. The leaders could discuss pressing national problems and formulate lines of common action to be followed during the next twelve months and decide the venue for the next meeting. It was left to the branch of the Congress in the city chosen, and the presidency in which the city was located, to raise the funds needed for the meeting.

The difference between the Congress and the earlier associations was that the Congress was an all-India body that *presumed* to reflect national aspirations and speak for the nation. To begin with, this was a hollow claim. But as the activities and the membership of the Congress expanded, and its programs gained wider support from the press and the public, as the British government shifted its stand and began to view the Congress as a seditious body, and as the Congress got disillusioned with the government's hesitating policies of reform and changed its tactics, the Congress *did,* indeed, become a genuine national organization that, in sixty-two years, brought independence to the country.

The development of the Congress up to 1947 can be divided into four broad stages:

1. 1885–1905: The moderate phase when the Congress attempts to work within the British framework to get the British to modify their policies.
2. 1906–1916: The split over aims and methods between moderates and extremists. The aim of the Congress shifts to the attainment of self-government.
3. 1916–1918: World War I and the home rule movement.
4. 1919–1946: The Congress under Mahatma Gandhi's leadership introduces a mass national movement. Also, a period when the limited British constitutional reforms institute communal electorates and the Congress gains experience in elective politics. The phase sees the emergence of the Muslim League as a major factor on the political scene.

During the first phase, which is our main concern in this section, leadership of the Congress was dominated by a small group of highly Anglicized persons who were mostly well-placed lawyers and professionals. These leaders met for three days in December every year and passed resolutions proposing miscellaneous reforms, such as:

- Greater Indian representation in the Indian administration
- Expansion of the central and provincial legislative councils through elections
- Separation of judicial and executive functions
- Higher age limit for the ICS examinations, with examinations to be held simultaneously in England and India
- Reduced military expenditures and home charges
- More higher-level jobs for the Indians in the army
- Abolition of the Arms Act forbidding Indians from owning arms
- Higher taxable minimum on incomes

This period has been called "moderate" because: (1) the leaders, relying entirely on the sense of justice of the British government, raised the issues of reform not as demands but as recommendations in the form of "petitions"; and (2) the leaders quite openly professed loyalty to the Crown and expressed faith in "constitutional" methods of approach. As W. C. Bonnerjea (the first president of the Congress) expressed it at the 1885 Congress session, "I think that our desire to be governed according to the ideas of Government prevalent in Europe is in no way incompatible with our thorough loyalty to the British government."[43] The same sentiment was reiterated as late as 1906 by Dadabhai Naoroji in his presidential address: "I for one have not a shadow of a doubt that in dealing with such justice-loving, fair-minded people as the British, we may fully rest assured that we shall not work in vain."[44]

The tendency of the Congress moderates to elect British ex-officials to the presidency of the party was also an indication of their desire to be looked upon favorably by the Britishers in England. However well meaning these British presidents may have been (and there were four of them until 1910), they were surely not nationalists as one would have expected a Congress leader to be.

The Congress during this first phase did try to maintain a national and secular character by getting delegates from all parts of India and seeing to it that people from all religious communities, particularly Muslim, were represented. In this respect, it was fortunate that it first met in Bombay because, at the turn of the century, Bombay was the most cosmopolitan of all cities in India (and probably still has that distinction), and the Muslims in Bombay were doing rather well as businessmen and professionals. During the period under review, it was Bombay that provided the only two outstanding nationalist Muslim leaders, Badruddin Tyabji and R. M. Sayani, who were elected as presidents of the 1887 and 1896 Congress sessions, respectively. Incidentally, Bombay also produced the two great Parsi leaders, Dadabhai Naoroji and Pherozeshah Mehta, who played an important role in the shaping of the Congress during the first phase.

In 1886, the National Conference of Surendranath Banerjee merged with the Congress. In the same year, the national and secular stance of the Congress got a sharper definition when Dadabhai Naoroji, in his presidential address at the Calcutta session, asserted that the Congress should have a political platform and discuss only those matters that affected the whole of India, steering clear of social questions. It is noteworthy that the number of delegates at Calcutta—they had been elected and not nominated—was 436 as against 72 in the first session, the number of Muslim delegates being 33 as against the original 2.

By the third session, held in Madras in 1887 under the presidency of Badruddin Tyabji, it was evident that the Congress was becoming a more broad-based organization: not only did the 120 members of the Madras Reception Committee include Hindus, Muslims, and Christians, but it collected a sizable amount of money from contributions made by the rich and the poor; the contribution of laborers and peasants often was no more than one *anna*.* Among the 607 elected delegates, a foreign observer noted 45 peasants and 19 artisans. The session was held outdoors and attracted over 3,000 spectators.

Unfortunately, 1887 was also the year when Sir Syed Ahmad Khan warned

---

*A cupronickel coin worth one-sixteenth of a rupee. The coin is no longer in circulation. The rupee is still the basic currency of India; about 40 rupees equal 1 U.S. dollar (2000).

Muslims not to join the Congress, which according to him was seditious and no friend of theirs. In the same speech, Sir Syed also declared that Hindus and Muslims were two distinct races; that representative institutions were unsuited to India because they would lead to a permanent subjugation of Muslims by Hindus; and that Indian Muslims should depend on the British to safeguard their interests. In 1888, Sir Syed established an anti-Congress association, the United Indian Patriotic Association, whose goal was to reveal Congress chicanery, to strengthen British rule, and to "remove those bad feelings from the hearts of the Indian people, which the supporters of the Congress are stirring up."[45] Fortunately for the Congress, the association had no program that could be carried out and no vitality; it languished for a while and then disappeared.

Despite Sir Syed's attacks, the number of Muslim delegates to the annual sessions of the Congress remained significant, and many middle-class Muslims even joined the Hindus in demanding that ICS examinations be held in India.[46] In the 1899 Lucknow session, where a formal constitution for the Congress was approved, "Muslims beat all previous records by sending 313 delegates out of a total of 739."[47]

However, although the declared goal of the Congress was "to promote by constitutional means the interest and well-being of the people of the Indian Empire,"[48] the British divide-and-rule policies, Sir Syed's overwhelming influence, Hindu revivalism, and the rise of the extremist faction in the Congress began to alienate the Muslims; between 1893 and 1905 the percentage of Muslim delegates fell to 7.1, as against the 13.5 for the period 1885–1892.

Though the Congress kept growing, the results it achieved were negligible. The Indian Councils Act in 1892 fell far short of Indian expectations because, though the act increased the number of nonofficial members of the Imperial Legislative Council to ten (out of sixteen), it did not concede the elective principle; the only change was that the government was now empowered to consult local bodies, university senates, chambers of commerce, and landlord associations before nominating the nonofficial members. London's argument was that elections would not work in India because "voiceless millions" remained "absolutely untouched" by an unrepresentative Congress.

A section of Congressmen became so disillusioned with the "politics of mendicancy" and the nonproductive "constitutional approach" that they began to call for "direct action" and "self-help." This section, dubbed the "extremists" by the British, was also reacting against the Tariff and Cotton Duties Acts of 1894 and 1896, which favored the British manufacturers at the expense of textile mill owners in India.

The extremists were influenced by many factors, not the least among them being the writings, speeches, and activities of Aravinda Ghose (1872–1950, popularly known as Shri Aurobindo) from Bengal and Bal Gangadhar Tilak (1857–1920) from Maharashtra (part of Bombay Presidency). Aurobindo, who had been educated in England and had failed the ICS examination because he could not pass the riding test, returned home to become a fiery nationalist, inspired by the French Revolution, Hindu revivalism, and the literature of Bankim Chandra Chatterjee (1838–1894).

Chatterjee, after retiring from service in the British Government of India, had turned to writing novels that combined neo-Hinduism with modernism. Chatterjee wrote passionately about India, "the mother," who should be worshipped by everybody. His most famous novel, *Anandamath* (Monastery of Bliss), written in Bengali and published in 1882, is largely a story of a dedicated band of patriots who defeat an Anglo-Muslim army to restore the motherland to the Hindus. One of the songs (hymns) in the novel, the "Bande-mataram" (Hail to the Mother) became the rallying cry of the emerging group of extremists. Because of its patriotic contents, the hymn also came to be sung in the open sessions of the Congress from 1896 on. After the crisis created by the partitioning of Bengal in 1905, "Bande-mataram" was adopted as the Indian National Anthem and used as such by the Congress until Independence. The British government banned it, but that only added to its popularity. Aurobindo, inspired by *Anandamath*, named his extremist newspaper *Bande Mataram* and wrote in one of the issues: "It is not in human nature to rest eternally contented with a state of subordination or serfdom. God made man in his own image, essentially and potentially free and pure.... Tyrants have tried but have they ever succeeded in repressing this natural love of freedom in man? ... [G]aining strength and inspiration from repeated failures and endless suffering, [freedom] has risen finally, to overthrow the oppressor for good."[49]

One must bear in mind that the environment in which extremism came to flourish was also influenced by the expansion of the press, by the new patriotic literature, and, of course, by Hindu revivalists such as Swami Dayanand and Swami Vivekananda (discussed earlier). These champions of a Hindu cultural renaissance preached that self-help, self-reliance, and service to the community would save the motherland and revive its former glory.

As a result, the extremists, unlike the moderates, not only rejected Congress "mendicancy" but shifted away from Congress elitism, secularity, and politics-only approach. Thus, Tilak, called Lokmanya (Beloved of the People) by the Indians, the Father of Indian Unrest by the British, and "the man who really blazed the trail for Extremism,"[50] by historian Sumit Sarkar, moved politics to the level of the masses, thus putting an end to elitism. And to win mass support, Tilak did not hesitate to use religion (thereby rejecting secularism) or take up social causes (rather than merely political ones).

The first evidence of Tilak's innovative use of Hindu symbols came in 1893, when he turned the Ganapati Festival, a traditional folk festival of Maharashtra associated with Ganesh (a popular Hindu deity), into a grand affair designed to appeal to both the classes and the masses. Tilak's festival became an annual event that contributed to cultural solidarity and provided Tilak with an ideal opportunity to preach militant nationalism. The success of this venture led Tilak in 1896 to organize Shivaji festivals and use the cult of Shivaji, the founder of the Maratha empire and the symbol of Hindu resistance to the Mughals, for the same political end: bringing a sense of unity among the masses and making them politically conscious.

In the meanwhile, the British Government of India under Viceroy Lord Curzon (1899–1905) made no pretense of hiding its hostility toward the Congress. Indeed, Curzon, whose contemptuous attitude toward the Indians has been noted earlier, stated that "one of my great ambitions while in India is to assist [the Congress] to a peaceful demise."[51] To achieve this end, Curzon decided to weaken the nationalist movement by partitioning the province of Bengal (1905) because, according to Curzon, "Calcutta is the center from which the Congress party is manipulated throughout the whole of Bengal, and indeed the whole of India."[52] Though Curzon claimed that the partition was intended to bring greater efficiency to the administrative system, his hidden agenda was to drive a wedge between the two major Indian communities by separating the Muslim majority in eastern Bengal from the Hindu majority in the western half. In anticipation of the partition, Curzon toured Bengal and tried to win Muslim support by informing his Muslim audiences that Islam would be dominant in the new province and invest them with a unity "which they had not enjoyed since the days of the old Mussalman Viceroys and kings."[53] Although apart from the pro-Congress Muslims there were many other important Muslims, including Syed Ameer Ali, a recognized champion of the Muslim cause and founder of the Central National Muhammadan Association, who condemned the partition, it was generally welcomed by the Aligarh School and many other Muslim associations in Bengal. In the long run, the partition did prove to have catalyzed separatist Muslim consciousness.

The partition had given the Congress a unique opportunity to foster a country-wide nationalist movement, but the moderates failed to rise to the occasion and take over the leadership of the popular movements of *swadeshi* (promote native industry and buy Indian goods) and the boycott of British and other foreign goods that had emerged so spontaneously in Bengal and then spread to other parts of India. These movements introduced the notion of passive resistance, which was to be used so effectively by Mahatma Gandhi later. The moderates tried to separate *swadeshi* from the boycott, accepting the former but rejecting the latter for being provocative and not in keeping with the moderates' faith in British liberalism. As a result, the extremists, who had dared to talk of *swaraj* (self-government, independence) as being their birthright, were the ones who managed to harness the mighty upsurge created by the partition and strengthen their position in the Congress.

The Congress was split, and though it would take some more years for the moderates to relinquish their hold over the Congress, it was plainly evident that time was against them. It is significant that whereas the moderate leaders included personalities from various religious groups, the principal extremist leaders were all Hindus. In the 1906 Calcutta session of the Congress, the effort of the Young Turks to get Tilak nominated for the presidential chair was rendered ineffective by the moderates who prevailed upon the eighty-one-year-old Dadabhai Naoroji to accept the presidency. Nobody dared to oppose the nomination of the "Grand Old Man of India," who captured the spirit of the occasion by declaring that all the "political principles" of the Congress, "the root of our national greatness, strength, and hope . . . are summed up in self-government," which was the "only and chief remedy" for India's poverty and backwardness.[54]

In 1907 the venue for the Congress was shifted by the moderates from Nagpur, the area of Tilak's support, to Surat, where Tilak was still an outsider. However, rumors that the four Calcutta resolutions—on self-government, boycott, *swadeshi,* and national education—were going to be dropped, and the chairman's refusal to let Tilak move an amendment resulted in pandemonium. The session, after two days of verbal and physical clashes (a sandal hurled at the podium struck the venerable figures of Surendranath Banerjee and Sir Pherozeshah Mehta), was suspended *sine die.* The split between the two factions became final in April 1908, when a committee set up by the moderate patriarchs drew up a constitution for the Congress. The constitution affirmed that the goal of attaining self-government would be achieved through *constitutional means,* "by bringing about a steady reform of the existing system of administration." It also required that delegates to future meetings of the Congress be elected by "recognized bodies of three years' standing" and be required also to confirm "in writing" that they would "abide by this Constitution." One of the reasons for the moderates taking this rigid stand was that they hoped thereby to win the favor of Viscount Morley, the new secretary of state for India (1905–1910), who was in the process of formulating reforms (the Morley-Minto Reforms, 1909, which will be discussed in the next chapter) for India. As far as Tilak was concerned, he was arrested in 1908, sentenced to six years' transportation to be served in Burma's Mandalay jail; Tilak was charged with exciting feelings of animosity and disloyalty toward Her Britannic Majesty's government.

The All-India Muslim League

As might have been expected, the rise of the extremists in the Congress created a feeling of apprehension in the minds of the Muslims. Muslims were disturbed by the covert anti-Muslim thrust of the antipartition agitation, the drive by the Hindus in the north to get the government to replace Urdu with Hindi as the official language in the courts, and the periodic disturbances created by Hindu cow-protection societies.

At this time of growing political consciousness among the Muslims, even Tyabji was won over by his erstwhile "enemies" in the Aligarh camp, and in 1903 he accepted the invitation to preside over Sir Syed's Mohammadan Educational Conference, which had been established in 1886 expressly to oppose the

Congress. In his presidential address, Tyabji said that "there is not a Musalman in India, certainly not in Bombay, who does not wish all prosperity and success to Aligarh."[55] And according to Aga Sultan Mohammad Shah (1877–1957, better known as His Highness the Aga Khan), *Imam* of the Ismaili community from 1885 to 1957, a prominent leader of the Muslims and a supporter of the Aligarh movement, the Congress "was already proving itself incapable of representing India's Muslims or of dealing adequately or justly with the needs and aspirations of the Muslim community."[56]

However, the leaders of Muslim opinion were divided on the course to be followed. Some still held that Sir Syed's loyalty-to-the-British policy, coupled with political neutrality, was the best path; others suggested that Muslims should enter the arena of agitational politics by forming an organization like the Congress that could represent the Muslims of the entire country.

In 1906 it was revealed that the new viceroy, Lord Minto (Viceroy, 1905–1910), and the new secretary of state for India, Viscount Morley, were planning to introduce reforms that would enlarge the Legislative Councils with "elected" Indian representatives. The Aligarh Muslims realized that the time had come for them to be a little more forceful in letting the government know of their fears and aspirations. Encouraged and advised by W. A. J. Archbold, the principal of Aligarh College, who had been in communication with the viceroy, a Muslim deputation, led by the Aga Khan met with Lord Minto in August 1906; the deputation was composed of thirty-five prominent Muslim aristocrats from various parts of India, though the bulk of them were from the north.

Lord Minto, who had helped to maneuver this meeting, felt that an expression of sympathy for the "hopes and aspirations" of the Muslim community would keep it loyal to the British and aloof from the Congress; he had also decided that this was "a capital opportunity for making clear our position . . . [of] *resolute impartiality between races and creeds* [of India]" (emphasis added).[57] The address presented to the viceroy by the deputation lauded the "inestimable benefits conferred by British rule on the teeming millions" of India, and then went on to point out that electoral politics would place the Muslims at the mercy of the Hindu majority; that the Hindus, by including in their numbers tribals and outcastes, have reduced the size of the Muslim population even further; and that the British should go beyond the numerical size of the Muslim community and bear in mind the status the community had enjoyed only a hundred years earlier, and the contribution of the Muslims to the defense of the empire. The address petitioned that competitive recruitment to services be eliminated, that Muslims be given proportional representation in the administrative services and assured seats on the judicial benches, and that a Muslim electoral college be formed to elect members of the councils.

The viceroy agreed that "in any system of representation . . . in which it is proposed to introduce or increase an electoral organization, *the Mahommedan community should be represented as a community and you justly claim that your position should be estimated not merely on your numerical strength* but in respect to the political importance of your community and the service it has rendered to the Empire. . . . I am entirely in accord with you" (emphasis added).[58]

That evening, an overjoyed British official wrote to Lady Minto congratulating the viceroy for "a work of statesmanship" that was "nothing less than the pulling back of sixty-two millions of people [the Muslims] from joining the ranks of the seditious opposition [the Congress]."[59] Britain had committed itself to separate Muslim electorates and laid the basis of communal politics that marred all developments in India from 1909 to 1947.

In December 1906, Muslim leaders met in Dhaka and formed the All-India Muslim League (AIML). Its aim was to promote loyalty to the British and to advance the interests of the Muslims through respectful representations to the government. In many ways, the Muslim League was a replica of the Congress in its early formative period: the Muslim League sought to integrate various local Muslim associations into an all-India body and, like the Congress in 1885, it swore loyalty to Britain and expressed a desire to work within the framework of the British administration. The differences were that AIML represented only one Indian community and that it was established when the Congress had already moved away from the politics of "mendicancy." There was, however, nothing to stop a Muslim from being a member of the Muslim League and the Congress at the same time; indeed, Muhammad Ali Jinnah (1875–1948), the future leader of the Muslim League and the Father of Pakistan, was for a long time a member of both organizations.

Conclusion

The first fifty years of British rule in India witnessed the high point of jingo imperialism and outright racism. The British did manage to perfect a system of administration that was efficient and, from the British point of view, fair, but it was officered by civil masters, not civil servants. These officers and their wives socialized only with each other and tried to recreate the "back home" environment by holding garden parties and dinner and dancing parties in their exclusive clubs. No Indian, of however high an official rank, could expect to be invited to these functions. British children were sent "home" to England for their education, and their parents looked forward to spending their vacations in England and returning there to retire. What is more, from 1863 on, the entire establishment of the central government, headed by the viceroy and his Executive Council, accompanied by wives and servants, migrated every summer from Calcutta to the cool heights of Shimla, 1,170 miles away (later, when New Delhi became the capital, the journey was shorter but by no means much cheaper). This arrogantly superior and aloof class of rulers never felt a real need to understand the people they ruled, and presumed that any criticism of their rule, however respectfully worded and however abundantly wrapped in sentiments of gratitude for the

White Raj, came from troublemakers who had to be suppressed.

The British never came to fully grasp the complexity of the bonds that linked the socioreligious movements to political movements. It was the combined impact of these movements that had brought India, by 1908, to a stage where faith in British rule had been corroded. Thus, the Hindu reform movements, even if they betrayed a streak of obscurantism, had created a social climate for change and modernization and contributed to the evolving national consciousness that was anti-Western and rooted in the indigenous cultural heritage. Again, the spread of Westernized education had given birth to a new intelligentsia that had the self-confidence to challenge the economic and moral basis of the British imperial system, and yet again, the modern vernacular and English-language press had provided a voice to the new intelligentsia—many of the political leaders, like Surendranath Banerjee, Aurobindo Ghose, and Tilak, had newspapers of their own—and government attempts to curb the press only made it more nationalistic and more strident in its demands.

A good example of the self-confidence, aloofness, and hauteur of the British is Viceroy Curzon, who came to India practically at the end of the period under review. Curzon did many good things for India, such as the expansion of irrigation projects and the protection of ancient monuments, but he also showed his total lack of understanding of the growth of Indian nationalism. As quoted earlier, he thought the Congress was "tottering to its fall," and he said that it was his greatest ambition to "assist it to a peaceful demise." It was this incapacity to sense the true sentiments of the intelligentsia that made Curzon so dense-headed and one of the most hated of viceroys. In 1904, he enacted the Universities Bill, which aimed at eliminating the more serious abuses in higher education. There was nothing wrong with that, but since he also increased government control over the universities without consulting Indian opinion, the act "convulsed educated India from one end of the country to the other."[60]

Curzon's second measure that inflamed Indian nationalist sentiment even more was the partition of Bengal in 1905, which, like the Universities Act, was administratively justifiable. It was the partition that forced the Congress to discard its faith in British liberalism and move away from its moderate and constitutional approach. The Congress, under pressure from the extremists, who represented the new spirit of self-assertion, declared *swaraj* to be its objective, and it also accepted the principles of *swadeshi* and boycott as legitimate weapons to fight British imperialism. Instead of "tottering to its fall," the Congress, though still a small body of intellectuals who had no significant connection with the masses, emerged as the implacable enemy of the British, and as a nationalist force that would lead India to independence.

One of the reasons for Curzon's plan to partition Bengal was, indeed, that it would hasten the demise of the Congress. Curzon believed that Calcutta was the nerve center of the Congress and that a divided Bengal would weaken the importance of Calcutta and, therefore, of the Congress. Curzon was wrong in his analysis, but his maneuver to drive a wedge between the Hindus and the Muslims by wooing the Muslims, followed by the establishment of the Muslim League in 1906, did introduce divide-and-rule policies that encouraged communal discord and ultimately led to the partitioning of the country. He may not have succeeded in destroying the Congress, but he did make it difficult for the Congress to remain the sole representative of Indian nationalism.

However that may be, the period when the British could say that they had brought law and order to the country was over. The next forty years would see the country convulsed by massive anti-British agitations.

In the paradoxical environment where the Congress never abdicated its stand that it was a secular national party, and where the British continued to find leaders of minority communities (Muslims, and later Sikhs and Scheduled Castes) to dispute the Congress claim, Congress leaders ultimately failed to forge true national solidarity. These leaders were also hampered in their efforts because the country lacked a tradition of political-social unity. A society held together by the interdependence of caste and religious ghettos could not be reshaped without consideration to religion.

After an initial phase, which had a semblance of unity, the Congress national movement got fractured in the early decades of the twentieth century when several key Hindu leaders began, consciously, to exploit the religious sentiments of the people. At the same time the establishment of the Muslim League paved the way for Muslims to break away from the Congress and identify themselves with an organization of their own, which from the very start was not national in character.

Notes

1. Quoted in R. C. Majumdar, gen. ed., *British Paramountcy and the Indian Renaissance*, Part II (Bombay: Bharatiya Vidya Bhavan, 1965), p. 382.

2. See T. E. Colebrook, *Life of Mountstuart Elphinstone*, Vol. II (London: Murray, 1884), p. 72.

3. Quoted in M. E. Chamberlain, *Decolonization: The Fall of European Empires* (Oxford: Basil Blackwell, 1985), p. 5.

4. See Majumdar, *British Paramountcy and Indian Renaissance*, p. 384.

5. Ibid., pp. 384–385.

6. Ibid., p. 401.

7. Quoted in Mark Bence-Jones, *The Viceroys of India* (New York: St. Martin's Press, 1982), p. 187.

8. Quoted in Reginald Reynolds, *The White Sahibs in India* (Westport, CT: Greenwood Press, 1970), p. 95.

9. Answer to Question 19, Select Committee of 1884.

10. Kate Mitchell, *India without Fable* (New York: Alfred A. Knopf, 1942), p. 121.

11. Reynolds, *The White Sahibs in India*, pp, 107–108.

12. Judith M. Brown, *Modern India: The Origins of an Asian Democracy* (New York: Oxford University Press, 1985), p. 96.

13. Letters from Curzon to Hamilton in 1902, Hamilton Correspondence, India Office Library.

14. Quoted in L. S. S. O'Malley, *The Indian Civil Service: 1601–1930* (London: John Murray, 1931), p. 173.

15. Quoted by Hamilton in a letter to Curzon in 1905, Hamilton Correspondence, India Office Library.

16. Quoted in Majumdar, *British Paramountcy and Indian Renaissance*, p. 502.

17. Ibid., pp. 296–297.

18. Quoted in M. Mujeeb, *Indian Muslims* (New Delhi: Munshiram Manoharlal, 1985), p. 448.

19. Quoted in Shan Muhammad, *The Growth of Muslim Politics in India* (New Delhi: Ashish Publishing House, 1991), p. 6.

20. Ram Gopal, *Indian Muslims: A Political History—1858–1947* (New Delhi: Asia Publishing House, 1959), p. 47.

21. Quoted in Anil Seal, *The Emergence of Indian Nationalism* (London: Cambridge University Press, 1971), p. 320.

22. Gopal, *Indian Muslims: A Political History*, p. 68.

23. Ibid., p. 66.

24. See Seal, *The Emergence of Indian Nationalism*, p. 323.

25. Stephen Hay, ed., *Sources of Indian Tradition* (New York: Columbia University Press, 1988), p. 193.

26. Gopal, *Indian Muslims: A Political History*, p. 66

27. Ibid.

28. Maulana Abul Kalam Azad, *India Wins Freedom* (Madras: Orient Longman, 1988), p. 8.

29. Quoted in Tarasankar Banerjee, "The Growth of the Press in Bengal vis-à-vis the Rise of Indian Nationalism (1858–1950)." S. P. Sen, ed., *The Indian Press* (Calcutta: Institute of Historical Studies, 1967), p. 43.

30. Ibid., p. 46.

31. *Bangabasi*, 16 May 1891. Quoted in Annual Report on Native Press of Bengal for 1891.

32. Quoted in Majumdar, *The British Paramountcy and Indian Renaissance*, p. 129.

33. Ibid., p. 131.

34. See Dhanpati Pandey, *Swami Dayanand Saraswati* (New Delhi: Publications Division, 1985), p. 122.

35. See Kenneth W. Jones, *Arya Dharm* (Berkeley: University of California Press, 1976), p. 146.

36. Majumdar, *British Paramountcy and Indian Renaissance*, p. 471.

37. Ibid.

38. Ibid., p. 473.

39. Ibid.

40. Ibid., p. 485.

41. Seal, *The Emergence of Indian Nationalism*, p. 162.

42. Quoted in S. R. Mehrotra, *The Emergence of the Indian National Congress* (Delhi: Vikas, 1971), p. 418.

43. Quoted in Iqbal Singh, *The Indian National Congress: A Reconstruction* (Riverdale, MD: The Riverdale Co., 1988), pp. 13–14.

44. Cited in R. P. Masani, *Dadabhai Naoroji* (New Delhi: Publications Division, 1975), p. 19.

45. Gopal, *Indian Muslims: A Political History*, p. 68.

46. Shan Muhammad, *The Growth of Muslim Politics in India*, p. 23.

47. Ibid., p. 24.

48. Ibid.

49. Majumdar, *British Paramountcy and Indian Renaissance*, p. 576.
50. Sumit Sarkar, *Modern India, 1885–1947* (Madras: Macmillan, 1983), p. 99.
51. Ibid., p. 29.
52. Curzon to Brodrick, February 21, 1905. Curzon Papers in India Office Library.
53. Gopal, *Indian Muslims: A Political History,* p. 91.
54. Cited in Iqbal Singh, *Indian National Congress: A Reconstruction,* p. 125.
55. Quoted in G. Allana, *Eminent Muslim Freedom Fighters: 1562–1947* (Delhi: Low Price Publications, 1993), p. 133. It is noteworthy that Allana does not include Tyabji in his list of eminent Muslim freedom fighters.
56. Shan Muhammad, *The Growth of Muslim Politics in India,* p. 53.
57. Ibid., p. 60.
58. Ibid., p. 66.
59. Gopal, *Indian Muslims: A Political History,* p. 100.
60. Sir Surendranath Banerjea [Banerjee], *A Nation in the Making* (London: Benn & Co., 1928), p. 175.

6

Constitutionalism and the Politics of Communalism

1908–1947

Lord Curzon was the last of the nineteenth-century British viceroys who could maintain an attitude of self-assured superiority that reflected Britain's pride in her global empire and her international stature. Blinded by his faith in Britain's imperial mission, Curzon never came to understand the intellectual and social ferment that was taking place in India. While Curzon's contempt for the Congress—for the entire educated Indian elite, for that matter—embittered even the moderates in the Congress, it was his ill-advised partitioning of Bengal that had the most far-reaching consequences for Britain and India: for the former, it marked the beginning of the end of British rule in India; for the latter, it marked the beginning of communalism that ended in the partitioning of the country.

The agitation that followed the Bengal partition introduced the complementary ideas of *swadeshi* and boycott that, in turn, strengthened the forces of nationalism. And it was this combination of nationalism, *swadeshi,* and boycott that was later used so effectively by Mahatma Gandhi to hasten the end of the empire. Incidentally, Gandhi, observing Indian developments from South Africa, where he was currently living and was still a relatively unknown figure in India, made the astute observation in 1908 that the partition had given birth to the "real awakening" of the Indian peoples and to a "new spirit" that were "tantamount to a demand for Home Rule." "That which people said tremblingly and in secret," wrote Gandhi, "now began to be said and to be written publicly. . . . People, young and old, used to run away at the sight of an English face; it now no longer awes them. . . . The spirit generated in Bengal has spread in the north to the Punjab and in the south to Cape Comorin."[1]

The British Government of India, after Curzon's departure, realized that new policies were needed to pacify the subcontinent. As a result, two broad approaches were adopted simultaneously: the introduction of constitutional reforms that gradually increased Indian participation in the local and central governments; and a policy of harsh repression aimed at suppressing troublemakers, who ranged from radical political leaders, editors of newspapers, and speakers at peaceful public gatherings, to bomb-throwing terrorists. A subsidiary, but important, component of the reforms policy was a calculated attempt to magnify the differences between Hindus and Muslims, and to favor Muslims so that, in Lady Minto's words, they were kept from "[throwing] in their lot with the advanced agitators of the Congress."* Ultimately, the reform and suppression approach failed to perpetuate British rule in India, but the divide-and-rule policy did succeed—if that is the right word—in destroying the possibility of India's gaining freedom as a single, united, country.

The beginnings of a new social-political climate that initially encouraged Muslims, and later other sectarian groups, to foster separate "nationalisms," can be traced to the Bengal partition (1905) and the establishment of the Muslim League (1906). The British, by helping to separate Muslims from the mainstream, created a situation where the Congress could not live up to its image of being a truly "national" organization and carry on a "national struggle" to bring independence to a unified state. However, it remains a moot point whether the Hindu leaders of the Congress, even in the absence of such a development, could ever have been able to detach their *dharmikta* (religiosity) from politics. We will have more to say on this subject later in the chapter.

The beginnings of communalism in modern India can be traced to the traumatic partition of Bengal. Until the turn of the century, Hindus and Muslims had their religious and social differences, but by and large they managed to coexist with little friction. The relations between the Hindus and the Muslims fell in the same category as the relations between Hindus belonging to different castes: they did business with each other but did not socialize with each other.

It is from the time of Curzon that the notion grew that one's religious commitment could gain one political and economic advantages at the expense of other religious communities. This new communalism came to be best displayed through violence against "the other" sectarian groups. The irritants of the past that had led to limited local trouble—such as cow slaughter (which troubled the Hindus) or a Hindu music-making group passing before a mosque (which the Muslims found offensive)—now became symbols of separatism.

The sense of community and ethnonationalism engendered by communalism is uniquely Indian. Focusing on the Muslim community in India, one finds that, other than religious unity (although there are wide differences between the

---

*Lord Minto was viceroy of India from 1905 to 1910.

Sunni, Shia, and other sects, like the Ahmedia), Muslims hold no tangible characteristics in common, such as *language* (Bengali-speaking Muslims cannot communicate, through language, with Tamil-speaking Muslims), *culture* (Bengali Muslim culture is vastly different from Tamil Muslim culture), or *race* (the Mughals and Pathans have contempt for Muslim converts from low-caste Hindus). In the ultimate analysis, it was the British who helped to create a sense of self-identity among the Muslim community as a whole by guaranteeing that the Muslims would achieve substantial gains politically and economically if they could forge a "national identity" as a counterpoise to the Congress.

The first truly communal Hindu-Muslim rioting took place in Bengal in 1906–1907, when Muslim masses, instigated by the pro-British leaders of the Muslim League, attacked the pro-*swadeshi* Hindus. According to a news report filed by the special correspondent of the *Manchester Guardian,* the lieutenant-governor of the newly created province of East Bengal and Assam, Bamfylde Fuller, used the police to back the Muslim rioters:

> I have almost invariably found English officers and officials on the side of Mohammedans. . . . And in Eastern Bengal this national inclination is now encouraged by the Government's open resolve to retain the Mohammedan support of the Partition by any means in its power. It was against the Hindus only that all the petty persecution of officialdom was directed. . . . When Mohammedans rioted, the punitive police ransacked Hindu houses. . . .
>
> Priestly Mullahs went through the countryside preaching the revival of Islam and proclaiming to the villagers that the British Government was on the Mohammedan side, that the Law Courts had been specially suspended for three months, and no penalty would be exacted for violence done to Hindus, or for the loot of Hindu shops, or the abduction of Hindu widows. . . .
>
> Fuller said in jest that of his two wives (meaning the Moslem and Hindu sections of his province) the Mohammedan was his favorite. The jest was taken in earnest and the Mussalmans genuinely believed that the British authorities were ready to forgive them all excesses.[2]

From 1906, the politics of communalism began to spread over the entire subcontinent and the self-perceptions of both Muslims and Hindus increasingly came to be identified with their religions. After independence, every disgruntled community in India, from the Muslims and Sikhs in the north and tribals in Bengal and Assam, to Other Backward Classes across the length and breadth of India, effectively extended the arena of the politics of communalism.

The Government of India Act of 1909: Communalism Institutionalized

After much debate and hesitation, the secretary of state for India, John Morley, with the support of the viceroy of India, Lord Minto, introduced constitutional reforms in 1909 that instituted a modicum of representative government in India. The Government of India Act of 1909, popularly known as the Morley-Minto Reforms, while making no provisions for a responsible government, did take the important first step of associating Indians with the executive and legislative branches of the Indian central and provincial governments.

The appointment of Indians to the executive councils did not amount to much: the viceroy nominated one Indian to his Executive Council and similar token additions were made to the provincial Governors' Executive Councils. The idea behind the appointments was, no doubt, to silence the Indian critics who reproached the British for not being able to locate from among the 300 million inhabitants of India even one qualified person who was fit to advise the viceroy or the governors. The impact of the act on the legislative bodies was more significant because the size of both the Imperial (that is, the Central) Legislative Council and the Provincial Legislative Councils was increased. However, the structure of the legislatures, while contributing precious little to the extension of democracy, did incalculable harm to the future of the country by giving a separate political identity to the Muslims.

The legislative bodies were composed of two groups: a nominated group, that was further divided between officials and nonofficials, and an elected group. The center, by maintaining a majority of official members, precluded any possibility of the government's policies being thwarted by the elected natives. In the provinces, though there was no requirement that the legislature be composed of a majority of officials, the combination of nominated officials and nominated nonofficials exceeded the elected nonofficials in all provinces except Bengal.

Furthermore, an examination of the electorates for the Imperial (or Central) Legislative Council reveals that the British not only gave the Muslims a special status but made them the only direct participants in the democratic process! The electorates were divided into four categories: (1) *General Electorates,* composed of nonofficial members of the provincial legislative councils that elected fifteen members; (2) *Landholders Constituencies,* in which two of the six elected seats were reserved for Muslims; (3) *Chambers of Commerce* in Bengal and Bombay returning one member each; and (4) Separate *Mohammedan Constituencies* in Eastern Bengal, Bengal, United Provinces, Madras, and Bombay that elected six members.

Thus, even if we presume that the members elected from (1), (2), and (3) would be mostly Hindus (technically these electorates were open to all, including Muslims, and did, in fact, contribute a significant number of non-Hindus), the fact remains that they were *indirectly elected,* whereas the Muslims were *directly elected* from (4).

A similar system obtained in the provinces: the General Electorate comprised members of municipal councils and district boards, university graduates, magistrates, pleaders, jurors, assessors, and persons paying a certain amount of property or professional taxes. In 1912, the total number of these electors, who returned 193 nonofficial members to nine provincial assemblies (not counting Burma), was 33,812![3] This is the beginning of so-called democracy in India: a General Electorate, which was not general, an enfranchisement of 34,000 persons in a country with a population of 300 million, with only Muslims given the right of direct representation.

1909–1919: The Decade that Changed the Nature of Indian Politics

British Repression

By the time the next set of reforms were introduced by the Government of India Act of 1919, the British in India were faced by a series of developments, the most significant being World War I, which confounded their attempts to maintain an unchallenged hold over the country.

The British responded to the growing restiveness in the country by reinforcing their coercive powers, on the one hand, and on the other, by making conciliatory gestures such as reunification of the two Bengals (1911) and issuing the Montagu Declaration of 1917, which announced that Britain aimed to increase the "association of Indians in every branch of the administration . . . with a view to the progressive realization of responsible government in India as an integral part of the British Empire." This declaration was followed by the Montagu-Chelmsford Report of 1918, which laid the basis for the constitutional reforms enshrined in the Government of India Act of 1919.

It was Lord Hardinge (viceroy, 1910–1916) who, convinced that the Bengal partition had created a "state of political unrest and terrorism," worked out the scheme for the reversal of the partition. However, the fear that united Bengal, even though it was shorn of Bihar and Orissa and Assam, would wield an undue influence over the Imperial Legislative Council (located, naturally, in Calcutta, the Imperial capital, which would now also be the site of the new provincial legislature), induced Hardinge to move the capital to Delhi.

Both these decisions were announced by His Majesty the King-Emperor George V at the spectacular imperial *durbar,* held in Delhi in December 1911, to honor his coronation earlier that year. If the intention of the *durbar* was to display the power, the glory, the might, and the majesty of the British sovereign, its success was unquestionable. Never in the history of India had the ruling chiefs of the entire country, and thousands of its notables, gathered at one place to bow their heads before their imperial master. But if the intention was to impress upon the natives that George V was confirming, by his presence, the stability and solidity of the new dynasty that was the true successor of the Mughals, the effort proved to be a total waste of the 660,000 pounds sterling that was spent on the *tamasha* (frivolous spectacle). That Hardinge's efforts had failed to moderate the activities of the terrorists and the revolutionaries became more than apparent when a bomb was hurled at him in December 1912 (a year after the *durbar*), when he was making his state entry into the new capital. Though Hardinge's wounds were not serious, the attempt on his life made it painfully clear that he was wrong in believing that his policies had put an end to violence.

The outbreak of World War I brought a new dimension into the political scene. Though the war was purely a European affair, India was made to contribute heavily to the British war effort—so heavily indeed that even Viceroy Hardinge admitted (in his biography) that India had been "bled white." The total war expenditure of the British Government of India was about 130 million pounds sterling, and over 1.2 million Indian troops and support staff were sent abroad to help in the war, which took a toll of 101,439 Indian lives. The impact of the war on Indian nationalist groups was varied, but as a generalization, it can be said that by 1919, because of the repressive measures of the government, few had any faith left in the British sense of justice and democracy. More important, British repression prepared the ground for Gandhi's massive noncooperation movement that would soon turn the entire nation against the rulers.

Both the conciliatory reform policies and the abhorrent repressive policies reflected the growing dilemma of the British, and in the long run both these policies proved counterproductive. At the heart of the problem was the view of the British that they needed absolute authority to maintain the supremacy of their rule. The British failed to realize that there was a symbiotic relationship between violent resistance and the demands of the reform-minded political leaders. The British tried, on the one hand, to shore up British authority by ruthlessly suppressing antiestablishment radical elements, and on the other, to bolster British authority by appeasing the politically conscious intelligentsia by introducing reforms that would entice them to associate themselves with the government. Unfortunately for the British, Indian society could not be compartmentalized, and repressive measures aimed at one section of society came to affect all of society; barbarous repression, regardless of whom it was aimed at, alienated everyone and led to a radical change in the outlook of the Indian political leaders, who now called for concessions that went beyond the 1919 reforms and so were wholly unacceptable to the British. Thus the Indian Press Act of 1910 may have been directed at those who published "seditious material," but since a broad definition of the term *seditious* could include any writing that was critical of the government, the act was used by local administrators to gag the freedom of the press, often on frivolous grounds.

In 1913, in response to the Hardinge bomb incident, the government passed the Indian Criminal Law Amendment Act, which made conspiracy an independent criminal offense and increased the discretionary powers of the bureaucracy to handle so-called seditious activity. In 1914, at the outbreak of World War I, the Criminal Law was superseded by the Defence of India Act, which gave the government extensive powers of arrest, detention, and restriction of individual freedom. The Defence of India Act, which denied the basic concepts of civil rights and liberty, authorized the government to institute summary trials by special tribunals that had the power to judge a person on hearsay evidence and order prison sentences from ten years to life, or even order the death penalty; the tribunals' sentences could not be appealed. The act also empowered civil and military authorities, in the name of public safety and on grounds of mere suspicion, to restrict a person's movements, to enter and search any residence or building, to arrest a person who was deemed to have contravened any rule made by the government under the act, and to detain him without trial. After the passage of this act, India was no longer ruled by law but by executive fiat.

The Rowlatt Acts, 1919

At the end of the war, the government, in unbecoming hurry, passed the infamous Rowlatt Acts, which every Indian in the Imperial Legislative Council had voted against. Intended to crush subversive movements, these acts provided for stricter control of the press, arrests without warrant, indefinite detention without trial, and *in camera* trials of political prisoners, without juries. These acts moreover denied the accused the right to know who his accusers were or to challenge the evidence on which he was being tried, while requiring ex-political offenders to deposit securities and forbidding them to take part in any political, educational, or religious activity.

The Rowlatt Acts, placed on the books in March 1919, aroused a storm of national protest and provided Mahatma Gandhi his first opportunity to emerge as the new leader of the country. On April 6, Gandhi launched an all-India *satyagraha* (truth-force or soul-force expressed through nonviolent civil disobedience) campaign by calling for a nationwide *hartal* (closing down of shops and businesses). The *hartal* was a tremendous success, although some cities did report incidents of rioting and violence.

The Jallianwala Bagh Incident: The Height of Repression

In 1919, the worst disturbances occurred in Punjab, which was simmering with discontent under the harsh and repressive government of Lieutenant-Governor Sir Michael O'Dwyer, who had used ruthless strong-arm methods to gain recruits for the army and raise funds for the war; Punjab had contributed 60 percent of the troops sent abroad and suffered the most from the economic drain caused by the war.

Gandhi's April 6 *hartal* was observed quite peacefully in the cities of Punjab, including Amritsar, the holy city of the Sikhs, which was shortly to become the scene of Britain's most notorious and unforgivable act of tyranny. On April 9, a huge procession of Hindu and Muslim citizens of Amritsar peacefully paraded the streets of the city to protest the arrest of Gandhi on the previous day. Sir Michael, having decided to use what he called "fist force" (as against Gandhi's soul-force), ordered the arrest and deportation without trial of the two highly respected Punjab leaders, one a Hindu and the other a Muslim, who had led the peaceful procession. On April 10, another peaceful procession of the citizens of Amritsar proceeded to the residence of the deputy commissioner to seek the release of their leaders. The procession was fired upon without provocation. Three persons were killed and many wounded.

There was no way that the enraged citizens could be stopped from rioting and wreaking vengeance against the British, which they did by setting fire to buildings and looting government offices and banks. In the riots a number of people were killed (including three Britons) and a number wounded (including a female British doctor). The crowds were fired upon again and again, and there were many more casualties.

April 11, the day the bodies of those killed by the police were carried in funeral processions, went off without incident, but the city was handed over to the military under General Dyer, who established a de facto martial law regime (officially proclaimed on April 15).

On the twelfth, the citizens of Amritsar decided to hold a public meeting in Jallianwala Bagh, a public garden (*bagh* is the Punjabi word for garden), on Sunday the thirteenth; the thirteenth also happened to be Baisakhi Day, an important festival that attracted hordes of pilgrims to the holy city. No one knew that the meeting had been prohibited at the last minute by General Dyer.

On the thirteenth, when thousands—men, women, and children—had gathered at Jallianwala Bagh, General Dyer decided to display the might of the British Empire by personally leading a contingent of his troops to the Bagh, and after stationing them at the only exit that the garden had, ordered them to fire on the dense, unsuspecting, unarmed crowd. After 1,650 rounds of .303 bullets had been expended and the ammunition exhausted, Dyer ordered the troops to turn around and march back to their barracks.

Later, speaking to the Hunter Commission that had been established to inquire into the massacre, Dyer said that he had, indeed, committed this "horrible act" because he "thought it would be doing a jolly lot of good and [the Indians] would realize that they were not to be wicked."[4] According to the official British report, the death toll was put at 379 (a more reliable source puts the figure at 1,000) and the number of wounded at 1,208.

After having performed his heroic duty, Dyer imposed a curfew order that denied any movement of people after 8:00 P.M. This meant that the dead could not be removed and were left to putrefy in the Bagh; worse, still, the wounded, whom Dyer said were not his responsibility to take to the hospital, were also left in the Bagh to suffer all night.

Following the massacre of the innocent, Dyer established a diabolical regime of terror, cutting off the water and electric supply to the city, erecting a platform for the public flogging of persons who showed any disrespect to their British masters, ordering everyone to salute passing Britishers and to "crawl with belly to the ground" in the street where a British lady doctor had been assaulted. The Martial Law Commission sat daily to deal out unappealable, summary "justice" that ranged from several years in prison to prompt execution.

Background of Mohandas Karamchand Gandhi (1869–1948)

Mohandas Karamchand Gandhi was born in the small princely state of Porbandar, in western Gujarat, where his father and grandfather had served as prime ministers. His parents, particularly his mother, were devout Hindus. Gandhi married at the age of thirteen and became a father at the age of eighteen, the year before he left for England to become a barrister-at-law.

Soon after his return to India, the young lawyer happened to get a job with an Indian firm in South Africa, where he lived and worked for twenty years (1893–1914). On his arrival in Natal, Gandhi was insulted and humiliated by a white man, who, on entering the first-class railway compartment in which Gandhi was rightfully traveling, got the police to eject him without even allowing him to collect his luggage. The shocking incident influenced Gandhi's decision to turn to politics and assume the leadership of a hapless Indian community upon which the white racist government was heaping unbearable indignities.

Gandhi's struggle to get the South African government to remove the disabilities imposed on the Indians soon became a full-time activity, and he gave up his practice to establish the Natal Indian Congress and devote himself to political work. Gandhi realized that he had to bring a sense of community to a host of Indians who belonged to disparate religions and castes and hailed from linguistically different parts of India, and to devise a political weapon that would be effective without pitting a defenseless community against the might of a despotic government.

Gandhi's solution was defiance through *satyagraha,* expressed as nonviolent resistance to injustice (civil disobedience). The philosophy of nonviolence was rooted in Hindu culture, though Gandhi was also inspired by Thoreau, Tolstoy, and the New Testament, especially the Sermon on the Mount. Civil disobedience had a spiritual content as well because it implied that if one did not disobey an unjust law, one had to pervert one's conscience and become party to injustice. A true *satyagrahi* (follower of *satyagraha*) broke the law openly and accepted the penalty for doing so without any show of violence.

Gandhi's tactic proved successful when his followers nonviolently refused to accept the degrading South African law that forced them to carry an identity card on their persons. Under Gandhi's influence, and following Gandhi's example, thousands of them peacefully accepted police violence and jail sentences.

Dyer was not the only one indulging in such violent repression. There had been disturbances in other parts of Punjab, too, and Governor Sir Michael took the extraordinary step of imposing martial law on the whole province, bombing and machine-gunning innocent villages from the air, using armored vehicles and armored trains to indiscriminately shoot at inhabitants within range, and gagging the newspapers so that news could be kept from the rest of the world.

Though it took six months before London was properly informed of Punjab developments, news of the atrocities, particularly of Jallianwala Bagh, did filter out and shock the Indian public long before that. The reaction of thinking Indians

The South African government was compelled to repeal most of the obnoxious laws in 1914, the year Gandhi returned to India. In 1915, the philosopher-poet Rabindranath Tagore hailed Gandhi as the *Mahatma* (literally Great Soul, but "saint" in common parlance) and that is how he came to be known to millions of his countrymen.

Before Gandhi emerged on the national scene in 1919, and before he assumed the role of supreme leader of Congress in 1920, he spent four years traveling around the country to acquaint himself with the life of the common people. During this period he was not wholly inactive. He established an *ashram* near Ahmedabad to train future *satyagrahis;* he went to Champaran, in Bihar, where he applied civil disobedience tactics to force the British indigo planters to stop exploiting local peasants; and he took up the cause of the underpaid millhands in Ahmedabad, organized a strike by them, and arbitrated a settlement between them and the mill owners. In the latter action, Gandhi also went on a hunger strike because he considered fasting an act of penance that helped cleanse the minds of the conflicting parties. He was later to use the hunger strike many times to pressure various groups, including the British government in India. Some have looked upon Gandhi's hunger strikes as a blackmail tactic.

However that may be, no one can deny that Gandhi was the most outstanding and conspicuous leader of India from 1920 to his assassination in 1948. It was Gandhi who brought politics down to the level of the common people of India. By discarding Western clothing and wearing a *dhoti* (a single piece of handmade cloth that was used by the poorest to cover the lower half of the body), traveling third class in railway trains, and most significantly, working for the uplift of the lowest castes of Untouchables, whom he gave the name Harijan (Children of God), Gandhi came to identify himself with the masses.

Gandhi's social-economic program was critical of large-scale industry and encouraged the revival of rural handicrafts and a decentralized economy that favored small, self-sufficient rural communities. Gandhi's greatest contribution to India was that, by allying fearlessness, truth, and action to nonviolence, he made the meekest Indian a courageous fighter for freedom. He could not eliminate violence from Indian politics, but he did manage to make nonviolence the unifying force for mass Indian nationalism.

is, perhaps, best expressed in the letter written by the Nobel Laureate Sir Rabindranath Tagore to the viceroy, along with which he returned the badge of his Knighthood:

> The disproportionate severity of the punishment inflicted upon the unfortunate people and the methods of carrying them out are without parallel in the history of civilized Governments....
> The very best that I can do for my country is to take all the consequences upon myself in giving voice to the protest of the millions of my countrymen surprised into a dumb anguish of terror. The time has come when badges of

honour make our shame glaring in the incongruous context of humiliation and I for my part wish to stand shorn of all special distinctions by the side of those of my countrymen who for their so-called insignificance are liable to suffer a degradation not fit for human beings.[5]

As an expression of sympathy for the people and an act of defiance against the government, the Congress held its annual session in Amritsar in 1919. Jallian-wala Bagh can be considered to mark the end of the era of cooperation between the Indians and the British. The British reaction to the Jallianwala incident was remarkably mild. After the Hunter Commission had investigated "the facts" of the Jallianwala Bagh massacre, Dyer was merely asked to resign and no action was taken against Sir Michael O'Dwyer. Indeed, prompted by Sir Michael, the London *Morning Post* launched a fund for General Dyer, "the Man who saved India," and raised over 26,000 pounds sterling.[6] O'Dwyer was, however, not forgiven by the Indians. He was shot dead in London in 1940 by one of the survivors of Jallianwala Bagh.

For a short book, we have spent much space in discussing British repressive policies during this period because they lay the foundation of what follows.

Indian Political Activism

The Home Rule Movement

The arrest of Aurobindo Ghose and Tilak in 1908 (see previous chapter) had deprived the Congress extremists of leadership and left the party in the hands of the moderates. World War I gave the moderates the last occasion to publicly protest their loyalty to the Crown and to make exaggerated claims that all Indians were ready "to rush to the front" to serve the just cause of the empire. The moderates hoped that their loyalty and India's contribution to the war effort would win Indians the right to be treated more equally: if India's tremendous contributions were helping to defend democracy and nationalism in Europe and to strengthen the ideal of national self-determination, surely India, too, had a right to advance toward self-government.

However, the days of the moderates were numbered. The limitations of the 1909 act, the ineffectiveness of the constitutional approach, British repressive laws, and the fall in the living standard of the majority of Indians owing to the war all contributed to the feeling that the time for talk was over and the time for action had arrived. With the release of Tilak from jail, in 1914, and the passing away of Gokhale and Pherozeshah Mehta, the last of the great moderates in 1915, Congress politics began to shift back to a more radical approach. In 1915, Tilak's extremist followers were allowed to reenter the Congress.

Tilak's persistent demand that India aim at gaining an autonomous government—a demand that had irked both the British government and the moderates in the Congress—now found support from a rather curious source. Mrs. Annie Besant (1847–1933), an energetic British social activist who had come to India in 1893 and been closely associated with the occult-slanted Theosophical Society (she claimed that she had been reincarnated several times in India), turned to the political arena in 1913 and become an ardent advocate of self-rule. In September 1915, Besant formally announced her decision to establish an all-India Home Rule League; in December, Tilak's faction also resolved to found an Indian Home Rule League. The goal of both organizations, which had also started their own newspapers, was the attainment of self-government within the British Empire.

The home rule movement spread rapidly throughout the country, and in 1917 the home member of the British Government of India wrote, in a confidential memo, that the "moderate leaders can command no support among the vocal classes who are being led at the heels of Tilak and Besant."[7] This was, of course, very troublesome for the British, who were fighting a major war and could not afford to have a law-and-order problem in India.

The Development of a Hindu-Muslim United Front

The British troubles were not limited to a radicalized Congress. They were compounded by the fact that many Muslim leaders, on whose support and loyalty Britain had depended so heavily, began to lose their faith in the British. And worse still, a potentially far more serious scenario developed when it appeared that the disillusioned anti-British Muslims were ready to join forces with the Congress to present a united defiance to British authority.

Muslim misgivings about the British were first manifested when Bengal was reunified in 1911. The act was viewed by the Muslims as a British gesture that placated the Hindus at the expense of the Muslims. At this stage, though the Muslims felt betrayed by the British, they had no faith in the Congress, either. But the feeling did arise that the Muslims must now learn to trust "the power of [their] own arm."[8]

The situation changed further a few years later when the Muslim League, in search of more Westernized leadership, invited the highly educated Bombay lawyer Muhammad Ali Jinnah (1876–1948) to join the Muslim League. Jinnah, who later would be the one man most responsible for the partitioning of India and the creation of Pakistan, was currently an ardent member of the Congress, and he refused to join the Muslim League because its objectives were not nationalistic enough. However, in 1913, after the Muslim League had amended its constitution to include the goal of attaining "a suitable form of self-government," Jinnah did join the league, but without giving up his membership of the Congress. Indeed, Jinnah made it his immediate task to forge greater unity between the two organizations and, thereby, between the Hindus and the Muslims.

Fortuitously, at this stage, Jinnah was helped in his efforts by a school of younger radical thinkers who had emerged in the Muslim community. They, too, began to voice their dissatisfaction with the imperial system and emphasized the need for joint Hindu-Muslim effort to achieve India's national goals. One of them, for example, was Maulana Abul Kalam Azad (1888–1958), who started an Urdu-language newspaper, *Al-Hilal,* in 1912; the paper, which became very popular, called on the Muslims to develop a sense of revolutionary nationalism and attacked the British for having planted the fear of the Hindu majority "in the minds of the Muslims." Azad, a nationalist Muslim, later became president of the Congress and was an important minister in independent India.

As a result of this new Muslim outlook, the goals of the Muslim League came to approximate those of the Congress, and Jinnah brought the two organizations nearer to each other by getting them to hold their annual sessions at the same time and place. The British attitude toward the Muslim League changed and they tried to create division within its ranks, just as they had endeavored to split the Congress when its demands appeared to become unacceptable. At the Muslim League's meeting in Bombay in 1915, where Jinnah wanted to, and did, move a resolution on self-government and constitutional reform, British officials encouraged rowdy dissidents to disrupt the proceedings and attack Jinnah and other liberal leaders, for not being "good Muslims" and for speaking in English instead of Urdu. The authorities backed the more orthodox leaguers who were suspicious of Jinnah's move because he had invited a number of Congress leaders to attend the league session.

Despite British efforts, the movement for Hindu-Muslim entente continued to gain real strength. In 1916, Jinnah became the president of the Muslim League, and in that capacity he negotiated the Lucknow Pact at a joint conference of the Muslim League and the Congress held in Lucknow in 1916. The pact became the basis for further cooperation and collaboration. It was composed of two parts: one presented the British with a joint demand that reforms be instituted that would raise India's status to that of an equal partner in the empire as a self-governing dominion. The other spelled out, province-wise, the percentage of seats to be allocated to the Muslims through separate electorates. The Muslims were given greater representation in all Muslim-minority provinces than was warranted by their population and, by the same token, a slightly lesser representation in Muslim-majority provinces.

The pact was hailed as a great achievement in the cause of national unity, although it gave official recognition to the system of separate electorates for Muslims and, more important, made the Congress look like an organization that represented only the non-Muslims, particularly the Hindus, of India. What the British had done by design—introduce communal electorates—the Congress accepted of its own volition. Thus the pact meant not only that the Congress had abandoned its stand against the politics of communalism but also spelled the end of a truly democratic, constitutional approach to nationalism.

With some ups and downs, the Muslim League and the Congress continued to cooperate with each other even after the leadership of the Congress fell into the hands of Mahatma Gandhi in 1920. In the years preceding 1920, Gandhi, working on his own, had also been trying to foster Hindu-Muslim unity. His approach was to fraternize with the Muslims and openly espouse their causes. One such cause was associated with the question of the caliphate.

Indian Muslims, particularly after the collapse of the Mughal dynasty, had begun to look upon the sultan-caliph *(khalifa)* of the Ottoman Empire, a Sunni ruler who was also the protector of Islamic holy places, as the head of the pan-Islamic world order. During the years 1911–1913, when the Balkan Wars eroded the Ottoman Empire, Indian Muslims began to get disturbed at the possibility of the Christian powers destroying the Ottoman Empire altogether, and the caliph of Islam along with it. Unfortunately for the British, Delhi's refusal, in 1912, to grant Aligarh Muslim College the status of a university came at a sensitive time and added to the general apprehension that Britain was becoming anti-Islamic. This feeling was reinforced when, on Turkey's entrance into World War I, on the side of the Axis Powers, some British statesmen made anti-Turkish and anti-Islamic statements that dismayed even the staunch Muslim loyalists.

Fearing that plans were afoot to depose the sultan-caliph of Turkey, Indian Muslims started a movement, under the guidance of the Ali brothers, Shaukat and Muhammad, that tried to put pressure on the British government to preserve the caliphate. The agitation was limited during the war, partly because it was treason to support an enemy power (Shaukat and Muhammad were both interned), and partly because Prime Minister Lloyd George gave an assurance that even after the war, the caliph would retain control over the holy places of Islam. The assurance was violated by Britain when, at the end of the war, it decided to dismantle the Turkish empire and abolish the caliphate.

Angered by these developments, Muslims in India began the Khilafat movement. In 1918, Gandhi had written to Viceroy Chelmsford on behalf of Shaukat Ali and Muhammad Ali, and though the brothers were released only in December 1919, the Muslims had come to appreciate Gandhi's sympathy and support for the Muslim cause. A month earlier, at the All-India Khilafat Conference, Muslims honored Gandhi by electing him president of the conference, in which many other Congressmen, Muslims as well as non-Muslims, participated. After their release, the Ali brothers continued to work with Gandhi, and it was in the Khilafat Manifesto written by Gandhi in March 1920 that he first elaborated the doctrine of nonviolent noncooperation, which was accepted as a campaign strategy by the Khilafat movement.

The agitation against the Jallianwala Bagh incident (1919) (see above), appeared to have established a bond of patriotism between the Hindus and Muslims. Gandhi managed to maintain the momentum of Hindu-Muslim unity by supporting the Khilafat movement, and although, as we shall see later, the unity was artificial and the two communities parted company within a few years, in 1920, the British had every reason to be alarmed that a united national front against them was in the making.

Terrorists, Revolutionaries, and Disaffected Masses

The story of the British predicament in India during this troubled era would not be complete without some reference, however brief, to the organized and unorganized rebellious groups that caused so much harassment to the British that laws such as the Rowlatt Acts had to be passed. By 1914, Indian "revolutionaries," who had first appeared in Bengal and Maharashtra, spread their disparate activities of assassination, bomb throwing, and looting of government offices to other parts of the country. Their aim was to terrorize the British officials and disrupt communications. Local insurrectionary groups, apart from making bombs, raiding arsenals for guns and ammunition, raising funds to buy weapons, and spreading revolutionary ideas among the Indian army units and the peasantry, began to establish contacts with revolutionary organizations of Indian émigrés abroad (the largest group being in America, which had established the Ghadar [Mutiny or Rebellion] Party) and conspire to overthrow the British Government of India.

The revolutionaries, in India and abroad, tried to gain support from Germany and Turkey, the enemies of Britain in World War I, but the conspirators were ill-organized and their subversive efforts proved utterly futile. According to one highly respected historian, "the flash-point of possible armed revolt had come and gone by early 1915,"[9] the year the extremely repressive Defence of India Act (discussed above) was passed. However, as another scholar has pointed out, these revolutionary activities did have a long-term impact on the development of Indian nationalism: "The sufferings of their emigrant countrymen enabled the Indian revolutionaries abroad to move beyond sporadic acts of terrorism towards organizing a mass movement with ambitious schemes for an immediate military seizure of power. Unsuccessful though these efforts were, they formed an important stage in the transformation of the elitist middle-class Indian nationalism into a popular movement. Gandhi, who was subsequently to implement much more successful methods of transforming the burgeoning nationalism into a mass movement than those employed by the revolutionaries, likewise began his mission among the suppressed Indian immigrants: those in Natal."[10]

World War I also saw an increase in the rebellious activities of the tribals and the spread of peasant and worker protest movements. British policies that aimed at exploiting the forest resources of India through conservation laws and regulations controlling the disposition of forest produce affected the lifestyle of the tribal communities and endangered their livelihood. For example, take the law that banned the system of *jhum* in certain tribal areas. *Jhum,* the practice of slash and burn followed by many primitive tribes, may have been destructive to the forest resources, but it was the only way certain tribes knew how to survive, and they could neither understand, nor accept, the government's interference in their lives. Tribes not following *jhum* also had reasons to be offended by other, similarly exploitative laws. When the war started and rumors began to float that the British were on their way out, tribals rose in revolt in many parts of India. They were put down by the same kind of ruthlessness the British were displaying elsewhere.

During the war, the situation of the peasantry, not good at the best of times, also deteriorated. The landlords, who had been forced to contribute to the war effort, reduced their losses by squeezing the peasantry. Excessive taxes and as-sessments resulted in the peasant debt to moneylenders doubling between 1911 and 1925 and in many peasants' losing their lands through mortgages or distress sales. The two bad harvests of 1918–1919 and 1920–1921 made matters worse. As a result many peasants fled their lands; others became rebellious and went so far as to organize no-tax movements. Like the tribals, the peasants were ready for someone to lead them against their exploiters.

The condition of the urban industrial working classes was somewhat different. They had a higher literacy rate and a higher living standard. The war had been good for them—employment had increased and wages had improved. However, when the war came to an end, many wartime industries had to be closed down and large numbers of workers laid off. This brought privation and suffering to the urban proletariat. As a consequence, in 1918, there were a series of strikes in Bombay, Ahmedabad, Kanpur, and Madras, and India saw the beginnings of a trade union movement. It was this discontent of the masses that Gandhi managed to channel into his mass-based national protest movement.

1919–1939: Constitutional Reforms, Gandhi, and a Fragmented Nation

During the twenty years between the two World Wars, the British never lost the capability of ruling India; the civil administrative structure remained strong and intact to the very end, and the British control over the army and the police ensured that the government could suppress demonstrations and riots anywhere in the country. What they lost, after Jallianwala Bagh, was the moral right to rule the country.

Up to World War I, the British still believed that their rule was based on the support and consent of the native rulers, landlords, and the propertied classes of India, who were seen as having vested interests and a genuine stake in the country. Since these classes had a direct contact with, and influence over, the peasantry and the common people, the British took it for granted that they also enjoyed the support of the Indian masses. The professional elite, represented by the Congress, "a microscopic minority" as it was dubbed, had no such vested interests and could therefore be ignored as irresponsible troublemakers. They were nationalists clamoring in the name of a nonexistent nation.

Because of this faulty assumption, the government viewed all signs of unrest only as matters of local law and order and lacked the vision to place the symptoms of restlessness in the larger context of the political arena. Missing the forest for the trees, the British failed to realize that the masses were being stirred into a new awakening, and as a result opposition of any type was seen as "revolutionary conspiracy" and dealt with as such. This basic flaw in the administration's outlook made it impossible for the rulers to recognize nationalism that was healthy and needed to be encouraged, and it also precluded the possibility of any British accommodation with Indian political leaders, who were growing in popularity and importance. On the contrary, the British strategy turned these leaders, and the masses that followed them, into enemies of the empire, to be suppressed, jailed, and tortured.

It was Gandhi who recognized the possibility of exploiting the universality of the Jallianwala Bagh issue to tap the widespread anti-British feelings among the Hindus and the Muslims, the elite and the masses, and thereby to draw the countryside and the cities to his cause. Gandhi was the first Indian leader ever to attempt to unify the polyglot peoples across the vast country, bring a sense of nationalism and common purpose to them, and turn them against what he called the "satanic" British Government of India. Gandhi's charismatic leadership changed the sociopolitical environment radically. His unorthodox pacifist political techniques baffled the rulers, and even his own followers, but they did bring revolutionary results.

Gandhi's immediate success in 1919 was limited. It would take many more years before he could effectively use *satyagraha* to weld the disparate fragments of Indian society into something akin to a nation. It also took the British some time before they could fully comprehend the strange new developments fostered by this saint-politician. In the meanwhile, the British hoped that the Montagu-Chelmsford Reforms, embodied in the Government of India Act (GOI Act) of 1919, would help to win over the moderate Indian political leaders, who had been reproaching the British for not sharing political power with Indians. But the reforms brought too little too late, and the politically conscious Indians were offended by the act, which gave a clear indication that the British still had no faith in the Indian leaders. The Congress rejected the act outright and refused to participate in the elections that were held under the new constitution.

The Government of India Act of 1919

The Government of India Act of 1919 reinforced the real governing authority of the viceroy, who, along with his Executive Committee, remained responsible to the British Parliament. The three Indians appointed to the seven-member Executive Council were no more than figureheads with little say in the making of policy.

The act set up a bicameral legislature at the center composed of an upper chamber, the Council of State, and a lower chamber, the Legislative Assembly. Though the powers of the legislature were still limited, the elected members formed a majority (over the official members who were expected to support British policies) and were directly elected. This concession did not amount to very much because the viceroy could reject a bill passed by the legislators or certify one as being essential even if the majority in the legislature did not agree.

The act divided the functions of the government between the center and the provinces. Key subjects such as defense, foreign affairs, customs, and relations with native states, were reserved for the former, and the remaining were made provincial subjects. In the provinces, too, some of the subjects, such as law and order, and revenue, were reserved for the governor and his Executive Council, while other, less important but more bothersome subjects (bothersome, because they offered more scope for public criticism), such as education, public health, and agriculture, were handed over—or transferred—to Indian ministers drawn from among the elected members of the provincial legislative councils. In this system of dyarchy, the Indian ministers were made responsible (answerable) to the legislature, but the governors, like the viceroy, were not. The electorate was enlarged and the elected members of the provincial legislatures now formed a majority, but as if to counter all the good that it had sought to do, the act not only perpetuated the principle of communal representation for the Muslims but extended it to include Sikhs in Punjab (as was done at the center), non-Brahmins in Madras, Marathas in Bombay (the last two had the intent of splitting Hinduism itself by segregating the lower castes from the upper castes), and to Europeans, Anglo-Indians, and Indian Christians.

This represented a gratuitous elaboration of the divide-and-rule policy that aimed primarily at setting off Muslims against Hindus, but also had the effect of creating animosity between the Sikhs and Hindus, and between the lower castes and the upper castes. The act fostered a multiplicity of sectarian identities and thereby further weakened the forces of nationalism. The story of the Sikh demand, after India's independence, for a separate homeland is a repeat in some ways of the successful Muslim bid for Pakistan. The virus of communalism, separatism, and inter-caste conflict that is so sorely afflicting the body politic of contemporary India can be traced to the 1919 act.

The 1919 act, while it made it practically impossible for India to ever have a truly democratic, secular, government, did otherwise extend the electorate to 1 percent of the adult population for the central legislature, and 3 percent for the provincial councils. And along with the 1935 GOI Act, it did provide Indians an opportunity to gain greater experience with electoral politics, which was to become the basis of parliamentary democracy in independent India. The Congress, while fighting the British every step of the way, did learn enough from the British system to establish a nationalist copy of the British structure that made it easy for the Congress to take over and run the country in 1947.

The Congress and the Flawed Gandhian Revolution

As we have seen, Gandhi came to national attention only in 1919, when he called for an all-India *hartal*. In 1920, after the publication of the Hunter Committee report made it amply clear that the British wanted to whitewash the Jallianwala incident, Gandhi on August 1, 1920, announced that he would launch a *satyagraha* movement. Although he had defined his South African strategy of nonviolent noncooperation and civil disobedience some months earlier in the Khilafat Manifesto (see above), this was the first time he actually introduced it to India as a whole.

It so happened that August 1 was also the day that Tilak passed away, removing the last hurdle in Gandhi's path to the assumption of leadership of the Congress. Yet it is worth remembering that both in 1919 and in 1920 Gandhi had called for his nationwide movements without consulting the Congress. That the Congress adopted the Gandhian program at its special session held in September 1920 is an indication of how quickly Gandhi's charismatic personality had won over a host of skeptical leaders. After 1920, Gandhi and the Congress became synonymous and Gandhi's philosophy of political action came to be identified with Congress ideology.

In December 1920, the Congress, under Gandhi's guidance, adopted a new constitution that changed the ad hoc nature of the organization into a genuinely democratic national one: district-level Congress Committees were to elect Provincial Congress Committees, which in turn would elect delegates to the annual National Congress presided over by an elected president with a one-year tenure. The provincial branches of the Congress were to use the regional languages for their local work. This was a wise decision though it would, after independence, lead to the demand (often accompanied by violence and bloodshed) for redrawing the provincial map and the establishment of linguistic states.

The most important provision of the Constitution was the creation of an All-India Congress Committee (AICC) (300 members) that had a permanent headquarters and met several times a year to discuss policy and oversee the program of work laid down at the previous Congress session. A much smaller, and more compact body, the standing Working Committee, was established to function as the Congress cabinet. The membership of the Congress was made more democratic than anything conceived by the British in their reform acts. Anyone who was twenty-one years old or older, and who paid an annual subscription of four annas (which was such a small amount that even day laborers could afford to pay it), could become a member of the Congress.

The goal of the Congress was proclaimed by Article 1 of the Constitution, which said that the "object of the Indian National Congress is the *attainment of Swarajya* [Self-rule] by the people of India by all *legitimate and peaceful means*" (emphasis added). The new Constitution not only signified the demise of the old Indian National Congress that had made fealty to the Crown the basis for its demands but created a structure that paralleled that of the British Government in India.

Gandhi and Satyagraha: An Explanation

In 1919, horrified by the Rowlatt Acts, Gandhi turned against the British and published his *satyagraha* pledge, which baffled and alarmed many Congressmen on account of its sheer novelty and apparent naivete. It shocked the moderates, who thought that Gandhi was not only cutting off their dialogue with the British but also rejecting Western civilization and industrialism, things that modernizing India needed; it baffled the extremists, because Gandhi's mass-based politics eschewed violence and demanded strict adherence to the all-embracing philosophy of *ahimsa* (nonviolence and love of mankind), which incorporated the rejection of materialism, owning no more than the bare minimum needed for daily use, avoidance of savory food, asceticism, truthfulness, and *brahmacharya* (continence, celibacy); and to most of the Westernized leaders of the Congress, it appeared that Gandhi was being naive in believing that the mere act of discarding fashionable western clothing for the dress of the commoner (made of handspun, hand-woven material called *khadi*) would somehow advance the cause of national unity. Nevertheless, the majority of Congress leaders were prepared to recognize the tactical value of *satyagraha* without accepting *ahimsa* as an article of faith. What they failed to realize was that Gandhi was trying to cast Indian nationalism in an indigenous mold.

Although Gandhi was not a doctrinaire Hindu, his culture and upbringing made it impossible for him to use terms and concepts that were not Sanskrit-based and associated with Hindu thought and mythology. His religious philosophy has been summed up as follows by J. B. Kripalani: "All these contacts [with Christianity, etc.] confirmed him in his own faith, Hinduism. . . . His Hinduism was based on the teachings of the Upanishads and the Gita. Like other great reformers in Hinduism he wrote a commentary on the Gita. He molded his life in accordance with the basic teachings of this scripture."[11] Throughout his life Gandhi remained a staunch believer in *karma,* the key Hindu doctrine of rebirth.

As a consequence, even though Gandhi addressed himself equally to all communities, the Sanskrit-based terminology he used—such as *ahimsa, swarajya* (self-rule), *purna swarajya* (complete self-rule), *Ramrajya* ("the rule of Lord Ram," which expressed Gandhi's notion of an ideal state based on the return to the golden age of Hinduism), *sarvodaya* (universal uplift), or even the very popular word *satyagraha*—was apt to appeal more to Hindus than to others. This exposed him, in due course, to the uncharitable and unjustifiable charge that he wished to impose Hindu culture on the Muslim minority.

Gandhi's *satyagraha* program had two parts to it. One was nonviolent noncooperation and the other civil disobedience; the second could follow the first or run concurrently. Nonviolent noncooperation included the surrender of titles and honors bestowed by the British, resignation from government office, withdrawal from government-affiliated schools and colleges, and boycott of elections, law courts, and foreign goods. Civil disobedience went a step further by calling for noncompliance with British laws (for example, by not paying taxes), or even the breaking of British laws (as happened when Gandhi defied the government's salt monopoly by making salt from sea water, discussed below). These actions had to be complemented by the establishment of national schools, the setting up of village *panchayats* to arbitrate disputes, the encouragement of village crafts (especially spinning and weaving), and the maintenance of Hindu-Muslim unity.

Gandhi's concept was novel and its acceptance depended on how far he could succeed in capturing the imagination of the people and getting them to identify with his program. Gandhi's boycott of foreign clothing was readily accepted by millions, who turned to wearing Indian-style clothing made of *khadi*. Indeed, *khadi* is worn by many Congress ministers even today, though all else that Gandhi preached has been totally forgotten. To a very large extent, Gandhi's popularity with the masses was based on the fact that this "semi-naked fakir," as Churchill had called him, was looked upon as a Hindu saint. The title Mahatma made him out to be a saint in the eyes of the peasants and commoners, who touched his feet to gain his blessing. This holy-man bit even influenced the middle classes, albeit the Hindu middle class.

End of Congress-League Detènte and a Jolt to the Raj, 1920–1923

Gandhi's support for the Khilafat movement was not opportunism, as it has sometimes been made out to be. He supported the Indian Muslims because, like them, he felt that the British prime minister, by breaking his pledge to maintain the Khalifa's control over the holy places of Islam, had shown scant respect for Indian sentiment. And Gandhi could not have had a better ally than Muhammad Ali, the leader of the Khilafat movement, who was a nationalist and had accepted Gandhi's noncooperation movement without any reservation. On the negative side, by sympathizing with Muslims over their distinctly self-centered concern for pan-Islamism, Gandhi did, indeed, give recognition to the fact that the Muslims could not divorce politics from religion.

Muslim acceptance of the Gandhian noncooperation strategy in 1920 may have appeared to herald a future era of joint Hindu-Muslim action, but perceptive persons noted that the Muslim Ulama had to issue a *fatwa* (religious injunction) to get most of the Muslims to participate in the noncooperation movement. Perhaps Gandhi should have listened to Tilak's advice, given just before his death, that Gandhi not "seek to introduce theology into [Indian] politics,"[12] but then Gandhi himself was not a believer in Western-style secularism. "For me," said Gandhi in 1922, "there is no distinction between politics and religion."[13] What also went unnoticed by many in 1920 was the attempted (attempted, because most were turned back at the border) migration of 18,000 Muslims from India to Afghanistan, from the infidel government of the British to *Darul-Islam* (World of Islam). This desire of the Muslims to live in an Islamic society, under

Islamic law, appears to be an abiding feature of the Muslim psyche.

Furthermore, the national integration and unity that Gandhi sought were, in due course, undermined by Jinnah's break with the Congress. Jinnah resigned his membership of the Congress in 1920 because he wholly disagreed with the Gandhian mass-based *satyagraha* approach; besides, Jinnah had no great respect for the Khilafat movement. Though this was in no way evident in 1920, Gandhi's policies gradually alienated Jinnah, who as time passed gave up his concern for national causes and reorganized the Muslim League so as to restrict its activities to the protection of Muslim interests. In hindsight, one may ask whether it would not have been more beneficial for the future of India if Gandhi had spent some energy and time wooing the less religious, more rational Jinnah than he did in lavishing his favors on the Khilafat Committee. But such an idea would never have arisen in Gandhi's mind because his vision of India, his goals, and his approach to politics were so vastly different from those of Jinnah.

When Gandhi launched the *satyagraha* campaign in 1920, most of the loyalist title holders and high officials did not respond to his call. The schools and colleges, too, after some initial interruption, carried on as before. However, the majority of Congressmen refused to participate in the elections that followed the 1919 act, and many electors kept away from the polls. Those who disagreed with Gandhi over the issue of elections formed the Liberal Party to work the dyarchy experiment, but lacking the respect of the British and the landlords, and the support of the Congress, they turned out to be an ineffective group and soon disappeared from the scene. One other party, the Justice Party, which was founded in Madras province to fight the elections, was not only non-Congress but anti-Brahmin, its thesis being that the Madras Congress was dominated by Brahmins who had traditionally exploited the non-Brahmins and monopolized all public offices.

Despite these setbacks, the noncooperation movement reached its climax in 1921 and was initially so successful that it nearly paralyzed the working of the government. According to Jawaharlal Nehru, Gandhi had managed to change the "demoralized, timid, and hopeless mass[es], bullied and crushed by every dominant interest, into a people with self-respect and self-reliance, resisting tyranny, and capable of united action and sacrifice for a larger cause."[14] Hundreds of thousands attended the symbolic burnings of imported cloth that was carried out in practically every township.

The most defiant demonstration was mounted on November 17, 1921, the day the Prince of Wales landed in Bombay for a state visit. Gandhi's call for a national *hartal* on that day was obeyed with such enthusiasm that the work of the government came to a halt in many cities.* In Bombay, too, where the Prince of Wales was to land, things went well for the Congress. At a beach not too far

---

*For a vivid description of how the *hartal* paralyzed normal life in Calcutta, see Nirad C. Chaudhuri, *Thy Hand Great Anarch! India 1921–1952* (New York: Addison-Wesley, 1987), pp. 18–21.

from where the prince was being received, 60,000 persons gathered peacefully to listen to Mahatma Gandhi denounce the British. After his speech, Gandhi ended the meeting by lighting a bonfire of foreign cloth. It was then that things got out of hand. After leaving the beach, many from Gandhi's audience turned into a mob of hooligans and began to beat up the Anglo-Indian and Parsi "toadies" who had lined the roads to cheer the Prince of Wales. The riots went on for five days and resulted in many deaths at the hands of both the mobs and the police.

While the *hartal* had passed off peacefully in most cities, there were some disturbances in some areas, though not so violent as in Bombay. No doubt the repressive measures of the government (by December, 40,000 Congress workers were in jail and thousands of others had been heartlessly beaten by the police) were also responsible for the movement's turning violent, but it had become apparent that strikes inflamed passions and could lead to bloodshed. Gandhi was mortified to see his followers fall into the trap of violence. There was bad news from other quarters, too. In the summer of 1921, a community of fanatical Muslims, the Moplahs, who lived on the Malabar coast, incited by the Khilafat propaganda, rose in revolt and directed their violence against the government and the local Hindus. The Moplahs established a "Khilafat kingdom," and in the process of doing so killed a large number of Hindus, raped Hindu women, desecrated Hindu temples, looted and burned Hindu homes and property, and forcibly converted some Hindus.

Conservative, religious-minded Hindus and Muslims in the rest of India reacted so differently to the Moplah incident that it affected the Congress-Khilafat entente and strained relations between the two communities. Arya Samaj activists, in an effort to reclaim the Hindus converted by the Moplahs, started the *shuddhi* reconversion movement, which was extended to outcastes who had converted to Islam much earlier in other parts of the country. Some prominent Muslim *ulama* responded by starting a counter-proselytizing movement, the *tabligh* movement, to strengthen Islamic faith in the outcastes who were targeted by the Arya Samajists. This collision course adopted by the two communities could not be anything but destructive to the cause of national solidarity.

As far as the Moplah Khilafat kingdom is concerned, the government managed to crush it by January 1922. In the following month, a mob of peasants and Congressmen attacked a police station at Chauri Chaura, in the United Provinces, and burned to death twenty-one Indian policemen by setting fire to the building. Gandhi was so shocked by the news that he ordered the Congress to suspend the noncooperation movement, which the Congress hastily agreed to do. However, many members of the Congress, including Jawaharlal Nehru, who was in jail, could not understand this sudden change of heart because, despite the violence, the *satyagraha* movement had been a great success. Later in the year, when things had become quieter, Gandhi's stock rose again when he was arrested for sedition and sentenced to six years in jail.

In 1922, after the Turkish sultan was deposed but allowed to remain caliph, the Khilafat movement also began to peter out; in 1924, the movement finally collapsed when the Turkish Republic abolished the institution of the caliphate altogether. In the same year, 1924, Gandhi, who had been released from prison because of an attack of appendicitis, tried to revive the understanding between Hindus and Muslims by undertaking a three-week fast. Gandhi's fasts can be traced to an ancient Hindu custom of "sitting *dharna*" that was followed by one who, having been denied redress to a grievance, would sit in front of the house of the person who had caused the grievance and fast until the evildoer satisfied the *dharna* sitter's demands to avoid condemnation by society. At first, Gandhi's fast appeared to have attained its goal when Muslim and Hindu leaders came to plead with him to give it up, but in reality the end of the Khilafat movement had spelled the end of Gandhi's role as peacemaker. The two communities soon drifted apart. The old Muslim fears of the majority community, abetted by the British divide-and-rule policies incorporated in the 1919 GOI Act, could not be allayed by the Congress or Gandhi.

Council-Entry and Renewed Hindu-Muslim Conflict, 1923–1927

By the end of 1922, even before Gandhi was arrested, it had become clear that enthusiasm for the *satyagraha* program had ebbed and that other means were necessary to carry on the agitation against the government. Several important leaders of the Congress felt that the solution lay in accepting the constitutional reforms and carrying on the fight from within the legislative councils. This would, of course, mean giving up the *satyagraha* boycott of the constitutional process and Gandhi's rejection of Western-style democracy. However, whereas these dissident leaders could understand the electoral system, they were not sure that Gandhi's vision of a classless, self-regulated society based on self-control of all the citizens and held together by spiritual unity could, if at all, be realized soon enough to provide the means for liberation.

To achieve their goal, dissidents like the well-known Congress leader Motilal Nehru (1861–1931), father of Jawaharlal, who had joined the noncooperation movement and given up his lucrative legal practice, his aristocratic life-style, and his membership of the provincial legislative council, formed the Swaraj (or Swarajya) Party in 1922. The Swarajists declared that they were an integral part of the Congress and would not discard the *satyagraha* principles. But by accepting the 1919 constitution, the Swarajists also had approved the religion- and caste-based politics being established by the British.

After a whirlwind campaign, the Swaraj Party contested the elections of 1923 and won a resounding victory over the moderates in the Liberal Party, who as mentioned above had broken away from Gandhi in 1919. Though the Swarajists were not equally successful in all the provinces, they, along with independents, formed big enough blocs to obstruct the work of the government, or at least to show up the weakness of the dyarchy system in which the government was not responsible to the legislative councils. Thus, in Bengal, for example, the Swaraj Party, supported by Hindu and Muslim independents, moved that all political prisoners jailed under various previous acts be released and on another occasion decided to throw out the budget. Nothing came of these moves, which were vetoed by the governor, but the nationalists had embarrassed the government and proved that it was autocratic in nature. Driven into a corner, the Bengal government, faced with the rise of violence in the state, promulgated a draconian Bengal Criminal Law Amendment Bill in 1925, that reintroduced the provisions of the Defence of India Act of 1914, giving almost unlimited authority to the executive to resort to summary trials, to search without warrant, and to jail persons on suspicion. In 1926, the Swarajists walked out of the legislature and ended their connection with the British constitutional system.

These tactics were duplicated in the central Legislative Assembly, where the Swarajists had established a coalition with Jinnah and his Muslim faction (who had been returned from the Muslim constituencies) to form what is loosely referred to as the Nationalist Party. Jinnah was still a nationalist and ready to work with the Swarajists for the early attainment of self-government. The activities of the Swarajists at the center had eminent visibility, and it goes to their credit that they exploited the situation to their full advantage. The high point was, no doubt, their audacious motion (adopted by a vote of 72 to 45) asking England to revise the Government of India Act of 1919 "so as to secure for India full self-governing Dominion Status within the British Empire and Provincial autonomy within the provinces"—in other words, to make the executive fully responsible to the legislature. As a result, the Swarajists diminished the prestige of the British and emerged as heroes in the eyes of the Indian public. Motilal Nehru's castigation of the British, in a speech he made in the central Legislative Council, raised the stature of every educated Indian: "We say we are absolutely fit for self-government, as fit as you are in your own island. This is what we say. Here [in the Legislative Council] we are occupying that position and you tell us as you would tell school boys: be good boys and you will be promoted to a higher form."[15]

One act of the government during this phase needs to be mentioned because it had traumatic consequences a few years later. In 1923, against the vote of the nationalists in the Legislative Council, the viceroy, to balance the central budget, doubled the tax on salt. In 1930, Gandhi was to use this tax issue in one of his most dramatic *satyagraha* campaigns. After his release in 1924, Gandhi, having accepted the Swarajist approach, retired for a few years from active politics and turned his attention to "constructive work," which to Gandhi meant village uplift and the removal of untouchability among the Hindus. Traveling from village to village, Gandhi popularized the traditional *charkha* (spinning wheel) for hand-spinning yarn because he believed that this would provide extra income to the impoverished peasantry. Gandhi himself worked the *charkha* for several hours every day, and all Congressmen were enjoined to spin a certain amount of yarn to set an example to the people; later the *charkha* became a national symbol and was given a central place in the Congress national flag. Gandhi also spent much time persuading the upper-caste Hindus to allow Untouchables to draw water from village wells and to let them enter Hindu temples; both these privileges were traditionally denied to outcastes. In the process of doing all this, Gandhi brought political consciousness to millions who otherwise had been left out of the mainstream.

With the shift of interest to local politics, the importance of the Congress as a national body had diminished and its nationwide organizational activity had begun to suffer. In 1925, Gandhi, recognizing the changed circumstances created by entry of the Swaraj Party into electoral politics, decided to withdraw from the Congress and hand over the organization to the Swaraj Party so that the machinery of the Congress could be used fully for political purposes. Gandhi could now devote himself entirely to social work under the aegis of the newly created All India Spinners Association that was funded by the Congress but had its own constitution.

Gandhi's "retirement" did not mean that he had divorced himself from Congress politics. Motilal Nehru, head of the Swaraj Party and virtually of the Congress, kept Gandhi informed of developments in the Congress and took the Mahatma's advice and attained his approval of all policy decisions.

But the troubles of the Congress did not end with this organizational change. Motilal Nehru moved a resolution at the annual session of the Congress in December 1925 that the Swaraj Party would withdraw from the legislatures if the government did not reform the constitutional system by early 1926. Many of the Swarajists did not agree with this pressure tactic and broke away to form factional parties that decided to participate in the 1926 elections. Further trouble came from the ultra-Hindu organization called the Hindu Mahasabha (the Great Hindu Community).

The Hindu Mahasabha had been established in 1906 by Madan Mohan Malaviya (1861–1946), a highly learned and deeply religious Hindu who was a loyal Congressman and who had been elected Congress president in 1909 and 1918. The Hindu Mahasabha had remained quiescent until the 1920s and came into prominence only when it joined the Arya Samaj in the *shuddhi* movement. In 1924, Malaviya, speaking at a special session of the Mahasabha, explained that the Mahasabha was a social organization that aimed at preserving and spreading Hindu culture, just "as the Muslims were doing," and that it supplemented and strengthened the Congress, which he said was a political organization. However, since the Mahasabha was in fact involved with politics more than with social and cultural activities, it reinforced the growing view that the Congress was a Hindu organization.

That the Hindu-Muslim drift was becoming serious was also evidenced by a statement made in 1924 by Muhammad Ali, the Khilafat leader who had once been an avid admirer and supporter of Gandhi, in which Ali remarked that, "however pure Mr. Gandhi's character may be, he must appear to me, from the point of view of religion, inferior to any Musalman, even though he be without character."[16]

There were still many moderate Hindu and Muslim leaders, Jinnah being one of the latter, who wished to see some form of cooperation between the two communities so that a united front could be presented to the British. These leaders convened an All-Parties Conference at Bombay in 1925 under the presidency of Mahatma Gandhi to frame a constitution. The work of the conference was aborted by representatives of the Mahasabha and other ultra-Hindu organizations who could not agree on the method of communal representation to be adopted in the proposed constitution.

At the popular level, too, there was a marked deterioration in Hindu-Muslim relations. Between 1924 and 1926 there were seventy-one cases of communal riots. The number of such riots in 1927 alone was thirty-one. The reason for this sudden increase was the assassination of an Arya Samaj leader, Swami Shraddhanand, by a Muslim fanatic. Shraddhanand, an outspoken supporter of the reconversion movement, was highly respected by the Hindus but hated by the Muslims. Hundreds were killed and thousands injured in these riots, often by the police firing on the unruly crowds. Violence was becoming an accepted factor of everyday life.

A New Surge of Nationalism: The Last Chance for National Unity, 1927–1929

Unknown to Indian leaders, the failed attempt by Motilal Nehru in the Central Legislature to get the British to amend the constitution had prompted secret correspondence between the viceroy and the secretary of state over the issue of setting up a commission to review the Indian Constitution. The correspondence lasted for three years and resulted in the British government's announcing in 1927 that an Indian Statutory Commission, headed by Sir John Simon, had been appointed to look into the Indian political situation and suggest the next stage of reforms. However, when the announcement disclosed that not even one Indian had been included in the commission's panel of seven members, all Indian parties expressed their disappointment and anger by deciding to boycott the commission. As a result, when the commission arrived in India in February 1928, it was greeted by *hartals,* strikes, and massive demonstrations. The slogan "Go back Simon" was heard across the nation. Several Congress leaders, Jawaharlal Nehru among them, were injured by wanton police attacks on peaceful demonstrators.

As the Simon Commission tottered toward failure, Lord Birkenhead, a member of the House of Lords who had been associated with the establishment of the Simon Commission, challenged "our critics in India" to put forward suggestions of their own for a constitution. This challenge induced the Congress and Muslim

League leaders to set up an All-Parties Conference to devise a constitution for India. The conference delegated the task to a committee chaired by Motilal Nehru and, therefore, was called the Nehru Committee. The report prepared by this committee (often referred to as the Nehru Report) made several important recommendations: first, that India should be granted dominion status and thus placed on a par with Canada and Australia; second, that the new dominion should have a federal government with a clear division of powers between the center and the provinces; and third, while there should be no special electorates or weighted representation for minorities, the interest of the minorities should be protected through provincial autonomy. This highly secular and democratic constitution, however well devised and progressive it may have sounded, could not have found favor in the eyes of so many sectarian groups fighting for communal gains. At any rate, it was rejected by Jinnah and the All-India Muslim Conference, who wanted the continuance of "separate electorates," and "weightage" and other "safeguards" for Muslims, including a minimum of one-third of the seats in the central and provincial legislatures. The Congress, trying to work out a compromise with Jinnah, was attacked by the Sikhs who, reacting to the Muslim demands, raised similar ones of their own. And the Mahasabhite Hindus sabotaged the whole affair by declaring that they would reject any settlement negotiated between the Congress and Jinnah.

As the years 1928 and 1929 rolled by, it became apparent that the temporary sense of unity created by the Simon Commission had evaporated. Indeed, this was the last time that Jinnah would even try to collaborate with the Congress. From now on, he would devote all his energies to unifying Muslims under the banner of the Muslim League and making the Muslim League the only spokesman of Muslims. The Hindu-Muslim divide came into sharp relief in the communal riots that broke out in various parts of the country. Only Jawaharlal Nehru, naive and optimistic, still felt that communalism "may be a giant today, but it has feet of clay. It is the outcome largely of anger and passion, and when we regain our tempers it will fade into nothingness. It is a myth with no connection with reality and it cannot endure."[17] He would learn otherwise as time passed.

The British were quite pleased to see that the Nehru Report was not making much headway with the Muslims and this is reflected in the secretary of state's advice to the viceroy: "A little more nursing of the Muslim party, it is suggested, would give a much more stable element of support to government in the assembly."[18] But the British were also worried that politics was turning left and that new socialist-minded leaders, such as Jawaharlal Nehru and Subhaschandra Bose (1897–1945),* the Young Turks (Jawaharlal was forty, but young compared to his father or Gandhi; Bose was only thirty-one) were taking the center stage. It

---

*Inspired by Gandhi, Bose resigned from the prestigious Indian Civil Service in 1921 and joined the Congress. However, he was extremely anti-British and, along with Jawaharlal, a member of the left wing.

was particularly bothersome that both these leaders were against the Nehru Report for seeking dominion status for India; they wanted *purna swaraj* (complete independence). In 1928, Jawaharlal and Bose, who had jointly established an All-India Independence League, were elected general secretaries of the Congress. Because of them, the Congress in its December 1928 session agreed that if the British did not grant dominion status *within a year,* the Congress would change its goal to *purna swaraj.*

After consulting with London, the viceroy, Lord Irwin, apparently in an attempt to forestall this event, made a public statement in October 1929 that it was "implicit in the declaration of 1917, that the natural issue of India's constitutional progress, as there contemplated, is the attainment of Dominion Status."[19] The statement made no mention of the granting of dominion status, just that it remained a distant goal. This supposedly conciliatory move of the viceroy was rejected with the contempt it deserved, and the Congress, at its next annual session, held at Lahore in December 1929, adopted the resolution that *purna swaraj* was the goal of the freedom struggle, though it was not to be achieved through violence. The Congress also declared that January 26 would be observed as Independence Day and the Congress tricolor national flag would be unfurled by all freedom-loving people. This had a tremendous symbolic value, and from 1930 to 1947, masses of people all over the country celebrated Independence Day every January 26. After independence, India adopted its republican Constitution on January 26, 1950, thus perpetuating the importance of the original date, although the name was changed to Republic Day; Independence Day had, by then, already been shifted to August 15, the day India actually achieved independence in 1947.

In the meantime, in 1929, because of a suggestion by the Simon Commission, the British government decided to invite representatives of various parties and groups to a round table conference in order to discuss the report of the commission. The Congress was not won over and, instead of collaborating with the British, Gandhi launched his biggest civil disobedience movement in 1930.

The Drawing of the Battle Lines: 1930–1935

Gandhi's Civil Disobedience Movement, 1930

Gandhi started his civil disobedience campaign over the issue of the state salt tax. In March 1930, he wrote to the viceroy that since the British, who had impoverished the dumb millions of India and reduced them to political serfdom, had no intention of granting dominion status, he, Gandhi, had to use organized nonviolence to "check the organized violence of the British government." In Gandhi's view, the tax on common salt, a basic necessity of life, was a heavy imposition on the vast numbers of the very poor, who had to use it even in their frugal meals. The government, according to Gandhi, was morally wrong in monopolizing the production of salt; therefore he had decided to break the law by going to the sea and making some salt for himself.

Gandhi's plan was simple but masterful. Soon after giving notice to the viceroy, Gandhi, accompanied by seventy-eight of his followers, walked 241 miles from his ashram near Ahmedabad to Dandi, a small village on the western seaboard. On April 6, Gandhi picked up some salt that lay thick on the beach and, by that act, destroyed the sanctity of the almighty British laws. The walk (later called the Dandi March or Salt March) was a leisurely one and had taken twenty-four days to complete, but that was how Gandhi had designed it because this gave a host of national and international reporters ample opportunity to spread the news and prepare the ground for a national movement. Thousands came to see Gandhi as he passed through the little villages, and thousands joined him in the march.

When Gandhi began his March, few could understand the significance of what looked like an eccentric, if not a weird, act. The British bureaucrats laughed at him and the intellectuals in the Congress were baffled. But Gandhi's enigmatic action soon produced the results he had been waiting for. Salt had no communal association, and Gandhi's defiance inspired people of all religions and provinces to follow his lead. Soon everyone was making salt or selling illicit salt. All Congress leaders joined the nationwide movement.

The government did not arrest Gandhi because that would have only fueled anti-British sentiment. However, the government could not just stand by and let itself become a laughingstock in the eyes of the populace. It ordered local officials to stamp out the illegal production of salt, and it imposed press censorship so that news of police brutality could not be reported. The movement was unimaginably peaceful, and however surprising it may appear, Gandhi's *satyagrahis* refused to react with violence even when they were being beaten unconscious by the police. The army was brought in where the gatherings were too large to be controlled by the police, and it often had to resort to firing at the crowds to get them to disperse.

Within a month, 60,000 arrests had been made, including that of Jawaharlal, but the movement did not abate. When Gandhi decided to increase pressure on the government, and the ordeal of his followers, by announcing that he would lead a group to occupy the saltworks at a place called Dharasana, he was finally arrested and interned, to be held indefinitely without trial under the viceroy's Ordinance Law. But 2,500 *satyagrahis* undertook the peaceful assault on Dharasana anyway. The manner in which they behaved in the face of ruthless police attacks stands as testimony to Gandhi's influence over his followers: "Policemen with steel-shod lathis [wooden staves] . . . charged over the level ground. The lathis fell on the marcher's heads. Not a single hand was raised. As the crack of each impact rang out clearly, the onlookers winced and gasped. One after another the marchers fell . . . stunned or tossing in agony with fractured skulls, their white khadi stained with red."[20] Of the 320 prisoners taken by the British at Dharasana, two died on the spot.

Gandhi's arrest led to *hartals* and boycott of British goods in many cities and agrarian unrest in the countryside. As a result, the number of those jailed across the country rose to 100,000 (12 percent of whom were Muslims) and the viceroy was forced to abandon the rule of law in favor of rule by ordinance.

The First Round Table Conference (RTC), 1930–1931

With the Congress noncooperating, the British decided to invite representatives of various Indian interest groups to the first Round Table Conference whose presence could prove that the Congress was an extremist body that did not represent the nation as it purported to do, and that Indian political life was hopelessly fragmented. Apart from Congress Hindu leaders, nationalist Muslims (not all of whom were Congressmen) were also left out of the invitation list. Among those nominated to attend the Round Table Conference were liberals, Hindu Mahasabhites, Muslims from Muslim national bodies and from Punjab and Bengal, Sikh leaders, and representatives of "depressed classes" (a sinister move to separate outcaste Hindus from caste Hindus), Princely States, Indian Christians, and Anglo-Indians. The main work of the first RTC was two-pronged: to formulate a constitutional structure for India and to resolve the question of safeguards for the minorities. While there was not much difference among the delegates regarding the constitutional proposals that envisaged a federal form of government with full responsibility to the provinces, there was no consensus on the communal issue. The first RTC was adjourned *sine die* after it had put down a loose set of recommendations that conferred neither dominion status nor responsible government but did strengthen the centrifugal forces of communalism.

Thus, while the Muslim stand on separate electorates and other safeguards hardened, the Sikhs, who constituted 11 percent of the Punjab population, also began to insist that they be given one-third of the seats in the Punjab cabinet and 5 percent, instead of the earlier 2½ percent, at the center. The Depressed Classes (Scheduled Castes of today), constituting nearly 30 percent of the whole population, were represented by the erudite Dr. B. R. Ambedkar, who also asked for safeguards for his community, the Untouchables and other underprivileged castes, through separate electorates. It, however, goes to Ambedkar's credit that although he was extremely desirous of ameliorating the living and social conditions of the 60 million Untouchables, he did not lose sight of the larger national goal. When the communal award (discussed below) was applied to the country, Ambedkar* saved the nation from being fractured further by accepting reservations for outcastes within the general joint electorates.

It is interesting to note that while the first RTC was in session, Sir Muham-

---

*Ambedkar did build up a party of the Untouchables that is still active today. A man of great learning and ability, Ambedkar was one of the chief architects of the Indian Constitution.

mad Iqbal (1877–1938),* in his presidential address to the Muslim League in December 1930, proposed that the Muslim majority areas of North West Frontier Province, Punjab, Sind, and Baluchistan should be amalgamated to provide the Muslims a consolidated Muslim state. For the next seventeen years, Iqbal's idea spread and gathered momentum and finally culminated in the creation of Pakistan in 1947.

At the end of the first RTC it became clear to the British government that all efforts at working out a constitutional solution for India would be futile without the cooperation of the Congress. Consequently, before the second RTC was held, Viceroy Lord Irwin, determined to break through the hostility of the Congress, decided to deal directly with Gandhi. To prepare the ground for this rapprochement, Lord Irwin, speaking to the Legislative Assembly in January 1931, paid an unexpected tribute to Gandhi: "No one can fail to recognize the spiritual force that impels Mr. Gandhi to count no sacrifice too great in the cause, as he believes, of the India he loves."[21] Following the speech, Gandhi, and the Congress Working Committee members were released from jail unconditionally.

During February and March, Gandhi had several meetings with the viceroy that concluded with the so-called Irwin-Gandhi Pact of March 4, 1931. In accordance with the pact, Gandhi called off the civil disobedience movement, the Congress agreed to participate in the next Round Table Conference, and Irwin released all political prisoners. Even though there was a general feeling of elation because Gandhi had negotiated with the viceroy as an equal, many Congressmen (including Jawaharlal Nehru) saw the pact as a surrender on the part of Gandhi. They were particularly unhappy with his acceptance of the federal system worked out in the first RTC, which provided for British control over defense and external affairs, as well as safeguards for the minorities. Even so, the Congress ratified the agreement and nominated Gandhi as its sole representative at the second RTC. Incidentally, if some in the Congress were not happy with the Irwin-Gandhi meetings, there were many in England, too, who saw no reason for the viceroy to bestow such honor on a subversive character. Churchill summed up the reaction of this group when he fumed about "the nauseating and humiliating spectacle of this one time Inner Temple lawyer, now seditious fakir, striding half-naked up the steps of the Viceroy's palace there to negotiate and parley on equal terms with the representative of the King-Emperor."[22]

The question as to why Gandhi changed his attitude toward the British remains to be considered. Perhaps the explanation lies in the deteriorating political situation. First, there was an upsurge of violence in the name of the freedom movement (some of it, provoked by the arrest of Congress leaders, was a spontaneous extension of the civil disobedience campaign and some the product of the revolutionary activity of armed radical groups); second, *hartals* and the boycott

---

*Iqbal was a pan-Islamist and an Urdu poet of great renown. He was invited to the second and third Round Table Conferences.

of foreign goods had begun to alienate the mercantile community; and third, the people had begun to lose interest in the *satyagraha* movement.

As far as violence is concerned, the 1930 large-scale armed uprisings in Peshawar (northwest India), Chittagong (Bengal), and Sholapur (Maharashtra), where law and order broke down for several days, were perhaps the most troublesome for the British, although the activities of the underground revolutionary organization, the Indian Republican Socialist Association, were no doubt more spectacular. The youthful members of the organization, all in their twenties, condemned the policy of nonviolence and drew their inspiration from the ideals of men like Guru Gobind Singh and Shivaji, who had fought against Mughal tyranny, and Washington and Lafayette, who had revolted against British despotism. One of the ranking leaders of this group, Bhagat Singh, courted arrest in 1929 by slipping into the Central Legislative Assembly and dropping two bombs from the visitors' gallery to the floor of the chamber to "make the deaf hear" the anguished cries of the exploited Indian masses.[23] No one was injured in the bomb attack and Bhagat Singh was given life imprisonment.

However, while in jail, Bhagat Singh and two of his co-revolutionaries, Sukhdev and Rajguru, were tried for their alleged involvement with an earlier conspiracy case that had led to the death of a junior English officer in Punjab. Though solid proof was lacking, the court ordered their execution. The three young revolutionaries, all in their early twenties, were hanged to death on March 23, 1931. A wave of profound anger swept across the country and, in the words of a prominent Congress leader, "it is no exaggeration to say that at [that] moment Bhagat Singh's name was as widely known all over India and was as popular as Gandhi's."[24] A few days later, the Congress, at its annual session held in Karachi on March 29, 1931, passed a resolution on the martyrs, despite opposition from Gandhi, placing on record its "admiration of the bravery, and sacrifice of the late Bhagat Singh and his comrades . . . and mourns with the bereaved families the loss of their lives. This Congress is further of the opinion that this triple execution is an act of wanton vengeance and is a deliberate flouting of the unanimous demand of the nation for commutation."[25] The Karachi session also approved the Irwin-Gandhi Pact but, while reaffirming that the goal of the freedom struggle was to attain *purna swaraj*, left room for the interpretation that dominion status could be accepted as an intermediary stage.

The Second Round Table Conference and its Sequel, 1931–1935

On his arrival in England, in September 1931, Gandhi made every attempt to show that the Congress was a national, not a sectarian, organization; that the Congress represented all communal groups, including the Muslims, Sikhs, and the Untouchables; and that Gandhi, as the only elected representative of a national organization, spoke for the country, while the other delegates, who had been nominated by the government, could not even speak for the minority groups they were supposed to represent. Gandhi's basic position was that the communal issue was an internal one for India to solve after the British had conceded responsible government. He was specifically against the notion that the Depressed Classes should be given separate electorates; this would have set the outcaste Hindus against the caste Hindus.

However, Gandhi gained little sympathy from the British government, which was not only loath to abandon the divide-and-rule policy that it had so carefully nurtured but could not forget that Gandhian boycotts had grievously hurt the Lancashire textile industry. (Annual cloth export to India had fallen from 26 million pounds sterling in 1929 to 5.5 million in 1931.) The RTC thus came to an end in December 1931 without having achieved anything. Thereafter London hardened its attitude toward Gandhi. Lord Willingdon, the new viceroy of India, too, reversed Lord Irwin's policy and passed a series of new repressive ordinances that empowered civil officials with near-military martial law powers. Willingdon, who considered Gandhi to be the "most astute and opportunist politician," had no desire to negotiate with Gandhi or the Congress.

Gandhi returned to India to find that the country was in the throes of political upheaval: thousands of political activists had been detained in Bengal, which was being ruled through draconian ordinances because of the resurgence of terrorism; in the Muslim-majority North West Frontier Province, the beloved Muslim leader Abdul Gaffar Khan, "Frontier Gandhi," had been arrested for expanding the civil disobedience activities of his Khudai Khidmatgars (Servants of God) and merging them with the Congress; and in the United Provinces, Jawaharlal Nehru had been arrested for organizing a no-rent campaign to secure relief for the peasantry. When Gandhi reached Bombay on December 28, 1931, he immediately sought an interview with Willingdon to discuss the situation with him and work out a formula designed to avoid further conflict, but was rebuffed.

Gandhi had no recourse but to start a new civil disobedience campaign, which he did on January 4, 1932. Within a week, Gandhi and all important leaders of the Congress, along with 34,000 other Congressmen, were behind bars; the figure rose to 48,500 by June. There were no trials and no hearings. The Congress was banned as an illegal organization.

With the Congress out of the way, and the civil disobedience movement losing the vigor it may otherwise have had, the minorities, especially the Muslims, began to enlarge their earlier demands. The British, on their part, saw the need to be sure of the support of the Muslims, now that war had been declared on the Congress. As Willingdon put it in a letter to the prime minister in July, "if the Muslims are now carried away in opposition we shall be faced with a situation in this country, which will certainly demand measures more drastic than any we have taken. We should have the whole force of the country against us, Hindus and Muslims. . . . We cannot afford to be wholly without friends."[26] In August, Prime Minister Ramsay MacDonald, on the grounds that Indian leaders had not been able to come to any agreement on the issue, announced his own communal award. The chief features of the award were:

1. Separate electorates were to be created for the Muslims, the Sikhs, the Indian Christians, and the Anglo-Indians.
2. Members of the Depressed Classes were to vote in general constituencies but certain special constituencies were also to be created for them.
3. Muslims were to retain their current weightage in provinces where they were in a minority.
4. Women were to be elected on a communal basis from special constituencies.
5. In Punjab, Muslims were to be given 51 percent of the seats, the Sikhs 18.8 percent, and the Hindus 27 percent.
6. In Bengal, Muslims were to be given 48.4 percent of the seats, the Europeans 10 percent, and the Hindus 39.2 percent.

The award was patently pro-Muslim. Practically speaking, it gave a statutory majority to the Muslims in Punjab, and de facto statutory majority to them in Bengal. As for non-Muslims (i.e., Hindus), even in provinces in which they were a minority they were not given any weightage.

The award fractionalized the electorate by dividing it into twelve separate constituencies and confirmed the British view that the idea of Indian unity was a myth. The worst feature of the award was that it departed from the previous communal approach by recognizing the right of the Depressed Classes to reserved seats and separate electorates. Gandhi (in jail near Poona), seeing how this posed the biggest threat to Indian unity, began on September 20, 1932, a "fast unto death" to protest the separation of caste Hindus from Hindu Untouchables and "to sting Hindu conscience into right religious action." After the initial shock was over, the announcement of the fast, in Nehru's words, produced "a magic wave of enthusiasm" among the Hindus, who opened their temples to the Harijans (Children of God, the name Gandhi had given to the Untouchables) and publicly broke bread with them—acts which symbolized the destruction of caste taboos. Ambedkar, initially unyielding, was persuaded to meet with Gandhi, and the two reached an agreement, popularly referred to as the Poona Pact (September 24), which eliminated separate electorates in return for a larger representation for the Harijans through reserved seats. Hindu leaders, including the ultra-conservative Malaviya, who had helped in the Poona Pact negotiations, passed a resolution declaring that "henceforth, amongst Hindus no one shall be regarded as an untouchable by reason of his birth and that those who have been so regarded hitherto will have the same right as other Hindus in regard to the use of public wells, public schools, public roads, and all other public institutions. This right shall have statutory recognition . . . and shall be one of the earliest Acts of the Swaraj Parliament. . . . It shall be the duty of all Hindu leaders to secure . . . an early removal of all social disabilities [imposed on untouchables, and their] admission to temples."[27]

The British government consented to modify the award on the basis of the Poona Pact. However, by concluding the Poona Pact, Gandhi had tacitly accepted the rest of the communal award. Also, the pact, by giving higher representation to the Harijans, confirmed the notion that backward, disadvantaged sections of society needed to be given weightage (and this notion is causing problems in contemporary Indian politics).

Gandhi's action, though condemned by some caste Hindus because it had won over the depressed castes at the expense of the upper castes, did in fact preserve the unity of Hindu society. He now turned his full attention to the uplifting of the Harijans, and though he was still in prison, he directed the publication of a magazine entitled *Harijan*. After being released from jail in 1933, he gave up all other activities for two years to carry out a massive campaign against untouchability. In May 1934, the civil disobedience campaign, which had already petered out because of the government's repressive laws, was officially terminated by Gandhi, and it was decided that the Congress, while neither accepting nor rejecting the communal award, would fight the forthcoming elections. Thereupon, the government lifted the ban on the Congress.

The Communal Repercussions of the Government of India Act of 1935

The British government followed up Ramsay MacDonald's Communal Award by holding a truncated third Round Table Conference in November 1932. The absence of the Congress made no difference to the preconceived proposals of the RTC, which were used by the British government to draft a White Paper in 1933. Soon thereafter, the Parliament set up a powerful Joint Committee on Indian Constitutional Reform to study the White Paper and make its recommendations. On the basis of the report issued by the Joint Committee in November 1934, the government introduced the India Bill in January 1935, which despite its denunciation by the right-wing faction of the Conservative Party led by Winston Churchill, was enacted into law in August as the Government of India Act 1935. The main features of the 1935 act were:

1. Burma was separated from India; two new governor's provinces were created, a Hindu-majority province of Orissa (separated from Bihar) and Muslim-majority province of Sind (separated from Bombay); and the Muslim-majority North West Frontier Province was raised to the status of a governor's province.

2. The eleven governor's provinces were given a new constitutional status that made them more independent and autonomous. In place of the old dyarchy, responsible government was introduced and control of all provincial subjects was placed in the hands of popular ministers responsible to the legislature. The governors had certain "special responsibilities," the most important of which were the prevention of any grave threat to the peace and

tranquillity in their provinces, the protection of the legitimate interests of the minorities and the rights of the services, and of the native Princely States that did not officially come under the control of the British government in Delhi. In the event of a breakdown of constitutional machinery, the governor was empowered to assume all powers of the government.

3. Provision was made for the establishment of a federal government for the whole of India, including the Princely States. One-third of the central legislative seats were allocated to the Princely States and they could be filled by nomination; the remaining two-thirds were to be elected from British India according to the communal award. The principle of dyarchy, eliminated from the provinces, was introduced at the center, ostensibly to provide Indians with experience in national politics. Ministers, responsible to the central legislature, were to be in charge of most subjects, except defense and external affairs, which were the sole responsibility of the viceroy, and the ministers also had limited control over federal finances. The viceroy had "special responsibilities," like those of the governors; besides, he could veto the acts of the assembly, certify legislation that the assembly had refused to pass, and even suspend the constitution. The viceroy was also given a new office of Crown Representative to deal with the Princely States because they had a special relationship with the Crown but none with British India. The native rulers of these states were expected to sign Instruments of Accession to join the new federation that could only come into being after 50 percent of the Princely States had joined the union.

4. Separate electorates for the legislatures were retained in accordance with the communal award, but as modified by the Poona Pact.

5. The franchise was extended from 6 million to about 40 million (from 2.8 percent of the population to about 18 percent) and now included all persons with any education, landholding peasants, small shopowners, and a proportion of the Depressed Classes.

1936–1947: Constitutionalism, Communalism, and Independence

Most Indian nationalist leaders were disappointed with the 1935 act because it had not only not mentioned dominion status but had denied a responsible government at the center. However, because a weak center and strong provinces with weighted Muslim representation satisfied Muslim demand, Muslim opinion on the whole was favorable to the new constitution.

The Congress rejected it, to quote Nehru, as "a new charter of slavery," but the Congress leaders were by no means unified on the issue. As we have mentioned earlier, by the time Gandhi and other Congress leaders were released from jail in 1933, the civil disobedience movement had collapsed and there was a general sense of apathy and alienation among the rank-and-file members of the Congress. In 1934, after the movement had been officially called off and the government ban on the Congress had been lifted, and Gandhi had announced his retirement from politics to devote himself to social reform, the Congress decided to participate in the 1935 elections that were being held under the old constitution. The Congress did remarkably well in these elections.

In the meantime, because of objections raised by the Princely States and other parties involved, the issue of a federal center was postponed and the viceroy went ahead with the program to hold the elections in 1937 to introduce responsible government in the provinces under the 1935 act.

Early in 1936 the Congress, at its annual session, decided to contest the provincial elections, but was still unsure whether it should accept office if a chance to do so came up. Later in the year the Congress, under the influence of the socialist-minded Nehru, currently president of the Congress, issued a manifesto declaring that the goal of Congress policy remained the "rejection of the Act" and that Congressmen would enter the legislatures (through elections) not to cooperate with the act but to "combat" it "and seek an end to it"[28] (by not taking office and forming ministries), because only by rejecting the act could the Congress reject the communal award that was inconsistent with the principles of democracy and true independence. The manifesto also stressed the commitment of the Congress to social and economic reforms that would reduce poverty and unemployment.

The 1937 elections, the first to be held under the 1935 act, and the first in which the Congress, not a host of *swarajist* "parties" associated with the Congress, *participated as a political party,* resulted in the Congress gaining nearly 70 percent of the vote cast, achieving a clear majority in six of the eleven provinces (including the Muslim-majority North West Frontier Province) and emerging as the largest single party in three others. The heady victory drove away Nehruvian ideas of noncooperation and, with the blessings of Gandhi, the Congress formed ministries in eight provinces.

The main reason for this amazing triumph was that the Congress, unlike the elitist Muslim League, had over the decades become a genuinely broad-based mass party. When the 1935 act extended the electorate to cover 11.5 percent of the population, many of the newly enfranchised citizens were cultivators and landholders who had been exposed to Congress propaganda and wooed by the local Congress leaders. A British Central Intelligence Officer's report from central India can be quoted as an example of what was happening across the country: "Many villagers observed fast on the day of the polling and broke it after exercising their franchise in favor of the Congress candidate. . . . Village voters bowed before the Congress candidate boxes as a mark of respect to Mahatma Gandhi."[29]

The Congress's success exhilarated the masses. The impeccably dressed, arrogant and aloof British ICS officers were now forced to salute the *khadi*-clad Indian ministers and take orders from the "criminals" whom these officers had put behind bars in the past. The British officers were mortified to hear "Bande-matram," the "national" anthem, being sung at the meetings of the provincial assemblies and to see the tricolor, the "national" flag, being hoisted on official buildings. It was no surprise that there was a massive increase in the Congress membership: from about 650,000 in 1936 to over 3 million in 1937, and to 4.5 million in 1938.

Jinnah Splits the Nationalist Movement

The failure of the Muslim League shocked its leaders. The Muslim League did not even win 25 percent of the reserved Muslim seats and, lacking a majority even in a single province, could not form any ministries. Jinnah tried to get the Congress to agree to form coalition ministries, but the Westernized, secular-minded Nehru rejected the proposal because it perpetuated communalism and because Nehru was convinced that the Congress victory had shown that there were only two forces in India that mattered: imperialism and nationalism, the latter represented by the Congress. The Congress, however, declared that elected members of the Muslim League who wished to participate in the provincial governments could do so by resigning from the Muslim League and joining the Congress. The Muslim League naturally reacted angrily to this call for self-annihilation.

Nehru's assessment of the electoral situation was not wholly correct. In the 482 electorates reserved for Muslims, the Congress had put up only 58 candidates, of whom 32 lost the election. In other words, most of the Muslim seats had been won by Muslim candidates who had stood as independents or who belonged to non–Muslim League parties that had no affiliation with the Congress. The Muslim League had secured 108 seats, which still made it the biggest representative of the Muslim community. It thus appears that the ghost of communalism had not been laid to rest by the elections and could reemerge if more Muslims were to move over to the Muslim League. And this is what actually happened in the next few years.

The Congress tried to reach out to the Muslim masses and middle-class intellectuals through mass-contact programs and publications in Urdu (the language with which the Muslims identified), but Jinnah countered by transforming the Muslim League into a Congress-style party of mass appeal, with the difference that his platform was based on the assertion that the "Hindu Raj" inaugurated in several provinces was out to destroy Islam and the Islamic minority community. Had not the Congress foisted the "positively anti-Islamic, idolatrous"[30] song, "Bande-matram,"* as the national anthem of India and forced children in schools and legislators in assemblies to sing it? Had the Congress provincial governments not encouraged

---

*The literal translation of the title is "Hail to the Mother." However, as used by the Congress over the decades, it had come to mean "Hail to the Motherland." The song, taken from a famous nineteenth-century Bengali novel was, in the story, an invocation to Mother goddess Kali made by rebels against Muslim conquerors, but for half a century it had been used by Congress nationalists for arousing patriotic sentiment against the British. The song had lost its original context for the largely Hindu Congress, though obviously not for the Muslims. The Congress had adopted only the first section of the song as the national anthem because these stanzas had no religious connotation.

Hindi at the expense of Urdu? Had they not prohibited cow slaughter in various places? And had they not discriminated against Muslim civil servants?

These accusations were based on isolated incidents, but they helped to create a myth that unified Muslim opinion and drew attention away from the reforms that had been introduced by the Congress ministries. As early as 1937, Jinnah, who had turned from being a nationalist into a bitter Muslim communalist, brought fear to the hearts of his audience when he said that "on the very threshold of what little power and responsibility is given, the majority community have clearly shown their hand: that Hindustan is for the Hindus." Jinnah went on to say that the 80 million Muslims, "as a well-knit, solid, organized, united force," had "their destiny in their hands."[31] Consciously or unconsciously, Jinnah had mooted the possibility of a separate Muslim state for the Muslim nation.

This view was strengthened by Fazlul Haq (the premier of Bengal who had joined the Muslim League) who, speaking at the annual session of the Muslim League in 1938, drew a chilling picture of conditions in Congress provinces where, he said, "riots had laid the countryside waste. Muslim life, limb, and property have been lost, and blood has freely flowed," and where, "Muslims are leading their lives in constant terror, overawed and oppressed by the Hindus . . . their mosques are being defiled . . . Muslim worshippers [molested] . . . [and] where Muslim officers have been unjustly treated or deprived of their legitimate rights."[32] The reports published in 1938 and 1939 by the League-appointed commissions to inquire into charges against Congress governments further made out that Muslims were finding it impossible to live under "Hindu Raj." It did not matter that independent British and Indian investigations found little justification for these charges.

By 1939, the cry "Islam in danger" had transformed the Muslim League into a militant mass party and put it on the path of *jihad* (religious war), and Jinnah had succeeded in creating the image, in Muslim minds, of the Congress being a Hindu organization. Hundreds of local branches of the Muslim League sprang up all over the country and the league adopted a green flag with a crescent moon on it (both the color and the crescent moon are symbols of Islam) to replace the Congress's tricolor (the flag had three horizontal colors of saffron, white, and green with a *charkha* in the central white band).

The Congress and the Hindu Right Wing

On the other extreme, for totally different reasons, the Hindu Mahasabha reemerged as an aggressive critic of the Congress. The Mahasabha accused the Congress of following policies that appeased the Muslims and were unfair to the Hindus. Like the Muslim League, the Mahasabha also believed that Indians did not constitute a single nation. In the words of Savarkar, the president of the Mahasabha in 1937, "India cannot be assumed today to be a unitarian and homogeneous nation, but on the contrary there are two nations in the main, the Hindus and the Muslims."[33]

It is worth noting that although Savarkar advocated a secular constitution for the country that would give equal rights and privileges to all Indian citizens, regardless of their religion, and where the recruitment to the services would be through merit, he was quite frank in expressing his hope that the Hindus, whom he referred to as the authentic natives of India, would monopolize power. Savarkar's provocative speeches justified Jinnah's conviction that the Hindus "after many centuries of British and Muslim rule [look forward] to the re-establishment of a purely Hindu Raj."[34]

World War II and Indian Politics

When the Second World War began in September 1939, the viceroy, who had already been given powers by Parliament to suspend many of the provisions of the 1935 Constitution, proclaimed India to be at war with Germany. He did this without consulting the Legislative Assembly or any Indian leader. He also suspended political reform for the duration of the war by passing the Government of India Act and the Defence of India Act, which gave the central government absolute power to suspend democratic freedoms (of press, assembly, etc.) and to enforce preventive detention (without consideration of legal rights).

The Congress leaders, while resenting the viceroy's action, condemned Nazi aggression and, on the grounds that only a free India could join a war for freedom and democracy, offered to support the war if India was given immediate self-rule or a categorical assurance that Indians would gain the right to self-determination after the war and be permitted to draft their own constitution through an elected constituent assembly. The Muslim League proffered support and cooperation to the British on two conditions: that the British make no constitutional changes without the consent of the Muslim League ("the only organization that can speak on behalf of Muslim India") and that Muslims be given increased representation in the Congress provinces.

Since the viceroy's response was basically noncommittal, the Congress high command ordered all Congress provincial ministries to resign in protest, which they did by December 1939; these provinces now automatically came under the autocratic rule of the governors. Jinnah, heartened by the Congress's withdrawal from active politics, called upon the Muslims of India to celebrate December 22 as Deliverance Day. It is the opinion of some scholars that the Congress decision was a serious mistake because it (1) deprived the Congress of the opportunity of influencing political developments during the war, and (2) enhanced the importance of the Muslim League by giving it greater political visibility and leverage.

Between 1937 and 1939, Jinnah's stature as the only true spokesman of the Muslim community grew rapidly, and many important Muslim leaders, who had so far remained aloof from both the Muslim League and the Congress, joined the league. This newfound prestige gave Jinnah the self-confidence to declare, in 1939, that India was composed of two nations and that no federal parliamentary system would be acceptable to the Muslims if it entailed the political dominance of the Hindus. In March 1940, at the annual session of the Muslim League, Jinnah became even more assertive and made the categorical declaration that "Mussalmans are a nation according to any definition of a nation, and they must have their homelands, their territory, and their state."[35] It was at this very session that a resolution was passed calling for territorial readjustments aimed at unifying Muslim-majority areas and establishing "independent states" in which the constituent units shall be "autonomous and sovereign." Though the term *Pakistan* was not used in the resolution, the resolution did lay the foundation for the future division of the country and later came to be referred to as the Pakistan Resolution.

In three short years, Jinnah had become the unchallenged leader of the Muslim League, which he had revived into a popular and powerful body that superseded all other organizations to become the lone representative of the Muslims of India. When the idea of Pakistan* had been first put forth by a group of Muslim students in England in the early 1930s it was denounced as chimerical, even by the Muslim League. As late as 1936, no one had given serious consideration to this notion. However, within three years of the Muslim League's debacle in the elections, the new force of communalism unleashed by Jinnah's "Islam in danger" theory had turned the idea of Pakistan into a practical proposition.

The Congress could still count on the loyalty of many nationalist Muslims, but the bulk of the Muslim community had rejected the Congress view of national unity. The Congress continued to condemn the Muslim League as a communal party and looked upon itself as a noncommunal national organization fighting for national independence, but Jinnah had rejected Indian nationalism in favor of Muslim nationalism. For Jinnah, the motherland was no longer India but those nebulous territorial units where the Muslims were in a majority. Nehru condemned the narrow-minded bigotry of the Muslim League as reminiscent of Nazism; Jinnah retorted that it was Congress fascism that had destroyed all hope of a Hindu-Muslim settlement.

Communalism, as we have noted earlier, had entered the Indian political scene with the British divide-and-rule policy that established a link between religious affiliation and political-economic gain. This had led the various communities—the most notable being that of the Muslims—to look inward and create a sense of solidarity by emphasizing their distinctly unique differences,

---

*The original term was *Pakstan* (Land of the Pure), and it was derived from the names of the Muslim-majority territorial units that were to be amalgamated to form the Muslim state, viz. Punjab, Afghanistan (i.e., North West Frontier [NWF] Province, where Indian Afghans live), Kashmir, Sind, and Baluchistan. Later spelled as Pakistan, the term came to also include Muslim-majority areas in Bengal and Hyderabad. The partition created East and West Pakistan, the former was carved out of Bengal and the latter incorporated NWF Province, Sind, Baluchistan, and a part of Punjab. Kashmir became an area of contention that has yet to be resolved.

and to design symbols that buttressed their feelings of separateness from each other. Until the mid-1930s, communal riots were still a local phenomenon. After 1937, Jinnah, a nonpracticing Muslim, exploited Islamic zealotry to consolidate the incipient notion of Muslim nationalism and spread a sense of "community" among Muslims who were, otherwise, widely separated by region, language, and class. As a consequence, by 1940 communalism had undergone a qualitative change and communal outbursts now became more organized and were directly connected with developments in the country's institutional politics. The fifty-seven communal outbreaks in the Congress provinces from 1937 to 1939 were serious enough, having caused 130 deaths and 1,700 other casualties, but the 1940 Pakistan Resolution foreshadowed nothing less than a countrywide civil war.

The Congress, apparently united in its stand regarding noncooperation and the resignation of its ministries, was in fact divided over issues of policy. Gandhi made the baffling statement that Britain should oppose the Fascists through nonviolence and not with arms. The moderates in the Congress were ready to support the British war effort, but only if Britain took the initial step of creating a provisional national government as a prelude to the eventual grant of independence. At the extreme left, represented by Subhaschandra Bose (elected president of the Congress in 1938 and 1939) wanted to exploit Britain's predicament by seeking the support of its enemies and starting an armed struggle for independence.*

By the end of 1940, when it had been made abundantly clear that the viceroy could provide no support to the stand of the moderates, the Congress had to decide on some concrete plan of action. The only alternative to cooperation was noncooperation and Gandhi, unwilling to embarrass the British government, hesitatingly started a half-hearted civil disobedience program on the basis of symbolic "individual *satyagraha*," and he prepared a list of hand-picked *satyagrahis* who would exercise their right to preach pacifism but not the goal of independence. By early 1941, the government, viewing the Congress action as an obstacle to the war effort because it interfered with the recruitment of Indians into the armed forces, arrested all the prominent leaders on Gandhi's list as well as 20,000 other Congressmen. This, more or less, ended Congress activities for the moment.

---

*Having been forced by Gandhi to resign after his 1939 election, Bose formed the Forward Bloc Party within the Congress to carry out his plan of action. In 1940, the Forward Bloc was banned and Bose was put under house arrest. In January 1941, just before his trial, Bose escaped, via Afghanistan and the USSR, to Germany, where he established the Azad Hind (Free India) Radio Station. Encouraged by the inflammatory broadcasts from this station, many of Bose's followers carried out acts of terrorism and violence against the British in India. In 1943, Bose went by submarine to Japan-held Singapore, where he organized the Indian prisoners-of-war (held by the Japanese) into the Indian National Army (INA), and established a Provisional Government of India. The INA was to fight along with the Japanese for the independence of India. With the collapse of Japan, his dreams came to naught; he is reported to have died in an air crash in 1945. Bose is still venerated by many in India as one of the great nationalist leaders.

However, by the end of 1941, the British once again galvanized Indian public opinion by insulting India's aspirations. The occasion was the framing of the Atlantic Charter by President Roosevelt and Prime Minister Churchill in August 1941. In a joint statement of peace aims, the two statesmen had included a section that said that they (Roosevelt and Churchill) respected the right of all peoples to choose the form of government under which they wanted to live, and that the two leaders wished to see sovereign rights and self-government restored to those peoples who had been forcibly deprived of them. Indians were naturally heartened by this declaration, but Churchill—the diehard imperialist who never wanted Britain to relinquish its hold on India—turned the hopes of the Indians into bitter anger when, speaking in the House of Commons in September, he made it emphatically clear that the Atlantic Charter did not apply to India.

Nevertheless, the British were conscious of the need to placate Indian feelings, particularly as it became apparent that Japan was about to enter the war, and so the viceroy released all political prisoners in December 1941. The situation for Britain became extremely serious when Japan, soon after it entered the war on December 7, advanced through colonial Southeast Asian states with lightning speed; by May 1942, it had occupied the Dutch Indies, overrun Malaya, captured the supposedly impregnable British naval base in Singapore, and pushed the British out of Burma.

In March 1942, Churchill appeared to do a turnabout: he announced that Sir Stafford Cripps, member of the War Cabinet, Lord Privy Seal, leader of the House of Commons, a prominent English socialist, and a champion of the cause of India's freedom, was going to India with a radically new scheme of constitutional reform that would help rally "all the forces of Indian life" to the defense of India against the Japanese invaders. In fact, Churchill had had no sudden change of heart but had been pressured by Roosevelt to take some suitable action to raise India's status to that of an independent partner so that the peoples of India would whole-heartedly fight for India and not for the prolongation of "England's mastery over them."[36]

With England at the receiving end of the massive Lend-Lease program, Churchill wanted to placate Washington, but since the idea of losing the empire was abhorrent to him, he allowed Cripps to carry proposals that had not been discussed with Indian leaders beforehand and that these leaders were bound to reject. According to Mark Bence-Jones: "[Viceroy] Linlithgow, who had not been consulted, regarded the scheme as dangerous and amateurish and nearly resigned; but in fact Churchill's real purpose was to show Roosevelt and American public opinion that Britain had done all she could to solve the Indian problem; and he was relieved when Cripps . . . failed to persuade either Nehru or Jinnah to accept his offer."[37]

Actually, Cripps had little new to offer. Apart from somewhat enhanced participation in the government, major changes were to come only at the end of the war, and those changes were neither meant to preserve the unity of India nor to strengthen the forces of democracy. The main points of the Cripps proposals can be summarized as follows:

1. The creation, "upon the cessation of hostilities," of a new Indian union that would have the status of a dominion.
2. A constituent assembly—composed of members elected on the basis of proportional representation in British India, and native rulers who would represent their states—to be established after the war to frame the constitution of the Indian union; the constituent assembly would sign a treaty with Britain to ensure protection of racial and religious rights of the minorities.
3. No part of India, the provinces or the native states, could be forced to join the union. These nonacceding territorial units could frame their own constitutions and gain the same status as the Indian union.

Although the proposals did not mention separate electorates for the constituent assembly, they did perpetuate the notion of proportional representation, and they did implicitly provide legitimacy to the Muslim League's demand for a separate state and held forth hope to the princes that they could remain separate from the Indian union. For one reason or another, Cripps proposals were turned down by all the Indian parties. The Congress rejected them on the ground that they not only failed to give India a responsible government immediately but that they contained the "novel principle of non-accession" of provinces and native states which was "a severe blow to the conception of Indian unity."[38] Gandhi was reported to have called the proposals "a post-dated check on a failing bank."

Surprisingly, even the Muslim League rejected the proposals, its objection being that the terms of nonaccession did not, unequivocally, accept the partitioning of India and the establishment of an independent Muslim state; moreover, the Cripps offer appeared to compel Muslims to enter the constitution-making body before the question of nonaccession could be taken up.

The Mahasabha could not agree to the proposals because they conflicted with its belief in the indivisibility of Hindu India, while Dr. Ambedkar condemned them because they were "calculated to do the greatest harm to the Depressed Classes and are sure to place them under an unmitigated system of Hindu rule."[39] The Sikh leader, Master Tara Singh, was dismayed because the proposals virtually conceded the demand for Pakistan, but had nothing to offer to his community; he informed Cripps that "we have lost hope of receiving any consideration. We shall, however, resist by all possible means separation of the Punjab from an All-India Union. We shall never permit our Motherland to be at the mercy of those [meaning Muslims] who disown it."[40]

The Quit India Movement

After the failure of the Cripps mission, the British decided to carry on the war without any further negotiations with the Congress, and that meant with any

Indian party because without the involvement of the Congress other parties did not matter. The viceroy, armed with draconian powers under the Defence of India Act, ignored the growing anti-British mood of the people, and concentrated on gagging the press and ruthlessly suppressing all signs of anti-British agitation within the country. In the same autocratic vein he ordered the local officials in the areas facing a possible Japanese attack to carry out a scorched-earth policy that would impede any Japanese advance. As the district officer posted in the Calcutta harbor recalls: "[Scorched-earth] orders came through to collect and immobilize all bicycles. . . . Then it was the turn of the country boats. Cycles [although counted in thousands] were not numerous in this riverain district, but boats there were by [many] thousands, and they were the lifeblood of the community. . . . It was later asserted by critics of the Government that the [confiscation] of boats made a significant contribution to the famine [the Great Bengal Famine of 1943] that developed in the following year."[41]

The poor, common people of India were not for or against the war, as such, and the 2 million plus who had joined the armed forces were mostly volunteers, but as the war continued, the populace came to be increasingly hurt by war-induced shortages, inflation, and the steep rise in prices (250 percent between 1940 and 1942) of daily-use commodities. The government was forced to try and alleviate the situation by introducing a rationing system for grain, sugar, and cloth but this encouraged hoarding, black marketing, and corruption. All this bred bitterness that, naturally enough, was directed against the British. News of British defeats at the hands of the Germans or the Japanese was received with great jubilation by the populace at large, especially by the Bengalis, who were waiting for Bose to return, with Axis help, to liberate India.

There was a spirit of militant defiance in the air, and Gandhi's philosophy of nonviolence seemed to have gone out of public favor. However, after the failure of the Cripps mission, when the splits in the Congress leadership created by the Cripps proposals had healed, Gandhi was back in power and in July 1942 helped to draft a resolution, later known as the Quit India Resolution, that called for an immediate end to British rule, on the understanding that a free India would do everything in its power to support the Allied war effort. This was a notable concession by Gandhi, who had all along stood by his policy of uncompromising pacifism. However, the resolution went on to say that if this appeal failed, the Congress, led by Gandhi, would be compelled to launch a widespread nonviolent struggle against the British.

To give Delhi time to think about the resolution, it was decided that the All-India Congress Committee (AICC) would meet on August 7 to reach the "final decision."[42] Prime Minister Amery, upon learning of this resolution, wanted to get the Congress leaders arrested forthwith and wired to Linlithgow:

Twice armed is he that has his quarrel just,
But thrice armed he who gets his blow in fust.[43]

The AICC met in Bombay on August 7, and on the following day passed the Quit India Resolution, simultaneously launching a mass civil disobedience struggle that aimed at gaining power, not for the Congress but for the "whole people of India." Gandhi in his speech said that, though he was still ready to negotiate with the viceroy, he was no longer ready to accept "anything short of complete freedom." He explained why the time for struggle had arrived: "If a man holds me by the neck and wants to drown me, may I not struggle to free myself directly? . . . Here is a *mantra*, a short one that I give you. You may imprint it on your hearts and let every breath of yours give expression to it. The *mantra* is 'Do or Die.' We shall either free India or die in the attempt; we shall not live to see the perpetuation of slavery."[44] According to Professor Hutchins, "by holding India in subjection, the British had abrogated any right to claim a higher moral standing for their side. Gandhi was thus willing to see the British opposed, during the war, if necessary by violence."[45]

In the early hours of August 9, before the Congress had worked out any specific plan to guide mass action, Gandhi and other Congress leaders were arrested and taken to unannounced destinations. Similarly, leaders outside Bombay were also taken into custody; the total number jailed was around 60,000. The government also declared the Congress to be an illegal body. With the leaders behind bars, there was no way that popular anger could be kept under control. There was a rash of spontaneous mass demonstrations right across the country, which took the form of marches, *hartals,* and violent assault on the symbols of government, such as police stations, post offices, courts, railway stations, railroad rolling stock, railway tracks, telephone lines, and telegraph cables. Terrorists and revolutionaries naturally took advantage of the situation and contributed their bit by resorting to bomb throwing and sabotage.

By the end of 1943, apart from damage to government property estimated at 2,735,125 rupees, 63 policemen had been killed and 2,012 injured.[46] The government's quick and ruthless response resulted in the police shooting and killing 763 persons, injuring 1,941, carrying out 2,562 sentences of public flogging and arresting 91,836 "miscreants"; the 57 army battalions brought in to help the police fired 68 times, killing 297 and injuring 238; and there were 5 cases of aerial bombardment. The collective fines imposed by the government amounted to 9,007,382 rupees. Although these statistics cover a period of seventeen months, the bulk of the action from both sides took place in August and September 1942. The severity of the British response is understandable because, as Linlithgow informed Churchill at the end of August, the Congress movement was "by far the most serious rebellion since that of 1857, the gravity and extent of which we have so far concealed from the world for reasons of military security."[47] Having called it a rebellion, Linlithgow treated it as such and struck it down "swiftly and decisively."[48] The Quit India Resolution had evoked a nationwide reaction, and except for the loyalist provinces of Punjab, NWF, and Sind, there was hardly a district that had remained unaffected. However, it is noteworthy that, though there was an absence of communal violence, the Muslim League went along with the government in denouncing the nationalist uprising as a rebellion.

In return for this demonstration of loyalty, Jinnah secured exemption for Muslims from collective fines imposed on recalcitrant localities, and this helped to strengthen his standing in the eyes of the Muslim community in the subcontinent.

It is also noteworthy that the leaders of the Mahasabha, the Sikhs, and the Untouchables maintained a neutral stand on the Quit India issue, and the Communist Party of India (CPI), guided by instructions from Moscow, was most forthright in its support of the British war effort: As a gesture of goodwill toward its ally, the USSR, Britain revoked the illegal status of the CPI in 1941. In 1942, the CPI condemned the Quit India movement and Subhas Bose's Indian National Army and, strangely enough, supported Jinnah's Pakistan resolution. For this, the CPI lost the respect of the nationalist Indian intelligentsia.

With all the Congress leaders in jail, 1943 was a quiet year, although Gandhi managed to create a stir by going on a twenty-one–day fast in February to protest the viceroy's charge that the Congress leaders, Gandhi included, were responsible for the violence that had been unleashed by the Quit India movement. Linlithgow, afraid that the fast might kill the seventy-three-year-old leader and cause even worse problems for the state, decided to release him for the duration of the fast. But Gandhi refused to be released and survived his self-imposed penance.

Then came the cataclysmic Bengal famine, which claimed nearly 3 million lives and was largely the result of the government's acts of omission and commission. The unimaginative scorched-earth policy that had led to the confiscation of the boats (described above), coupled with the rationing of petrol, meant that grain from the grain-surplus areas could be transported neither by boats nor by trucks to the grain-short areas. The shortages were aggravated by unchecked profiteering and black marketeering. What is more, the British heartlessly rejected an American offer of grain, apparently because they were not averse to punishing the troublemaking Bengalis.

The villagers, who had been forced to sell even their seed-grain, could no longer depend on their own resources, and lacking the money to buy the exorbitantly high-priced grain in the open market, fled from the impoverished countryside to beg and starve to death in the streets of Calcutta. As a local district officer recalls, "Those were the days when the streets of Calcutta and the railway platforms were all littered with dead bodies, and women reduced to mere skeletons, almost bare bodied, with dead children around and babies on their breasts and the beggar's bowl beside were a common sight in and around Calcutta."[49] The gruesome Bengal famine turned even the nonpolitical Indians in the civil and military services more nationalistic and disloyal to the Raj.

It was left to Lord Wavell (commander-in-chief of the Indian army and a member of Linlithgow's Council), who was made viceroy in October 1943, to curb the ravages of the famine, which he did with military efficiency, and the province soon returned to a state of normalcy. In the following year, when the tide of war had shifted in favor of the Allies and the Indian political environment was quiescent, Wavell, afraid that Gandhi, who was suffering from a severe attack of malaria, may die in jail, released him on medical grounds. On his release, Gandhi tried to revive negotiations with the viceroy. He wrote to the viceroy that he would get the Congress Working Committee to renounce civil disobedience if the British could make a declaration that India would be granted independence immediately. Nothing came of Gandhi's efforts because neither Delhi nor London could accept his conditions.

Jinnah's Growing Prestige

The absence of the Congress from the national political scene from 1942 to 1945 gave Jinnah a splendid opportunity to expand the activities of the Muslim League and consolidate his support among the Muslim masses. In 1942, Jinnah defined for the first time the territories that should constitute his Pakistan; they included Assam, Bengal, Sind, Baluchistan (not a province but an administrative district), Punjab, and the North West Frontier Province. In 1943, Jinnah's leadership and program got a further boost when Rajagopalachari, a prominent Congress leader from Madras who had not been jailed because he had not supported the Quit India Resolution, accepted the partitioning of India as a viable basis for a settlement with the Muslim community. The full measure of Jinnah's success became evident in the postwar 1946 elections, the first to be held after 1937, when the Muslim League won 439 of the 494 Muslim electorates in the provincial legislatures and 100 percent of the Muslim seats for the central legislature.

After his release in 1943, Gandhi, who had been kept informed by Rajagopalachari of his exchanges with Jinnah, decided to open talks with Jinnah. In his discussions Gandhi, who had earlier consistently maintained that any "vivisection" of India would be a sin, accepted the formation of a Muslim state (after the attainment of freedom) that would unify "contiguous Muslim-majority *districts*" in the northwest and northeast, but suggested that certain subjects, like foreign affairs and defense, should be administered centrally. The talks failed because Jinnah refused to accept a "moth-eaten Pakistan" that was not given total sovereignty.

The talks were condemned by the Sikh and the Hindu minority communities in Punjab, the Hindu minority community in Bengal, and by the Mahasabha. Though Gandhi's valiant efforts to break the political impasse had resulted in a major setback for the Congress, they were a clear indication of how important the Muslim League had become in the last six years. Congress, obviously, could no longer speak for the whole of India. Nehru's 1937 statement that the communal Muslim League had no place in the freedom struggle and that there were only two forces that mattered—nationalism and imperialism—now sounded hollow. Gandhi's move had also strengthened the British position that, since the Indian leaders could not settle the problem by themselves, it was left to Britain to *impose* a solution, and that in doing so, Britain would be justified in putting the Muslim League on par with the Congress.

On his part, Wavell, backed by his provincial governors, was convinced that the agenda for constitutional reforms in India needed to be moved forward before the war came to an end. His proposals to London called for setting up an interim government in Delhi representing all the major parties and establishing some mechanism for writing a new constitution. London balked at his proposals and delayed a decision for eight months until the Allies had secured Germany's surrender. Finally, on June 14, 1945, after his proposals had been approved by Churchill, Wavell announced that he would meet with twenty-two representatives of the Congress, the Muslim League, the Sikhs, and the Scheduled Castes (the new name for the Depressed Classes that had now been placed on an official schedule—that is, on an official list) to form a new Executive Council, as an immediate step toward self-government. This council, would, for the moment, administer the country under the viceroy and help to prosecute the war against Japan. Wavell also announced that a new constitution would be drawn up in due course by the Indians themselves.

The imprisoned Congress leaders were released on June 15, and the Congress Working Committee decided to participate in the conference with the viceroy, although he had made his well-known pro–Muslim League bias more than obvious by proposing parity between "caste Hindus" and Muslims and, by inference, making the Congress the representative of the former and the Muslim League the representative of the latter.

The conference, held in Shimla from late June to mid-July, succeeded in gaining agreement regarding the powers and functions of the Executive Council, but trouble arose when the viceroy asked the representatives to present lists of their nominees, from which the viceroy could select the council members. The Congress, refusing to be identified with "caste Hindus," wanted to have the right to include Muslim and Scheduled Caste Congressmen among its nominees. The representative of the Scheduled Castes, however, rejected this proposition and also demanded that the number of Scheduled Caste members on the Council be the same ratio to population as was applicable to the Muslim members. As for the Muslim League, it raised several objections:

- Jinnah rejected the procedure because it did not guarantee that all Muslim members of the council would be members of the Muslim League.
- Jinnah, who in 1929 had sought one-third representation in the council, was now not even satisfied by the viceroy's offer of Muslim-Hindu parity because, according to Jinnah, there was a possibility that minority nominees voting with "caste Hindus" could place Muslim League nominees in a minority. As a safeguard against such an occurrence, Jinnah wanted bills, opposed by the Muslim League members, to be passed with a two-thirds majority or by some other such formula.

- Jinnah wanted the principle of Pakistan to be accepted before the Wavell plan was introduced.

Wavell, unable to get Jinnah to modify his inflexible stand, decided to abandon his proposals and dissolve the conference. By capitulating to Jinnah, Wavell further weakened the possibility of India's gaining independence as a unified country.

The Collapse of the Empire: The Last Twenty-Four Months

At the time the Shimla conference failed, no thinking person, however optimistic, could have imagined that within eighteen months Britain would, itself, unilaterally, set a date for its withdrawal, or that the Raj would actually come to an end in twenty-four months.

Immediately following the Shimla conference, there were two major developments outside India that had a vital impact on Indian politics: one was the replacement of Churchill's Conservative government by the Labor Party, which had won a landslide victory in the July national elections (the Labor Party had all along been sympathetic to India's aspirations for freedom); the other was the sudden collapse of Japan (August 14) after the dropping of atom bombs on Hiroshima and Nagasaki (the issue of war could no longer be used by Britain to postpone political change in India).

What was of even greater import to the future of India was that Britain emerged from the war with its economy shattered and had neither the finances nor the will to continue to hold India by force. Not only was the empire no longer a paying proposition, but there was a growing popular sentiment in England, and abroad, against imperialism and the perpetuation of the empire. Also, "Britain was now heavily dependent on American aid, and the United States was not in the least sympathetic to the continuation of the British empire in India."[50]

Turning to affairs in India, we can view them in the following order, even though many events overlap each other:

The British Announcement Regarding Constitutional Reforms

In September 1945, Wavell announced that, for the fulfillment of the goal of "early realization of full self-government in India" (the term *independence* was still avoided), elections to the provincial and central legislatures would be held in December 1945/January 1946, an Executive Council formed soon thereafter, and a constitution-making body convened as soon as possible.

INA Trials

Even before the collapse of Japan, the Allied forces in Southeast Asia had made prisoners of about 20,000 officers and men of Subhaschandra Bose's Indian

National Army (INA), many of whom were from the British army units that had capitulated to the Japanese. Since in the eyes of the British they were traitors, the government decided to try them for treason.

The trials opened in the Red Fort in Delhi in November 1945, when a group of three officers—a Hindu, a Muslim, and a Sikh—was brought before a British military tribunal. The British action was technically correct but politically unwise. The government should have known that there was widespread sympathy for the INA and that by putting a Hindu, a Muslim, and a Sikh in the dock together, the government was only helping to unify anti-British Indian sentiment. The selection of the Red Fort as the venue for the trials was also unwise because of its association with the Mughals and, in particular, with the trial of the last Mughal emperor after the uprising of 1857.

As the trials proceeded, mass demonstrations in which all the communities participated and that had often to be suppressed by police firing spread through practically all major cities of India, with Calcutta taking the lead because of Bengali sentiment for Bose and the Forward Bloc (over a hundred demonstrators were killed in Calcutta by the police firing).

The Congress added to, and exploited, the anti-British hysteria by organizing relief for the families of the INA prisoners and by setting up a defense committee, headed by Nehru, to defend the three officers. The courtroom provided a forum for the impassioned nationalistic speeches of the defense lawyers, which were reported widely by the press and helped to transform the three INA officers into symbols of India's fight for freedom.

The British, on realizing that the situation had become explosive and was getting out of control, ended the trials by pronouncing relatively light sentences on the three officers and by releasing other INA detainees. The Congress, having created an agitational environment reminiscent of the old civil disobedience days, felt that it had won a great victory and proved its capacity to lead the nation.

The Elections

The results of the 1945–46 winter elections brought a major surprise. While the Congress outdid its 1937 success and could legitimately claim that it was the most popular party in the country, the surprise was that the Muslim League won *all* the reserved Muslim seats in the Central Legislature and 446 out of a total of 495 reserved Muslim seats in the provincial elections, proving thereby that the Muslim League had indeed won the right to be considered the sole and undisputed representative of the Muslims of India. The Congress, not counting the NWFP, did extremely poorly in the reserved Muslim constituencies.

The Congress could still claim that it represented the nation: it had routed all other parties in the general constituencies to capture 57 seats (out of a total of 102) in the Central Legislature and secured an absolute majority in eight of the eleven provinces, including the Muslim-majority North West Frontier Province;

and it had put up non-Hindu candidates, including Muslims, in the general constituencies and most of these candidates had won the elections. However, even though the Congress formed ministries in eight provinces and the Muslim League could do so only in two (Bengal and Sind) of the four Muslim-majority provinces (Bengal, Sind, Punjab, and NWF Province), the fact remained that, viewed from the point of reserved Muslim electoral seats, the Congress did not represent the Muslims in ten of the eleven provinces. In this regard, the Muslim League success had made the demand for Pakistan more viable.

The Mutiny of the Armed Forces

The riots, strikes, and violence that had come in the wake of the INA trials had also politicized the Indian personnel in the British-Indian armed forces, particularly those in the Royal Indian Navy and the Royal Indian Air Force. The most serious occurrence of unrest was the mutiny of the sailors in the naval units in Bombay. Trouble started in February 1946, when ratings of the Signals School in Bombay went on a hunger strike to protest poor living conditions and racial discrimination. Ratings from other units joined the strikers and the mutineers seized several ships in Bombay harbor; imprisoned the officers in their cabins; raised the Congress, Muslim League, and Communist flags on the mastheads; and turned their guns on Bombay. The government temporarily lost control of the situation and the striking sailors marched through the streets of Bombay demanding that the government not only redress their grievances but release the INA prisoners, as well as the other, purely political prisoners.

The naval strike spread to Karachi and other ports, and at its height brought disaffection to seventy-eight ships, twenty shore establishments, and 20,000 ratings. There were exchanges of artillery fire between the ships and the government forces. The situation was so critical that Admiral Godfrey threatened to destroy the navy with the use of air power. If that had been done, the history of India may have changed and the country might have gained independence through an armed uprising. There are reasons to believe that the air force officers, who also had gone on token sympathetic strikes at several stations in the country, including Bombay, may have refused orders and joined the 300,000 workers in Bombay who were on a sympathy strike. The workers' strike had led to street fighting and the setting up of barricades, and two battalion of troops had to be brought in to quell them. Over two hundred civilians were killed and over a thousand wounded.

According to Maulana Azad, the president of the Congress, "this was the first time since 1857 that a section of the Defense Forces had openly rebelled against the British on a political issue. . . . All these developments convinced the British that they could no longer rely on the armed forces unless the political problem of India was satisfactorily solved."[51]

Curiously, though, the naval mutiny was underplayed by all concerned. The British obviously could not admit to losing control over the armed forces, while the Congress and the Muslim League, who were readying themselves for a constitutional assumption of power, could not afford to be seen as supporting a military rebellion. Indeed, it was the Congress and the Muslim League leaders who persuaded the ratings to lay down their arms. The naval mutiny had lasted less than a week, but it did help to precipitate the transfer of power.

The Cabinet Mission

In February 1946, London announced that a mission composed of three cabinet members would soon leave for India to draw up a scheme for self-government. The cabinet mission arrived in March, and after meeting with the representatives of the various parties and groups and coming to the conclusion that there was no possibility of getting these groups to come to a unanimous agreement, it published, on May 16, 1946, a plan that tried to preserve the unity of India while attempting to satisfy Muslim aspirations. Significantly, the cabinet mission, in the introductory section of its plan, provided detailed reasons as to why the establishment of Pakistan would not solve the religious-minority problem nor prove structurally viable (the emergence of Bangladesh in East Pakistan has proved the Mission's foresight).

The cabinet mission's long-term constitutional plan for the union of India can be briefly described as follows:

1. The Union of India would embrace British India and the Indian Princely States, both of which would contribute to the membership of a central executive and a central legislature. The powers of the center would, however, be limited to foreign affairs, defense, and communications; all other subjects would be the prerogative of the provinces (this would eliminate the fear of a Hindu-controlled center exerting an undue influence over the few Muslim-majority provinces). In the union legislature, no communal matter was to be acted upon except by the majority vote of the community concerned (this provided a further safeguard for the Muslims).

2. The provinces would be highly autonomous and would retain all the subjects and powers not ceded to the Union. The provinces would also be free to form groups with common executives and legislatures (this would allow Muslim-majority provinces to unionize) and determine which provincial subjects should be held in common.

3. The Princely States would retain all subjects and powers not ceded to the union.

4. The newly elected provincial assemblies, in ratio to the provincial population, would elect members, on communally proportional basis, to a constituent assembly that would also have representatives from the Princely States. The constituent assembly would draft a new constitution.

5. In advance of drafting a constitution, but after the rights of the citizens, minorities, and tribals were set up, the provincial representatives to the constituent assembly would divide into three sections. One section would be composed of Hindu-majority provinces; the second of Muslim-majority provinces in the northwest (NWF Province, Punjab, and Sind) and administrative district of Baluchistan; and the third of Muslim-majority provinces in the northeast (Assam and Bengal). Each of these groups would draw up its own constitution (this was meant to satisfy Jinnah's Pakistan plan).

6. Ten years after the constitution had been framed, any province, by a majority vote of its legislature, could opt out of the section to which it was allotted.

Soon after the above proposal was published, the cabinet mission also announced a short-term plan that called for an interim government wholly composed of Indians (except the viceroy) to be set up immediately under the old constitution. In June 1946, the viceroy opened negotiations for the interim government.

Despite the bickering and mutual attacks, the league, on June 6, and the Congress, on June 24, accepted the mission's long-term proposals. The league did so on the presumption that the proposals would result in the "establishment of complete and sovereign Pakistan."

However, even before the Congress announced its decision, a deadlock arose over the composition of the interim government. Jinnah demanded parity with the Congress in the Executive Council and the right to nominate all the Muslim members, a proposal first mooted by Wavell in the Shimla conference (see above). The Congress, holding fifty-seven seats in the Central Legislature against the Muslim League's thirty, rejected both of Jinnah's demands on the grounds that the Congress must have a larger representation and that the Congress had the right to nominate a Muslim if it so desired. Having failed to get the Congress or the Muslim League to come to an agreement, the viceroy, on June 16, stopped all further discussions and announced that he was inviting fourteen persons to serve as members of the interim government: six were Hindu members of the Congress (including one Scheduled Caste), five were members of the Muslim League, and the remaining three were a Sikh, a Parsi, and an Indian Christian. The viceroy added that if either of the two parties rejected his coalition government plan, he would go ahead and try to make the interim government as representative as possible of the parties that had accepted the May 16 cabinet mission's long-term plan.

Since the Congress had yet to declare its acceptance of the May 16 long-term plan, the Muslim League, calculating that the political situation was in its favor, hurriedly accepted the viceroy's proposal. However, on June 24, the Congress announced its acceptance of the long-term plan but rejected the interim government proposal. According to his own declaration (that all parties that had accepted the long-term plan would be represented in the interim government), the viceroy could not proceed with the formation of the interim government without Congress participation. The Muslim League felt outwitted and attacked the viceroy and the cabinet mission for dishonesty and breach of faith.

The Muslim League was also troubled by the Congress's interpretation of the cabinet mission's constitutional program. The most troublesome of the interpretations came from Nehru, who was more blunt than the other Congress leaders in making his views known. A genuinely secular and democratic person, Nehru was not pleased with the way in which pro-Congress Muslims in the NWF Province or in Kashmir had been ignored in the cabinet mission plan. And in any case, Nehru's notion of independence did not jibe with the conditions imposed by the plan on the process of constitution making by a sovereign nation. It is, therefore, understandable that he would make a statement such as he did on July 10, 1946: "We are not bound by a single thing except that we have decided to go into the Constituent Assembly."[52] The British would have no right to interfere with the business transacted by the Indian delegates in that sovereign body.

Jinnah was naturally angered by such statements because, to his way of thinking, they proved that the Congress could not be trusted to carry out the cabinet mission plan or to safeguard the rights of Muslims in a united India. On July 29, the Muslim League made a total turnabout and rejected the mission's proposals. Jinnah declared that the Muslim League would no longer follow constitutional methods but "make trouble," and he fixed August 16, 1946, as Direct Action Day, when Muslims were to begin their struggle for Pakistan. The Muslim League ministry in Bengal declared that day to be a public holiday, and frenzied Muslim mobs, promised immunity from police interference, began to roam the streets of Calcutta indulging in arson, looting, and killing. Hindus and Sikhs retaliated with attacks of their own, and by the end of the three days of the "great Calcutta killing," nearly 5,000 were dead, 15,000 injured, and about 150,000 rendered homeless; it was finally the army that suppressed the riots. *This was the biggest and bloodiest outbreak of communal violence under the British regime so far.* Communal rioting spread from Calcutta to East Bengal, then to Bihar (where 7,000 were butchered), and in early 1947, to Punjab. It is estimated that by February 1947, 12,000 lives had been lost. Such communal riots became a regular feature in many cities until independence partitioned the country.

Jinnah may have believed that he was using the time-honored techniques of mass agitation that the Congress had employed so effectively, but there was a qualitative difference between his campaign and those of the Congress. The Congress's nonviolent civil disobedience campaigns, even if they turned violent, were directed against the British and attempted to draw the nation into the struggle for national freedom; Jinnah's campaign, on the other hand, was directed against the Hindus, a *jihad* against the infidel that could lead to civil war.

With the Muslim League's withdrawal, Wavell was obliged to work with the Congress to form the interim government. Nehru, who had been elected president of the Congress, was sworn in as the vice-president of a Congress-dominated interim government on September 2, 1946. Wavell continued to pressure Nehru to negotiate a settlement with Jinnah and get him to participate in the interim government. Jinnah, who was also concerned about the Muslim League's getting isolated, on October 26 agreed to let league members take office, even though he had not gained his demands of parity and the right to nominate all the Muslim members. However, he had no desire to offer genuine cooperation; his intention, on the contrary, was to work from within the interim government to wreck it. The league's representatives created divisions and put obstructions in the path of Nehru, whose leadership they refused to recognize. To add to the troubles of the British, Jinnah also declared that Muslim League members who had been elected to the Constituent Assembly would not take part in the assembly's meetings until the Congress had categorically and unconditionally accepted the cabinet mission plan that provided for a province, or a group of provinces ceding from the union.

Realizing the need to break the impasse, Prime Minister Attlee made a last-ditch effort to bring the leaders together by inviting Jinnah, Nehru, and Baldev Singh (as representative of the Sikhs) to London. The talks, held in early December 1946, failed to break the deadlock. A few days later, on December 9, when the Constituent Assembly held its inaugural session, the Muslim League boycotted the proceedings and Nehru proposed an "objectives resolution" that the goal of the new constitution would be the establishment of "an independent sovereign republic." The resolution, passed in January 1947, confirmed the Muslim League's fears that the Congress was bent on moving ahead without regard to the league's views, and provided the league another reason for not accepting the cabinet plan. Congress leaders thereupon demanded that the Muslim League, because it had not yet revoked its rejection of the cabinet mission plan and had not joined the Constituent Assembly, should be asked to resign from the government, failing which, the Congress itself would withdraw from the interim government.

Practically a year had passed since the cabinet mission had been appointed to resolve India's political problems. The mission's efforts had proved futile, and the sorry state of India's affairs had become even sorrier.

The Call for Khalistan: Another Log in the Fire of Communalism

A new element of turmoil came from the friction that was developing between the Sikhs and the Muslims in Punjab. The Sikhs, a minority Punjabi community, had achieved remarkable solidarity since the turn of the century. Although they were demographically disadvantaged (14 percent of the Punjab population and less than 2 percent of the national population), the Sikhs were a prosperous section of Punjab society and contributed nearly one-third of the provincial revenue. More important, from the British point of view, they made good soldiers and constituted about 20 percent of the country's armed forces. The British recognized their importance and, as noted above, in the communal award of 1932, granted them separate electorates, though not the weightage they demanded.

Until the 1940s, the Sikhs had cooperated with the Congress while continuing to seek constitutional safeguards for their community. In 1944, Master Tara Singh, the head of the Akali Party (whose strength was rooted in its control of the Sikh religious institutions and which had emerged as the dominant Sikh religious-political party), perturbed by the possibility that Punjab would be made a part of Pakistan, declared that the Sikhs were also a separate nation and should be given the right to have an independent homeland. In 1946, Tara Singh wrote to the cabinet mission that the Akali Party preferred a united India, but if Pakistan was formed, it would insist on a separate Sikh state. Soon thereafter the Akali Party officially adopted a resolution calling for the establishment of a state called Sikhistan or Khalistan (Land of the Pure). -

During all the communal troubles from 1942 to 1947, the government of Punjab had remained in the hands of a non–Muslim League party (the Unionist Party) that was a coalition of Muslim, Hindu, and Sikh landed interests. However, the Unionist government, not being able to suppress the violence organized by the Muslim League's "direct action" units, resigned on March 2, 1947, clearing the way for a Muslim League takeover. The rumor that this decision was about to be taken had brought large crowds of Sikhs and Hindus to the Punjab Legislative Assembly, and when the decision was announced on March 4, it created pandemonium. Master Tara Singh, who was also there, unsheathed his sword and, brandishing it, shouted "Death to Pakistan" (Pakistan *Murdabad*) and "The Sikhs will rule" *(Raj karega Khalsa)*. Tara Singh had declared his own "direct action." The communal clashes that followed were marked by sickening savagery; within a few days thousands of people had lost their lives and hundred of thousands had fled their homes.

Partition and Independence

As we have seen, communalism and communal violence had made all schemes of a constitutional settlement unworkable. Except for Gandhi, who continued to trudge from one communal conflagration to another to try and bring back Hindu-Muslim understanding, not many any longer believed that independence was possible without some kind of partition; even the Congress had veered round to this position.

London hastened the process by announcing on February 20, 1947, that, come what may, Britain had decided to transfer power to some form of central government or to existing provincial governments "by a date not later than June 1948," and that Lord Louis Mountbatten had been appointed as the new viceroy to carry out the task. Mountbatten took over the viceroyalty on March 24, 1947. In actuality the British were not transferring, but abandoning power.

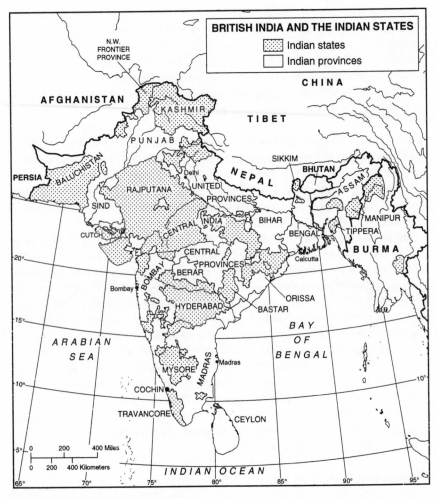

British India and the Indian States

Mountbatten, forty-six years old, had been commander-in-chief of the South-east Asia Command during the war and was known for his bold and quick decisions; he was also a cousin of the king-emperor, which gave him considerable political stature and a certain sense of confidence. He was a man in a hurry and he gave himself six months to reach a solution; as it turned out, he needed only two. After meeting all the leaders, Mountbatten came to the conclusion that there was no possibility of finding a solution that could keep India intact. By the end of May he had drawn up a partition plan that, after being approved by London, was presented, on June 3, to the leaders of the Congress, the Muslim League, and the Sikhs, who all accepted it. Mountbatten then disclosed that the transfer of power would take place within seventy-five days, on August 14, 1947.

The Mountbatten plan divided the subcontinent into three parts. Two of these areas, separated by a thousand miles, were to constitute Pakistan: a western wing, or West Pakistan, composed of NWF Province, Sind, Baluchistan, and *Muslim-majority districts* of Punjab (western Punjab); and an eastern wing, or East Pakistan, which would include *Muslim-majority districts* of Bengal (East Bengal), and the *Muslim-majority district of Sylhet* in Assam. The rest of British India—the six Hindu-majority provinces (Bihar, Orissa, United Provinces, Central Provinces, Bombay, and Madras), Assam minus Sylhet, and the Hindu- and Sikh-majority districts of eastern Punjab and West Bengal—would constitute independent India. Power would be transferred to the two governments, each of which would be granted dominion status with the right of secession. The transfer of power would also end the Crown's paramountcy over the Princely States, which would then have the option of joining one of the dominions or remaining unattached; the last was an impractical option, as the Princely States were to soon realize. By August 15, 1947, the 500-odd Princely States (except for three, including Hyderabad and Kashmir, which later were a source of trouble) located in non-Pakistan India had, through persuasion, acceded to the dominion of India.

Mountbatten had given very little time for the immense task entailed by the partition: new boundaries had to be drawn in Punjab and Bengal, the armed forces had to be divided, civil and military materials had to be apportioned, and civil and military officials not opting to serve in the dominion in which they happened to be located had to move over to the other dominion. Most of these issues were handled in a fairly efficacious way, but the Boundary Award came only on August 14. It had been delayed to the last hour to avoid a preemptive Hindu-Sikh attack on Lahore, which was to go to Pakistan, or a similar Muslim attack on Calcutta, which was awarded to India. As the subcontinent approached August 14, most of the country remained relatively calm, but in Punjab there was an unprecedented flare-up of communal violence.

Since every person in Punjab knew that, regardless of where the boundary line was actually drawn, the western districts of the province would go to Pakistan and the eastern districts to India, local interest groups began an organized onslaught on the minority groups to get them to flee to the other side, leaving their lands and properties behind. Thus, in anticipation of the partition, armed Muslim mobs in the western districts unleashed an orgy of violence not witnessed anywhere in the country until then. Hundreds of thousands of men, women, and children were slaughtered mercilessly, the dead bodies left around to be devoured by jackals and vultures. The Hindus and Sikhs displayed similar ferocity in eastern Punjab. It is calculated that over 10 million people were uprooted and fled to India or Pakistan as refugees. Neither the British nor the interim government headed by Nehru were prepared for this holocaust.

The coming of independence—to Pakistan on August 14 and to India on August 15—was celebrated with great abandon everywhere except in Punjab, which remained in the grip of communal frenzy for another two months. Theoretically, communalism, having fulfilled its purpose, should have died with the birth of Pakistan. Unfortunately, it continued to flourish. In fact, one can conclude that communalism, more than anything else, has thwarted the process of nation building in the independent nation-state of India.

Notes

1. Quoted in R. C. Majumdar, gen. ed., *The History and Culture of the Indian People: Struggle for Freedom* (Bombay: Bharatiya Vidya Bhavan, 2nd Edition, 1978), p. 61.

2. Ibid., pp. 56–57.

3. Sneh Mahajan, *Imperialist Strategy and Moderate Politics: Indian Legislature at Work 1909–1920* (Delhi: Chanakya Publications, 1983), p. 71.

4. Quoted in Reginald Reynolds, *The White Sahibs in India* (Westport, CT: Greenwood Press, 1970), p. 184.

5. Quoted in Sachchidananda Bhattacharya, *A Dictionary of Indian History* (Westport, CT: Greenwood Press, 1977), p. 514.

6. Geoffrey Moorhouse, *India Britannica* (London: Paladin Grafton Books, 1984), p. 172.

7. Quoted in Majumdar, *Struggle for Freedom*, p. 253.

8. Shan Muhammad, *The Growth of Muslim Politics in India* (New Delhi: Ashish, 1991), pp. 135–136.

9. Sumit Sarkar, *Modern India: 1885–1947* (Delhi: Macmillan India Limited, 1983), p. 149.

10. Don Dignan, *The Indian Revolutionary Problem in British Diplomacy: 1914–1919* (New Delhi: Allied Publishers, 1983), p. 23.

11. J. B. Kripalani, *Gandhi: His Life and Thought* (New Delhi: Publications Division, 1991), p. 337.

12. Iqbal Singh, *Indian National Congress: A Reconstruction, Vol II: 1919–1923* (Riverdale, MD: The Riverdale Company, 1989), p. 163.

13. Quoted in Susanne Hoeber Rudolph et al., *Gandhi: The Traditional Roots of Charisma* (Chicago: University of Chicago Press, 1983), p. 4.

14. Jawaharlal Nehru, *India and the World* (London: Allan & Unwin, 1936), pp. 172–176.

15. Quoted in Hugh Tinker, *India and Pakistan: A Political Analysis* (New York: Frederick A. Praeger, 1968), p. 23.

16. Quoted in Ram Gopal, *Indian Muslims: A Political History, 1858–1947* (New Delhi: Asia Publishing House, 1964), p. 166.

17. Quoted in M. J. Akbar, *Nehru: The Making of India* (London: Viking, Penguin, 1988), p. 217.

18. Quoted in Meena Gautam, *Communalism and Indian Politics* (Delhi: Pragati Publications, 1993), p. 47.

19. Quoted in Majumdar, *Struggle for Freedom*, p. 464.

20. Geoffrey Ash, *Gandhi* (New York: Stein & Day, 1968), p. 291.

21. Quoted in Bence-Jones, *The Viceroys of India* (New York: St. Martin's Press, 1982), p. 258.

22. Ibid., p. 259.

23. Gurdev Singh Deol, *Shaheed Bhagat Singh: a Biography* (Patiala, Punjab: Punjabi University, 1969), p. 58.

24. P. Sitaramaya, *The History of Indian National Congress*, Vol. 1 (Bombay: Padma Publications, 1946), p. 456.

25. Quoted in Deol, *Shaheed Bhagat Singh*, p. 101.

26. Quoted in Gautam, *Communalism and Indian Politics*, pp. 112–113.

27. Quoted in Majumdar, *Struggle for Freedom*, p. 523.

28. See Sarvepalli Gopal, *Jawaharlal Nehru: A Biography, Vol I: 1889–1947* (Cambridge, MA: Harvard University Press, 1976), pp. 206–207, 210, 214, 217–218.

29. Quoted in D. A. Low, *Eclipse of Empire* (Cambridge: Cambridge University Press, 1991), p. 94.

30. The attack was made at the 1937 annual session of the Muslim League.

31. Quoted in Richard Sisson and Stanley Wolpert, eds., *Congress and Indian Nationalism* (Berkeley: University of California Press, 1988), p. 37.

32. See Gopal, *Indian Muslims: A Political History*, p. 258.

33. Ibid., p. 264.

34. Majumdar, *Struggle for Freedom*, p. 613.

35. Stephen N. Hay, ed., *Sources of Indian Tradition*, Vol. 2 (New York: Columbia University Press, 1964), p. 286.

36. See the section on India in the *Foreign Relations of the United States, Diplomatic Papers, 1942*. The papers reveal that Roosevelt had been advised by the State Department and the Foreign Relations Committee of the U.S. Senate that "India should be given a status of autonomy."

37. Bence-Jones, *The Viceroys of India*, p. 285.

38. "The Cripps Mission to India," *International Conciliation*, Vol. 381 (New York: Carnegie Endowment for International Peace, June 1942), p. 340.

39. Ibid., p. 347.

40. Ibid., p. 352. See also Khuswant Singh, *The History of the Sikhs*, Vol. 2 (Delhi: Oxford University Press, 1991), p. 250.

41. Roland Hunt and John Harrison, *The District Officer in India, 1930–1947* (London: Scolar Press, 1980), p. 218.

42. For fuller details see, Majumdar, *Struggle for Freedom*, pp. 643–650.

43. Quoted in Penderel Moon, *The British Conquest and Dominion of India* (London: Gerald Duckworth & Co., 1989), p. 1114.

44. See quotes in Francis G. Hutchins, *India's Revolution: Gandhi and the Quit India Movement* (Cambridge, MA: Harvard University Press, 1973), p. 201; and Bipin Chandra et al., *India's Struggle for Independence* (New Delhi: Penguin Books, 1989), p. 459.

45. Hutchins, *India's Revolution*, p. 203.

46. Figures in this and the following paragraph are taken from Hutchins, *India's Revolution*, pp. 230–231.

47. Quoted in Sarkar, *Modern India, 1885–1947*, p. 391.

48. Ibid., p. 273.

49. Hunt and Harrison, *The District Officer in India: 1930–1947*, p. 218.

50. M. E. Chamberlain, *Decolonization: The Fall of the European Empires* (Oxford: Basil Blackwell, 1985), p. 22.

51. Maulana Abul Kalam Azad, *India Wins Freedom* (Madras: Orient Longman, 1988), p. 142.

52. Gopal, *Jawaharlal Nehru*, Vol. I, p. 326.

Part III
Independent India
Search for National Identity

7

Jawaharlal Nehru, 1947–1964

The Shaping of a New Order

Regardless of all the trauma associated with partition, as far as Britain and the Congress were concerned, the transfer of power in 1947 was peaceful; the Congress took over the government as a running concern with all the old institutional control apparatuses remaining intact and in place. The most important of these, no doubt, was the civil bureaucracy headed by the elitist Indian Civil Service (ICS) that was a powerful, nonpolitical organ of the central government; the ICS carried out central policies and supervised the administration of the entire country. The name Indian Civil Service was changed to Indian Administrative Service (IAS), and Indians replaced the departing British officers, but the "steel frame," as the British had called it, continued to serve in its multifunctional national capacity. There were other central (railways, customs, income tax, etc.) and state services (provincial civil service, provincial police service, etc.), too, that carried on without much disruption.

One very valuable legacy from the British, though less visible than the IAS, was the highly disciplined and experienced army that has largely maintained its old structure and traditions of training and service. The nonpolitical army, relatively small in size (because a part of the original British-Indian army had left for England and another had been acquired by Pakistan), that was inherited by independent India proved its professionalism, fighting skill, and loyalty to its motherland within weeks of partition, when the Kashmir War (discussed below) broke out. There was some debate over the feasibility of retaining the "imperialist" ICS-style bureaucracy, but none over the acceptance of the armed forces into the new body politic.

The transfer was also smooth because the Congress, organized as it was from the district level, through the provincial level, to the national level, had a national structure and it could, using the machinery of parliamentary democracy, move into all levels of political authority in the country as a whole. The Congress, as a monolithic party, thus initially helped to maintain a sense of national unity and solidarity. (The fact that the Congress was *not* a genuine political party but an umbrella organization under which many small parties with differing ideologies coexisted would cause problems later.) These advantages were, however, counterbalanced by two formidable handicaps: (1) the government was faced by a highly fragmented and communalized society that had yet to be welded into a nation, and (2) it had to deal with the immense social, economic, and political problems created by partition.

The Tasks of State Building and Nation Building

As we have seen in the previous chapters, pre-British traditional India had no concept of an all-India political unit, though the traditional Hindu socioreligious society had an overarching religious unity, symbolized by the pilgrimage centers that dotted the entire map of the subcontinent. The Hindu, in the practically autonomous world of his caste, lived in relative freedom, touched by politics only to the extent that the ruler, Muslim or Hindu, impinged on his space through wars or taxes. This was a system of relatively peaceful coexistence: the castes coexisted, as did the peoples of various religions—each in its own ghetto—doing business with each other but living their entirely separate social and personal lives.

The British period brought a radical change to the old order that replaced traditional coexistence with an environment of mutual suspicion and hostility. The rise of nationalism (a wholly new phenomenon) and the struggle for freedom gradually politicized the peoples of the country and made them conscious of the fact that the British government was not "their government." Simultaneously the British, although they made every attempt to thwart the growth of nationalism by encouraging separatist and communalistic tendencies, did introduce democratic institutions to satisfy Indian nationalistic impulses.

These two developments changed the relationship of the people as a whole to politics, making them participants in the fulfillment of national aspirations; and the relationship of the castes, classes, and religious communities to each other, making them competitors for economic and political advantages. Thus the struggle for freedom at one level gave birth to the concept of nationalism and a unified Indian political state, while on another level it undermined that very concept by generating parochial and communalistic trends associated with caste, class, and religion. The consequence of the partitioning of the country on the basis of the Muslim communal demand had the effect of weakening the frail all-India nationalistic impulse engendered by the Congress and of strengthening the already relatively well-developed forces of localism and communalism.

In 1947, a free India emerged as a new state in the international state system, but it was neither a state proper, connoting a well-defined territorial entity (the

Princely States had yet to be absorbed; the issue of independence-demanding frontier tribes, such as the Nagas, had yet to be resolved; and the borders with China had yet to be settled), nor a state in the accepted sense of "nation-state." That the Indians had meekly accepted a part of the country as their state was, itself, an indication of how little headway had been made by modern nationalism. It is, therefore, not wholly shocking that the people would turn their wrath against each other rather than against the British. Is it not amazing that not one British was killed during partition, while thousands of Indians died at each other's hands?

In other words, the new state of India had yet to establish itself as a unified modern state. It was the task of the new government to establish the territorial integrity of the state as well as to mold it into a nation-state by articulating aggregative national goals and national aspirations that could bring social and political cohesion to a country where many divisive, counterproductive patterns of thought and behavior had become deeply entrenched during the decades of India's struggle for independence.

Jawaharlal Nehru, the most outstanding leader of independent India and its prime minister for the first seventeen years of its existence, tried to achieve the latter end by fostering a national identity based on the ideals of secularism and democracy. He aimed to do so by strengthening the democratic institutions, inherited from an "illegitimate" foreign power, by giving these institutions a genuine *secular, democratic content.*

Unfortunately for Nehru, the popular Gandhian tactic of civil disobedience, which had been used to harass the alien British government and undermine the source of its legitimacy, had also subverted the democratic principle that the people should seek relief for their demands through established institutions. As a consequence, while this democratic principle had yet to be universally understood and accepted, the disruptive Gandhian legacy could readily be employed against the legitimate Indian government itself. Fifty years after partition, the opposition parties (including the Congress in the regional states where it is not in power) continue to indulge in the politics of strikes, riots, and violence, and to ignore the rule of law and the peaceful approach to the resolution of conflict. Civil disobedience today often takes ridiculous forms: for example, students in schools and colleges, if they find an examination too difficult, go on strike, torch the examination hall, and beat up the invigilators.

The young Indian state had also to deal with religion-based separatist attitudes that had found their way into many political parties. Except for the Congress, which claimed to be nondenominational, many other parties, such as the Akali Party and the Mahasabha, openly and avidly identified themselves with one religion or another, and advocated militancy. Even where the Congress was concerned, Gandhi's unique notion of religion had come to be closely identified with that organization, and this, too, became an obstacle in Nehru's path to secularism.

Problems of Partition

Even as the new government began its state-building and nation-building endeavors, it had to face several unforeseen problems that were created by partition—problems that were intensified by the centrifugal forces carried over from pre-partition India and which called for prompt attention.

Refugees and Communalism

First, and foremost, the young, inexperienced government had to settle the millions of refugees who had poured into eastern Punjab, and the lesser numbers that had crossed over from East Pakistan into West Bengal. Apart from the logistics of resettlement, which took years to achieve, the Indian government had to placate anti-Pakistan and anti-Muslim passions aroused by the Punjabi refugees and their horror stories.

The West Bengal situation appeared to be better because there was no massive migration of the Punjab-type from East Pakistan. But as time passed the predicament in West Bengal turned out to be worse than in Punjab. West Pakistan had cleansed western Punjab of the Hindu and Sikh population with one fell stroke; the exodus from East Bengal, on the other hand, continued into the early 1970s, by which time practically all the Bengali Hindus, who had formed 22 percent of the East Pakistan population in 1951, and been reduced to less than 11 percent in 1961, had been driven out of the country. This apparently never-ending tragedy did not allow passions to cool in West Bengal or, for that matter, in the rest of India. After 1971, when East Pakistanis overthrew the Pakistan government and established independent Bangladesh, a wholly new problem arose when Bangladeshi Muslims began to infiltrate India through the porous borders of Assam and West Bengal. Today, it is estimated that there are over 1.5 million Bangladeshi Muslim illegal immigrants in India. It is not surprising that many Indians, mostly Hindus and Sikhs, would like to see these Bangladeshis forced to leave the country.

Partition and Gandhi's Assassination

The refugee problem, in turn, also meant that India could not establish an amicable relationship with Pakistan. In mid-January 1948, Gandhi, who was then in New Delhi, went on a fast to get the Hindus to treat their Muslim brethren, who had remained behind in India, better and to get the government to pay its monetary debts to Pakistan. The government responded to Gandhi's fast by making the payment to Pakistan, and the local Hindus also temporarily stopped attacking Muslim homes and refugee camps. Gandhi broke his fast, but not all Hindus were happy with Gandhi's stand and, on January 30, an extremist Hindu linked with the Mahasabha and the militant Rashtriya Swayamsewak Sangh (RSS: National Volunteer Force) shot and killed the Mahatma at his evening prayer meeting.

There was a massive, spontaneous outpouring of sentiment for Gandhi, and people from all levels of society felt a sense of personal loss and wept openly for their beloved Mahatma. The whole world paid tribute to the lonely seeker of truth who had given up his life in the cause of principled politics. However, the pity is that India, while perpetuating the memory of Gandhi by naming streets after him and putting up his statutes, soon forgot his message of humanity, compassion, and nonviolence. The right-wing Hindu extremist organizations made a quick recovery and reemerged as a dynamic factor in the further communalization of the politics of the country.

Partition, Communalism, and the Princely States

Another issue created by partition, and also affected by communalism, was related to the accession of the Princely States to India. As noted in the last chapter, all the 550 Princely States within the borders of India, except for Hyderabad, Junagadh, and Kashmir, had acceded to India by August 15, 1947. The nonaccession of these three states (Hyderabad and Junagadh, Hindu-majority states under Muslim rulers, were surrounded on all sides by Indian territory; Kashmir, a Muslim-majority state with a Hindu ruler, had borders that touched both Pakistan and India) proved a source of trouble to the new government of India. The problem of Junagadh was resolved with relative ease: When Junagadh (a small kingdom in the state now known as Gujarat) endeavored to accede to Pakistan, India just took over the state (November 1947) on the grounds of "internal disorder." A plebiscite held in early 1948 proved that the population was overwhelmingly in favor of accession.

In early 1947, before the decision on partition had even been taken, the Muslim ruler of Hyderabad (a large Princely State in southern India, second largest in the subcontinent) declared his intention to remain independent, and he created a "voluntary" Muslim militia to stay in power. India signed a Standstill Agreement* with Hyderabad and gave it a year to make up its mind. Hyderabad did not help its cause by lending $62 million to Pakistan or by allowing the militia to terrorize and harass the Hindus who constituted over 80 percent of the state's population. On September 13, 1948, India moved troops into the state and took "police action" to restore law and order. By September 18, Hyderabad had acceded to India.

The scenically beautiful northern state of Jammu and Kashmir (popularly referred to as Kashmir), the largest of the Indian Princely States, posed a different kind of problem. The Hindu *maharaja* of Kashmir ruled over a population of

---

*A Standstill Agreement was a transitional expedient that fell short of accession. By signing such an agreement, a state allowed the dominion concerned to handle defense, external affairs, and communications (subjects that the viceroy had controlled) but retained its internal sovereignty.

4 million, 77 percent of whom were Muslims. The *maharaja,* having jailed Sheikh Muhammad Abdulla, the nationalist Muslim leader of the popular, largely Muslim, National Conference Party with pro-Congress leanings, tried to retain his independence by signing a Standstill Agreement with Pakistan. Immediately after partition, Muslims in southwest Kashmir, backed by Pakistani "raiders," rose in revolt against the *maharaja.* The *maharaja,* knowing that he would not be able to repulse the raiders who were supported by Pakistan, turned to Nehru for help, but Nehru accepted Kashmir's Instrument of Accession only after Sheikh Abdulla had been released from jail and installed as head of a reconstituted government of Kashmir.

Indian troops reached Kashmir on October 27, 1947, in time to save Srinagar, the capital, and the Kashmir Valley, but they could not, by January 1948, when the United Nations–imposed cease-fire came into effect, get the Pakistani army to vacate the western half of the state. It was resolved at the United Nations that a plebiscite would be held to determine the wishes of the Kashmiri people, but since India and Pakistan interpreted the resolution differently, the plebiscite was never held. In due course, India, by a constitutional amendment, made Kashmir an irrevocable part of the republic of India.

Pakistan named the area under its control "Azad Kashmir" (Free Kashmir) and has not accepted this *de jure* merger of Kashmir with India, insisting that Muslim-majority Kashmir must separate from "Hindu-dominated" India. As time passed, Pakistan leaders also discovered that they could recover their declining popularity within the country by inflaming popular passions over the Kashmir issue. Thus, as one Pakistani political commentator points out, in 1965, when "the political situation in [Pakistan] had deteriorated" terribly, Pakistan decided to start a war with India "to focus attention once again on the people of Kashmir."[1] Pakistan lost the war, but not its interest in Kashmir. In 1990, Pakistan's Prime Minister Benazir Bhutto, "her support base wiped out by malfeasance and misrule, desperate to save herself, whipped out the Kashmir card, always the least expensive route to popularity in Pakistan . . . [and] came out in open support of secession."[2]

The current insurgency in Kashmir may have been inspired by Pakistan's calls for *jihad* and by Pakistan's material aid (money and guns) and support (military training and safe havens), but its roots can be traced to the communalism that gave birth to Pakistan: the notion that religion is reason enough to demand a separate homeland. From the end of 1988 to the present (2000), the militants and terrorists in Kashmir (many from Pakistan, Afghanistan, and other Middle Eastern Islamic states), in several fundamentalist Muslim organizations backed by Pakistan, have kept Kashmir in a continuous state of unrest and tension by driving the Hindu population out of the valley, assassinating prominent pro-Indian Muslims, and bombing government offices, police stations, and communication centers. This forced New Delhi to impose president's rule over the state (i.e., it replaced the locally elected government with central executive rule) from 1990 to 1996 and use armed police and the military to restore law and order. The

The Perpetuation of Communalism

Communalism, which did not disappear with the establishment of Pakistan, continues to affect Indian politics and society. The effects are most significant in four major areas. First, a large percentage of Muslims in the provinces and Princely States that form the union of India did not migrate to Pakistan. Since they had supported the cause of Pakistan, their continuance in India (there are over 120 million Muslims in India today in a population of nearly a billion) was, and to a lesser extent still is, considered by many Hindus as anomalous. These Muslims are often looked upon with suspicion, though as citizens of the Indian Republic, they are constitutionally equal to all other citizens of India.

Second, communalism, which had resulted in the establishment of Pakistan, confirmed the notion that a community, on the basis of its religious or ethnic identity, could demand a separate homeland. As a consequence, communities such as the Sikhs (who had talked of Khalistan even before partition), the Nagas, and the Kashmiri Muslims have, at one time or another after independence, risen in rebellion against India and demanded secession from the union. The government has had to crush these insurgencies through the use of armed police and military force (the Kashmiri secessionist movement has yet to be wholly quelled).

Third, the birth of Pakistan aroused such bitter communal passions that, nearly fifty years after partition, the relations between Pakistan and India remain estranged. The two countries have fought three wars that can all be related to communalism.

Fourth, worst of all, communalism and the fanaticism associated with it have penetrated Indian society deeper than it ever had before independence. "Communalism," says the educator Gaurinath Sastri, "has become an integral phenomenon of socio-political life in India. . . . The communalization of Indian politics and the creation of communal 'Vote Banks' and the political catering or appeasement to these 'Vote Banks' have an important bearing on communal conflict in the country."[*] In many areas, the politicians, the police force, the civil servants, and the courts have become a willing party to communal disturbances that have now extended from religious conflict to contentions based on caste, ethnicity, or linguistic differences.

---

[*]Gaurinath Shastri, "Foreword," in S. K. Ghosh, *Communal Riots in India: Meet the Challenge Unitedly* (New Delhi: Ashish Publishing House, 1987), p. viii.

---

internal war in Kashmir is not yet over, though the 1996 state elections have restored a modicum of civil government in the state.

Partition and the Economy

Partition also had an immediate impact on the Indian economy because it upset the economic integrity of the subcontinent. For example, the areas that came to constitute Pakistan produced a surplus of wheat, cotton, and jute, but were short of coal and sugar and had hardly any cotton or jute mills, while the territories that came to form the Indian union were grain-short and needed all the cotton and jute they could get for their mills.

After the lapse of fifty years the trade and commercial issues between the two countries have yet to be fully settled. What needs to be emphasized here is that the severe food shortage caused by partition in 1947 was regarded as "one of the prime causes"[3] of the state of emergency declared by the Indian government soon after independence; food had to be imported from abroad for many years after partition.

The Nehru Era: 1947–1964

On August 15, 1947, India achieved full freedom, but for constitutional reasons it had only gained the status of a dominion in the British Commonwealth. It was only on January 26, 1950, when the Indian Constitution came into force, that the sovereign republic of India was established. Until then, the political system demanded that India have a governor-general as the symbolic head of state. At the request of Jawaharlal Nehru, head of the interim government, and Rajendra Prasad, president of the Constituent Assembly, Mountbatten was invited to serve as the first governor-general of independent India. After Mountbatten retired from this post in 1948, he was succeeded by Rajagopalachari, whom we mentioned earlier in connection with his talks with Jinnah after the Quit India movement was launched; Rajagopalachari was replaced on January 26, 1950, by Rajendra Prasad, who became the first president of the republic of India.

Nehru was already a nationally recognized and much-admired leader when he became prime minister in 1947. He retained that office until his death in 1964. He was, no doubt, a great statesman and thinker, whose abiding commitment to democracy, secular politics, and social justice has had a great impact on India's formative years. Nehru was appalled by communalism and narrow-minded religious attitudes because they not only hurt his sense of values but, more so, he saw in them a threat to national unity. Nehru knew that the nineteenth-century Western notion of nationalism had lost its meaning and utility in the West, but as he said, "for us in India, we have to build true nationalism, integrating the various parts and creeds and religions of our country, before we can launch out into real internationalism."[4]

As we have seen in our discussion of the legacy of partition, Nehru came in at a time when the country was facing a disastrous situation. However, he and his handpicked cabinet, composed of outstanding Indian statesmen, politicians, and thinkers (Nehru's cabinets always included members who represented Muslim, Sikh, Harijan, and Christian communities), tackled the task of national consolidation and reconstruction with admirable energy and devotion. In time, the principle that cabinets should represent all important minority communities became a permanent feature of future Indian governments.

Toward National Integration

The Constitution

The Constitution of India was adopted by the Constituent Assembly in November 1949, and it became the law of the land on January 26, 1950, establishing India as a sovereign, democratic, republic. The Indian Constitution, perhaps the longest of all modern written constitutions, is an impressive document that borrows much from the politically liberal states of the West, but, more importantly, enshrines the collective aspiration of all pre-partition Indian leaders that the state would "promote the welfare of the people by securing and promoting . . . a social order in which justice, social, economic, and political, shall inform all institutions of the national life" (Article 38).

The Constitution is federal in nature, but provides the central government with reserve powers so that, in the face of the divisive tendencies released by partition, a strong center would ensure the future integrity of the nation. The central government, if national interest so demands, has the right to legislate on any subject, even if it is on the list of state subjects. The center has the prerogative to invoke "presidential rule" to suspend any state government and bring it under direct central control for a period of six months, after which elections must be held in the state and the democratic political system restored.

The Constitution, by ensuring the universality of laws that transcend both the citizens and the government; by discarding the British-imposed communal electorates; and by introducing universal suffrage, confirms the secularity of the union. Although there was a risk in introducing universal suffrage in a country where the illiteracy rate was about 86 percent, the experiment has proved eminently successful in leading India toward democracy inasmuch as it has proved that illiteracy does not mean that the peasant masses do not have a shrewd understanding of what is good for them. It is a different matter that in a resource-poor country, democracy has also brought some unhealthy tendencies that heighten factionalism and corrupt practices. For the structure of the government, see diagram below; the Parliament, particularly its lower house, represents the sovereign will of the people.

The main features of the Indian Constitutional system are as follows:

1. *The President.* He or she is elected by Parliament and state legislatures, is the head of state and symbol of the nation, and exercises his or her executive power through the prime minister and the prime minister's cabinet. The president has emergency powers whereby he or she can, if the law and order in any state breaks down and the situation is considered to pose a threat to the unity of the country, remove the elected government of the state and introduce President's Rule. This kind of extraordinary power was held by the viceroy in British India and had been condemned by the Congress, but for reasons explained earlier, the president was given similar powers by the

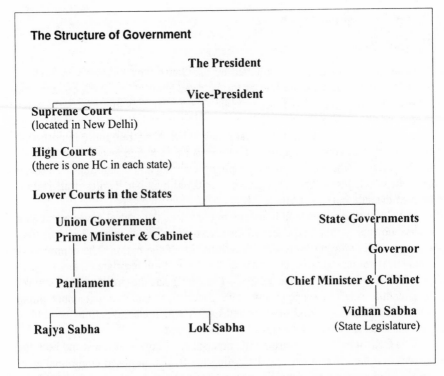

The Structure of Government

The President

Vice-President

Supreme Court
(located in New Delhi)

High Courts
(there is one HC in each state)

Lower Courts in the States

Union Government
Prime Minister & Cabinet

State Governments

Governor

Parliament

Chief Minister & Cabinet

Vidhan Sabha
(State Legislature)

Rajya Sabha   Lok Sabha

Constitution. Since the President's Rule is imposed at the advice of the cabinet, it opened the possibility of the central government misusing this power, and that, indeed, came to pass under prime ministers who followed Nehru.

2. *The Vice-President.* He or she is elected by both houses of Parliament. The vice-president is chairman of the Rajya Sabha and takes over as president if the latter dies in office.

3. *The Judicial System.* India has a single judicial system with a Supreme Court at the center and a High Court in each state; the High Court oversees the lower courts of the state. The judiciary is independent of the executive and the legislatures, and the judges have no involvement with politics. The chief justice and the fourteen judges of the Supreme Court and the chief justices and other judges of the High Courts are appointed by the president in consultation with sitting judges. The High Courts superintend the work of the lower courts, whose judges are appointed by the governor of the state in consultation with the High Court.

4. *Union Government.* After an election, the head of the majority party in Parliament is appointed prime minister (PM) by the president. The PM selects his or her own cabinet of ministers who are also from the majority party in the Parliament; they, too, are sworn in by the president. The execu-

tive is answerable to the legislature. All this makes the executive's relationship with the legislature much closer than it is in the United States.

5. *The Parliament.* The Parliament is composed of two houses: the Lok Sabha (House of the People, or Lower House) and the Rajya Sabha (Council of States, or Upper House). The Lok Sabha, as the country's main lawmaking body, is supposed to hold central importance in the Indian parliamentary system, however its work has come to be overshadowed by the executive. The Lok Sabha is composed of 545 members, 543 of whom are directly elected through universal suffrage from nationwide constituencies, and its normal life is five years. (It can be shortened if the cabinet loses a vote of confidence and resigns, and another government cannot be formed. Thereupon the Lok Sabha is dissolved and fresh elections held.)

The Rajya Sabha is composed of 250 members, a few of whom are nominated; one-third of the remaining are elected every two years by the Vidhan Sabhas (legislatures of the states), which gives it its English name, Council of States. Like the House of Lords in England, the Rajya Sabha is a weak chamber, though it can originate bills (which can only become law if the Lok Sabha approves them) and does review bills moved in the Lok Sabha (it cannot reject them but can improve the language and content). The Rajya Sabha cannot be dissolved.

6. *State Government.* The government of each of the twenty-five states of the Indian Republic is similar to that of the union government. The governor, like the president at the center, is the constitutional head of the state. The governor, often a retired civil service officer, is appointed by the president on the recommendation of the prime minister for a term of five years. Like the president, the governor holds the formal executive power, which is actually exercised by the chief minister and his or her cabinet (just as the prime minister and his or her cabinet do at the center) who are sworn in by the governor. If, for some reason, the state cannot form a stable government, or if law and order in the state breaks down, the state can be brought under President's Rule. In this case, the governor has the authority to take over all executive power and govern the state under the guidance of the center.

The chief minister is the leader of the majority party in the Vidhan Sabha and selects his or her own ministers from the majority party in the Vidhan Sabha to form the state cabinet. Both the chief ministers and the ministers are sworn in by the governor.

The Vidhan Sabha (state legislative assembly), like the Lok Sabha at the center, is directly elected through universal suffrage in the state for a term of five years; it is the lawmaking body of the state and represents the "will of the people of the state." It is not surprising that over the decades, the members of the state legislative assemblies (MLAs) have become truly representative of the masses; this is reflected in the increase of non-English-speaking MLAs who have close links with their constituencies.

The Constitution provides the country with the institutional means to facilitate an orderly national integration and social assimilation. For example, the fundamental rights (equality, freedom, right against exploitation, freedom of religion, property, and cultural and educational rights) abolish Untouchability, forbid the practice of Untouchability in any form, and prescribe that no citizen shall be discriminated against on grounds of religion, race, caste, sex, or place of birth. Among the rights and freedoms, the Constitution guarantees the freedom of conscience and the right to profess, practice, *and propagate* religion, subject to public order and morality. However, no institution supported by federal funds can offer religious instruction. Provision is made to help the advancement of the disadvantaged Scheduled Castes and Scheduled Tribes by reserving seats for them in the Lok Sabha and the Vidhan Sabhas.

In its Directive Principles of State Policy, the Constitution contends that, in making laws, it is the duty of the State to be guided by certain principles such as social welfare, an equitable economic system, decent working conditions for the workers, equal pay for men and women, compulsory free education (after ten years of the inauguration of the Constitution; over 50 years later, the clause has yet to be enforced), improvement of public health (which includes the center's endeavor to introduce prohibition of liquor and drugs), banning of cow slaughter (on economic grounds), and protection for women and children from exploitation.

The Constitution gives official recognition to fourteen (a later amendment increased the number to fifteen*) languages, prescribes that Hindi is the official language of the union, and gave the country fifteen years to shift over from English to Hindi. Unfortunately, there was strong opposition to the language policy from non-Hindi-speaking peoples in the south because the imposition of Hindi as the national language was seen as giving preference to the north at the expense of the south. The language policy heightened pressure on the government to establish linguistic states where the recognized local language could be used as the medium of instruction and official communication. As a consequence, fifty years after independence, English has yet to be replaced by Hindi.

The Reorganization of the States

Pre-independence India was composed of two parts: British India, divided into governor's provinces, and Native India, comprising 550 autonomous Princely States that had direct treaty relations with the Crown of England. Many of the governor's provinces had grown haphazardly, expanding as the British gained new territories from their wars of expansion and came to absorb geographically different areas with disparate cultures and languages. Many felt that for a proper

---

*Assamese, Bengali, Gujarati, Hindi, Kannada, Kashmiri, Malayalam, Marathi, Oriya, Punjabi, Sanskrit, Sindhi, Tamil, Telugu, and Urdu.

development of the country the old administrative boundaries should be redrawn on linguistic lines.

The Dissolution of the Princely States. As far as the Princely States were concerned, they had acceded to the Indian union by signing an Instrument of Accession, but this did not mean that they had been fully integrated into the Indian administrative system; the instrument had only replaced the paramountcy of the Crown of England with that of the government of India, and the Princely States still retained their autonomy and residual sovereignty. Immediately following independence, the task of fully integrating the Princely States into the union was brilliantly performed by Sardar Vallabhbhai Patel, deputy prime minister and minister for states and home affairs.

The first step in the process was the creation of three categories of states under the Constitution: Part A, Part B, and Part C states (please note that the term *province* was replaced by the term *state*). One hundred eleven of the very small Princely States were merged with the nine old British provinces* that were now designated Part A states; 275 other small and medium-size Princely States were integrated into five large unions, each of which was placed under a council of princes who elected a *rajpramukh* (chief of state) from among themselves. The rulers of the three large Princely States of Kashmir, Hyderabad, and Mysore became *rajpramukhs* of their own territorial units. These five unions and the three units formed Part B states, and had to develop their own elected legislatures and cabinets responsible to the legislatures. Lastly, the remaining sixty-one medium-size states (some of which were merged with each other) and the three centrally administered Chief Commissioner's Provinces (Ajmer, Coorg, Delhi) were placed directly under the administration of the central government and constituted the Part C states.

Later, these three categories of states were dissolved and reorganized (discussed below) and by 1962, India had fifteen states (please note that this is how the administrative political units of the country would be known henceforth), and eight centrally administered union territories.† As a result of these changes, the Princely States lost their identity and the princes their right to rule; each prince was given a "privy purse" (i.e., an income; some privy purses were very big) but reduced to the level of an ordinary citizen of India. The integration of the Princely States into the Union was a major achievement.

The Formation of Linguistic States. In contrast to the relatively peaceful absorption of the Princely States, the reorganization of the country into linguistic states was accompanied with violence and political trouble. Before independence, the Congress itself had divided British India into language-based

---

*Punjab, United Provinces, Bihar, Bengal, Assam, Orissa, Central Provinces, Madras, and Bombay.

†After 1962, more states were carved out of the existing ones. Today India has twenty-five states and seven union territories.

Hindi as a Nonunifying Factor!

There were several reasons why Hindi failed to get established as the national unifying language. First, Hindi was considered the dominant language of the country and, supposedly, 75 percent of the population in fifteen of the twenty-eight states (the Part A, B, and C states) spoke Hindi. In fact, many so-called speakers of Hindi, like the Punjabis, did not actually speak that language.

Second, the proponents of Hindi turned "official" Hindi into such a Sanskritized language that even the people whose languages are Sanskrit-based (i.e., all northern Indian languages), and who could have very easily learned Hindi, were turned against it. Instead of accepting English and Urdu words in current use, the Official Language Committee, in charge of preparing a Hindi lexicon, created such bizarre words as *agnirathyantraviramsthan* (fire-vehicle-station) for "railway station,"* a term every illiterate peasant understands and uses.

Third, the non-Aryan Dravidian peoples of south India, whose languages (Tamil, Telugu, Malayalam, and Kannada) are not Sanskrit-based, felt that Hindi was being imposed on them and that Hindi, as a national language, would always give northerners an advantage over southerners.

To make matters worse, agitations against Hindi in the south coalesced into a Dravidian movement against the Brahmins, who had dominated political and social life for centuries and were now attacked as representatives of the northern Aryan invaders who had "enslaved" the south; the Dravidians held that they were a nation entitled to sovereign independence. The Dravidian movement lost ground after Dravidian-language–based linguistic states were established.

---

*See D. B. Vohra, *A Panoramic History of the Indian People* (New Delhi: Munshiram Manoharlal, 1992), p. 276.

"Congress provinces," where the local branches of the Congress could use the local languages to facilitate their organizational and propaganda work. After independence, however, the Congress was hesitant to accept linguistic provinces because of the fear that this would increase local friction and tensions and strengthen the forces of division. The local political leaders, who had exploited the cultural and historic consciousness of *their language area* to gain power, were naturally disappointed. Many linguistic groups that were spread across the borders of two, sometimes three, states found themselves in a disadvantaged position as linguistic minorities.

Nehru resisted demands for linguistic states for six years, hoping that Hindi would gain acceptance as the national language in less than the fifteen years allowed by the Constitution and the need for linguistic states would disappear.

The Telugu-speaking people, who were located in an area that covered parts of Madras state and Hyderabad, and who had a well-developed historic consciousness of being descendants of those who had once ruled the powerful Andhra empire, were the first to agitate for a separate state. The center resisted, but when a Gandhian Telugu nationalist, Potti Sriramalu, fasted to death (December 1952) fighting for the creation of the Andhra Pradesh (*pradesh* means state), New Delhi gave in and Andhra state was established in 1953.

The demand for linguistic states was whetted by the success of the Telugus. Trouble was already brewing between Gujaratis and Marathis in Bombay, a huge state that included the entire Gujarati-speaking area but not all of Marathi-speaking area. The Gujaratis wanted to be separated from Bombay. The Marathis wanted Maharashtra (The Great State), a state that would cover most of the erstwhile Maratha empire, or at least unite the Marathi-speaking territories in Bombay, Hyderabad, and Madhya Pradesh. There were similar demands for a Kannada-speaking state (that would include most of Mysore but also extend into Hyderabad and Madras), a Malayalam-speaking state (that would cover Cochin, most of Travancore, and a part of Madras), and a Tamil-speaking state that would automatically be created if the areas where the people spoke Telugu, Kannada, and Malayalam were taken out of the old British-created Madras Province. Among the other important contestants one must mention the Sikhs in Punjab, who wanted a Punjabi-speaking state.

In 1953, when Andhra emerged as a separate entity, the center set up the States Reorganization Commission to consider the whole question of redrawing state boundaries. The commission, after two years of deliberation, produced a report that warned against "local loyalties" being allowed to undermine "national loyalty," but at the same time, it recommended some boundary changes. The response from the advocates of linguistic states was, however, so violent that an alarmed Nehru could not help bewailing that "the poison" of "communalism, casteism, provincialism and all that" had come to taint the very leadership of the Congress Party.[5] Nevertheless, in September 1956, the twenty-seven Part A, B, and C states currently in existence were reduced to fourteen states and six union territories. The boundaries of all states except Bombay and Punjab were redrawn to conform to the dominant language of the area. The commission also ignored the demands of Nagaland and Jharkhand for separate tribal states.

The commission's attempt to retain Bombay as it was angered the Marathas, who organized the Samyukta Maharashtra Samiti (United Maharashtra Committee) and launched a violent agitation for the creation of Maharashtra. In 1960, the center accepted the inevitable and divided Bombay into the states of Gujarat and Maharashtra, giving the city of Bombay to Maharashtra. This left the issues of Punjab and Nagaland unresolved. These areas exploded into violence in the post-Nehru era and are discussed later in the chapter.

In 1957, the movement for linguistic provinces appeared to have released centrifugal forces that, in the words of Rajagopalachari, were "bound to prevail" and bring "political anarchy" to India.[6] By 1964, when Nehru left the scene, the doomsayers had been proved wrong and India had successfully resolved the first major national crisis. Indeed, as time was to prove, the reorganized states strengthened the federal system and the unity of India. It did, however, mean that English would remain the link-language for interstate and state-center communications for a long time, and would perpetuate the English-speaking elite who formed no more than 4 percent of the population.

The Integration of Foreign Enclaves into the Union

The British departure from India had left behind several small French and Portuguese colonial enclaves. The biggest was Portuguese Goa, located on the west coast south of Bombay. In 1950, Goa had a population of about 650,000, of whom 800 were Portuguese and other Europeans. Portugal also held three tiny enclaves located in Saurashtra—Daman, Diu, and Haveli (total size: 314 square miles)—that were separated by a thousand miles from Goa. The French had five possessions, also at varying distances from each other, the biggest being Pondicherry, an insignificant port south of Madras.

On gaining independence, India opened negotiations with Portugal and France regarding the transfer of these territories to the Indian union. Nobody believed that these enclaves had any right to continue to exist as foreign colonies or that they would not revert to India. The French, in a very civilized manner, resolved the issue of their possessions by 1954. In 1952, on the basis of a referendum held in Chandernagore (located in the vicinity of Calcutta), that enclave reverted to India; in 1954, negotiations between New Delhi and Paris concluded with the administration of the remaining four territories being handed over to India. These arrangements were formalized in a treaty signed by the two countries.

Portugal, however, displayed a more inflexible stand and failed to be persuaded by diplomatic means. In 1951, Lisbon amended its constitution and converted its possessions in India into an overseas Province, thereby foreclosing any discussion regarding the reversion of these territories to India. Nehru continued to stress the need to solve the problem peacefully, but national sentiment demanded some kind of forceful action. In 1955, the cold war brought a new twist to the situation: that year Premier Bulganin of the USSR and Nikita Khrushchev, first secretary of the Soviet Communist Party, visited New Delhi and made a statement that India had every right to take over the Portuguese colonies; the U.S. secretary of state, John Foster Dulles (who had condemned Nehru's policy of nonalignment as "immoral"), issued a joint statement with the foreign minister of Portugal, confirming that Goa was a province of Portugal. India reacted to the statement by ordering Portugal to close its embassy in New Delhi. Ultimately, in 1961, despite a barrage of criticism from the U.S.-led Western camp, India moved troops into Goa and in twenty-six hours the process of the integration of foreign enclaves into the Indian union was concluded.

Working for Development and Social Justice

Jayaprakash Narayan, the head of the Socialist Party, who had worked with Nehru for decades before the Socialist Party was forced to leave the Congress in 1948 (see below), has summed up Nehru rather well. He says that Nehru "had the soul of a poet, a most kindly heart and sensitive mind that reacted instantly to poverty and human misery . . . [and he] had the unique good fortune, among thinkers and revolutionaries, to have the opportunity . . . to put his ideas into practice."[7]

Nehru's idea was "to bring the whole picture of India's future—agricultural, industrial, social, and economic—into a single framework of thought and action,"[8] so that "every man, woman and child in this country has a fair deal and attains a minimum standard of living."[9] This was a noble goal and Nehru, who dominated Indian politics, tried to realize it through his brand of socialism, which was a combination of ideas borrowed from the Fabians, Marx, and Gandhi. Nehru failed to achieve his aim during his lifetime, but his socialist beliefs got embedded in Congress ideology and his five-year-plan approach got institutionalized.

Pushed by Nehru, the Congress in 1955 passed a resolution that declared that India must aim at establishing a "socialistic pattern" of society; unfortunately, nobody until today has been able to define that phrase satisfactorily. As time passed, the gap between the abstract Nehruvian ideals and the concrete reality of the Indian social-political scene increased, and Nehru's ill-defined notion of socialism became an obstacle to the country's economic development: the public sector grew larger, more unwieldy, more bureaucratic, more inefficient, and less productive. In contrast, the small private sector remained efficient and productive, even though it was hemmed in by bureaucratic controls. The need to speed up India's progress forced the Congress, in the 1980s, to reduce the emphasis on the "socialistic pattern" and in the 1990s to practically abandon the ideology altogether and shift to a freer market approach.

Nehru failed in his endeavor because even though "from the end of 1950 the Government of India was basically a one man show,"[10] he was no dictator and had to work in a national and international environment that was not always congenial. Apart from the problems created by shortages, a growing population, mass illiteracy, and communalism, Nehru had to compromise with his opponents within the Congress and the Parliament, and divert massive amounts of scarce funds to defense, particularly after the war with China in 1962.

Nehru and the Congress Party

When the Congress formed the national government in 1947, it was a party that had no coherent, well-defined ideology, and it suffered from factionalism and infighting; the party was broadly split among the village-oriented Gandhians, the

Hindu Conservatives led by Sardar Patel, and Nehru's progressive left wing, all with significantly different ideologies. If Nehru was to carry out *his* policies, he needed to either get them approved democratically by his contentious colleagues or make the Congress a subservient, pliable body. After finding the former approach frustrating, Nehru made the Congress more pliant by gaining control of its organization. His ascendancy over the Congress was helped to a degree by fortuitous circumstances. Gandhi's death in 1948 reduced the status and voice of the Gandhians and Patel's death in 1950 removed one of the leading Conservatives from the scene.

However, unlike the Gandhians, who had never really been too involved in active politics, the Conservatives were a formidable group with some remarkably outstanding leaders like Sardar Patel and Purushottam Das Tandon. As long as he was living, Patel, as deputy prime minister and minister of home affairs, represented the Conservatives in the government, and he openly disagreed with Nehru over several important issues. For example, Patel was partial to Hindu nationalism, which Nehru abhorred; Patel did not favor a conciliatory approach toward the Muslims or Pakistan, which Nehru did; and Patel's support of private enterprise and property rights went against Nehru's socialistic ideas.

In 1948, pressured by Patel, the Congress adopted a new Constitution that withdrew membership from all those who were members of another party that had a different constitution or program. Nobody could fault this move, which was intended to cleanse the Congress of fissiparous tendencies. The Congress, after all, had been an umbrella organization under which many parties had coexisted, including the Congress Socialist Party, founded by Jayaprakash Narayan in 1934, with which Nehru had had an intimate association. The new Congress Constitution forced Narayan and his followers to leave the Congress. Through this move, Patel may have meant to undermine Nehru's support in the Congress, but as it turned out, he did Nehru a favor: Nehru could now elaborate his own design of socialism without being hindered by the more dogmatic views of Narayan.

In August 1950, when the Congress was considering various candidates for the post of party president, Patel supported Tandon, who was condemned by Nehru as having "a communal and revivalist outlook."[11] Nehru would much rather have had the Gandhian Acharya Kripalani take over as president. When Tandon did get elected, Nehru took this as a personal affront and even toyed briefly with the idea of resigning from the prime ministership. However, he finally chose to stay on and fight the Conservatives and crush their opposition in the Congress. Nehru used his popularity and political stature to get the plenary session of the Congress to adopt various resolutions that supported his views on subjects such as communal relations and relations with Pakistan. He then secured a vote of full confidence from the Congress Parliamentary Committee. Patel's death in December 1950 weakened the Conservatives, and Nehru, having proved that he was indispensable to the Congress, proceeded to undermine Tandon by refusing to serve on the Working Committee of the Congress as constituted by Tandon as Congress president. Caught in a bind, the members of the Working Committee decided to resign and invite Nehru to reconstitute the committee. The outcome was that Tandon was forced to step down and let Nehru replace him as president of the Congress. After four years in that position, Nehru gave up that office, but only after handing it over to a person of his choice.

The Congress did not, as Tandon alleged, become "the slave of the Government," and it still remained a home for many different, if not contradictory points of view, but it did become "a junior partner"[12] of the prime minister. However, the trend set by Nehru was not a healthy one, and later, when his daughter, Indira Gandhi (1917–1984; Gandhi was her husband's surname; he was not related to Mahatma Gandhi), became prime minister, she did make the Congress a servile body.

It was Nehru, controlling the presidency of the Congress and prime minister-ship of India, the two most important offices in the country, who oversaw the planning-for-progress programs.

Toward a Socialist Economy

The notion of planning for economic development was not new to Nehru or the Congress. The Congress had, in 1938, established a National Planning Committee of which Nehru was chairman. In 1944, eight prominent industrialists had published "A Plan of Economic Development of India" (popularly known as the Bombay Plan), which envisaged utilizing $30 billion to double agricultural production, and triple industrial output in three five-year plans. It was purely a paper plan, but did excite considerable interest among Indian intellectuals. Also in 1944, the Indian Federation of Labor issued a People's Plan that was based on the assumption that all agricultural land would be nationalized and industry would be under government control. The Bombay Plan looked to a mixed economy, the People's Plan to a purely socialist economy.

When Nehru became prime minister of independent India, he had few choices. Given the poverty of the country and the backwardness of its industrial development, no one questioned the need for the state to play a major role in economic development. The only question was how far the state should go in its endeavors to control the economic arena. Nehru was not a communist and had no desire to duplicate the USSR model; he was at best a democrat-socialist who was anxious that India develop rapidly and increase its wealth so that poverty could be eliminated and living standards raised. Nehru wanted the state to introduce, encourage, and oversee the development of large-scale and small-scale economic enterprises, the former publicly owned and the latter cooperatively run. He also agreed that there was room for the private sector to contribute to the overall growth of the economy, but it was through planning above all that all these changes could be brought about.

Land Reform. The Congress had long debated the issue of land reform, and so immediately after independence, despite all its other major preoccupations, it established an Agrarian Reforms Committee (December 1947). The committee's recommendation to the Constituent Assembly was that the land system associated with *jagirdars* and *zamindars**—the semiautonomous intermediaries between the government and the peasants, who exploited the peasantry and perpetuated feudalism—must be ended and a ceiling imposed on land holdings to reduce disparities in the rural economy. The recommendation became the basis for the directive principle in Article 39 of the Constitution that said, in part, that the state shall ensure that the "economic system does not result in the concentration of wealth and means of production to the common detriment."[13]

The first step in the land reform program was aimed at the intermediaries, and in the 1950s, guided by policies formulated by the central government, the Vidhan Sabhas passed *zamindari abolition* bills (land was a state subject). This program of land reform eliminated *jagirdars* and *zamindars,* allowing them to keep only the land that was being cultivated under their personal direction. The rest of the land was bought from the landlords and distributed to those who actually cultivated it. Although the program resulted in the emergence of a significant number of very rich farmers (the *jagirdars* and *zamindars* who managed to retain much of their land by turning into farmers), it did bring the government in direct contact with all cultivators, most of whom were poor and could now benefit from lower taxes and state programs such as public works, education, and health. With limited surplus land available, the program could not, however, eliminate tenancy or ameliorate the condition of landless labor.

The second step in the land reform program attempted to impose ceilings on land holdings, but there was no consensus on the issue. Since the richer landowning Congress members in the Vidhan Sabhas were reluctant to enact laws that would take away their lands, the program had limited success. The ceilings introduced differed from state to state, and many of the bigger landowners managed to circumvent the law through various devices; the easiest method was to partition the land and transfer parcels of it to relatives and friends, each given the maximum possible. The surplus land available to the government for redistribution thus amounted to very little.

The third step was the introduction of cooperatives that would help the

---

*As explained earlier, a *jagirdar* was a holder of a *jagir* (a parcel of land) given to him in return for his loyalty to the ruler. Technically, the *jagirdars* were not owners of the lands allotted to them, but in practice the *jagirdars* had established hereditary rights over their *jagirs*. They paid no land revenues to the state and "ruled" the *jagirs* as private fiefs: they appointed land officers to assess and collect taxes on their behalf, and they often had their own police force to enforce their regulations. The *zamindars* were owners of their estates and had no administrative responsibilities except the collection of taxes, of which they paid a fixed amount to the state and kept the bulk for their own use; they often overtaxed the peasantry under their control.

weaker sections of the rural community by providing credit and assistance with marketing and processing. Unfortunately, the scheme resulted in large government-run credit societies and service cooperatives that had little contact with and little impact on the small landholder. After visiting China in 1954, and having been impressed by the Chinese cooperative farming experiment, Nehru got the Congress to pass a resolution in 1959 that nonofficial, small-size, voluntary cooperatives run by village *panchayats* should be introduced to service agriculture and prepare the villages for joint farming. This smacked too much of socialism and provided Nehru's right-wing critics an opportunity to attack not only this program but all of his other domestic and foreign policies. The critics eventually left the Congress to form a new conservative party, the Swatantra Party. Nehru never gave up the idea of cooperative farming, but he stopped trying to enforce it. The idea died a slow natural death.

To sum up, the land reform program succeeded in eliminating the *jagirdars* and *zamindars,* but failed to redistribute land or bring relief to the tenant farmer and the landless labor; the landless still constitute about 27 percent of rural households. Instead of the social revolution in village India (where nearly 75 percent of the population lives) that Nehru had aimed at, the land reform program actually helped the richer peasants to become richer, and thanks to their excessive influence over local politics, strengthened the forces of casteism and parochialism. No "socialistic pattern of society" emerged in rural India.

The Five-Year Plans. As mentioned above, Nehru was committed to a coordinated program of planned development in which the state was to play the leading role. This approach was institutionalized with the establishment of the National Planning Commission (NPC) in 1950 (with Nehru as the ex-officio chairman) and the launching of the first Five-Year Plan in 1951. The Five-Year Plans (FYPs) have become a fixture of India's development policy.

The NPC is a powerful institution that formulates policies that affect all aspects of national life. It not only decides how the central funds, foreign loans, aid money, and foreign exchange allocated to it are distributed among the states but can implement key projects on its own initiative. The NPC is an extraconstitutional body of experts that is not accountable to the Parliament, though the appointment of one or more ministers as members of the NPC has helped to increase communication between the expert and the politician. The NPC's plans are, however, published in advance and are thoroughly analyzed and discussed in the Parliament and closely scrutinized by the press and the public. All five-year plans affirm their commitment to growth and the reduction of inequalities. One of the important elements in the plans is the fixing of the ratios of investment outlays in the public and private sectors.

The First Five-Year Plan (1951–1956) began with limited resources (c. $10 billion; equally divided between the public and private sectors) and inadequate data. It achieved, however, several very laudable results: a 17.5 percent increase in national income; a 10.5 percent rise in personal income; 11 million tons of extra food; a 660 percent increase in the fleet of locomotives; a 400 percent increase in the holding of railway wagons; a 168 percent increase in engineers; and so on. The industrial growth index rose from 105 in 1950 (base year 1946) to 170 in 1956. The most important contribution of the first FYP to India's future development was, no doubt, its huge multipurpose dam projects such as Bhakra-Nangal, which alone aimed at producing as much electricity as the whole country had in 1950 and increasing the land under irrigation by 1.3 million acres.

The Second Five-Year Plan (1957–1961), backed by the "socialistic pattern" resolution passed by the Congress in the previous year, was much bolder and closer to Nehru's notion of socialism. In practice, this meant that there was heightened emphasis on industrial development and an increase in the role of the public sector; of the nearly $15 billion outlay, the private sector was allocated only $4.8 billion. The main targets included the tripling of steel production by installing three huge steel plants; the tripling of power production; an increase in cement production by 240 percent, and in coal production by 160 percent; the state was also to take charge of ventures such as atomic energy, heavy machinery, aircraft, and shipbuilding. Unfortunately, this meant that the outlay for agriculture had to be reduced from 35 percent in the first plan to 17.5 percent in the second.

The plan turned out to be too ambitious and difficult to fulfill because of population growth, the depletion of foreign reserves (aid had to be sought from the U.S.–Europe-organized Aid to India Consortium), and the incapacity of the states to raise the funds they were supposed to contribute. There was severe shortage of food grains in 1957–1958 and this caused a 50 percent rise in food prices, forcing the government to take over the wholesale trade in food grains and sign the first PL480 agreement with America for the import of food.

The Third Five-Year Plan (1961–1966) mentioned the phrase "socialist pattern of society" as a basic objective and made self-sufficiency in food grain production one of the main targets. The notion that limited foreign aid would not undermine India's self-reliant approach to development led to the acceptance of $4.3 billion from the Aid to India Consortium to finance the plan. The 1962 war with China shifted resources to defense, but the shortages in funds for the plan were somewhat compensated by the war aid provided by the United States and the Soviet Union. However, when the Indo-Pakistan War broke out in 1965 (the year following Nehru's death), development was hampered because the United States and the consortium halted aid, and national funds had to be diverted to war needs on a massive scale. India devalued the rupee by 36 percent to gain foreign exchange through an increase in exports, but this thwarted industrial production because imports became prohibitively expensive. Despite these handicaps, steel production increased from 4.3 million tons to 7 million tons, and India rose to the seventh rank among the industrialized countries of the world.

Nehru's achievements were many and substantial; the most important, no doubt, was his contribution to strengthening the democratic base of Indian polity and laying the foundations of an independent economy. However, his five-year plans, although also a legacy of Nehru, did not "pave the way for socialism but promoted capitalist enterprise in both industry and agriculture."[14]

The Party System

Many political parties had emerged before 1947, and theoretically, the parliamentary system established by the Constitution of India made them important to the future development of democracy in India. The Congress, as the largest and most broad-based of all the parties, had an advantage over the other political groups and became the dominant party in independent India—a position it was to hold for fifty years. But the Congress was hardly a political party in the true sense of the term. It had been a nationalist movement of protest, and a host of parties with differing ideologies, ranging from the left-wing Socialist Party to the right-wing Forward Bloc, had thrived under its auspices. Not wanting to antagonize any section of society, the Congress could not afford to have a well-defined, coherent ideology. Of the various presidents of the Congress since 1919, Lala Lajpat Rai was an ardent Arya Samajist; Malaviya was a staunch Hindu Mahasabhite; Bose was a militant revolutionary; Nehru was an agnostic, secular socialist wanting to industrialize India; and Gandhi believed in nonviolence, village-based economic development and held that religion could not be divorced from politics.

On the achievement of independence, Mahatma Gandhi had rightly recommended that the Congress disband itself and allow genuine political parties, with well-defined ideologies, emerge from its midst. On various grounds, the Congress chose not to heed Gandhi's advice and proceeded to turn itself into a political party with a historic mission of reshaping Indian society.

The new Congress Constitution of 1948 shifted the goal of the Congress from the expulsion of the British to the engineering of a social revolution in the country, but this did not bring unanimity within the party over issues of policy. Nehru, in order to get the party to approve his program of socialism, had to gain ascendancy over it, which he did by weakening the inner organization of the Congress. Although Nehru's programs did not bring the panacea he had promised—50 percent of the people remained below the poverty line—he commanded the unswerving support of the Congress until his death. As the distinction between government and party became amorphous, the oppositional factions within the Congress, denied the opportunity to share power with the dominant faction, became critics of the government and often broke away from the Congress to form opposition parties, such as the Swatantra Party (see above). Such opposition parties (and more of them emerged after Nehru) remained offshoots of the Congress with little new to offer in the way of ideology or program.

The ruling Congress Party had no real competitors on the national level. The left, represented by the socialists and the communists, claimed to be national in character, but in actuality its strength was confined to some regional pockets. The right-wing parties showed similar weaknesses: the Swatantra Party, which survived until 1974, was critical of Nehru's socialist policies and stood for secularism and a free market; the Jan Sangh, a Hindu nationalist party associated with the militant RSS, was popular in northern India for several decades until it merged with other organizations with similar ideology. In the 1952 Lok Sabha elections, the first to be held under the Constitution, the percentage of votes gained by the *national* parties was as follows (the votes not accounted for below went to *regional* parties or independents):

Ideology	Party	Percentage of Votes
Centrists	Congress	45 percent*
Left-wing	Socialists	16 percent
Left-wing	Communists	3 percent
Right-wing	Jan Sangh	3 percent (includes Swatantra)

The results in the 1957 and 1962 elections were similar:

Party	1957	1962
Congress	48 percent*	46 percent*
Socialists	11 percent	13 percent
Communists	9 percent	10 percent
Jan Sangh, etc.	6 percent	15 percent

The political system could perhaps have become more democratic than it was if there had been at least another national party of the stature of the Congress and a two-party system based on differing ideologies had evolved. The country had to wait for three decades, after Nehru's death, for such a development to take place.

As against the slow development of opposition parties with a national stature, regional parties with strong parochial roots and interested primarily in local politics emerged quite early and undermined or displaced the local branches of the Congress. This resulted in a complex pattern of party politics where the Congress, which was still the single biggest national party, had to maintain its position through fragile alliances with regional parties and the smaller all-India parties. Thus, in 1955 in Andhra, and in 1960 in Kerala, the Congress made

---

*In all these years the Congress retained 73 percent of the seats in the Lok Sabha.

agreements with minor local parties to defeat the challenge of the Communists. Although many of the regional parties were single-issue parties that disappeared from the scene when the issue was resolved (for example, the Samyukta Maharashtra Samiti, at one time a very powerful party that had mobilized Marathi-speaking people to fight for their own homeland, faded away after the Maharashtra state was established), some of the state parties did take root and began to gain increasing representation in the Parliament.

The most important of the state parties in Nehru's time, and they have continued on into the present, were the Dravida Munnetra Kazhagam (DMK, or Dravidian Progressive Federation) in Tamil Nadu, the Akali Dal in Punjab, and the National Conference in Kashmir. The former two had begun to give trouble to the center, but gained state power only in the post-Nehru era; the National Conference under Sheikh Abdulla, on the other hand, was responsible for getting Kashmir to accede to India (see above) and has remained the main ruling party in Kashmir until today (January 2000).

The DMK is an offshoot of the Dravidian movement, started in 1922, to protest the Aryan-Brahmin domination and exploitation of the non-Aryan Dravidians, the original inhabitants of the south who formed 97 percent of the population. In 1944, the movement became more militant and began to demand an independent homeland for the Tamil-speaking Dravidians. In 1949, the DMK was formed and carried on the agitation until 1957, when it opted for the parliamentary route to power and after its electoral success in 1963 dropped its demand for an independent Tamil homeland (Tamil Nadu). However, following the 1967 state elections, when it finally assumed the government of Madras, the DMK did change the name of the state to Tamil Nadu. Also in the 1967 national elections, all the twenty-five DMK candidates for the Lok Sabha won their elections and made the party the third largest opposition party in Parliament. The DMK success came when it broadened its appeal from caste to regional nationalism.

Unlike the DMK, the Akali Dal (discussed in the last chapter) was a religious-cum-political Sikh party that had already gained prominence in the later years of the Raj. Its leader, Master Tara Singh, had agitated for Sikhistan (or Khalistan), a homeland for the Sikhs, before independence, but nothing had come of the movement. At partition, the Sikhs from western Punjab (which became a part of West Pakistan) migrated to eastern Punjab in India. When the states were reorganized, Punjab came to include Hindi-speaking and Pahari-speaking (Pahari is the language of the people living in the hills of eastern Punjab) peoples. The Akali Party demanded that, in keeping with the other linguistic states, a Punjabi-speaking state (Punjabi Suba) be created. The demand, resisted during the Nehru era, was finally granted in 1966 and the Akali Party came to power in the new state in 1969.

One party, the Communist Party of India, which was technically an all-India party, gained its greatest success in the regional areas of Kerala and West Bengal.

After having tried to carry out a mass-based violent revolution in the south, it turned to the parliamentary route and in 1957 formed the government in Kerala. This government tried to introduce rapid economic and social changes by carrying out a land reform program and nationalizing education, but these policies, particularly the latter, came under attack from the Congress (representing the middle classes) and the Catholic Church, which is a strong force in Kerala. The agitation and disturbances that followed led the center to impose President's Rule in 1959, and the Congress, in alliance with other parties, was returned to power in 1960.

To sum up, until 1964, the Congress remained the dominant national party and, with some local alliances, retained its hold over the state governments.

India's Foreign Policy

When India gained independence, the cold war had already established the framework for international relations and dragged the European empires in Africa and Asia, which had yet to be dismantled, into the orbit of East-West conflict. Prime Minister Nehru, who also assumed the external affairs portfolio in 1947, hated imperialism with a passion and had a certain sneaking respect for socialism, but he was convinced that India should remain nonaligned and have friendly, cooperative relations with both the United States ("to whom destiny has given a major role in international affairs") and the Soviet Union ("the other great nation of the modern world").[15] Nehru's nonalignment policy was not isolationist; India tried to help the national liberation movements in Africa and Asia and endeavored to get the heads of the newly independent countries to accept his views on nonalignment.

Nehru's nonalignment policy (dubbed "immoral" by Secretary of State Dulles) was wholly unacceptable to the United States, which had made its crusade against communism the basis of its entire foreign policy. The United States did accept India's offer to mediate in the Korean War and help resolve the problem of the repatriation of American and Korean prisoners-of-war. India also played a significant role in the 1954 Geneva Conference, which brought about a settlement between France and Vietnam.

However, after the Korean War was over, the American attitude toward the People's Republic of China hardened to such a degree that Washington refused to recognize the Communists as the legitimate government of China; that honor, until 1972, was conferred on the Nationalist Party in Taiwan. India's continued efforts to get the People's Republic admitted into the United Nations obviously did not help India's relations with Washington. America's military aid to its ally, Pakistan, only strained them further.

Despite all the misgivings about Nehru in Washington, America and India had no direct clash of interests. The friction was over the vastly differing attitudes the two states had toward other countries such as China and Pakistan.

Pakistan was ill-disposed toward India, and had placed itself firmly on the side of America by joining the Central Treaty Organization (CENTO) and the South East-Asia Treaty Organization (SEATO), which constituted the central segments of the arc of America's communist-containment cordon that ran from South Korea and Japan in the east to the North Atlantic Treaty Organization (NATO) in the west.

India, on the other hand, though wanting better relations with Pakistan and the United States, was friendly to the Soviet Union and China, the enemy that was being contained by Washington. After 1954, when the United States extended military aid to Pakistan, India had to turn to other countries for its military hardware. This strengthened the American view that Pakistan was a friendly country and India an unfriendly one, though not an enemy. Despite their troubled relationship, America could not totally ignore India, "the biggest democracy in the world"; in fact, it provided India with much-needed food and technological aid.

The major challenge to India, surprisingly enough, came from China, a country with which Nehru had maintained the friendliest of relations. The British had left India with 2,000 miles of its northern border with Tibet and China not wholly demarcated. Soon after coming to power in 1949, the Chinese Communist government quickly occupied Tibet and was anxious to get India to vacate the special posts in Lhasa that India had inherited from the British. Nehru, perhaps to counter the Pakistan pact with America, signed, in a bit of a hurry, the Panch Sheel agreement* with China in 1954, which reduced Tibet to a position of vassalage to Beijing.

In 1955, Nehru's dream of Afro-Asian cooperation appeared to be fulfilled at the Bandung Conference, where India played a leading role in getting the heads of Afro-Asian states to meet and adopt Panch Sheel as their common platform. Many leaders had not been happy at the idea of Communist China, a satellite of the Soviet Union, being invited to a conference of nonaligned countries, but while they initially irritated Nehru by their posture, they were soon won over by the mild visage presented by Prime Minister Zhou En-lai. By the end of the conference, Zhou had managed to enhance China's, and his own, image in the Third World and emerge as a great Third World leader. Nehru perhaps did not realize that helping China to the world stage may have been a mistake, because despite all the consideration shown to it, China's actions on the Tibetan border remained hostile to India. By 1958, the Chinese were openly attacking India for allegedly helping the Tibetans, who had risen in rebellion against the harsh Chinese military occupation. In 1959, when the Dalai Lama was compelled by

---

*Panch Sheel is a Sanskrit term meaning "Five Principles." The five principles of coexistence in the treaty were: (1) mutual respect for each other's territorial integrity and sovereignty; (2) mutual nonaggression; (3) mutual noninterference in each other's affairs; (4) equality and mutual benefit; and (5) coexistence.

circumstances created by the Chinese to seek refuge in India, relations between India and China soured further because Beijing took the view that by giving shelter to the Dalai Lama, India was playing "the imperialist game." China, for military purposes, had also built a road through India's northwest territory, Aksai Chin (in northern Kashmir), to connect Lhasa with Urumchi, the capital of Sinkiang. When asked about it, Beijing not only declared that that area was part of China but laid claim to thousands of square miles of other Indian territory that supposedly had been usurped by Britain. All signs of friendship evaporated and tensions on the border escalated, though Nehru never believed that China would go to war.

But China, denouncing India's "offensives," did go to war, without of course declaring one. On October 20, 1962, Chinese troops came through the high passes in the northeast and across the border in the high plateau of the northwest and invaded Indian territory, mauling the surprised Indian troops that came in their way. A month later, having humiliated India, the Chinese announced a unilateral cease-fire, turned around, and marched back to the line of actual control in the northeast, but kept much of the territory they had occupied in the northwest (this was to protect the road they had built in Aksai Chin).

Nehru, realizing that India's defense policies had been faulty and had resulted in shortages in equipment, turned to world leaders for help. The quickest response came not from nonaligned nations but from America, which promptly began to airlift supplies to Delhi, and from Britain. The Soviet Union, "[not wanting to make] a gift of India to the American imperialists,"[16] saved Nehru's "neutrality" stand by announcing that it would immediately deliver the fighter aircraft (MIG-21s) it had promised to India before the China war. This was poor comfort and Nehru, it is said, never recovered from the slap the Chinese had delivered to his commitment to nonalignment and peaceful coexistence. China and India did not break diplomatic relations, but they withdrew their ambassadors and relations between the two countries remained strained for the next fourteen years; only in 1976 did China and India exchange ambassadors again. The war did help to bring a temporary sense of unity and nationalism to the Indian people. However, India's status in the international community declined perceptibly and "even nonaligned friendly countries fell under the newly prevailing spell of regarding India as a weak and, consequently, unimportant country."[17] India had learned a bitter lesson: a country's greatness is measured in terms of its military capacity, not its commitment to peace.

Nearer home, Pakistan exploited the deteriorating relations between India and China by drawing closer to Beijing and demanding, in February 1963, that the state of Kashmir be transferred to Pakistan.[18] Having just fought a war with China to defend its territory in Kashmir, India could hardly be expected to take this rather absurd suggestion seriously. Pakistan's announcement in June that it had made a defense arrangement with China did not augur well for the future of India-Pakistan relations. President Ayub Khan, Pakistan's military ruler, however, waited for Nehru's passing away before mounting a military attack on India.

The End of the Nehru Era

Nehru suffered a mild stroke in January 1964, but he refused to take a complete rest as advised by his doctors or slow down his harsh pace of work. On the night of May 26, 1964, he worked as usual before going to sleep. Next morning he got up in pain. His abdominal aorta had ruptured. He soon went into a coma, and at 2:00 P.M. he was pronounced dead. The heart of India stood still and millions grieved the passing of the country's most beloved son. According to his last will and testament, a handful of Nehru's ashes were thrown into the Ganga and the rest scattered over his beloved Kashmir,* the Himalayas, and the four corners of India.

After his death it was discovered that Nehru had copied out the following lines from Robert Frost and kept them on his desk:

> The woods are lovely, dark and deep,
> But I have promises to keep,
> And miles to go before I sleep,
> And miles to go before I sleep.†

No words could have given a better illustration of Nehru's mind—the mind of a man who once observed: "I want work and work and work. I want achievement. I want men who work as crusaders. . . . I want you to do big things. I want you to build India."[19]

Since this book began with a reference to commentators and analysts who deplore the current social-political situation in India and believe that the country's troubles are related to the decay, if not the death, of the Nehru-created politics of secularism (see Preface to the Second Edition), it is time for us to examine Nehru's secularism. That Nehru was secular minded is a fact. He was so at two levels: personally, he was not at all religious minded and was genuinely disturbed by casteism and communalism; on a nonpersonal level, Nehru had faith that the Constitution provided a framework to foster secularism in the country. Although the word *secular* did not appear in the Constitution, it was presumed that universal suffrage and protection of individual rights would, in due course, change social attitudes and help separate the private sphere from the public one.

Nehru's personal understanding of secularism was not necessarily accepted, or even understood, by other leaders in the Congress, let alone by the peoples of

---

*Nehru was born in a Kashmiri Pandit family in Allahabad, but he never forgot his origins or his love for his homeland in Kashmir—Nehru's ancestors had moved from Kashmir to India in the early eighteenth century.

†From "Stopping by Woods on a Snowy Evening" by Robert Frost in *The Poetry of Robert Frost,* edited by Edward Connery Lathem. © 1951 by Robert Frost, © 1923, 1969 by Henry Holt and Co., Inc. Reprinted with permission from Henry Holt and Co., Inc.

India. The view expressed by Vice-President Radhakrishnan in 1956, for example, must have caused immense distress to Nehru: "The religious impartiality of
the Indian State is not to be confused with secularism or atheism. Secularism as
here defined (i.e., in the Constitution) is in *accordance with the ancient religious
tradition of India*"[20] (emphasis added).

The Indian Constitution, unlike the constitutions of the West, could not create
a wall of separation between church and state because the majority of people in
India, the Hindus, had no religious establishment that could be defined as a
church. The Hindus, belonging to vastly diverse groupings, did live their lives
according to well-defined religious prescriptions (caste regulations, notions of
pure and impure, etc.), but had no organizational views (on subjects such as
abortion and birth control) that demanded state compliance. But India also had a
number of better defined and organized religious (e.g., the Muslims and the
Sikhs) and socially deprived (the Harijans and tribals) communities that had been
prompted by the British to fight the Hindus for a greater share of political power.
The Indian Constitution tried to replace the British-engendered communal approach by introducing the notion of citizenship to the peoples of the country,
making them equal in the eyes of the state.

However, the divide-and-rule policies of the British had so communalized
society that even if the new government could have established strong, noncor-
rupt institutions and removed partiality from political activity, it would have
taken a very long time to achieve the standard of education and affluence needed
to eject communalism from the body politic. While education has yet to reach the
bulk of the population and the poverty level remains high, politics in the re-
source-scarce country has become corrupted and politicians increasingly exploit
communal friction to gain their ends. The Constitution may project the idea of a
secular state, but it cannot create a secular society; and nothing demonstrates this
more dramatically than the rapid increase in the frequency of communal riots at
the end of Nehru's premiership—from 26 in 1960, to 1,170 in 1964.[21]

Throughout his years in office, Nehru continued to be troubled by "the growth
of this religious element in our politics, both on the Hindu and the Muslim
side,"[22] and repeatedly expressed the view that "religion in India will kill that
country and its peoples if it is not subdued."[23] Just a month before his death, and
seventeen years after partition, it must have saddened Nehru to admonish his
countrymen once again, in a broadcast to the nation, March 26, 1964, that they
must earnestly work for communal harmony: "Pakistan came into existence on
the basis of hatred and intolerance. We must not allow ourselves to react . . . in
the same way. We must live up to our immemorial culture and try to win over
those who are opposed to us. To compete with each other in hatred and barbarity
is to sink below the human level and tarnish the name of our country and our
people."[24]

Nehru never came to fully comprehend the roots of Hindu-Muslim friction.
His belief that the Hindus as a majority community had a duty to placate

Muslims' fears and exercise self-control even when the Muslims acted aggressively[25] was well intentioned but ill considered. Unfortunately, Nehru projected this thinking to the laws of the country and laid the basis for even greater future dissension between the two communities. This happened when Nehru, highly conscious of the need to ameliorate the lowly position of women in Indian society, moved to legislate their status. However, not wanting to hurt Muslim sentiment so soon after partition, he allowed the Muslim women to continue to be governed by their personal Islamic laws and focused attention only on Hindu women. Thus the 1949 Hindu Marriage Validating Act legally approved the traditionally forbidden intercaste marriages; the 1955 Hindu Marriage Act gave Hindu women the right of divorce denied in traditional Hindu personal law; and the 1956 Hindu Succession Act and an Adoption and Maintenance Act gave Hindu women the right, equal to that enjoyed by men, to inherit property and to adopt a female child, who would receive the same rights as an adopted male child.

These acts were revolutionary in nature, and Nehru was proud to get them enacted, even though many leading conservative Hindus, including Rajendra Prasad, India's first president, opposed them vehemently. However, since the Hindu Code Bills affect only the Hindus, the constitution does not provide a uniform civil code for the country. The Muslims, as we shall see in the subsequent sections, have refused to allow the state to interfere with their personal law, and post-Nehru Congress governments have acceded to their demands. This has helped the strengthening of the right-wing Hindu opposition groups and the emergence of the Hindu nationalist Bharatya Janata Party that is currently vying for national power; the BJP has gained support from the Hindu community that believes the Congress is biased in favor of the Muslims and has made the Hindus, in what is "their country," less equal than the Muslims. It has to be said that Nehru, however unwittingly, did harm the cause of secularism by allowing a major religion of India, Islam, to abridge fundamental rights and, thereby, reduce the sanctity of the constitution.

We can conclude this section with the broad generalization that Nehru was an outstanding statesman who, until his death, held on to a noble vision based more on his Westernized outlook than on his understanding of Indian society, of a modern India held together by the ideals of secularism, socialism, and democracy. He was right in believing that India's past was an obstacle in the path of the country's modernization; he was, however, wrong in thinking that the past could be willed away.

Notes

1. Tariq Ali, *Pakistan: Military Rule or People's Power* (New York: William Morrow, 1970), p. 132.
2. M. J. Akbar, *Kashmir: Behind the Vale* (New Delhi: Viking Penguin, 1991), p. 219.

3. Mark Bence-Jones, *The Viceroys of India* (New York: St. Martin's Press, 1982), p. 312.

4. Sarvepalli Gopal, ed., *Jawaharlal Nehru: An Anthology* (Delhi: Oxford University Press, 1983), p. 331.

5. See Selig S. Harrison, *India: The Most Dangerous Decades* (Princeton: Princeton University Press, 1960), p. 286.

6. C. Rajagopalachari, *Our Democracy* (Madras: B.G. Paul and Co, 1957), p. 17.

7. Jayaprakash Narayan, "Foreword," in Benudhar Pradhan, *The Socialist Thought of Jawaharlal Nehru* (Gurgaon, Haryana: Academic Press, 1974), p. vii.

8. Sarvepalli Gopal, *Jawaharlal Nehru: A Biography,* 3 vols. (Cambridge, MA: Harvard University Press, 1984), Vol. II, p. 198.

9. Ibid., p. 200.

10. Ibid., p. 304.

11. Ibid., p. 93.

12. James Manor, *Nehru to the Nineties: The Changing Office of the Prime Minister in India* (Vancouver: UBC Press, 1994), p. 165.

13. *Constitution of India,* 8th ed. (Lucknow: Eastern Book Company, 1988), pp. 28–29.

14. Gopal, *Nehru,* Vol. III, p. 294.

15. B. R. Nanda, *Indian Foreign Policy: The Nehru Years* (Delhi: Vikas Publishing House, 1976), p. 3.

16. Strobe Talbott, trans. and ed., *Khrushchev Remembers: The Last Testament* (Boston: Little Brown, 1974), p. 311.

17. Arthur Lall, *The Emergence of Modern India* (New York: Columbia University Press, 1981), p. 167.

18. Gopal, *Nehru,* Vol. III, p. 258.

19. Gopal, ed., *Jawaharlal Nehru: An Anthology,* p. 213.

20. Quoted in P. C. Chatterji, *Secular Values for Secular India* (New Delhi: Published by Lola Chatterji, 1984), p. 15.

21. Ibid., p. 260.

22. M. J. Akbar, *Nehru: The Making of India* (London: Viking, 1988), p. 141.

23. Ibid., p. 183.

24. Gopal, ed., *Jawaharlal Nehru: An Anthology,* p. 336

25. See, Gopal, *Nehru,* Vol. III, p. 172.

8

Indira Gandhi, 1966–1984

Authoritarianism and the
New Communalism

By the time Nehru left the scene, India had established a fairly strong democratic structure (universal suffrage, elections, state assemblies, national Parliament, a parliamentary system of government, free speech, and a free press), but the system was hollow and lacked the democratic values and ideology that could make it the basis of Indian unity. In the West, the developmental sequence was that strong unitary states with effective universal legal systems emerged first, then came nationalism, and democracy followed as the last stage. In India, the process was reversed. India had gained the shell of democracy that was supported neither by a strong, effective state or true nationalism. Nehru had faith that somehow the institutions of democracy, backed by a broad commitment to the ambiguously defined notion of secularism, would help to introduce the integrating ideologies of a nation-state. And, in the process, threats to India's unity—posed by regionalism, secessionist tendencies, religious differences, casteism, illiteracy, and conservative traditional practices—would be overcome. Nehru's faith was misplaced.

Post-Nehru India: The Rise and Fall of the Nehru Dynasty

In the post-Nehru period, the basic contradictions inherent to democracy in a backward, poor state became increasingly evident, and the diversity, complexity, and size of the country made their resolution even more difficult. No one questioned the need for India to be a strong state to face its enemies abroad and guide national development within. The question was: How does one achieve this end?

Some Important Dates and Events, 1964–1984

1964–1966	**Interim prime minister, Lal Bahadur Shastri (Congress)**
1965	India-Pakistan war
1966	Shastri dies
1966–1967	**Interim prime minister, Nehru's daughter, Indira Gandhi (Congress)**
1967	*Fourth Elections for Lok Sabha*
1967–1971	**Prime minister, Indira Gandhi (Congress)**
1971	*Fifth Elections for Lok Sabha*
	Indira's faction, Congress (R), wins overwhelming victory
1971–1977	**Prime minister, Indira Gandhi (Congress (R))**
1971	Establishment of Bangladesh
	War with Pakistan
1975	Indira declares national emergency
1977	*Sixth Elections for Lok Sabha*
1977–1979	**Prime minister, Morarji Desai (Janata)**
1979–1980	**Caretaker government under Prime Minister Charan Singh (Janata [Secular])**
1980	*Seventh Elections for Lok Sabha*
1980–1984	**Prime minister, Indira Gandhi (Congress (I))**
1982	Beginning of Sikh insurgency in Punjab
1983	President's Rule imposed in Punjab
1984	Indian army attacks Sikh insurgents in the Golden Temple
	Indira Gandhi is assassinated on October 31

India could not wait for the long-drawn-out process for the true Westminster system to get rooted in the country. It could, however, readily or more easily adopt the viceregal model that had given extraordinary powers to the center so that it could maintain firm control over the country. And that, with some significant differences, is what happened.

One major difference was that the Indian prime minister, who assumed many of the powers of the British viceroys, represented a party and was elected, not appointed, to office. If the prime ministership had changed hands between different parties, the office may not have become as authoritarian as it did. Unfortunately, except for four years, the Congress managed to remain in power from 1964 to early 1996. Furthermore, until 1991 Nehru's family emerged as the ruling dynasty and contributed two charismatic prime ministers—Indira Gandhi (Nehru's daughter) and Rajiv Gandhi (Indira's son)—who held that office for a combined period of twenty-one years. Jawaharlal Nehru, a decade before he became prime minister, once wrote a humorous piece of self-appraisal that is worth quoting because of its relevance to how Indira and Rajiv evolved as power holders: "Jawaharlal . . . has all the makings of a dictator in him—vast popularity, a strong will directed to a well-defined purpose, energy, pride, organizational capacity, ability, hardness, and, with all his love of the crowd, an intolerance of others and a certain contempt of the weak and inefficient.... His overmastering desire to get things done, to sweep away what he dislikes and build anew, will hardly brook for long the slow processes of democracy.... Therein lies danger for Jawaharlal and India."[1]

When he was prime minister, Nehru had preeminent personal authority, and he could also play the game of politics with finesse (witness the Tandon affair), but he never did anything to undermine the democratic functioning of the party or the country. His daughter and grandson, lacking his self-discipline and his vision for India, turned democracy into a patrimonial system that personalized and corrupted power and impaired the proper functioning of the party, the cabinet, the Parliament, the judiciary, and the bureaucracy by diminishing their authority and political role. By 1996, the Congress had lost much of its prestige and become a moribund party.

Lal Bahadur Shastri: Interim Prime Minister, 1964–1966

At Nehru's death in 1964, an informal caucus of five regional party bosses (later known as "the Syndicate"), organized by Kamaraj, the president of the Congress, selected Lal Bahadur Shastri as the interim prime minister. Even Morarji Desai (1897–1995), a strong-minded representative of the Congress right wing and a senior minister in Nehru's cabinet, who believed that the office should rightfully be his, accepted the verdict. Shastri had a mild, self-effacing personality and was no doubt chosen by the Syndicate on the presumption that he would be amenable to Kamaraj's "collective leadership" approach. Indira Gandhi was added to Shastri's cabinet as minister for information and broadcasting.

Pakistan, as mentioned earlier, had been waiting for Nehru's death to start a war with India. Equipped by the United States with sophisticated modern weapons, such as Patton tanks and F-86 Sabre jets, and fortified with an alliance with China, Pakistan felt confident that it could defeat a weak and ill-prepared India. And when war did come in 1965, India was indeed not immediately ready for it.

Pakistan tested India's readiness by attacking outposts in the remote Rann of Kutch, on the grounds that they were within Pakistani territory. After Pakistani tanks had rolled unhindered through ten miles of the Rann, Pakistan proposed a cease-fire and allowed a United Nations commission to demarcate the border. This was a diversionary tactic that boosted Pakistan's confidence, and it now turned to its real target: Kashmir. By August, the U.N.'s peacekeeping mission in Kashmir had reported thousands of violations of the cease-fire line by Pakistani armed "volunteers" infiltrating the state. Pakistan had hoped to surprise India by capturing Srinagar airport and fomenting an anti-Indian uprising of the Muslim-majority of the state. Pakistan was not wholly correct in its estimation of India's unpreparedness and totally wrong in its belief that the Muslims of Kashmir supported Pakistan.

By mid-August the situation had become so intolerable that Shastri publicly declared that "force would be met with force" and ordered the Indian army to push the Pakistani troops disguised as civilian volunteers out of Kashmir. A full-scale war followed. If Pakistan had thought that it could humiliate India as China had done in 1962, it was mistaken. The Pakistani army was thoroughly defeated, 450 of its tanks destroyed, and Indian troops reached the outskirts of Lahore, Pakistan's largest city, before a cease-fire (September 23, 1965) was accepted by both sides under the auspices of the United Nations. At this stage, the Soviet Union stepped in and invited Shastri and President Ayub to Tashkent to work out a peace agreement. Shastri negotiated a very promising agreement with Ayub, but before he could return home to receive the plaudits of a grateful country, he died of a massive heart attack on January 10, 1966.

India under Indira Gandhi

Phase I: Consolidation of Power, 1966–1970

The death of Shastri created another crisis for the Syndicate. Morarji Desai once again staked his claim for the post of prime minister. The Syndicate, anxious to maintain its hold over that high office, wanted a pliable individual (which Desai could never be) and got the shy, relatively inexperienced Indira Gandhi to contest the election. The Congress Parliamentary Party, influenced by the Syndicate and other Congress leaders, and equally by the fact that Indira Gandhi was Nehru's daughter, chose her over Desai by a vote of 355 to 169. The huge crowd that had gathered outside the Parliament House waiting for the verdict hailed the decision with cheers and shouts of "Indira Gandhi *Zindabad*" (Long Live Indira Gandhi) and "Jawaharlal Nehru *Zindabad*" (Long Live Jawaharlal Nehru).

Being Nehru's daughter had helped Indira Gandhi, but once in power she was to prove that she was nobody's puppet and had her own agenda for India. She did have a retiring personality (which may have misled the Syndicate), but she was strong-willed and definitely not inexperienced in Indian politics. She was, after all, the granddaughter of Motilal Nehru and the daughter of Jawaharlal Nehru, and had spent her entire life in a political environment. From 1950 until Nehru's death in 1964, Indira had lived in her father's residence and served as his official hostess. During these fourteen years she had ample opportunity to observe and participate in the inner workings of the Congress Party, campaign for her father in his constituency, witness the process of political decision making, and meet various heads of state at home or abroad. By 1966, she also had been directly involved with the Congress Party as a member, at one time or another, of its Working Committee, Central Election Committees, and Central Parliamentary Board; and she had been elected president of the Congress in 1959.

In a letter to Rajiv, written after her election as prime minister, she quoted a line from Robert Frost: "How hard it is from being king, when it's in you and in the situation."[2] This does not sound very self-effacing! In due course Indira Gandhi was to display an imperious, authoritarian streak and successfully ensured the perpetuation of the Nehru dynasty. Her political mode was, nevertheless, in keeping with the popular Indian tradition that sanctions the continuity of power-wielding families and places them on a higher pedestal than ordinary human beings. Nehru had hated it when people came up and touched his feet; Indira Gandhi was quite pleased to accept such adulation as a traditional gesture of affection.

In 1966, Indira Gandhi's position appeared to be quite tenuous; by 1970, her power was unassailable. Within these four years Indira Gandhi had split the Congress Party and established her left-oriented faction, cleansed of the Syndicate and the old guard, as the dominant new Congress Party (Congress R, discussed below) and one which was under her absolute control. An analysis of how and why this happened not only reveals the direction that democracy was taking but also sheds light on the complexity of the economic and political issues involved.

Gandhi became prime minister at a time when the nation faced many difficulties. Not counting the endemic problems of poverty and illiteracy, the most critical issue concerned the economic plight of the country, though religious and communal tensions and the Punjab linguistic agitation were only marginally less important.

Before turning her attention to economics, Indira Gandhi took a major step in resolving the ongoing Sikh agitation for a Punjabi *suba* (state or entity), which was not only a source of Hindu-Sikh communal troubles but posed a threat to internal peace. In 1955, the States Reorganization Commission (see above) had left the Sikh demand for a Punjabi-speaking state unanswered because Nehru had been unsympathetic to the Sikh aspirations, considering them to be based on religion, not language and culture. Since the Akali Party, like the Muslim League, combined religion with politics, and since prominent leaders of the Akali Party who were directing the agitation were the very ones who had raised the call for a Sikh homeland before independence, Nehru was not wholly wrong in his views.

In 1965, Sant (an honorific for a holy man) Fateh Singh, a highly respected and honored Sikh leader, threatened to fast unto death (as Potti Sriramalu had done for the establishment of Andhra Pradesh in 1952) for Punjabi Suba. However, on the advice of the center, he postponed the fast because of the exigency created by the Indo-Pakistan War. This, and the fact that the loyalty of Punjab, a border state from where the war had been staged, was important for India's unity, and that many Sikh regiments had fought valiantly in the war, probably impressed Indira Gandhi to take the bold decision she took to satisfy the Sikh demand. Moreover, their demand was no longer for a Sikh-majority state but for a Punjabi-speaking state, which the central government, having accepted the linguistic state principle elsewhere, could not deny.

Soon after a cease-fire had been declared and Indira Gandhi became the interim prime minister, she reorganized the Punjab state by separating the Hindi-speaking territories that had a non-Punjabi population into a new state, Haryana. Incidentally, the Punjabi-speaking Punjab state so created also turned out to be a Sikh-majority state (Sikhs formed about 52 percent of the population; the rest were Punjabi Hindus); however, for the moment a critical internal crisis appeared to have been resolved. In fact, the Sikh problem never went away and finally exploded in the 1980s in a demand for an independent homeland, Khalistan, and led to Indira Gandhi's assassination.

Unlike Punjab, the economic situation did not lend itself to a quick resolution. The country had suffered from the failure of the monsoons in 1965 and 1966 (they would also fail in 1967), and this had produced famine conditions in many states, food shortages throughout India, a rise in food prices, and inflation. At the same time, foreign exchange reserves, already reduced by the 1965 war (and the resulting suspension of U.S. economic aid to both India and Pakistan), were further depleted to finance grain imports. This, in turn, hurt Indian industry because it was starved of foreign exchange. The government estimated that it would take the country three years to recover from the economic setback. Therefore, it postponed the fourth Five-Year Plan (scheduled for April 1966) to 1969. Reviewing the situation, Indira and the Congress leadership decided to liberalize the economy by decontrolling several commodities so as to allow "the market much fuller play."

The only way out was for India to seek wheat from America against credits and, if possible, also hard-currency aid. With this purpose in mind, Indira Gandhi visited Washington in 1966. Her visit by all counts was tremendously successful, and President Johnson promised to supply the much-needed wheat and also $900 million worth of nonproject aid. On her return from the United States, Indira Gandhi took another important economic step: she devalued the rupee by 36.5 percent (from 4.76 to 7.50 to the dollar), ostensibly to increase foreign-exchange earnings by correcting the imbalance between exports and imports; devaluation made exports more attractive in the international market (which would bring more foreign exchange to India) and imports more expensive for Indian consumers (which would save hard currency).

However, Indira Gandhi's visit to the United States, where she had remained silent on American aggression in Vietnam, and her devaluation of the rupee, were severely criticized by the Congress left wing and the leaders of the opposition. Her critics denounced her for succumbing to American pressure and for taking actions that were meant to appease Washington. To counter this impression and to regain her popularity, Indira Gandhi (who was also, like her father, an anti-imperialist at heart) broke her silence on Vietnam and criticized the American decision to bomb Hanoi, the North Vietnamese capital, and

Haiphong, North Vietnam's biggest port. The United States, without any explanation, reacted to what it viewed as Indira Gandhi's pro-USSR stand by cutting the food supplies and reducing aid. Indira Gandhi felt humiliated by this breach of an agreement made by the president of the United States, and she never forgave the Americans for the gratuitous insult. Ironically, American action turned out to be good for India because it inspired Indira Gandhi to embark, in 1966, on a concerted drive to increase food production by introducing high-yielding varieties of hybrid wheat and rice seeds in favorable areas and ensuring that fertilizers and water (required for hybrid varieties) would be available to the farmers in those areas. The resulting "green revolution" was so successful that within a few years India became self-sufficient in grain production.

However, in immediate terms, the continuing food shortages coupled with the rise in prices owing to devaluation angered the people, who naturally directed their ire at the government. The opposition parties took advantage of the situation and contributed to a wave of anti-Congress sentiment, the first such phenomenon since independence. The divisions in the Congress Party and the infighting among its leaders also had a negative impact on the lower levels of the party and created local rifts that reduced the prestige of the Congress as a whole. Many, including some key regional leaders, left the Congress Party and joined the opposition groups.

For all these reasons, the Congress did far worse in the fourth general elections (1967) than it had in the three earlier ones. The Congress strength in the Lok Sabha fell from 358 seats to 283. At the state level, of the seventeen states, the Congress failed to gain majority in eight and formed governments in four other states with shaky alliances. Although the Congress still remained the biggest party in the country (none of the opposition parties emerged with the stature of even the weakened Congress party), its image had been badly shattered. The election results nevertheless augured well for Indira Gandhi because several of the old guard lost their seats while many of Indira Gandhi's followers won their elections. During the sixty days of the election campaign Indira Gandhi had traveled 15,000 miles and spoken at 160 public gatherings, projecting and reinforcing her image as a national leader. She spoke, not in the name of the Congress, but in her own name, and she referred to the masses as "her family" and "her children." Obviously, it was her intention to establish a direct link between herself and the peoples of India, bypassing all party institutions. And she was so successful in doing so that one day the country would willingly accept the slogan "Indira is India."

While Indira Gandhi's success in the 1967 elections meant that no one would dare question her right to be a candidate for the prime ministership, it did not yet mean that she was wholly free of the controls exerted by the Party bosses. Under party pressure Indira Gandhi was forced to compromise with Desai, to make him deputy prime minister and give him the finance portfolio, even though he had openly attacked her for being an incompetent amateur. Moreover,

Kamaraj, who represented the power of the Congress chief ministers and the state-level Congress organizations, embarrassed her by backing policies that she found impossible to carry out.

Indira Gandhi realized, as Nehru had in 1951, that to maintain and ensure a strong central authority she needed a freer hand to revitalize the Congress and restore its sagging image so that it could regain its old hegemonic stature. Like her father, she had no patience with scheming, petty-minded politicians; unlike her father, she also had no great regard for the Congress Party as it was constituted. Nehru had gained ascendancy over the Congress through the support of the Congress bosses in the states (including Kamaraj, one-time chief minister of Tamil Nadu and head of the Tamil Nadu Congress), but since Indira Gandhi's fight was with the Syndicate (composed of chief ministers or Congress bosses of various states) she could not depend on the current Congress organizations in the states. Under these circumstances it was clear that Indira Gandhi could gain a preeminent position only by eliminating all opposition within the Congress, turning that organization into a pliable body, and making the office of the prime minister the focal point of all power and authority.

To achieve this goal, Indira Gandhi turned her factional dispute with the Congress leaders into a populist ideological crusade for socialism. Since bad harvests, food shortages, rising prices, inflation, recession, and unemployment had alienated the masses and the intelligentsia, Indira Gandhi decided to discard the policies of economic liberalization introduced by Shastri and revert to Nehru's socialistic programs. But she could not carry out these programs until the party dispute had been settled in her favor.

The February 1969 mid-term elections in several states brought further losses to the Congress, and Indira Gandhi felt that the time had come to declare her hand. In July she, without informing Desai in advance, divested him of the finance portfolio and personally took over the ministry so that she could carry out the left-oriented policies that he had resisted. Her first act as finance minister was to issue an ordinance nationalizing fourteen of the leading private banks. Desai was so outraged at the manner in which he had been ousted as finance minister that he also resigned from his post as deputy prime minister and withdrew from the cabinet to join the opposition leaders in the Congress.

With Desai out of the way, Indira Gandhi then got the Lok Sabha to pass the Monopolies and Restrictive Practices Act that, in the name of public interest, placed restrictions on the private sector. This and the nationalization of banks were outright attacks on the conservatives inside the party and obviously were not meant to gain their approval or support; what Indira Gandhi had aimed at, and did gain, was the approbation of the people who admired her for having taken such bold action against the reactionaries in the Congress. Her actions, which, according to Mary Carras, brought her "national recognition and popular acclaim,"[3] were viewed by Indira Gandhi herself as "the beginning of a bitter struggle between the common people and the vested interests in the country."[4]

In 1969, "socialist" Indira Gandhi finally got the opportunity she had been waiting for to enlarge her skirmishes with the "reactionary" party bosses into a full-fledged battle for leadership. The unexpected death that year of Zakir Hussain, the president of India, gave Indira Gandhi the occasion to defy the Syndicate: she put up her own candidate for the office of president. Since the president of India is elected indirectly by the free vote of all legislators of the state assemblies and the members of Parliament (MPs), the presidential election divided the Congress Party between the supporters of the official (i.e., the Syndicate's) nominee and those that backed Indira Gandhi's candidate, V. V. Giri, vice-president of India and a former labor organizer.

Giri won the election. Following this success Indira Gandhi's supporters in the Congress submitted a requisition for a special meeting of the All-India Congress Committee to elect a new Congress president. The Congress high command responded by expelling Indira Gandhi from the Congress for "indiscipline." This caused a split in the Congress, and by the end of 1969 there were two Congress parties: Congress (O) (O for Organization) and Indira's Congress (R) (R for Requisitionists). Although neither Congress (R) nor Congress (O) formed a majority in Parliament, Indira Gandhi's position as prime minister was confirmed by a majority vote in the Lok Sabha; her support had come from not only the Congress (R) MPs but also from members of other smaller parties, particularly the left-wing parties.

To continue her socialist policies, Indira Gandhi tried in 1970, but failed by one vote, to get Parliament to amend the constitution so that a law could be passed to abolish the privy purses of the dethroned princely families. She thereupon got a presidential order issued (September 1970) that derecognized the princes. This move, too, was frustrated by the Supreme Court, which declared that the presidential order was unconstitutional and therefore illegal (December 1970). On similar grounds, the Supreme Court had declared the bank nationalization act to be invalid. Obviously, if Indira Gandhi was to carry out her socialist policies she needed to get Parliament to amend the constitutional clause concerning the fundamental right to property. Since she could only do this if she had an overwhelming majority in Parliament, she had either to wait for the election year, 1972, or call for elections immediately. That she chose the latter course proved how self-confident Indira Gandhi had become in the last two years.

Phase II: Indira Gandhi Establishes One-Person Rule, 1970–1977

Indira Gandhi's First Victory

On December 27, 1970, Indira Gandhi announced that elections would be held in March 1971, a year ahead of time. Her stunning victory at the polls, though no doubt helped by the success of the green revolution, affirmed the fact that Indira Gandhi had established her socialist credentials (one of her last populist acts before the elections was her announcement, in January 1971, that the government was allocating 500 million rupees for the creation of new employment opportunities in the rural areas) and gained massive nationwide popularity. Her party program was summed up in the simple but highly appealing slogan, *"Garibi Hatao"* (Remove Poverty). The old Congress, led by Desai, responded with the unimaginative, inane campaign slogan, *"Indira Hatao"* (Remove Indira).

By holding the Lok Sabha elections a year before they were due, Indira Gandhi broke the nexus between the parliamentary and the state elections (until 1971, both were held at the same time) and forced the voters to focus only on her future in Indian politics. The people's verdict was Indira Gandhi's first great political victory: her party won 315 of the 515 Lok Sabha seats; Congress (O) returned sixteen members. Congress (R) had taken over as the single, dominant, ruling party of the country.

Indira Gandhi's Second Victory

The year 1971 was one of glory for Indira Gandhi for another reason, too. In 1971, as a result of national elections held in 1970, the government of Pakistan, basically a government run by West Pakistanis, was faced with the proposition that the Bengali leader Sheikh Mujibur Rehman, whose Awami League Party had campaigned for regional autonomy and won an overwhelming vote in East Pakistan (which comprised 60 percent of the population of Pakistan), would have to be accepted as prime minister. There was jubilation in East Pakistan because it appeared that the Bengalis were at last going to share power in their country and not continue to be treated as second-class citizens.

The government of Pakistan, instead of working out a compromise solution with Rehman, decided to imprison him and suppress the Bengali movement for greater autonomy by allowing the Punjabi- and Pathan-dominated Pakistani army to go on a rampage in Dhaka, the capital of East Pakistan; it is estimated that 100,000 were killed in this so-called Operation Searchlight, launched just days after Indira Gandhi's phenomenal success at the polls. Pakistani action heightened Bengali resistance and led to a civil war that sent nearly 10 million to flee the country and turn up as refugees in India.

This put India in an awkward predicament. If India intervened, and the situation demanded that it do so, it would have to be military intervention. India, however, could not afford to go to war with Pakistan because that could provoke a reaction from America and China, the allies of Pakistan and its arms suppliers. This triangular relationship was more than confirmed when, at the height of the East Pakistan crisis, the national security adviser to President Nixon, Henry Kissinger, flew from Pakistan to Beijing on a secret mission to work out a rapprochement with China that resulted in the July 16 announcement that Nixon would visit China in early 1972—the announcement took the world by surprise. Kissinger's warning to Delhi, given during his visit to India that preceded by a few days his cloak-and-dagger secret trip to Beijing, that the United States would not come to India's aid if the Chinese intervened in a Pakistan-India war, took on a more ominous significance.

It must be said to Indira Gandhi's credit that she was not intimidated by any of these developments and that she prepared for the inevitable confrontation with Pakistan with several very wise moves. First, she countered the Pakistan-China-America menace by signing a twenty-year Treaty of Peace, Friendship, and Cooperation with the USSR (August 1971) that included a clause enjoining the two parties to come to each other's aid in the event of a security threat. Of course, the Americans were not pleased. Second, Indira Gandhi decided to go, in October-November, on a three-week trip to Belgium, Austria, England, France, West Germany, and the United States, to apprise the heads of these states on the gravity of the situation and to explain to them why the crisis was not a "conspiracy by Hindu India," as Pakistan claimed it to be. She also planned to explain why India was reluctant to take any drastic action in East Pakistan, although the 10 million refugees were becoming a threat to India's security and a drain on her resources.

Ironically, Pakistan—by making a preemptive air strike on December 3 against Indian air bases in Indian Punjab, manifestly to warn India that if it interfered in Bengal it would have to fight on two fronts—saved India from being the first to start the war. On December 4, the Indian army entered East Pakistan in support of the Bengali people's *Mukti Bahini* (Liberation Army), and on December 6, Delhi recognized the People's Republic of Bangladesh. By December 16, with the Pakistani army's surrender (93,000 officers and men) to the Indian commander in charge of the East Pakistan operations, the war was over. India promptly withdrew all its forces from Bangladesh, leaving Rehman to establish the government of independent Bangladesh. The Indian armed forces had been equally successful on the western front and captured 5,000 square miles of enemy territory. President Nixon's "tilt" toward Pakistan and his ordering of the U.S. Seventh Fleet into the Bay of Bengal had had no impact on India.

The resounding victory, apart from adding to the popular stature of Indira Gandhi, cut Pakistan down to size (never again would America or any other country be able to equate Pakistan with India), and India emerged as the major power in South Asia. But the dramatic developments had a negative side. To a discerning mind, the emergence of Bangladesh only proved that the 1947 partition had in no way ended the vigor of the communal forces of national disintegration. The successful breakaway of East Pakistan not only provided an encouraging example that secessionist groups in India could follow, but goaded a humiliated Pakistan to seek revenge on India by supplying the Sikh and Muslim insurgents in Indian Punjab and Kashmir with funds, military training, weapons, and safe haven. The situation in Punjab in the 1980s and in Kashmir in the 1990s became so critical that, for all practical purposes, it took on the proportions of an internal war. But these troubles were still a long way off and cast no shadow on India's euphoria of 1971.

From Political Dominance to Dictatorship

In 1972, Indira Gandhi, riding high on the crest of national adoration, further secured her hold over national power by gaining a landslide victory for her party in the nine states in which elections were held that year as scheduled. Also in 1972, Pakistan's prime minister, Zulfiqar Ali Bhutto, was forced to visit India to secure the release of the Pakistani prisoners of war and make a settlement with Indira Gandhi that in the future neither country would resort to war over Kashmir and that the issue of Kashmir would be resolved bilaterally without involving the United Nations or other powers. Indira Gandhi had regained international respect for India.

Internally, Indira Gandhi's position of political dominance had now surpassed that of Nehru: she had achieved practically absolute control over the party and the Parliament and over the central government and the states. This allowed her to establish a unique, one-person rule. Indira Gandhi had successfully used the structures of democracy (party organization, election campaigns, voting system, state assemblies, and Parliament) to gain her position of dominance, but she now proceeded to empty these structures of their democratic content. Depending on her immense popularity as the savior of the poor, and confirmed in her belief that she had obtained a direct mandate from the nation, Indira Gandhi discarded the normal, democratic procedures that ensure that power flows from the bottom upwards. Instead of taking counsel from the Congress (R) committees, the Parliamentary committee, or even from members of her cabinet, she formulated her policies on the basis of advice given to her by a coterie of personal friends and advisers. She made personal loyalty a test for loyalty to her Congress and the country.

In the words of Myron Weiner, Indira Gandhi also "had a patrimonial view of Indian politics. She saw the political system as a kind of estate she inherited from her father, which she believed should be transmitted to her heirs."[5] Indira Gandhi turned Congress (R) into a personally run establishment. The system of intraparty elections at the district, state, and national levels that had provided the organization with a democratic structure fell into disuse because Indira Gandhi took it upon herself to appoint office-bearers in various state and national Congress committees and to nominate chief ministers in the states (the chief ministers were previously democratically elected by the states' Congress parties). Thus, Indira Gandhi had eliminated worrisome dissent and debate in the party but also robbed it of inner-party democracy; she held no party elections in the Congress Party led by her as long as she was alive, and her example was followed by her son, Rajiv Gandhi (prime minister, 1984–1989).

The new politics took on the traditional *durbar*-style: Indira Gandhi was the empress, and the cabinet ministers, state chief ministers, and Congress leaders were her courtiers, fawning on her and waiting her pleasure. Indira Gandhi's favorites gained various offices in the government and the party while those who fell out of her favor were ousted from their offices unceremoniously. Common people gathered every morning at her house for *darshan* (the blessing one gains by seeing the face of a deity) of Indira Gandhi or to touch her feet and hand her petitions for help, which she passed on to her aides for disposal. Likewise, the cabinet ministers ran *durbars* of their own, as did the states' chief ministers and the states' ministers.

Along with favoritism came bribery and corruption. All parties needed money to fight the increasingly expensive elections, and money could come primarily from big business houses. Indira Gandhi and Congress (R) had turned left, but businessmen and capitalists, knowing that Congress (R) would be in power for a long time to come, supported the party with secret "black money" cash funds— cash black money because Indira Gandhi had banned (open) political donations by joint-stock companies. And as socialistic policies increased the state's role in issuing licenses to private businesses for setting up economic enterprises, import- ing materials from abroad, gaining bank loans, and so on, a nexus between politicians and businessmen, based on bribery, corruption, and nepotism, was established; and since the bureaucrats, who actually issued the licenses and the permits, were the intermediaries, they also became politicized and corrupt. Indian businessmen gave lavish gifts and bribes to influence the ministers in charge of the ministries they dealt with, but more important, since ministers came and went, they used graft to establish particularistic relationships with high-level bureaucrats who were posted for more definite periods in these ministries.

In 1972, newspapers began to reveal cases of corruption involving ministers of the central government who were reported to have taken donations for the Congress from smugglers and mafia bosses in return for certain favors. Before long it came to be generally known that "suitcases full of currency notes" were being sent to the prime minister's house by various persons interested in receiv- ing favors from Indira Gandhi. One of the worst scandals concerned Indira Gandhi's son, Sanjay (1946–1980) who, though he had no fitting credentials, was given a permit to set up a car factory. The site was fixed in Haryana, on the outskirts of New Delhi, and the chief minister of Haryana transferred 300 acres of prime land to Sanjay at a nominal price. And though no car rolled out of the so-called factory, Sanjay collected a huge amount of money from fictitious investors who represented industrialists out to please the young man (he was in his twenties) and his mother. It was strange that Indira Gandhi, committed to socialism, permitted her own son to indulge in the most corrupt form of private enterprise!

All these scandals, however big, may never have mattered if Indira Gandhi could have delivered on her election promise to "remove poverty." But that was not to be. By 1972, India had no doubt made major advances in the production of fertilizers and energy, in nuclear research, technology, education, and family planning, but not enough to provide sufficient food and jobs to the growing population. Food shortages and a rise in food prices were once again making the population restless.

Initially, Indira Gandhi had appeared determined to live up to her image as the Great Socialist. In 1971, she got Parliament to pass the 24th and 25th Amendments to the Constitution, whereby Parliament gained sovereign authority and the power to amend even the fundamental rights in the Constitution and the state gained the right to decide what compensation was to be paid for properties acquired by the state. These amendments removed judicial constraints and allowed Indira Gandhi to enforce her earlier plans to strip the rulers of the erstwhile Princely States of their privy purses and to nationalize the banks (both acts had earlier been overturned by the Supreme Court). In 1972, Indira Gandhi also introduced moves to nationalize 106 Indian and foreign-owned general insurance companies, 214 privately operated coal mines, and 46 textile mills, and to take over the management of the Indian Iron and Steel Company (IISCO).

However, all these acts did little to shore up her socialist image because in 1971 India saw the beginning of a three-year drought that affected 180 million people in its first year; in 1972–73, prices rose by 22 percent, causing a wave of strikes (there were over 12,000 protests in Bombay alone) and food riots across the country; in 1973–74 industrial production fell by 7 percent, and prices and inflation rose further (in Bihar and Gujarat the inflation rate in 1974 was over 30 percent). The 1973 world oil crisis further exacerbated India's problems. The increase in the price of imported oil affected the prices of all industrial products; the rise in the price of fertilizers had a particularly adverse impact on the production of food. Later in that year, the government, having distributed all the buffer stock it held, had to swallow a bitter pill and import 2.2 million tons of food grain from the United States.

In 1974 Indira took a surprise decision to carry out a nuclear test. Her reason for doing this was not quite clear. Perhaps she wanted to confirm India's independent foreign policy and its sovereign right to take such as action. Or it could be that Indira wanted to divert national attention away from her economic troubles. Whatever her reasons, the detonation did astound the world and catch U.S. intelligence unaware; however, since India had not violated any U.S. agreements, Washington could do no more than harshly criticize India's accomplishment. The detonation elated the Indian nation but proved of no help in alleviating Indira's internal difficulties. To the relief of the West, Indira Gandhi did not carry out any more tests during her remaining years in office. The test did confirm India's nuclear option, and 24 years later, in 1998, India went overtly nuclear.

The Beginning of the End

Indira Gandhi's socialist political facade began to crumble. Radical slogans did not fill hungry stomachs, and the people were not interested in the takeover of private economic enterprises; they wanted food and a control on the spiraling food prices. The memories of the Bangladesh victory and Indira Gandhi's successful fight with the reactionaries of the Old Congress were forgotten and replaced by the picture of a corrupt mother who allowed her even more corrupt son to fraternize with hoarders and profiteers and dominate the Delhi political scene. Incidentally, when one of her ablest bureaucrat-advisers, P. N. Haksar, tried to warn her about Sanjay's activities, Indira Gandhi was so incensed that she promptly relieved Haksar of his duties.

Indira Gandhi had made great promises to the people but appeared to be doing little to live up to those promises. While hunger and privation led to mass demonstrations, a growing army of frustrated, unemployed, educated youth added to the government's difficulties by creating disturbances in the universities and colleges, fueling political protest. In March 1973, half a million people took part in a "Great March" on Parliament to express their dissatisfaction with corruption and deteriorating economic conditions.

Under these circumstances one would have expected Indira Gandhi to have been more sensitive to the demands of the railway workers, who were threatening to go on strike. On the contrary, Indira Gandhi considered the strike to be a challenge to her political authority and declared it to be illegal. When a million railway workers did strike in 1974, Indira Gandhi decided to teach them a lesson. The army was called out, thousands of workers were jailed, and brutal "official violence" was used against the rest, who were terrorized to end the strike. The strike ended within a few weeks, but Indira Gandhi's action shattered what little was left of her socialist image.

Indira Gandhi's strategy of personalized leadership and the concentration of power in her own hands also proved counterproductive. All troubles were now blamed on her as the single source of India's problems. The insurrection against her began in Gujarat and Bihar, where Indira Gandhi's handpicked, but incompetent chief ministers had failed to keep matters under control. Youth violence and mass agitation in these states caused a breakdown of law and order and led to the dissolution of the state assemblies.

In Bihar, the aging but nationally recognized political leader Jayaprakash Narayan (popularly known as JP), once a socialist but now converted to Gandhianism, came out of retirement to lead a mass national movement to topple Indira Gandhi and her government. JP believed that the parliamentary system led to confrontation between parties, factionalism, communalism, corruption and waste; Indira Gandhi had only brought out the worst in the system, and her authoritarian, immoral, and corrupt government had eroded democratic and social values. He wanted the people to go back to the days of Mahatma Gandhi and launch a national peaceful *satyagraha* (the hallmark of Mahatma Gandhi's political philosophy) to bring about a total revolution based on *sarvodaya* (welfare of all); the revolution was to establish a federation of village republics that would be the centers of the country's political and economic life.

Though JP's aim was to establish a partyless democracy, he invited the opposition parties, including the communal Jan Sangh and the Rashtriya Swayamsevak Sangh (RSS), to work together to overthrow Indira Gandhi because that was the inevitable first step toward *lok-niti* (people's rule). Not all opposition leaders agreed with, or even understood, JP's program, but the notion of joining hands against Indira Gandhi's autocratic rule was very appealing; a Janata Front (Popular Front), an alliance of opposition parties ranging from the left to the right, soon came into existence. The first success of the Janata Front came in June 1975, when it defeated Congress (R) in the special elections held in Gujarat.

The Allahabad High Court Verdict. On the same day that Indira Gandhi learned of her defeat in Gujarat, she also received news of the Allahabad High Court decision that she had been found guilty of election code violations in the 1971 election. The case had been brought against Indira Gandhi by one Raj Narain, who had been defeated by her in the 1971 elections; Narain had accused Indira Gandhi of electoral malpractice (bribery, corruption, using officials and official vehicles for electioneering purposes, etc.). And though after years of hearings the Court had rejected most of the charges and found her guilty of only minor infractions, the charge was still "corrupt electoral practices." This made her election invalid and took away her seat in Parliament; without a parliamentary seat she could no longer continue as prime minister.

Indira Gandhi could, and did, appeal to the Supreme Court for a reversal of the decision. Since that would take time, she asked for a stay of judgment. The Supreme Court allowed her to remain prime minister until her appeal was heard, but disallowed her from taking part in the proceedings of Parliament.

To avoid this anomalous situation, Indira Gandhi should have stepped down from office, but her twenty-nine-year-old son Sanjay, and the Congress (R) high command, convinced her that she should not do so because her leadership was "indispensable" to the country. Since Indira Gandhi believed that she was the only one who could "save" the country in its dire hour of need, she did not need much convincing.

Imposition of Emergency Rule. The Supreme Court decision came on June 24. On the following day, June 25, JP and other opposition leaders, speaking at a mass rally in Delhi, denounced Indira Gandhi for establishing a fascist dictatorship, demanded that she resign, and called on the people to start a mass national movement to oust her if she did not step down voluntarily. The fact that JP was following Gandhian tactics may have given him and his followers a sense of legitimacy, but what they were forgetting was that Mahatma Gandhi had used these tactics during the nationalist struggle to paralyze a foreign, imperialist government. JP was calling on the people to undermine their own Indian government. It was particularly disturbing that JP was encouraging civil, police, and military officials of the government "not to hesitate to revolt against those directives that are 'unethical and immoral' in character. Your loyalty," he said, "is to the national flag and the constitution, not to the Prime Minister. . . . If an order appears to your conscience as something against the popular will and the national interest, *then it is your duty not to obey such an order"* (emphasis added).[6] Apart from inciting the officials, whose duty it was to uphold the structural unity of the country, to revolt, JP, unlike Mahatma Gandhi, was also ready to discard a peaceful approach for a violent one. "If the problems of the people cannot be solved democratically, I will also take to violence," said JP.[7]

JP's statements and actions were often ambivalent and contradictory: He spoke of "party-less democracy" while encouraging an alliance of opposition parties and campaigning for opposition candidates (for example, in Gujarat). He made simultaneous references to *satyagraha* and violence-based "total revolution" that would usher in "people's governments." And he received funds from industrialists, though he talked of village-based economy. JP's biggest supporters came from the ranks of the educated urban middle classes. Whichever way one views JP's formula for the overthrow of the Congress government, it has to be admitted that JP's mass movement would have eroded the democratic institutions and values that had evolved since 1947.

Indira Gandhi's response to the June 25 challenge of Jayaprakash Narayan was to get the president of India that very day (June 25, 1975) to declare a state of National Emergency on the grounds that the security of India was "threatened by internal disturbances." Indira Gandhi's action, too, was hardly meant to strengthen democracy; she had not even consulted the members of her cabinet before approaching the president. Under the Emergency, all the opposition leaders, including JP, were promptly arrested, censorship was imposed on the press, demonstrations and strikes were banned, and civil liberties guaranteed under the Constitution were abrogated. During the twenty-one months of the Emergency rule, over 110,000 persons were arrested and detained without trial. The undemocratic democracy of the viceregal days was back again.

Indira Gandhi's claim that she had nipped a conspiracy against the state backed by foreign enemies of India is debatable, but what is not debatable is that Indira Gandhi bolstered her dictatorial powers by imposing the Emergency. Soon after the declaration of Emergency, Parliament amended the electoral law and exonerated Indira Gandhi of the offenses for which she had been found guilty. It also amended the Constitution to deny the courts the power to review a presidential proclamation of emergency (38th Amendment) and the right to consider electoral disputes involving the president, the vice-president, the prime minister and the speaker of the Lok Sabha (39th Amendment). Another amendment, the 42nd, permitted the government to prohibit "anti-national" activities and further reinforced the powers of the prime minister in relation to those of the legislature and the judiciary.

Along with the imposition of Emergency, Indira Gandhi announced a populist Twenty-Point Program of economic reform that aimed at reducing inflation, liquidating rural indebtedness and bonded labor, providing aid to needy students, punishing tax evaders, and bringing discipline to the industrial sector (e.g., strikes were forbidden) and the bureaucracy. While the trains did run on time, most of the goals of the program were never achieved; ironically, it was the industrialists who were helped by the program because they could keep the workers' wages down without fear of strikes.

Indira Gandhi's biggest success during the period of her dictatorship—also the cause of her undoing—was that she managed to build up her son, Sanjay Gandhi, as her political heir. Sanjay, who was neither a member of the government nor a high office holder in the Congress, was given the privilege of speaking and acting on his mother's behalf. And Sanjay soon made loyalty to his person a measure of loyalty to his mother. His word was seen as a command from his mother, and Sanjay used this extraconstitutional authority to publicly chastise and humiliate chief ministers and high civil officials who did not kowtow to him.

Sanjay had a Five-Point Program of his own that incorporated some worthy plans, such as family planning and slum clearance. But the manner in which he carried out these plans made his excesses even more painfully unbearable than those of his mother's; for example, about 10 million persons, mostly men and mostly poor, were forcibly sterilized (hundreds were literally dragged in from the roadside to undergo vasectomies), and slum dwellings were demolished without giving their inhabitants a proper alternative place to live (in Delhi some of the Muslim slum dwellers who offered resistance were shot and killed by the police).

With the press gagged, the opposition leaders in jail, the intelligentsia silenced, and self-serving sycophants (one of whom had introduced the slogan "Indira Is India") giving her encouraging reports of India's progress, Indira Gandhi never came to know how badly her popular image had been bruised by Sanjay and the widespread misbehavior of the police and other officials who, under the protection of the Maintenance of Internal Security Act (MISA), arbitrarily harassed and terrorized innocent persons for payoffs.

The Final Humiliation

The year 1976 had otherwise been a good one: there were no food shortages, inflation was under control, the state of the economy was healthy and improving, and real national income had gone up by 6.5 percent in 1975 and by 3 percent in 1976. However, at the end of the year, Indira Gandhi was still thinking of deferring the elections by another year. But then, in January 1977, as unexpectedly as she had imposed Emergency, Indira Gandhi announced that elections would be held in March. In anticipation of that event she released the opposition, lifted the censorship on the press, and announced that political rallies and public meetings would be permitted. All political observers were caught by surprise. No one had believed that Indira Gandhi would relinquish her dictatorial power so readily.

Why did Indira Gandhi take this decision (and it was very much her personal decision)? Was it because she genuinely believed in the democratic system? Or was it because she thought that she had, indeed, won the hearts of her people and that they would prove their faith in her by returning her to power? Or did she want to legitimize the Emergency and the constitutional changes she had introduced? Or was it because, as it was widely rumored, an astrologer had told her that this way she could provide legitimacy to Sanjay's political status and ensure that he would succeed her as prime minister? (In her announcement Indira Gandhi had referred to Sanjay's Five-Point Program in such a way that it was equated to official government policy.)

Whatever Indira Gandhi's reason or reasons, she was astute enough to give the opposition hardly any time to prepare for the elections, thus tilting the electoral scale in her favor. Unfortunately for her, and fortunately for the future of Indian democracy, the four major opposition parties,* under the guiding hand of Jayaprakash Narayan, submerged their individual identities and formed the Janata (People's) Party; this meant that the Janata could put up one candidate for each candidate fielded by Indira's Congress and thereby avoid a split of votes between the individual parties that formed the united front. It also did not bode well for Indira Gandhi that in February one of her senior cabinet ministers, Jagjivan Ram, the recognized leader of the Harijans, left Indira Gandhi's Congress to establish his own party, Congress for Democracy, and declared his intention to collaborate with the Janata Party.

Though Congress (R) was much better organized and much better funded than the hastily formed Janata, the Congress election slogan, "For Progress and Stability—Vote Congress" was rejected by the nation in favor of the Janata slogans that exhorted the people to remember the excesses of Indira Gandhi's government and vote Janata if they wanted to replace "Dictatorship and Slavery" with "Bread with Freedom and Democracy." Over 60 percent of the electorate, nearly 200 million persons, turned out for the elections, and the Janata Party won a clear victory over the Congress, gaining 298 seats (as against Congress's 153) out of total of 539 Lok Sabha seats. The humiliation of Indira Gandhi was complete when the election results revealed that neither she nor her beloved son Sanjay had been elected from their "safe" constituencies.

The Janata was led by Morarji Desai, who after the Congress had split and he had been dismissed from the cabinet by Indira Gandhi in 1969, had remained with Congress (O). Desai became the prime minister and chose Charan Singh of the Bharatiya Lok Dal as the deputy prime minister.

A few months later the elected Congress (R) governments in nine states were dissolved on the grounds that Congress (R) in these states had won only 9 out of the 300 parliamentary seats, which according to Janata meant that the Congress (R) no longer had the confidence of the people. In the new elections, the Janata

---

*The parties were: Congress (O); Jana Sangh, a pro-Hindu party; the Bharatiya Lok Dal, whose leader, Charan Singh, represented the prosperous agricultural classes in Uttar Pradesh; and the Socialist Party.

Party and its allies carried all nine states. The Janata's position was further strengthened when, in July 1977, its candidate, Sanjiva Reddy, was elected India's new president. The Janata had, however, not helped the cause of constitutionalism by using the presidential rule to dismiss the nine state Congress ministries on the rather arbitrary and undemocratic argument that they had "lost the confidence of the people."

Phase III: The Janata Interlude, 1977–1979

The Janata success could have been a great turning point in the history of contemporary India. It could have led to the establishment of a two-party system and placed democracy on a firmer footing. However, despite the Janata's success, the elections proved that it did not have a national base; the Janata had gained 222 of its 298 seats from the northern Hindi-speaking states, but only 6 seats from the four southern states from where the Congress gained 92. Furthermore, the Janata was not a unified political party. It was an alliance of convenience, and once in power the major parties that had amalgamated for purposes of the elections began squabbling for office; friction also arose over their different, often contradictory, ideologies. Having shared the ministries among these parties, the government lacked unity and could not formulate any cohesive policies.

On the whole the Janata carried on the foreign and internal policies of the government it had toppled. The Janata had declared that it would liberalize the private sector, encourage small-scale industries, expand primary education, create 40 million new jobs, and improve the quality of life in the villages (ensure clean drinking water for all the villages and bring electricity to half of them), but by the time the Janata government fell in 1979, it had made no fundamental changes in Indira Gandhi's economic policies. Desai, who had been dismissed by Indira Gandhi for opposing the nationalization of banks, did not even undo that policy!

The most important contribution of the Janata to Indian politics was that it eliminated the repressive, undemocratic laws and practices that had been introduced during the Emergency. The intelligence organizations that had been misused by Indira Gandhi to blackmail friends and foes were cut down in size; the authority vested in the prime minister's secretariat was reduced; political prisoners were released; the freedom of the press was restored; and the courts were given back their judicial authority. The Janata amended the Constitution to revoke the extraordinary authority placed in the hands of the executive at the expense of civil and legal rights by Indira Gandhi's 42nd Constitution Amendment Act. Other than this, the record of the Janata was a dismal one. All the evils of black marketeering, profiteering, tax evasion, smuggling, and the hoarding of goods in short supply (to raise their prices) made a comeback. Desai's son, Kantilal, like Indira's son Sanjay, became a national disgrace because he used his father's name to become extremely wealthy through bribery and corruption, and like Sanjay he was protected by his parent.

As these scandals spread, the Janata leaders brought down their prestige even further by publicly attacking each other's credentials and bickering over the division of power. It also did not help the Janata's image when it undermined non-Janata state governments, mostly those that were still run by the Congress Party, by encouraging defections. Nor were the Janata's continued attacks on Indira Gandhi received well by the populace at large. This was particularly so after October 1977, when the Janata arrested her on charges that were so flimsy that the magistrate released her within two minutes of the case being brought before him. However, the unthinking, narrow-minded Janata leaders did not stop their highly personalized campaign against Indira Gandhi and a year later jailed her once again for a week. It is true that they were only using the techniques used against them by Indira Gandhi and Sanjay during the Emergency, but unfortunately their short-sighted behavior ensured that political vendetta would become a part of India's future political life.

Indira Gandhi's popularity had begun to surge again, but before she came out of retirement to reenter the political arena wholeheartedly, she decided to purge Congress (R) of "disloyal" followers, many of whom had distanced themselves from her after her defeat and criticized her for the Emergency and its excesses. Indeed, some had gone so far as to join hands with the Janata. Her solution, true to her character, was simple: she split the party once again, calling her faction Congress (Indira)—Congress (I) for short. The older body became Congress (S), "S" for its president, Swaran Singh. The appellation Congress (I) implied that the party would now be an even more personally run organization than Congress (R) ever had been. Loyal, subservient officials were appointed (as against being elected) at every level of the Congress (I) organization, and state chief ministers were handpicked by Indira or her son, Sanjay. Indira Gandhi saw little need to change her pre-1975 political style.

On the political scene in 1978, the Janata's smear campaigns of character assassination had only helped to make a martyr of Indira, and the forgiving Indian populace, disillusioned by Janata failures, welcomed her comeback. Indira Gandhi's untiring trips around the country and her shrewd wooing of the suffering lower castes and the minorities brought astounding successes. Congress (I) did remarkably well in the 1978 state elections, and Indira was returned to the Lok Sabha in a by-election in November 1978. The Congress (I) was now the official opposition party.

By 1979, the economy had begun to flag, and there was an alarming rise in prices of consumer goods. In July 1979, Desai's government fell because some of the members of the coalition withdrew their support from him or left the Janata altogether. Charan Singh, basing his strength on his Bharatiya Lok Dal Party, became the next prime minister, but he headed a minority government that ironically sought the support of Congress (I) to remain in power. Within a month, Indira Gandhi withdrew that support, and the president, seeing that no stable coalition was in the offing, dissolved Parliament and called for general elections in January 1980.

The Janata interlude had contributed little to democracy and even less to secularism. The merger of the Jan Sangh, representing militant Hinduism, with the Janata Party not only gave respectability to Hindu nationalists but, by the same token, impaired the secularity of Congress (O), the leading body of the coalition. Many leaders of Jan Sangh refused to accept the proposition that they should, at the very least, break their relations with the RSS. Strangely enough, Desai, the leader of Congress (O), did not think that this dual membership should be taken seriously by Janata.[8] In 1980, most of the Jan Sangh members left Janata and formed the Bharatiya Janata Party (BJP), which later rose to become the biggest single party outside the Congress and a serious contender for national power.

Phase IV: Indira Gandhi's Last Term and Her Assassination, 1980–1984

The Second Indira Wave

The collapse of the Janata had given ample evidence that the evolution of a two-party system was a hopeless dream. It had also proved that, even when given an opportunity, the opposition had no credible, alternative program to present to the nation other than a mild variation of the one followed by Indira Gandhi's Congress.

The 1980 elections brought out the old fighting spirit in Indira Gandhi. She traveled 40,000 miles in sixty-three days, visited 384 constituencies, and addressed 1,500 rallies. Her slogan "Vote Congress (I) for Order, Stability, and Progress" appealed to people who were disgusted with the Janata era and hardly considered Charan Singh or Jagjivan Ram, the other two contenders for prime ministership, as all-India leaders. The landslide victory gained by Congress (I) (351 seats, for a two-thirds majority in Parliament) was a personal triumph for Indira Gandhi, and for Sanjay, nearly 150 of whose youthful followers had been returned to the Parliament.

The Congress (I) victory confirmed the fact that it was the only national party; it had gained votes from across the country and from all social groupings, ranging from caste Hindus to the Muslims, the Sikhs, the Scheduled Castes, and the Scheduled Tribes. The most important group among those that had voted against her was the middle-class intelligentsia.

Once Indira Gandhi was back in power, she began to display her old tendency of trying to achieve a position of unassailable authority. Apart from avoiding internal party elections (not a difficult proposition, since she had already turned the Congress into a one-person party) that may have produced local leaders with independent bases of political power, she appointed pliant chief ministers in the states and nonentities in the central cabinet. The consequent weakening of the state party organizations would, in time, produce several negative results, but for the moment it satisfied Indira Gandhi to hold all the strings in her hands.

Immediately after the national election, Indira Gandhi, basing her decision on the precedent set by the Janata government in 1977, got the president to dissolve nine opposition-controlled state assemblies. In the reelections that followed, Sanjay Gandhi established his political credentials and justified his mother's expectations for his future political career by planning the strategy of the elections and using his Youth Congress to run the electioneering campaigns; Congress (I) gained eight of the nine states. Sanjay, like his mother, used his position to nominate several of the new chief ministers in the Congress states, some of whom soon proved that loyalty to the Gandhi family was no substitute for political competence. Indira Gandhi, however, had full trust in her son and accorded Sanjay a more formal status in the party by making him general secretary of the All-India Congress Committee (AICC). It was generally understood that Sanjay was the heir-apparent and was being groomed to take over the rulership of the country after his mother.

Despite all the power that she had accumulated in her person, Indira Gandhi's last term in office, ending with her assassination in 1984, was not an easy one. Many of her troubles stemmed from her personality. She had developed a deep-seated sense of insecurity that did not let her trust anyone around her except Sanjay. Her paranoia reached a point where even the giver of friendly advice was seen as an enemy out to destroy her. She was convinced that any trouble that arose in the country was the creation of her internal enemies or the work of a "foreign hand" (this usually referred to the CIA). Sanjay went even further in making loyalty the touchstone for judging the worth of political and bureaucratic officials. As a result, both in the political arena and in the higher echelons of the civil bureaucracy, many crude, incompetent sycophants came to replace highly sophisticated persons of recognized talent and integrity. As Indira Gandhi put it, "Am I to blame if I entrust sensitive jobs to men who may not be very bright but on whom I can rely?"[9] It is a sad reflection on the state of affairs that the president of India, Giani Zail Singh (president, 1982–1987), who had been nominated by Indira Gandhi, could publicly say that "if Madam asks me to pick up a broom and sweep the floor, I would happily do so";[10] that the chief minister of Maharashtra could declare that "I am a nominee of Indiraji . . . [and] I am going to stay in office as long as I enjoy Mrs. Gandhi's blessings";[11] or that the chief minister of Andhra Pradesh, while admitting that he did not even know how he came to be given that post, added that "all I can say is that I want to remain close to her."[12]

Indira Gandhi's arbitrary approach to national politics alienated the intelligentsia, but because she had been hurt by the opposition of the intelligentsia during the Emergency, Indira Gandhi refused to recognize the need to placate this class and gain its confidence and support; as an astute politician she should have been particularly conscious of the role of the press. However, in her estimation, "half the people calling themselves intellectuals are under American influence which works to our disadvantage. The other half, under Russian influence, have also [turned against us]."[13] Obviously it was futile to try and bring about a reconciliation. Gradually, even the moderate intellectuals, a majority in 1980, who had hoped that Indira Gandhi, chastened by her 1977 failure, would provide the healing touch to fractured Indian politics, became disillusioned.

Indira Gandhi's personalization of power burdened her with so many petty problems of bureaucratic and political decision making, better handled by her subordinates if only she had trusted them, that she was left with little time to grapple with the larger issues of national importance, many of which were wholly new to the country and demanded much careful rethinking of old policies. But then, according to some analysts, Indira Gandhi "was not a policy-oriented leader."[14]

Externally, the Soviet invasion of Afghanistan in December 1979 brought the cold war to South Asia. India, believing that American-style verbal attacks would only harden the Soviet position, tried to use quiet diplomacy to influence the Soviets to withdraw their troops. At the same time India condemned the American decision to renew military aid to Pakistan because it was perceived as a threat to Indian security. India should have known that it was too weak a country to have any impact on the superpowers. So while the Soviets got drawn deeper into a messy war, the Americans committed $3.2 billion in arms (including F-16 fighter planes) and economic aid to Pakistan, the friendly "frontline state." India, wanting to retain its military superiority over Pakistan, could only respond to this unforeseen development by increasing its own defense expenditures.

Indira Gandhi did try to underscore India's importance as a major regional and Third World power by holding the Asian Games in New Delhi in 1982, the summit meeting of the Non-Aligned Movement (NAM) in March 1983 (Indira Gandhi took over its chairmanship), and the meeting of the Commonwealth Heads of State in November 1983. These were prestigious, lavish, and spectacular events, but were hardly significant in the larger world context. If these activities were intended to impress the Indian public, they proved to be total failures. External affairs meant little to Indians, who were in the throes of rapidly escalating internal wars. In fact, from the very first year of her return to office, Indira Gandhi was forced to turn her attention away from foreign policy initiatives, other than the few activities mentioned above, to internal problems.

However, before she could do so, she suffered a very painful and tragic personal loss. In June 1980, soon after he was appointed general secretary of the AICC, Sanjay, while flying a small plane that had not yet been approved for flight, died in a crash. Indira was so depressed and heartbroken that she appeared to lose all interest in her work. At this point, Rajiv Gandhi (1944–1991; prime minister, 1984–1989), Sanjay's elder brother and a pilot for Indian Airlines, who had shown little interest in politics and was happy living a comfortable, private life with his Italian wife, Sonia, and his children, was pressured to resign his job and join his mother. In 1981, Rajiv was elected to the Lok Sabha from Sanjay's constituency, and in 1983 he was made a general secretary of Congress (I). Rajiv now became Indira Gandhi's successor as prime minister.

With Rajiv ensconced as her confidant, adviser, and putative successor, Indira became much more of her old self and began to display her earlier vigor in handling the various crises that were emerging in the 1980s. What distinguished the current explosion of internal conflicts (from the scattered, localized pre-1980 communal incidents) was that they were large-scale, *organized* protest movements that involved large territorial units and large segments of the population. Two of these outbursts of mass unrest, in the border states of Assam and Punjab (after Indira's death in 1984, Kashmir would join the group of troubled border states), turned into separatist movements that undermined central authority and posed a threat to national security.

Assam and the Northeast. By 1980, northeastern India comprised the relatively more populous state of Assam and five tribal states (Arunachal Pradesh, Nagaland, Manipur, Meghalaya, and Tripura) and one union territory (Mizoram) with smaller populations. The tribal states had been hesitatingly carved out of the old British province of Assam in the hope that this concession would end tribal insurgency and satisfy the demand of the tribes for autonomous homelands. On the whole, the creation of these states brought peace to the area (the Mizoram unrest did not end until it gained statehood in 1987), though secessionist guerrilla groups, particularly in Nagaland, Manipur, and Tripura, have continued to periodically attack the local authorities. The main reason for this is that some tribals still feel that their lifestyle and culture are threatened by the influx of non-tribal "foreigners"—Assamese and Bengali Hindus and immigrant Bangladeshi Muslims.

The crisis in the much larger state of Assam, too, arose out of a similar fear of immigrants, primarily the thousands of Bangladeshis who had sought refuge in Assam during the Bangladesh war (1971). The Assamese, a majority of whom are Hindus, had long hated all Bengalis (most of whom were also Hindus) who, during the British era, had come to dominate the provincial administration and after independence begun to control Assam's economy; in the urban areas of Assam in 1980, the Bengali-speaking population outnumbered the Assamese-speaking people. The fact that many of the new immigrants were illegal and Muslim gave the issue a communal coloring.

The Assamese perception was that large numbers of these Bangladeshi Muslims, illegal immigrants, had been placed on the electoral rolls to provide the Congress with a "vote bank" (a popular term in India indicating an assured bloc of votes). Consequently, a popular demand arose that the electoral rolls be revised. Matters came to a head in December 1979, when parliamentary elections were declared and Assamese students established the All Assam Students' Union (AASU) to lead a mass demonstration against the holding of elections until the government had carried out "Four Ds": *detected* the illegal immigrants, *disenfranchised* them, *deported* them to Bangladesh, or *dispersed* them to other parts of India. The AASU was backed by the new regional party, Asom Gana Parishad

(Assam People's Council, or AGP) and the United Liberation Front of Assam (ULFA), as well as Hindu fundamentalist organizations such as the RSS.

The fury of the movement not only kept the elections from being held but it shut down the vital petroleum industry in Assam, which was still a major source of oil, and made it difficult for the tea estates owned by non-Assamese to function. For three years New Delhi held several rounds of talks with the leaders of the AASU to define the term "illegal" and finally agreed that those who had entered the state after 1971 would be deported. But the AASU rejected the offer and launched a more aggressive campaign against the so-called foreigners that caused such widespread violence and civil unrest that New Delhi had to suspend the state government, introduce President's Rule, and send in armed forces to help the local police in maintaining law and order.

Since, under the Constitution, the President's Rule could be imposed for only one year, state elections were held in February 1983. Yet Assam was not ready for the elections, and in any case the electoral rolls had yet to be revised. Indira Gandhi could have extended the President's Rule, but she unwisely went ahead with the elections, presumably because the installation of a Congress government in Assam would strengthen the center's hold over the state. The elections only exacerbated the political situation because most Assamese boycotted the elections. The confrontation exploded into violent clashes in which entire communities and whole villages were wiped out; nearly 5,000 men, women, and children were massacred in cold blood, and 300,000 people forced to flee their homes.

With only 2 percent of the electorate turning out to vote, the Congress victory was a farce and the Congress government, established on the basis of this electoral success, lacked all legitimacy. The so-called duly elected government could carry on only with the use of state terror. The leaders of the opposition refused to negotiate any further with New Delhi, and violence, though on a reduced level, continued until 1986, when Rajiv Gandhi's government reached a settlement with the Assamese.

Punjab. The Punjab crisis was even more serious than the one in Assam. In Assam the demand for autonomy never developed into a movement for independence; in Punjab it did.

As noted earlier, the Akali agitation for a Sikh homeland that had started before partition had been temporarily dissipated with the creation of a Punjabi-speaking state by Indira Gandhi in 1966 on linguistic, not communal, grounds. However, after its borders had been redrawn, Punjab was a Sikh-majority state; even though the Sikh majority was marginal (about 55 percent), it gave hope to some Akali factions that their goal of establishing *Khalsa raj* (Sikh rule) was now achievable. But the Sikhs were not a monolithic body under the control of the Akalis; indeed, a very large number of Sikhs were members of the nondenominational Congress Party. In immediate terms, the only way the Akalis could gain any political power was by forming an alliance with non-Congress opposition parties. It was just through such a maneuver that the Akali Party had managed to form a coalition government in 1967. Although that alliance had been so unstable that its government lasted only eight months, the Akalis had learned a useful tactic. They used this tactic to return to office from 1969 to 1971 in a coalition with Jan Sangh, the radical Hindu party, and again from 1977 to 1980 in an alliance with the Janata Party, when the Janata was in power at the center.

In 1980, as prime minister, Indira Gandhi dissolved the Punjab government along with those of eight other states (see above). The elections that followed brought back the Congress to power in Punjab. From 1966 to 1980, the Akali Party had been moderate in its policies, as can be seen in its readiness to form alliances with other parties. However, the Akali Party had never given up its belief that it was the "very embodiment of the hopes and aspirations of the Sikh Nation and as such [was] fully entitled to its representation," a sentiment that was endorsed by the working committee of the party in a resolution adopted at its meeting in Anandpur Sahib in 1973.[15] The resolution also spelled out the party's main goal that the Sikh nation should have preeminent political power in Punjab, the homeland of the Sikhs, its own capital at Chandigarh (then serving as a capital for Punjab and Haryana), and greater control over its water and land assets. The central irrigation plans that envisaged a network of canals connecting Punjab with the neighboring states was seen as a device for depriving Punjab of vital water resources.

It is significant that the demands of the Anandpur Sahib resolution were raised eight years later, in 1981, only after Indira Gandhi's policies had personalized and nationalized regional issues and made center-state relations confrontational. The Akali Party presented the center with a list of grievances alleging discrimination against the Sikhs and demanded that the center accept the main objectives of the Anandpur Sahib resolution. The agitation was radicalized by the All-India Sikh Student Federation (AISSF), which was disenchanted with the moderate, factionalized Akali leadership. Religion and politics had been so enmeshed that secular Sikhs could stand aloof only at the risk of being called traitors to the Sikh cause.

The central government began negotiations with Akali leaders that went on for nearly three years without any agreement. In the meantime, an anti-Akali, fanatic fundamentalist, Sant Jarnail Singh Bhindranwale, who had been encouraged and supported by Sanjay Gandhi and Zail Singh during the Emergency to split the Akali Party, became a popular leader by his own right, turned against his mentors, and began to lead a violent agitation for an independent Punjab. He created an armed group of do-or-die terrorists who assassinated prominent persons opposed to the demand for Khalistan. Bhindranwale established his military headquarters in the holiest of the Sikh temples, the Golden Temple at Amritsar, from where he directed his heavily armed followers to assassinate his opponents and civil and police officials, carry out indiscriminate killings of Hindus (men, women, and children) to strike terror in the hearts of the non-Sikh population, torch railway stations, and bomb government buildings. The religious warrior-leader became a hero in the eyes of the Sikh community, particularly of the Jat Sikhs, an agricultural caste that forms the majority of the Sikhs. By 1983 most Akali factions, too, had found it politically expedient to join the antigovernment violence.

As law and order in Punjab broke down and civic life became chaotic, Indira Gandhi employed her heavy-handed policy of bringing in the armed forces to quell the unrest. Her lack of tolerance for any political opposition kept her from winning over the moderate Akalis, but why she did not stem the Punjab trouble by entering the Golden Temple and arresting Bhindranwale before things got out of hand remains a mystery. However, in June 1984, she finally did order the Indian Army to flush out Bhindranwale from the Golden Temple (Operation Blue Star). The army, having no idea that the Golden Temple, under the guidance of a retired Indian Army Sikh general, had been turned into a veritable fortress with all kinds of sophisticated weapons, walked into a trap. When it came under fire, the Indian army, although it had been directed not to damage the temple, was forced to employ its own heavy weapons.

The operation ended in two days. Bhindranwale and hundreds of his followers were killed or had committed suicide and large quantities of arms and ammunition were recovered from the temple buildings. Hardly a Sikh anywhere in India was not shocked, angered, and humiliated by the desecration of the Golden Temple. Some Sikh troops (about 2 percent of the total number of Sikhs in the armed forces) mutinied and went on a rampage, shouting "Death to Indira Gandhi." In one regiment they even killed their Hindu commander. Many Sikh members of the Parliament resigned their seats.

The operation turned Bhindranwale into a martyr, and now the cause of Khalistan was taken up by even those who had rejected the idea earlier. Sikh high priests excommunicated the Sikh president of India, Zail Singh, and a Sikh union minister, Buta Singh, declaring them to be *tankhaiya* (apostates) for their role in Operation Blue Star. Many political figures, including Indira Gandhi and her entire family, and high army officers involved with Operation Blue Star, were put on hit lists. Sikh secessionist organizations abroad, the most active being in England, Canada, and America, heightened their demand for Khalistan and funneled money into Punjab to help finance and arm the extremists, who were now also supported by Pakistan, to help them to continue their terrorist activities. "India," according to the historian Khuswant Singh, "had to pay a very heavy price for the miscalculation, the heaviest being the assassination of the miscalculator, prime minister Indira Gandhi."[16] It would take several years for a modicum of normalcy to return to Punjab.

Kashmir. Though the crisis of Kashmiri separatism would arise later, it can be said that Indira Gandhi's authoritarian approach was also responsible for laying the seeds of future trouble in that state. In 1982, when the veteran nationalist Kashmiri leader Sheikh Abdulla, the head of the National Conference, passed away, his son, Farooq Abdullah, took over as head of the party and the post of chief minister. Farooq was a popular figure, and the National Conference did well under his auspices, defeating the Congress in the state elections. The National Conference had been the preeminent party in the state ever since partition, but Indira Gandhi, in her new mood of not allowing any opposition party (even one that was committed to the unity of the country) that showed even a hint of independence to exist, bribed members of the state assembly to shift their support away from Farooq so that he could be removed. Farooq was toppled in July 1984, the month following Operation Blue Star. This, as we shall see below, was the beginning of India's troubles in Kashmir.

Andhra Pradesh. Andhra Pradesh provides another example of Indira Gandhi's personalized style of government. In 1980, on her return to power, Indira Gandhi, following the practice she and Sanjay had adopted in other states, chose a loyal, though incompetent chief minister for Andhra Pradesh. In 1982, after Rajiv Gandhi had entered politics, he happened to visit Andhra Pradesh. The chief minister received him in such a servile and obsequious manner that Rajiv, who unlike Sanjay detested such behavior, publicly rebuked the chief minister. Rajiv's manner was taken as an insult to the whole of Andhra, and N. T. Ramarao ("N.T.R."), a popular film star, asserted "Telugu pride" by forming a party called Telugu Desam (Homeland of the Telugu-speaking People) Party, which defeated the Congress in January 1983. Rajiv may have been "Mr. Clean," as he was dubbed by the people who had been disgusted with Sanjay's corruption, but his arrogance and haughty temper were in keeping with the feudal style adopted by his mother.

As was her wont, Indira Gandhi saw N.T.R. as a threat, so in August 1984 she ordered the governor of Andhra Pradesh to remove him from office. N.T.R. was losing popularity and would have lost the next elections, but Indira Gandhi's action gave him a new lease on political life. He flew to Delhi with all the assembly legislators who supported him and paraded them before the president to prove that he was still democratically, and legally, the chief minister. All of India was aghast at the "rape of democracy," and Indira Gandhi got out of this awkward situation by dismissing the governor on the grounds that he had acted without her knowledge. In September N.T.R was once again chief minister of Andhra.

The Assassination of Indira Gandhi

A month later, on October 31, 1984, Indira Gandhi was shot to death by her Sikh bodyguards. Hindu hoodlums in Delhi, encouraged by some local Congress politicians, rioted and took revenge by massacring entire Sikh families and burning and looting their homes and places of business; perhaps several thousand innocent Sikhs were killed in the orgy of anti-Sikh violence. Mob violence against the Sikhs occurred in a few of the other states, too, but at a lesser scale than in Delhi.

Hindu communalism completed the work of the Sikh communalists and deepened the schism between the two communities that has not yet been fully bridged. It has not helped matters that over a decade and a half after Indira Gandhi's assassination, the perpetuators of the Delhi holocaust have yet to be punished or the victims of the riots compensated.

An Assessment of Indira Gandhi

As a broad generalization it can be said that Indira Gandhi's performance in the field of foreign policy was far better than that in the realm of domestic affairs.

Foreign Affairs

By 1984, India had gained self-sufficiency in food production and was no longer dependent on America's food grain aid that had often forced New Delhi to accept humiliating demands from Washington. The dismemberment of Pakistan and the establishment of Bangladesh in 1971 had raised India's status as a major regional power, as did the exploding of a nuclear device in 1974. The United States continued to tilt toward Pakistan, and Pakistan became a major partner of America in South Asia after the Soviet invasion of Afghanistan, but this did not keep Washington from gradually realizing that India was not a stooge of the Soviet Union and that Indira Gandhi's post-1980 economic policy, which liberalized controls over the private sector and opened the country to foreign investment, made India attractive to American corporate interest. (In 1984, America was India's biggest trading partner.) In 1983, seventeen years after Indira Gandhi had first become prime minister, it was a far more self-confident India that held the meeting of the nearly a hundred Non-Aligned Nations. This was the high point in Indira Gandhi's foreign policy, and she displayed her leadership capacity by using the conference to reactivate the languishing north-south dialogue and, more important, to promote south-south cooperation. The year 1983 also saw India's first move toward regional cooperation, when it formally inaugurated the scheme for South Asian Regional Cooperation (SARC).

Indira Gandhi may not have settled all the problems of foreign policy—there were tensions in India's relations with neighboring countries, particularly with Pakistan; Indo-Chinese relations had yet to be normalized; and rapprochement with America had not yet taken place—but when she left the scene, India had regained more or less the international dignity it had enjoyed under Nehru, and was accepted as a power to be reckoned with.

Internal Affairs

Indira Gandhi's record as a national leader was a dismal one. It is, perhaps, best summed up in a statement by an astute observer of Indian politics, Vir Sanghvi, who said that Indira Gandhi had destroyed or subverted most of the institutions of Indian democracy. She pretty much killed the Congress Party, which was one vehicle, especially under her father, Nehru, of ensuring that a vast country like India was ruled by consensus. She destroyed the powers of the chief ministers and damaged the federal structure. She pressurized the judiciary and sapped its independence by appointing mediocre judges and transferring to inconsequential and uncomfortable outposts those judges who dared to assert their independence. She damaged the independence of the bureaucracy by calling for a "committed civil service." She politicized the army by using it for civilian purposes and manipulating promotions. She turned the cabinet into a joke by vesting unprecedented and sweeping powers in her personal staff and in her sons. And she prevented any rivals from emerging within the party—peopling it with thieves and scoundrels.[17]

The result of these developments was that in the 1980s, India began to face a growing crisis of governability. Not only Indira Gandhi at the center but political leaders in the states had only two overriding concerns: to achieve power through electoral advantages gained by sacrificing all democratic and secular principles, and to hold on to power by perverting all democratic institutions.

For the first goal, politicians did not hesitate to exploit communal or caste differences; draw on primordial loyalties; corrupt the process by massive use of undeclared funds acquired from smugglers, profiteers, and black marketeers; or co-opt criminal elements to create turmoil and terrorize the voters. For the second, the power holders fractured and weakened the once nonpartisan, politically impartial institutions of bureaucracy and police by rewarding (through better jobs and promotions) those officials who proved their loyalty by carrying out illegal orders and by punishing (through transfers and delaying of promotions) those who resisted them. Thus law and order were perverted, the efficiency of the services was reduced, and honest officers were replaced by dishonest ones, who (following the example of the politicians) replaced standards of integrity and impartiality with bias and corruption. In the 1970s the politicians were leaning on the officials to go easy with the criminal elements who had helped the politician in the elections. In the 1980s, "quite a few of the notorious names in the world of crime . . . were no longer in need of low-level political support. A few had entered the legislature themselves; many more had friends in the state cabinets or in the Union Cabinet."[18]

India was in obvious need of a leader with vision who could stem the tide of political decay. In the beginning, it appeared that Rajiv Gandhi would be that leader.

Notes

1. Sarvepalli Gopal, ed., *Jawaharlal Nehru: An Anthology* (Delhi: Oxford University Press, 1983), pp. 566–567.

2. Tariq Ali, *An Indian Dynasty* (New York: G.P. Putnam's Sons, 1985), p. 153.

3. Mary C. Carras, *Indira Gandhi in the Crucible of Leadership* (Bombay: Jaico Publishing House, 1980), p. 3.

4. *The Hindu,* August 5, 1969.

5. Myron Weiner, edited by Ashutosh Varshney, *The Indian Paradox: Essays in Indian Politics* (New Delhi: Sage Publications, 1989), p. 89.

6. *Hindustan Times,* New Delhi, February 16, 1975.

7. Ajit Bhattacharjea, *Jayaprakash Narayan: A Political Biography* (New Delhi: Vikas, 1975), p. 137.

8. See James Manor, ed., *Nehru to the Nineties: The Changing Office of the Prime Minister in India* (Vancouver: UBC Press, 1994), p. 201.

9. Inder Malhotra, *Indira Gandhi: A Personal and Political Biography* (London: Hodder & Stoughton, 1989), p. 228.

10. Ibid., p. 21.

11. *India Today,* April 15, 1982, p. 21.

12. Ibid., March 15, 1982, p. 24.

13. Malhotra, *Indira Gandhi,* p. 228.

14. Myron Weiner, *The Indian Paradox,* p. 253.

15. Quoted in Rajiv A. Kapur, *Sikh Separatism: The Politics of Faith* (Delhi: Vikas, 1986), p. 221.

16. Khuswant Singh, *A History of the Sikhs, Vol. 2: 1839–1988* (Delhi: Oxford University Press, 1991), p. 378.

17. Quoted in Pranay Gupte, *Vengeance: India After the Assassination of Indira Gandhi* (New York: W.W. Norton & Company, 1985), pp. 71–72.

18. N. S. Saksena, "The Home Front: Law and Order," in D. R. Mankekar, ed., *Indira Era: A Symposium* (New Delhi: Navrang, 1986), p. 58.

9

The Decline of the Congress, 1985–1996

The Emergence of Hindu Nationalism and Caste Politics

Under the Indian Constitution, when a prime minister dies in office, the Parliamentary Committee of the party in power elects his or her successor. However, the assassination of Indira Gandhi created a vacuum that could have been hazardous to national stability, and President Zail Singh, realizing the danger, set aside all parliamentary conventions and promptly installed Rajiv Gandhi as the interim prime minister (October 31). Zail Singh's action was immediately legitimized by the 497 Congress (I)* members of Parliament, who elected Rajiv as party leader. On November 12 he was also unanimously elected President of Congress.

Rajiv Gandhi: The Last of the Nehru Dynasty, 1984–1991

Rajiv Gandhi started his high career with certain handicaps. He had been in politics for less than four years (having been reluctantly brought into politics after the death of his brother in 1980), a member of parliament for three, and general secretary of Congress for two, and had never held a ministerial post. All this spelled political inexperience. That he went on to choose his advisers from his elitist school buddies, who also had no political experience, did not prove to be of much help either.

On the positive side, Rajiv was the fourth-generation heir to the Nehru dynasty's political capital, and he had national recognition and the sympathy of the nation

---

*Henceforth referred to as "the Congress," because all other Congress factions had, for all practical purposes, disappeared.

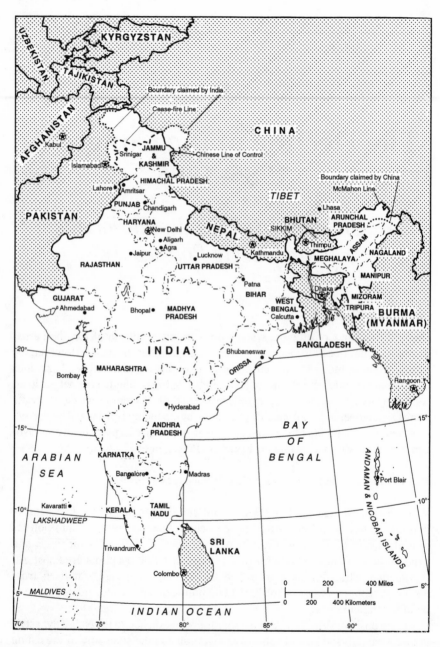

Political Map of India

Some Important Dates and Events, 1985–1996

1985	*Eighth elections for Lok Sabha*
1985–1989	**Prime minister, Rajiv Gandhi (Congress)**
	Beginning of secessionist movement in Kashmir
1989	*Ninth elections for Lok Sabha*
1989–1990	**Prime minister, V. P. Singh (Janata Dal)**
1990–1991	**Prime minister, Chandra Shekhar (Samajwadi Janata Dal)**
1991	*Tenth elections for Lok Sabha*
	Rajiv Gandhi assassinated while on an election tour
1991–1996	**Prime minister, P. V. Narasimha Rao (Congress)**
1992	Babri Masjid incident and communal riots
	Right-wing Hindu party, Bharatiya Janata Party (BJP), emerges as opposition party

shocked by the assassination of his mother. Rajiv, unlike his brother and mother, also had a clean public image (he had been dubbed "Mister Clean" even before he became Prime Minister) and had impressed the people with his handsome demeanor and youthful desire to lead India into the age of technology and science. Having become prime minister at the age of forty, he was the hero of the youth generation that constituted two-thirds of the electorate. His predilection for private enterprise and modern management methods also brought him enthusiastic support from the growing professional and business classes. Indeed, Rajiv had excited the imagination and hopes of the entire nation.

Within weeks of his becoming prime minister, Rajiv Gandhi declared parliamentary elections for December 24, 1984, and, riding a sympathy wave, he was returned to power with the largest number of seats ever won by any party and the highest-ever proportion of votes—the Congress had acquired 401 of the 515 seats in the new Lok Sabha.* It was a massive victory.

The Congress made similarly impressive gains in the state elections that followed in February–March 1985. Rajiv Gandhi, indeed, had received the people's mandate, but it must be borne in mind that, however well intentioned Rajiv may have been, and there is no doubt about the sincerity of his initial approach to power, Rajiv's inheritance included a divided nation, separatist movements, a highly centralized and personalized government, a federal system that was collapsing, a weakened and politicized bureaucracy that could not maintain law and order, and an undemocratic, criminalized party of corrupt sycophants. Rajiv had to have an extraordinary sense of commitment, inner moral strength, and, most important, po-

---

*The total strength of the House was 535 seats but, for various reasons, polling for 20 seats had been postponed.

litical sagacity, to clean up the political system. Unfortunately, he lacked these qualities. By the end of his term Indian politics was once again in disarray, and Rajiv had revived his mother's authoritarian and populist policies. The two main problems that came to undermine Rajiv's endeavors at nation building were his political naïveté that kept him from formulating coherent, long-term policies and the growth of corruption that undermined his credibility.

However, Rajiv Gandhi started off on a good footing, and his fresh, more open approach to old problems, and his obvious desire to solve them through a policy of reconciliation, won the respect of even his adversaries. For example, soon after the elections, L. K. Advani, general secretary of the opposition Bharatiya Janata Party (BJP),* remarked that, "When you talk to [Rajiv] you get the impression that he wants change, and this gives hope for the future."[1]

During the first year-and-a-half, Rajiv did appear to be doing everything right. Several laws were passed in 1985 that were intended to make political life "cleaner." One was the Anti-Defection Bill that prohibited elected members of Parliament and state legislatures from changing their party affiliation during the term of the legislature. This so-called "floor crossing" had made a mockery of party loyalty, and several state governments had been brought down by legislators, lured by promises of personal gain, defecting to an opposition party. Under the new law any elected representative who wanted to join another party had to resign and seek reelection.

Another law changed the statutory limits on election expenses and allowed businessmen and business houses to make "open" donations to political parties. This was a salutary move, because the growing cost of electioneering had forced all parties, including Congress, to elicit secret donations from business houses. This practice had added another dimension to rampant political corruption: corporations that made huge under-the-table cash donations to political parties expected favors in return, such as higher quotas of licensed commodities and permits for the import of scarce materials. A party in power was also expected to overlook the corporations' undeclared incomes; illegal contributions could, after all, be made only from illegal sources. As a result, the amount of black money circulating in the country had begun to undercut national revenues and create an underground black economy.

It was not surprising, therefore, that following the new law, Rajiv's government began to crack down on big businesses for tax evasion. Nearly 3,500 search-and-seizure operations were carried out in 1985 under the direction of the finance minister, V.P. Singh, leading to the recovery of millions of dollars of concealed income and the arrest of many well-known businessmen. At the same time, Rajiv's government cut taxes and relaxed controls on the private sector to help facilitate its healthy development and for the generation of a new corporate culture. Rajiv, while not publicly disparaging socialism, displayed an obvious leaning toward the capitalist system.

---

*Advani became president of the BJP in 1986.

Rajiv exhibited a similar positive approach to social problems by setting up the post of ombudsman and passing a law that put restrictions on the amount that could be given as dowry because the dowry system often placed an unbearable burden on the parents of the bride.

The most spectacular of Rajiv Gandhi's early achievements were in Punjab and Assam, where he forged accords with the moderate dissident leaders and restored the political process. In Punjab the Akali Party was split between extremist militants—who were responsible for bomb explosions in cities inside and outside Punjab and, allegedly, for the blowing up of an Air India plane with 329 aboard off the Irish coast—and moderates led by Sant Langowal. Rajiv released Langowal from jail and signed an accord with him in July 1985. Although the details of the accord, which included the transfer of the union territory of Chandigarh to Punjab, had yet to be worked out, state elections followed in September and ended the Presidential Rule that had lasted nearly a year.

Even though extremists assassinated Langowal in August, the elections went ahead and Langowal's faction, the Akali Party (Langowal), came to power with a landslide victory; significantly, there was a 70 percent turnout of the registered voters. This did not stop the extremists from continuing their activities, but it looked as if the democratic process had been reinstituted in Punjab under Chief Minister S.S. Barnala.

Similarly, the peace accord signed with Assamese dissidents (All Assam Students' Union and the Asom Gana Parishad or AGP) in August 1985 ended the anti-immigration agitation. The center accepted the proposition that all illegal immigrants who had entered the state between 1966 and 1971 would be deprived of voting rights and citizenship for ten years, and those who had arrived after 1971 would be deported. The sitting legislature (elected in 1983), popularly perceived as lacking legitimacy, was dissolved, and fresh elections held in December 1985 brought the AGP to power. And in the settlement of ethnic disputes, the brightest spot was the 1986 accord that ended the twenty-year-old state of emergency in Mizoram and turned the underground, militant rebel leader Laldenga into a civil leader: he became chief minister of the newly created Mizoram state.

All who were interested in the return of normalcy to the country and an improvement in center-state relations welcomed Rajiv's political successes in Punjab and Assam. Even the fact that the local parties, and not the Congress, had won electoral victories in these states was seen as a welcome development in party politics. Rajiv had placed national affairs above narrow party considerations. At the same time, Rajiv's promise that he would revitalize democracy within the Congress Party by holding party elections (last held in 1969) for Congress committees at all levels strengthened the impression that he was keen to reverse Indira Gandhi's policy of concentrating power in the hands of the Congress president. Speaking at the Congress centenary celebrations at Bombay in December 1985, Rajiv had the temerity to stand before the much older stalwarts of the party and denounce the "brokers of power and influence" in the Congress "who dispense patronage to convert a mass movement into a feudal oligarchy"[2] and who, according to Rajiv, thrived on slogans of caste and religion.

Rajiv Gandhi's blatant attack on the old guard pleased the youthful members of the party, but naturally alienated a host of aging regional leaders who had a narrower, more parochial view of politics and who did not share Rajiv's larger vision; they, for example, saw the Punjab and Assam elections as Rajiv's failure to foster Congress Party interests. Rajiv's democratization program, if he had indeed carried it out, perhaps could have replaced the conservative elements in the Congress with more forward-looking younger members, but this was not to be. The intraparty elections and the anticipated reorganization of the Congress never did take place.

1986–1989: The Years of Disarray

After a year of promise and hope, Indian politics drifted back into the pattern established by Indira and Sanjay Gandhi, where power was highly personalized and centralized, where ideals were replaced with greed for personal gain, where national interests were lost in the clamor of parochial demands, and where long-term policies gave way to ad hoc responses. In the final analysis, Rajiv not only failed to stem the trend that was contributing to the weakening of the democratic institutions and the corruption of the bureaucracy, but he actually strengthened it. As early as 1986, it started becoming apparent that Rajiv's party-building and nation-building plans had begun to unravel.

Rajiv's attempt to clean up the Congress was honest but flawed. He never fully realized the importance of the old guard that kept the party organization functioning in the states despite a pattern of corruption. Without the support of the states' Congresses, the national organization could do precious little to reform the party. Rajiv talked of training a new cadre of Congress workers and replacing old state leaders with fresh blood, but he had to carry out this colossal task without stopping the day-to-day work of the party, and that posed a dilemma. Thus, for example, to run the state elections in 1985, Rajiv had no recourse but to depend on the very leaders whom he had criticized as "corrupt power brokers" and whom he had wanted to eliminate.

The bigger blow to his program came when Rajiv Gandhi was forced to postpone Congress intraparty elections (scheduled for mid-1986) that were rightly conceived as an important first step in bringing back democracy and legitimacy to the party. First, it came to light that party officials who had been appointed by Indira Gandhi, anxious to ensure their own election, had started packing the party rolls with bogus members and that "over 60 percent of the enrolled members were either nonexistent or were not eligible for membership."[3] Second, Rajiv began to have apprehensions that his trusted lieutenants were planning to use the elections to enhance their own control of the party by getting their supporters, not Rajiv loyalists, elected to key posts. Third, Rajiv, since his popularity had already begun to decline, was faced with the possibility that many of the old stalwarts he was trying to push aside could use their considerable local following to get elected and thereby further weaken Rajiv's position within the party.

The postponed elections were never held and Rajiv abandoned his party reform program. As a consequence, Rajiv's weak attempts at party reform had only factionalized the disunited party even further. Under the circumstances, the question of infusing the party with a new ideological spirit did not even arise.

In 1987, after the Congress had lost several crucial elections in various states, Rajiv found it expedient to revert to the methods employed by Indira Gandhi. He consolidated his hold over the party at the center and tried to influence the fragmented state and local leadership by courting the very power brokers he had been so contemptuous of. He even brought back Sanjay's hooligans in the Youth Congress to help him carry out his newly adopted strong-arm tactics. He also deliberately began to espouse a populist, leftist posture in economic policies. However, none of this helped because internal factional bickering was weakening the Congress in several of the Hindi-speaking heartland states (Bihar, Uttar Pradesh, Madhya Pradesh, Haryana, and Rajasthan) that had been the stronghold of the party. Several of the best persons in Rajiv's government from these states left the Congress to join the opposition. As the leader of such a disorganized and corrupt party—corruption, which Rajiv was supposedly out to destroy, had made a raging comeback—Rajiv could hardly be expected to lead the country on the basis of a unified national vision.

Corruption and Authoritarianism

Of all the members of Rajiv's cabinet, V. P. Singh, the minister of finance, was most forceful in carrying out the economic liberalizing program while at the same time rooting out corruption in the private sector. Singh was an honest, hardworking, valuable minister, but within a year or so, as Rajiv's troubles in various quarters began to mount, Rajiv found it practically expedient to transfer Singh out of the Finance Ministry. Singh's zealous crackdown on corrupt businessmen, many of whom had close relations with top-ranking Indira loyalists and were major contributors to the Congress party, was no longer welcome. Singh was transferred to the Defense Ministry in January 1987. Rajiv's action damaged his clean image because the general public viewed Singh's transfer as "a victory for those business houses that wanted him out of finance."[4]

Unfortunately for Rajiv, Singh now turned his attention to the procurement department of the Defense Ministry and on April 9 announced that he was ordering an enquiry into a contract, signed when Indira Gandhi was prime minister, for the purchase of submarines from a German company. The company had paid an Indian agent 300 million rupees (over U.S.$20 million at the current exchange rate) as commission, although under the Government of India rules no middlemen were to be involved in defense contracts. Singh was harshly attacked by his cabinet colleagues and the Congress high command for ordering the probe, which was bound to reflect negatively on the Nehru family and the Congress Party. Rather than withdraw the probe, Singh resigned from the government on April 12, 1987.

Freed from the constraints of office, Singh now began to air his criticism of the Congress publicly, and this led to his expulsion from the party in 1988. The Janata Dal (JD), an alliance of centrist, national-level, opposition groups, promptly offered Singh, whose resignation and expulsion had gained him national prominence, the post of party president, which he accepted. As the head of an opposition party and the new "Mister Clean," he could now launch a campaign against Rajiv's corrupt government in earnest.

Singh was the first person to mention corruption in government, as something quite different from the ubiquitous corruption in the parties, and nothing that Rajiv could do would wash off the tarnish. The situation only became worse when, within days of Singh's resignation, Swedish radio announced that Bofors, a Swedish armament company with which Rajiv had signed a U.S.$1.25 billion contract for howitzers in 1986, had paid bribes to senior Indian politicians, most of whom were close associates of Rajiv. The government tried to dismiss the issue by saying that it was a foreign conspiracy to destabilize India, but few believed this and, in a public opinion poll carried out in August 1987, 44 percent thought that the prime minister was personally involved in the bribery racket.[5] The Bofors scandal was to haunt Rajiv for the rest of his term. Every month that passed revealed more and more damaging evidence, and Rajiv, by refusing to establish a parliamentary enquiry committee, provided grist for the rumor mill. Ten years later, in January 1996, five years after Rajiv had been assassinated, it was revealed that "documents obtained from Sweden established that Bofors was contractually bound to pay some 2,500 million rupees (72 million U.S. dollars) as kickbacks into secret Swiss bank accounts."[6]

In September 1987, Rajiv, in what was seen as an act of desperation, had the offices of the *Indian Express*, the newspaper that had most persistently investigated the corruption scandals, raided by armed police on the grounds that the paper had evaded customs duties in the purchase of printing machinery. Once again Rajiv's petulant behavior backfired and shocked not only Indians but the whole free world; a headline in *The New York Times* the next day read: "Intimidation Effort Seen."

In 1988, Rajiv got the parliament to pass a draconian anti–civil liberty legislation, the 59th amendment to the Constitution, which, though restricted to Punjab, gave the security agencies the powers to shoot to kill, arrest and confine civilians without due process, and impose press censorship. Another bill, the Defamation Bill, which made it a crime for any newspaper to criticize an act of the government, had to be withdrawn in the face of massive public opposition.

These were the last acts of an increasingly undemocratic, authoritarian government attempting to retain its hold over power. But the people had been disillusioned: the Congress was practically effaced in the Haryana state elections in 1987 and in mid-1988 it lost almost all parliamentary and state assembly seats in the by-elections in the electorally critical Hindi heartland states. All this implied that the Congress was ill-prepared for the forthcoming 1989 parliamentary elections.

Ethnic, Communal, and Caste Conflicts

If democracy fell by the wayside under Rajiv's imperious approach to politics, Nehruvian secularism, too, did not have much of a chance for growth. Despite the hope held out by the accords, the prospect of long-term peace in Punjab and Assam failed to materialize.

In Punjab, the Gandhi-Langowal accord had assured the Sikhs that, among other things, the city of Chandigarh would be transferred to Punjab on January 26, 1986, and that Haryana state, which also had its capital in Chandigarh, would be compensated by the transfer to Haryana of certain Hindi-speaking villages in Punjab. On January 25, when the Punjab government had made all the preparations to celebrate the transfer of Chandigarh, New Delhi announced that the date of transfer had been postponed. The unexpected action, whatever the reasons behind it, was shocking. It was slap on the face of the moderate Akali leadership and Chief Minister Barnala.

Rajiv had probably taken this action because of his need to mollify Haryana, which had not accepted the accord because it affected the state adversely, and where elections were due in June 1986. Even if one accepts the argument that Rajiv, having lost Punjab and Assam to non-Congress parties, could not afford to lose Haryana, it does not explain why he delayed decision on such a vital issue to the last minute.

Barnala, whose position had been severely weakened, came to be looked upon as a stooge of New Delhi, and factions of his Akali Party began to desert him in the belief that the Sikhs could not achieve their goals through constitutional means. This mood was exploited by the extremist Sikhs who increased their terrorist activities; the number of terrorist killings rose from 64 in 1985 to 620 in 1986, 883 in 1987,[7] 2,329 in 1988,[8] and over 1,700 in 1989.[9] The cry for Khalistan acquired new vigor, and Akali leaders could maintain their positions of leadership only by refusing to condemn the terrorists; some even made common cause with them. The terrorist attacks against Hindus, Sikh moderates, and police officials managed to put fear into the hearts of the civil population and the law-enforcing agencies. In late 1986 the terrorists flaunted their reach by assassinating a top general in far away Pune; the general was India's army chief at the time of Operation Blue Star.

In 1987, Rajiv responded to the deteriorating situation by suspending the state government and putting the state under Presidential Rule, which meant under direct central control. In 1988, Rajiv got Parliament to pass the 59th amendment to the Constitution, which gave the center power to extend President's Rule up to three years. (How like what the British had done in the bad old colonial days!) Instead of trying to understand the socioeconomic causes that lay behind the Punjab trouble, Rajiv declared the problem to be a law-and-order one and unleashed a reign of state violence. Having dismissed the moderate Barnala and his moderate faction, Rajiv thought that he could restore peace to Punjab by negotiating with the militant leader, J. S. Rode (who was released from prison for this purpose), but the effort was fruitless. In 1989, Rajiv turned once again to the moderates and promised to curb the powers of the police, bring back the political process through elections, and punish those who had been involved in the 1984 Delhi carnage. But the prime minister had lost political credibility, and no one believed in his capacity to shift away from the policy of drift. Punjab remained in a state of unrest through 1989, the year when the Congress lost the parliamentary elections and Rajiv his post of prime minister.

Likewise, Rajiv could not deliver on the Assam accord, which had brought the six years of political turmoil and the campaign against "foreigners" to an end. Since the laws made it difficult to prove illegal immigrant status, the AGP government could do little to expel or disenfranchise illegal aliens. The United Liberation Front of Assam (ULFA) distanced itself from an increasingly unpopular government and returned to its old militancy. ULFA had a well-organized and well-equipped army; it gradually enlarged its underground activities and set up a parallel government that taxed the villagers and traders; harassed the high executives of big businesses houses (such as the multinational tea corporations) and blackmailed them into paying millions of rupees; punished the citizens who broke its laws; and assassinated politicians and officials to prove that it was a force that could not be ignored.

Simultaneously, another militant ethnic Assamese group, the Bodo, emerged to heighten communal violence and tensions by demanding that a Bodoland be carved out of Assam territory north of the Brahmaputra river. The unrest in the state was a major consideration in the center's decision to delay the 1989 parliamentary elections in Assam.

In Kashmir, the government that had been propped up by the Congress after the dismissal of Farooq Abdullah in 1984 for "anti-nationalism" did not have the respect of the people and was so corrupt and unpopular that President's Rule had to be imposed on the state in early 1986. It took six months for Rajiv to fashion a "Rajiv-Farooq accord," an alliance of convenience between the National Conference and the state Congress party that brought Farooq back to power. However, since the details of the alliance were not made public, Kashmiri Muslims began to view Farooq as a stooge of New Delhi. In the words of M. J. Akbar, "it was a tainted alliance,"[10] and Farooq lost credibility.

For the first time anti-Indian Muslim fundamentalists, who did not need much backing from Pakistan, emerged on the Kashmiri political scene and started their agitation for independence or secession. Matters became worse in 1987, when the Kashmiris witnessed the most fraudulent elections ever held in the state; Farooq won the rigged elections, but he and Rajiv had lost Kashmir. Thousands of educated, unemployed youth, alienated by the corruption in government, joined the militants and discarded the language of peace for Kalashnikov rifles. The Punjab story began to unfold in the valley, with one difference: the population of the valley was primarily Muslim, and the mountainous border between Kashmir and Pakistan gave the rebels easy access to Pakistani arms and training.

In 1989, the last year of Rajiv's rule, the state capital, Srinagar, "experienced almost weekly rioting,"[11] and though the number killed in the state as a whole was still very limited, the situation was soon to assume the proportions of a civil war. A number of National Conference members publicly deserted the party, and in August 1989, "while large numbers celebrated Pakistan's Independence [August 14], just a handful attended the August 15 [India's Independence Day] function addressed by Farooq Abdullah."[12] The trouble in Kashmir soon added a wholly new dimension to India's security problems. In January 1990, the center dismissed the ineffective Farooq government and imposed President's Rule, which remained in force until September 1996.

Among other ethnic-cum-communal troubles, mention should be made of the violent agitation started in 1986 by the Nepali-speaking hill people in the district of Darjeeling in West Bengal, who also demanded an independent homeland, Gorkhaland. The Gorkha National Liberation Front (GNLF) destroyed roads and bridges, disrupted work at the tea estates (the district is one of the major tea-producing areas of India), and brought the local government to a halt. Rajiv first tried to use the agitation to undermine the prestige of the Communist Party–led government of West Bengal, but after the strife had lasted twenty-seven months, he helped in bringing peace to the region (October 1988) through a settlement negotiated between GNLF and the West Bengal government. This was one bright spot in the otherwise dismal picture of ethnic-cum-communal troubles.

Hindu-Muslim Relations

From the time of independence, Hindu-Muslim communal clashes had continued to mar relations between the two communities in many localities of India. But in the larger context of national politics, except for the National Conference in Kashmir and the Muslim League in Kerala, the Muslims had no organized voice. The Congress, increasingly more interested in votes than in social change, had assured itself of Muslim support by catering to the demands of the backward-looking orthodox Muslim *ulama* (clerics).

By the 1970s, the Muslim population had risen significantly; according to the 1981 census, Muslims constituted 11.4 percent of the population. Consequently Muslims, outside Kashmir and Kerala, tried to use their vote banks to advance their causes, one being the recognition of Muslims as a Backward Class that should be granted reservations in educational institutions and the like, along with other Backward Classes. In 1977, the Muslims, aggrieved by the actions of Sanjay Gandhi during the Emergency, used their newfound electoral strength by voting for the Janata. But since the short-lived Janata government had brought no great rewards, the Muslims reverted to their traditional support of the Congress in the 1980 elections. Of all the political parties, the Congress was still seen as offering the best protection to the Muslims because of its commitment to pluralism. With the Congress in power, Hindu-Muslim relations retained their stable, though uneasy, equilibrium. This situation underwent a radical shift in the 1980s with the rise of the Hindu nationalist Bharatiya Janata Party (BJP) and the decline of the Congress Party.

Until 1980 the Hindu parties, such as the Jan Sangh (which gave birth to the Bharatiya Janata Party in 1980), had failed to harness the Hindu vote or make any significant impact on the politics of the country. But all this changed in the mid-1980s, when it had become abundantly clear that, in the forty years that the Congress had been in power, it had done little to create a civic, political culture that could be the basis for a national identity. Perhaps this was so because Congress leadership believed that India's "sacred geography" and its cultural heritage that promoted tolerance, pluralism, and syncretism already provided the basis for an all-embracing national identity; therefore, no conscious effort was necessary to convert a tenuous hypothesis into a "living national culture" that could weld the disparate religious, linguistic, and ethnic categories into a new unity. Furthermore, it was presumed that Nehruvian democratic socialism based on a secular, constitutional ethos (embodied in a sovereign Parliament, a free press, and an independent judiciary) and a self-reliant economy would provide a sense of collective confidence and help to create "a modern state within the framework of India's culture."[13]

Whatever the reasons, the Congress under Indira Gandhi and Rajiv Gandhi had confused nation building with state building and identified itself with the state. The leaders legitimized their hold on power by declaring that they were saving the nation from instability and disunity. To achieve their "noble" end, they diminished the sovereignty of the Parliament and the autonomy of the judiciary, made a mockery of the federal system by reducing state chief ministers to a position of servility, undermined the institutions of law and order, and corrupted the bureaucratic system. Worse still, in the name of national unity they did not hesitate to use the state's power to suppress all opposition, resorting even to state violence. As a consequence, instead of fostering a civic political culture and a sense of national unity in India, Indira's and Rajiv's policies had precipitated the rise of militant Sikh nationalism in Punjab and militant Muslim nationalism in Kashmir.

Although popular Hindu reaction to Sikh fundamentalism and Muslim fundamentalism had created a basis for the emergence of a larger Hindu identity, it was Congress policy toward the Muslims, particularly Rajiv's handling of the Shah Bano case, that contributed to unifying Hindu sentiment.

Shah Bano, a destitute, divorced Muslim woman, had gone to court to seek alimony from her affluent husband, who had denied her a reasonable maintenance allowance. The case went all the way up to the Supreme Court and was decided in her favor. However, the Supreme Court judgment created a stir among the Muslims throughout India because the decision, according to the *ulama*, went against the teachings of Islam and interfered with the Muslim personal law, which alone could decide the question of maintenance. Shah Bano's husband got the *ulama* to issue a *fatwa* (verdict based on Muslim law) to that effect.

Many educated, forward-looking Muslims, men and women, hailed the court decision, but the conservative Muslim fundamentalists, who also controlled the vote banks, raised the cry "Islam in danger" and played on the insecurities and fears of a largely backward Muslim community. Rajiv, against the advice of all progressive Muslims (a Muslim member of his cabinet resigned in protest), undid the work of the Supreme Court by getting the Parliament to pass (in February 1986) the Muslim Women (Protection of Rights on Divorce) Bill, which recognized the authority of the Muslim personal law in matters of divorce and maintenance. Thus, Rajiv not only intervened in favor of the retrogressive elements in the Muslim community, but he also abandoned the fundamental principles of secularism and equality. A sectarian religious practice was made a part of the Constitution and of the "secular" laws of the country.

Rajiv's blatant attempt to gain the Muslim vote by proving that the Congress was a protector and ally of the conservative Muslims led by obscurantist mullahs gave the Hindu nationalists an opportunity to condemn the Congress for "betraying the majority community by pandering to Muslim fundamentalism, and conceding the two nation theory in all but name."[14] The critics pointed out that the Congress had not hesitated to ignore Hindu sentiment when it replaced Hindu personal law with the Hindu code bills (see above) but showed no reluctance in acceding to the demand of the non-Hindu religious communities to carry on under their respective personal religious laws.

Though Rajiv's action, not without reason, had created a perception in the Hindu mind that the Congress was pro-Muslim, it is a pity that the Hindu Code Bills were dragged into the Hindu-Muslim controversy; the Hindu Code Bills were a piece of progressive legislation that had done much to improve the lives of Hindu women. What the country needed was a common civil code that could have helped to ameliorate the condition of all women in the country; such a code would also have promoted the unity of the nation.

The Shah Bano controversy no doubt was helpful in unifying Hindu sentiment, but it was the Ayodhya Babri Masjid (mosque)–Ram Temple issue that gave Hindu nationalism its real boost. The Babri Mosque is said to have been built in 1528 by the Mughal emperor Babur on the site of a temple that marked Lord Ram's birthplace Ramjanmabhoomi, which Babur had razed. During the next 450-odd years, Hindus made seventy-six attempts to regain control of the shrine; the first attempts were made even before Babur had passed away. In 1860, the British effected a compromise between the two communities by letting the Muslims retain the mosque while allowing the Hindus to build a small structure outside the mosque for their worship of Ram.

A few years after independence, the main entrance to the mosque and the Hindu structure was locked up to avoid the growing confrontation between the two communities, but in the 1980s the Vishwa Hindu Parishad (VHP), backed by the militant Hindu organization, the RSS, made its main objective to "liberate" Ramjanmabhoomi. As the VHP campaign gathered force, in 1986 the local authorities were directed to unlock the Hindu shrine on the grounds that the action posed no risk to law and order.

This was Rajiv's attempt to balance his pro-Muslim stand in the Shah Bano case with a pro-Hindu stand in Ayodhya. Thus, he hoped to gain both the Muslim and the Hindu votes. Rajiv's tactic was totally counterproductive. The Hindus gave credit for their victory to the VHP and the BJP, and the Muslim attitude towards Rajiv's government soured. The mosque, which was in disrepair and hardly being used, suddenly became the symbol for Muslim solidarity, and various Muslim organizations came together and formed the Babri Masjid Coordination Committee to fight for the title of ownership. As both communities hardened their stand, communal riots broke out across the country. Rajiv, mired in the Bofors scandal and not wanting to alienate either community on the eve of the national elections, nevertheless refused to intervene and left it to the courts to decide the matter. This vacillation cost him dearly.

On October 17, 1989, Rajiv announced that elections to the Lok Sabha would be held on November 22, 24, and 26, thus giving the opposition parties hardly any time to formulate a unified strategy. But within weeks, under the guiding hand of V. P. Singh, a working alliance called the National Front was established between Singh's Janata Dal and three regional parties. The National Front worked out a coordinated electoral strategy with the BJP and the Left Front, composed primarily of the Communist Party of India (Marxist), or CPI(M), and the Communist Party of India, or CP(I).

Meanwhile, the VHP accelerated its Ramjanmabhoomi program and declared that a million devout Hindus would gather at the Ayodhya site on November 9 to lay the foundation of a magnificent $8 million temple, for which donations were being collected from Hindus across the country and abroad. The universal popularity of the program among the Hindus can be gauged from the fact that even V. P. Singh, known for his secular outlook, commented that since the Hindus felt so strongly about Ramjanmabhoomi it would be proper to let them build a temple there. While the VHP's Ayodhya movement stimulated Hindu nationalism, it was the BJP that used the opportunity to emerge as the political party that championed the Hindu cause.

Foreign Affairs

During his tenure as prime minister, Rajiv continued to uphold India's traditional stand of nonalignment, though he also made an attempt to improve relations with countries on both sides of the cold war by visiting various capitals, including Washington and Beijing. There were, however, no radical shifts in policy, and India's major concerns remained restricted to South Asia.

Mutual suspicions continued to mar relations between India and Pakistan, partly because America, with Pakistan as the staging ground for its anti-Soviet operations in Afghanistan, was providing sophisticated weapons to Pakistan and turning a blind eye to Pakistan's nuclear program. In addition, Pakistan was actively involved in training and financing the dissidents in Punjab and Kashmir. A new irritant was added to the relations between the two countries when China signed a nuclear cooperation agreement with Pakistan in 1986, the same year that the Punjab accord collapsed and Sikh terrorists increased their activities. In early 1987, when the press reported that Pakistan had acquired nuclear weapons capability, members of the Indian Parliament demanded that India develop a nuclear weapon of its own. Indo-Pakistan relations at times became explosive, but Rajiv did try, with considerable success, to diffuse the volatile situation by holding summit meetings with Pakistan. By early 1989, both countries had agreed not to strike at each other's nuclear facilities, and later in the year Pakistan gave some verbal assurances that it would not assist Kashmir terrorists.

The major change in regional relations concerned Sri Lanka, where ethnic trouble between the majority Sinhalese community and the Tamils (who formed about 18 percent of the population and were located mostly in the Jaffna peninsula, across the straits from Tamil Nadu) had led to Tamil insurgency. The Tamil guerrillas—the Liberation Tigers of Tamil Eelam (LTTE; *eelam* means "homeland" or "state")—found sympathetic support among their Tamil brethren in Tamil Nadu. By the mid-1980s, Sri Lanka was in a state of brutal civil war. Even though Colombo felt aggrieved that India's state of Tamil Nadu was offering sanctuary and training to the guerrillas, New Delhi could not ignore the sentiment of Indian Tamils who felt that Delhi should intervene on behalf of LTTE. In 1987, when Sri Lankan forces had isolated Jaffna and tried to starve the Tamil population there into surrendering to Colombo, Rajiv was forced by internal political considerations to violate international protocol and airdrop relief supplies to the besieged Tamils. However, he also hastily signed an accord with Sri Lanka to provide an Indian peacekeeping force to help Colombo negotiate with the LTTE and bring back law and order in Jaffna. Unfortunately, the peacekeeping force failed to suppress the insurrection, suffered heavy losses of men and arms, and came to be viewed as a hostile occupying force. Soon, both the Sri Lankan government and the leaders of the LTTE were demanding that the peacekeepers be withdrawn.

In 1989, Rajiv, advised by the Indian military chiefs, agreed to withdraw the forces. Obviously, the intervention and the accord had not been a success, but Rajiv had managed to achieve two of his main goals: (1) the moderate Indian Tamils had become disillusioned with the recalcitrant LTTE leaders and stopped supporting them; and (2) India's position as a regional power that would not brook any outside country coming to the aid of Sri Lanka was confirmed.

The 1989 Elections: The Second Janata Coalition Government (1989–1991)

On the eve of the 1989 elections, the outlook for the Congress was not encouraging: the Congress was a junior coalition partner in the National Conference–led government in Kashmir; it had lost Haryana to the Lok Dal Party; Assam was under Asom Gana Parishad rule; West Bengal and Kerala were under the CPI(M); Andhra Pradesh was under the Telugu Desam Party; and Karnataka was under the Janata Party. Punjab, Tamil Nadu, Nagaland, and Mizoram were under Presidential Rule. The Bofors scandal had deeply impaired the popular image of the Congress even in the Congress-governed states, and Rajiv's indecisive approach to the Ayodhya issue had alienated both Muslims and Hindus.

The situation in 1989 was much the same as Indira Gandhi had faced in 1977, and the results of the elections were also similar: the Congress lost the elections, and though it did win the largest number of seats (197 of the 529 Parliament seats) of any party, it fell far short of the majority needed to form a government. The major opposition gains were: Janata Party, 143 seats; BJP, 85; and CPI(M), 32. The most dramatic gain, no doubt, was made by the BJP, which had raised its representation from the 2 seats it had won in 1980, to 85. The electorate once again had proved that it had far greater acumen to judge political performance than it was given credit for. The peoples of India had rejected a corrupt and unjust government.

In December 1989, V. P. Singh, with the backing of the BJP and other smaller parties, was sworn in as prime minister of a minority National Front government that had won only 145 seats (of which the Janata Party had contributed 143). Singh was faced with the same problems (quarrels over office and personality clashes) that Morarji Desai had faced in 1977, and Singh's government did not last even as long as Desai's—it fell in November 1990 when the BJP withdrew its support.

History appeared to repeat itself when the Uttar Pradesh leader, Chandra Shekhar, with a following of 58 members, became prime minister with the support of Rajiv Gandhi's 197 Congress Members of Parliament (as had Charan Singh with Indira Gandhi's support in 1979). Chandra Shekhar proved pliant to Congress pressures, but in March 1991, when the Congress staged a walkout from Parliament to protest the illegal surveillance of Rajiv Gandhi, Shekhar resigned; his government had lasted four months. The president called for fresh elections in May.

Such short-lived, unstable, minority governments could not carry out any of their major programs envisaged by V. P. Singh or Shekhar. However, Singh's government did take two actions that made a long-term impact on Indian politics. The first was Singh's announcement that his government intended to implement the Mandal Commission Report; the Commission had been set up under the First Janata Government in 1979 and its report had been published in 1980 when Congress was back in power. The Commission had recommended that, in addition to the 22.5 percent reservation in educational institutions, government service, and political bodies that was already granted to Scheduled Castes (the Untouchables) and Scheduled Tribes, a 27 percent reservation should be awarded to Other Backward Castes (OBCs) in these fields. Mandal had classified 3,743 lower castes, comprising nearly 53 percent of the population, as "backward."

Singh's decision was widely, and very strongly, criticized by the well-placed upper castes as cheap populism and by the BJP, which saw the move as dividing the Hindu community. It was because of the BJP's withdrawal of support that V. P. Singh's government had fallen, but Singh's action was irreversible. The Supreme Court, in response to the petitions challenging the legality of the Mandal recommendation, granted a temporary stay against implementation, but this could only delay the inevitable: the time had arrived for democracy to recognize the masses of vote givers who had been exploited by the upper-caste politicians.

The change was certain to affect the Congress in the Hindi-speaking heartland where it had depended so heavily on the elite leadership of the upper-caste Brahmans, Rajputs, and Bhumihars. The southern states, reacting against centuries of Brahman domination, had introduced reservation quotas much earlier, and since political power there was wielded by middle-lower castes, the caste issue was less explosive in the south than in the north.

The BJP, whose support came primarily from upper-caste Hindus, tried to counter the adverse effect of the Mandal recommendations by galvanizing upper- and lower-caste Hindu opinion on the Ramjanmabhoomi issue. The BJP leader, L. K. Advani, shifted national attention away from the Mandal Report to *Hindutva* (polity based on Hindu ethos) by launching a *rath-yatra* (pilgrimage in a chariot)—the "chariot," ostensibly like the ones used during the times of the Mahabharata, was constructed on the chassis of an automobile. The pilgrimage started at the Somnath temple in Gujarat on September 15, 1990, and after wending its way through western, central, and northern India, it was scheduled to end at Ayodhya on October 30, the auspicious day chosen by holy men to start construction of the Ram temple.

The *yatra* was very popular with the Hindus, who came out in the hundreds of thousands to greet Advani. Advani's pilgrimage highlighted the "oneness" of the Hindu religion and the sacred land, which was unified by hundreds of Hindu holy places that dotted the entire country, from Dwarka and Somnath in the far west; Tirupati, Rameshwaram, Madurai, and Kanyakumari in the south; Bhabuneshwar and Puri in the far east; and Amarnath, Benaras, Hardwar, and Ayodhya in the north.

Advani was exploiting the fact that many temples, such as Somnath, that had been repeatedly looted and destroyed by the Muslims,* become symbols of Hindu humiliation at the hands of the Muslims and evoked memories of the rapacity and cruelty of the Muslim rulers. Most Hindus know little of Emperor Aurangzeb's reign except that he had issued a general order that all the schools and temples of the Hindus were to be destroyed[15] and that hundreds of temples, particularly the Vishvanath temple at Benaras and the Vishnu temple at Mathura, had been actually demolished. That the Muslim rulers had built mosques over many of the razed Hindu temples was also a well-known fact.

The Ayodhya issue gave the BJP an opportunity to replace the failing Congress attempt to establish a national secular cultural identity based on the Nehruvian interpretation of India's past (that emphasized the more secular emperors, like Akbar,

---

*Somnath was destroyed for the first time in the eleventh century by Mahmud of Ghazni and for the last time by the Mughal emperor Aurangzeb around 1665.

and the commingling of Hindu and Muslim customs and beliefs) with the idea that only the Hindu ethos (*Hindutva*) could provide a unifying basis for the Indian nation. According to the BJP, the Congress was using its so-called secular-democratic commitment to pluralism to justify the continuation of divisively distinct communities and nonsecular traditions (for example, the Muslim personal law).

The government, not wanting to risk a major communal clash between Hindus and Muslims over Ayodhya, arrested Advani before he reached Ayodhya, which only added to Advani's national stature.

The second action of Prime Minister Singh had to do with Kashmir. In December 1989, Kashmiri militants, wanting to put pressure on New Delhi to release their arrested comrades, kidnapped the daughter of Mufti Mohammad Sayeed, a Kashmiri leader who had joined Singh's government as home minister; the kidnapping took place in Srinagar. Since such a high-level terrorist-organized kidnapping had never taken place before, the government was caught by surprise and handled the affair very clumsily. The confused government gave in to all of the terrorists' demands, including the one that obliged New Delhi to free the prisoners before Sayeed's daughter was released.

Joyous crowds in Srinagar celebrated the militants' first major success against the government in New Delhi. "The situation in the Valley started deteriorating rapidly after this kidnapping. . . . [The television coverage brought] the Kashmir issue back on the center-stage of national and international agenda."[16] An ineffectual government had conferred legitimacy on insurgent movements that ranged from "the largely secular Jammu and Kashmir Liberation Front (JKLF) to the more religiously oriented and pro-Pakistani Hizb-ul-Mujahideen (HUM), which sent their recruits across the border to Pakistan where they were provided with training, organization, and weaponry."[17] The breakdown of law and order in the state resulted in the dismissal of the Farooq government in 1990 and the imposition of the President's Rule.

The 1991 Elections and the New Face of Indian Politics

The three main contenders in the May 1991 parliamentary election were the Congress Party, the Janata Dal, and the Bharatiya Janata Party. The polling, for logistical reasons, was scheduled to be held on May 20, 23, and 25. However, the last two days were shifted to June 12 and 15 because Rajiv Gandhi was assassinated on May 21 during his electoral campaign in Tamil Nadu; the assassin was a woman suicide-bomber who detonated an explosive device hidden under her clothes as she offered a garland to Rajiv. The suspicion that she belonged to the LTTE was later proved to be correct.

Rajiv's assassination shocked the nation, and fears were expressed that the void created in India's biggest party by his death could lead to the country falling apart. There was no one in the Congress who had been groomed to take over the party in such a contingency, and Rajiv's death revealed the extent to which the once-majestic

Congress had become deplorably servile to a single leader. It was a sad reflection on the state of the party that it turned to Rajiv's Italian-born wife, Sonia, and offered her the leadership of Congress, which Sonia wisely declined. The choice then fell on P. V. Narasimha Rao, a relatively unknown Andhra politician who had at one time served as a minister in the central cabinet; Rao, seventy years old, had had a heart operation and spoken of retiring from politics. As far as the collapse of India was concerned, Indian politics once again proved the doomsayers to be wrong. The country was mature and resilient enough to take another major tragedy in its stride.

The outpouring of sympathy for Rajiv's family produced a wave of empathy, but it was far less sweeping than the one that had marked the 1984 elections following Indira's assassination; in 1984 Congress had won 415 seats in a House of 541; in 1991 its representation rose from the 197 seats it had occupied in 1989 to 227 (the number increased to 251 after the by-elections later in the year), which made it the biggest party but kept it marginally short of being the majority party.

Looking at the polls, we find that there was a major shift in the voting pattern that did not presage well for the future of the Congress. Overall, the Congress was most successful in the four southern states,* where it gained 86 of the 129 parliamentary seats (the BJP won a mere 5 seats). The Congress also did well in Maharashtra, Orissa, and some of the smaller states in the north and northeast. As expected, it lost to the CP(M) in West Bengal (gaining 5 seats to CP(M)'s 27), but unexpectedly it lost badly to the BJP in Gujarat (4 seats to 20).

However, the Congress's biggest debacle was in two of the Hindi belt's larger states, Uttar Pradesh and Bihar. These states had once been the strongholds of Congress, and Uttar Pradesh, the most populous state of the Union, was particularly important because it returned 85 members to Parliament; significantly, it was the home state of all the prime ministers of India before Rao. That the Congress, in the 1991 elections, could only win 5 seats in Uttar Pradesh was a sorry confirmation of how ineffective the party machine had become in that state. The BJP, on the other hand, reflected its vigor and dynamism by gaining 50 seats in Uttar Pradesh. Even the Janata Dal won 22 seats! Worse still, not one Congress candidate was elected from Bihar. The biggest victor there was the Janata Dal, which gained 28 seats (the BJP won 5).

Politics in Bihar and Uttar Pradesh had shifted from the hands of the dominant elite upper castes (who in the past had the local influence to deliver the lower-caste and minority votes to the Congress) to the middle-status Backward Castes that favored the Janata Dal, the party that had given the Mandal recommendations a legal status, and the BJP, the party that stood for the greatness of Hindu culture.

The 1991 elections were also markedly different from all previous elections because for the first time ever the Congress faced another major party, the BJP, who had a clear-cut platform that differed sharply from that of the Congress. The BJP was a party that related nationalism and patriotism to the establishment of *Hindutva*, a

---

*Andhra Pradesh, Karnataka, Kerala, and Tamil Nadu

polity based on the distinctive Hindu culture and social ethos that, according to the BJP, could bring stability and strength to the country as a whole and ensure that all the peoples of India, irrespective of their religious orientation, would be able to live in peace and security. While the BJP's efforts to rebuild the Ramjanmabhoomi Temple symbolized its broad aspiration to be identified with the 80–plus percent of India's population, its announced aim to spur national growth by liberalizing the economy won it the support of the important middle class that had become disillusioned by Rajiv Gandhi's retreat to socialism. Above all, the BJP projected the image of a cohesive, well-disciplined party led by a number of highly capable leaders who had, so far, not been tainted by any corruption scandals.

The BJP emerged from the 1991 elections as the second biggest party with 119 seats, a big improvement over the 85 it had gained in 1989. As expected, the BJP had done best among the upper-caste Hindus (who had been angered by the Congress's policies that pandered to the Muslims and by V. P. Singh's acceptance of the Mandal recommendations), not so well among the lower castes (that favored the Mandal Report and, therefore, the JD), and least well among the Muslims (the BJP approach to the mosque/temple issue had put it squarely on the side of the Hindus versus the Muslims). The BJP consolidated its success at the national level by also winning power in four Hindi belt states: Himachal Pradesh, Madhya Pradesh, Rajasthan, and Uttar Pradesh (where Ayodhya is located).

V. P. Singh's Janata Dal made a poor showing in the election, and its parliamentary representation was reduced from 143 seats to 55. It was surprising that JD's Mandal platform had failed to make much headway among the 75 percent of the deprived population of India (composed of Backward Castes, Scheduled Castes, and Scheduled Tribes). The only state in which JD gained the majority of the parliamentary seats was caste-ridden Bihar (where Backward Castes constitute 52 percent of the population and the minorities, mostly Muslim, 13 percent). Its success there was attributable to the charismatic and popular Bihari leader, Laloo Prasad Yadav, a member of the Yadav (or Jadav) Backward Caste, who garnered practically all the backward and minority votes campaigning for the end of the "centuries-old Brahman supremacy."[18]

India Under Prime Minister Narasimha Rao: 1991–1996

In July 1991, Narasimha Rao was sworn in as the ninth prime minister of India. No Congress prime minister before him had ever faced as complex and difficult a set of problems. Most of these problems—associated with secessionist movements, terrorism, the Mandal Report, hardening of caste and regional identities, and the BJP—had produced a situation of ungovernability and political instability. But the issue that took precedence over all others was the economy, which had hit the lowest point since independence and was in a state of collapse.

However harshly historians may condemn Rao for the handling of the other crises, they must laud him for the boldness with which he introduced reforms that altered the direction of the Indian economy and gave it fresh impetus for growth. Rao's government, by reducing controls on the private sector, liberalizing the foreign trade regime, and opening the country to foreign direct investment and joint enterprises, practically jettisoned the Nehruvian model that had guided India's economy for forty-three years.

The New Economic Face of India

When Rao assumed power, the country was in the throes of a terrible economic crisis. The growth rate of the GDP had halved in the previous year, the wholesale price index had more than doubled, inflation was soaring, and industrial production was stagnating. In 1991, India's foreign exchange reserves had been depleted to such a degree that the Reserve Bank of India was forced to sell some of its gold stock to keep the country from defaulting on its international debt. India's fragile economy appeared to be on the verge of total collapse.

It goes to Prime Minister Rao's credit that despite his weak position in the Parliament as head of a minority government, he appointed a farsighted economist, Manmohan Singh, to introduce economic policies that many industrialists and political parties were certain to find unpopular: the industrialists, who had a monopoly on a growing, closed market, felt uneasy at the prospect of competing with better-manufactured foreign goods in an open market; and political parties, such as the socialists, the Janata, and the BJP, on principle were against foreign penetration of the national market.

Within days of being sworn in as finance minister, Manmohan Singh declared that he planned to cut government spending, devaluate the rupee (to make exports cheaper and imports dearer), deregulate the licensing system (easing controls on the private sector), expose the economy to foreign competition by opening the market to foreign investment and joint enterprises, and stop subsidizing sick public-sector industries. Singh's short-term aim was to gain a loan from the International Monetary Fund, which had insisted that India take such actions to gain the loan; his long-term goal was to stabilize the Indian economy by reducing internal and foreign debt, and to integrate India with the global economy. By adopting these policies, India had made a deliberate decision to move away from the Gandhian belief in self-reliance, which had resulted in isolationism, and Nehruvian socialism, which had resulted in economic stagnation and low productivity.

Singh's bold initiatives surprised the world, but many doubted the minority government's capability to carry out programs that did not find favor with vested interests in the public and the private sectors in India. However, even though the path chosen was not easy, and the execution of the reform policies had to be periodically tempered to suit changing political needs, the critics, by and large, were silenced by the very positive results that followed in the wake of the reforms. Within a year India's foreign exchange reserves, which had touched a low of $1 billion (a two weeks' import cover) in 1991, rose to $2 billion, and then to $6 billion in 1993, $9.5 billion in 1994, and $14.67 billion in 1995. The budget deficit dropped from 8.4 percent of the GNP in 1991 to 4.8 percent in 1995, while in real terms the GDP grew from 2.5 percent in 1991 to 5.5 percent in 1994–1995.[19]

The new market-friendly approach began to draw a response from foreign investors as approvals for projects involving up to 51 percent foreign equity were made automatic, and important sectors such as petroleum production, refining, and distribution, energy projects, telecommunications, and automobile manufacturing were opened to foreign companies. The response of the foreign investors was cautious in the beginning but speeded up as they realized that the reforms were there to stay. Direct foreign investment was less than $200 million in 1990–1991. It rose to $585 million in 1992–1993 and then to $4.7 billion in 1993–1994. In 1995, when the United States had identified India as a "big emerging market" with a middle class of nearly 150 million, Commerce Secretary Ronald Brown visited India and within days concluded transactions worth $7 billion. The figures above, of course, indicate commitments and not the actual utilization of the moneys.

By 1996, foreign investors from America, Japan, Germany, France, Italy, and other advanced economies, though still wary of the Indian political climate, had begun to establish their industries and businesses in India; American corporations such as IBM, McDonnell Douglas, Motorola, Texas Instruments, Ford Motor Company, Kellogg, and Pepsi Cola emerged as "the second biggest foreign investors, after expatriate Indians."[20] In 1994, even the Communist government of West Bengal revamped its industrial policy to welcome private corporations to invest in that state. As a result, West Bengal attracted $2.6 billion of domestic and foreign investments between January and August 1995, 380 percent more than in the corresponding period in 1994.[21]

The new economic policies started the process of liberating India from the thraldom of suffocating bureaucratic controls and contributed to the creation of a dynamic, new social-economic environment that is perhaps best described in an article published in *Business World* by Gurcharan Das, a well-known playwright, novelist, columnist, and a former high executive officer of Procter and Gamble. To write this piece, Das spent several months in 1995 traveling through India's remote villages and its bustling cities. Although several of the prominent personalities he met in his travels differed sharply in their comments, either praising Rao ("He doesn't realize it, but Narasimha Rao came out of the *Jurassic Park* in 1991 to become the biggest revolutionary in India since Gautam Buddha") or condemning him with equal vigor ("Do we really need Kellogg's corn flakes?" or "We are unleashing a culture of greed and permissiveness"), Gurcharan Das himself was very impressed with what he witnessed in his travels:

> The defining image of my journey is 14-year-old Raju in khaki half pants in Maraimalainagar village, between Madras and Pondicherry, who hustles around tables serving . . . south Indian coffee and spends the Rs [rupees] 400 a month [$13] that he earns in the cafe on computer lessons. He says that he wants to grow up and run a computer company one day, just like his [U.S.] role model

Bilgay [Bill Gates of Microsoft fame], the richest man in the world. Raju defines a profound new mindset as social scientists call it, a new way of looking at the world, that I found again and again during my travels around India from June to September 1995. I encountered it every day, in the hopes of the young, in the way people talked, in the way they stood at street corners, in the way mothers thought about their daughters. . . .

The spirit of the age—of an India approaching the end of the 20th century—is reflected in the vast number of rags-to-riches stories. . . . [Because of reforms and prosperity in the 1980s] the middle class started to grow rapidly, but rural demand also exploded for everything from washing powders to black and white TVs. However, by far the single biggest factor in opening the floodgates of entrepreneurship is the liberalization of 1991. It has unleashed pent-up energies and created a new confidence among young people and a feeling that "they can do it. . . ."

It is slowly beginning to dawn on Indian business that superior companies are built by superior people. . . . Almost every industrialist I talked to said that his biggest challenge is to find men and women of ability to manage crucial positions in his company. This is the most profound change I witnessed in the business world after the reforms. . . .

If there is one word that captures the mood of the country after the reforms, it is "confidence." Everybody I talked to, without exception, believed that their children and grandchildren would be better off than they had been. This was true in the slums of Bangalore, among the residents of Bartoli village in Uttar Pradesh, in middle class homes in Calcutta, among teachers, taxi drivers, shopkeepers, lawyers, politicians, painters, trade unionists, and bureaucrats across the country.[22]

Several critics of the government feared that the reforms would make the rich richer (which they have) but not help in alleviating poverty. This, too, was proven false. The poverty level, according to official data, fell from 25.5 percent of the population in 1987–1988 to 18.9 percent in 1993–1994. And as *The Economist* pointed out, "In the subsequent two years GDP [had] exceeded 6 percent annually, and this must have reduced poverty [further]."[23]

Internal Politics: The Decline Of Congress Party

Prime Minister Rao was far less successful in handling the country's political problems than he was in dealing with its economic ones. Most of the political problems had emerged before he came to power; however, the rise of the BJP as a contender for national government was a wholly new issue.

In dealing with these concerns, Rao was handicapped not only because he headed a minority government that was constantly under attack by the opposition parties but also because Rao's uncharismatic personality and style of work encouraged Congress leaders, who had strong power bases in their own states, to put themselves forward as challengers for leadership. Rao managed to ride out the troubles and complete the entire five-year term of office despite predictions that he would fail. Nevertheless, his predilection for postponing decisions on crucial issues in the hope that somehow time would resolve them, his manipulation of the party to preserve his position, and his tacit acceptance of corruption reduced his effectiveness and damaged his image and that of the Congress Party.

Rao's Political Vicissitudes

Despite the political uncertainty that surrounded him at the time he assumed office, at the beginning of his ascendancy Rao managed to gain popular favor by appearing to establish a style of government that emphasized a conciliatory, consultative, and moderate approach.

One of Rao's early actions concerned the Ramjanmabhoomi-Babri Masjid issue (hereafter, the Temple-Mosque issue) that had begun to overshadow national politics. In September 1991, Rao managed to get a bill through Parliament that sought to return both places of worship to the status quo of August 15, 1947. The BJP government in Uttar Pradesh tried to bypass this legal hurdle by acquiring a parcel of land next to the mosque where Vishwa Hindu Parishad could build the temple, but the Supreme Court, then in the process of hearing the claims of Hindu and Muslim bodies, issued a stay for the construction of any structures on that land.

With the Ayodhya issue temporarily out of the way, Rao turned his attention to Punjab where, by 1992, anti-insurgency operations had weakened the militant separatist movement to such a degree that Rao, against the suggestions of more cautious advisers, decided to risk holding elections in the state. Though all Akali parties boycotted the elections, and though the turnout was a mere 20 percent of the electorate, the elections of February 1992 brought back civil government to the state. The return of normalcy was welcomed by the majority of the people, as became evident when municipal elections later in the year saw a turnout of more than 70 percent despite calls for boycott by several Akali factions. The days of terrorism were not quite over, but militancy had finally been crushed. Punjab had returned to the national fold. Normalcy was also brought back to Assam where the militants, led by the United Liberation Front, had also become a spent force and were subdued by the end of 1992. Rao could do nothing, however, to reduce the state of turbulence in Kashmir, which remained the last major dark spot on the Indian political scene through the five years of Rao's tenure.

In another potentially very positive action, soon after assuming power Rao decided to bring back democracy to the Congress Party by holding intraparty elections, last held twenty years earlier. This was a massive exercise and held great promise, but the promise was never fulfilled. After the elections, it appears that Rao had second thoughts about their impact on his position within the party. Fearing that some of the members of the elected Central Working Committee, the policy-making body of the Congress, might prove too powerful to handle, Rao, in his capacity as the elected president of the party, managed to get half the committee to resign. Although the reason he gave for this rather undemocratic action was that the committee lacked representation from women, Scheduled Castes, and Scheduled Tribes, in actuality, Rao was safeguarding his dominance of the party by keeping new leaders from emerging. Among those who had been pressured to resign were Sharad Pawar from Maharashtra and Arjun Singh from Madhya Pradesh, both very able and highly respected leaders of the party.

Rao's desire to dominate the party was also revealed in his refusal to establish the Congress Parliamentary Board, which took decisions on crucial legislative matters, and the Congress Central Election Committee, which made final decisions regarding candidates for elections. As a result, the party's democratic process was perverted, and Rao used the pliant Central Working Committee and the powerless Provincial Congress Committees to maintain himself in absolute power in the style of Indira Gandhi. If Rao had had any intention of ending nepotism and corruption within the party and rehabilitating the image of the moribund Congress, he would never have followed this path. Rao's maneuvers gained him the reputation of an amoral politician who was willing to sacrifice the party to keep himself in power. The fund of popular goodwill that he had so far earned began to dwindle.

However, in immediate terms it was Ayodhya that proved to be Rao's nemesis. In July 1992, after months of relative inaction, the VHP heated up the Ayodhya issue by declaring that it had decided to go ahead and lay the foundation of the temple. Rao should have responded to this threat with resolute action, such as the dismissal of the BJP government in Uttar Pradesh and the imposition of central control over the state, or the dispatching of central forces to occupy the disputed site, as many in the Congress had advised him. But he did not do so because either action would have cost Hindu votes. Hoping that the courts would somehow relieve him from confronting the problem, Rao thought it more prudent to negotiate with the VHP for a postponement of action for three months.

The result of Rao's vacillation was that, on December 6, 1992, a mob of 300,000 impatient, fanatical volunteers (*kar seva*) of the VHP, who had tired of waiting, took matters in their own hands. In defiance of the center and the courts, but with the tacit backing of the BJP government, they stormed the mosque and demolished it within a few hours. Rao reacted to the Ayodhya incident by dismissing the BJP government in Uttar Pradesh (later, the governments in the three other states under BJP control were also dismissed), arresting some of the BJP leaders, and banning five "ultracommunal" organizations, including the VHP and the RSS. Rao also made a hasty promise to build a mosque and a temple on the Ayodhya site.

None of this, however, kept the Muslims and secular-minded Hindus from blaming Rao for not having taken firm action during the preceding months when it had become obvious that a flare-up was in the making.

Nor could Rao's belated actions stop the outbreak of communal violence, the worst that India had witnessed since 1947. As many Hindus gloated over their victory and angry Muslims took to the streets to protest, religious hatred engulfed the country, spreading death and destruction through many of its major cities. Both Hindus and Muslims were killed in the riots, though it was the Muslims who suffered the most. By the end of December 1992 over 1,000 persons had died in communal violence. Communalism was already a fact of everyday life in India, but this was a wholly new kind of communalism. It was espoused by organized groups that were openly using religion for political advantage by poisoning Hindu-Muslim relations at the national level.

The Ayodhya incident appalled the nation. Many believed that the country was on the verge of a total collapse of law and order. Every thinking person, Hindus included, deplored the bigotry that had led to the senseless destruction of the mosque. Liberal-minded intellectuals, particularly the Westernized ones, wrung their hands in anguish because they saw secular India being taken over by militant Hindu fundamentalists.[24] One scholar, referring to the "rottenness afflicting the Indian state," wailed that "in today's India religion is the first refuge of scoundrel politicians, patriotism the last retreat of the baffled and defeated."[25]

The situation was actually far more complex than reflected in these responses. Though the savagery released by religion-based passions cannot be condoned, one has to look at the larger picture of post-1947 developments to comprehend the Ayodhya explosion. After Nehru, whose unrealistic notion of secularity had, more or less, died with him, not much effort had been made to understand the issue of nation building in a socioreligious society. Because Hinduism is *not* a religion in the sense the term is used for Judaism, Christianity, and Islam—with a common scripture, creed, or rituals—the emergence of Hindu fundamentalism, per se, was impossible. However, there is a national ethos associated with Hinduism that pervades the everyday life of the majority of the people in the country. The BJP had managed to exploit this ethos temporarily to produce a broad sense of Hindu nationalism, but it was impossible for the BJP, as it soon learned, to use this ethos to create a monolithic Hindu society in a population deeply divided by caste, language, and region. The Ayodhya incident may yet provide the impetus for Indian thinkers to reexamine Western models of secularism that appear to be inapplicable to India and produce an Indian paradigm that integrates secularism with the national ethos.

Bombay was worst hit by the riots. Hindu policemen had deliberately allowed Hindu mobs, directed by the militant Shiv Sena (Army of Shivaji, named after the Maratha hero who had defeated the Mughals and established a Hindu kingdom), to seek out and kill Muslims and loot their property. The Muslim response came on March 12, 1993, when Muslim underworld criminals in Bombay carried out seven sophisticated car-bomb explosions that damaged the stock exchange and other Bombay landmarks, killed 270 persons, and injured 1,200 in a conspiracy that led from Bombay to Pakistan and Dubai. Altogether, nearly 1,300 died in the Bombay riots, and over 1,000 were wounded. The Bombay bombings revealed for the first time the extent to which organized criminal elements were being protected by crooked politicians, and it was this nexus of crime, corruption, and politics that would soon become the main target of public outcry.

To the credit of the cosmopolitan citizenry of Bombay, however, because of their universal outpouring of sympathy for the victims and their condemnation of the police, the riots did not produce long-lasting scars; in Bombay, the Muslims and Hindus, more or less, returned to their traditional relations based on mutual tolerance. Peace was also restored to other parts of India, though the Muslim-Hindu divide had widened in some areas. Just as the prospect of rebuilding the temple had temporarily galvanized Hindu sentiment, the destruction of the once-decrepit mosque had "become a symbol of identity for millions of Muslims."[26] However, it is significant that in a nationwide poll carried out immediately after the Ayodhya incident, 52.6 percent of the respondents disapproved of the demolition of the mosque, and 52.9 percent felt that the BJP had broken the law. At the same time, ironically, popular opinion in all the states (except Gujarat and the four southern states) had swung in favor of the BJP at the expense of the Congress.[27]

Rao came under much public criticism for his handling of the Ayodhya issue. His image within the party declined further when he silenced his critics in the cabinet by packing off one to become the chief minister of Maharashtra and downgrading the post of another.

In 1993, Rao's reputation, and that of the Congress Party, suffered another setback when a broker involved in a $1.7 billion security-trading scam revealed that he had personally handed Rao a suitcase filled with 10 million rupees (over $300,000) in cash as a secret campaign donation. The Central Bureau of Investigation (CBI) later exonerated Rao, but no one believed the CBI because the bureau was under Rao's control. During his remaining years in office, Rao could never overcome the general impression that he was a corrupt politician. His loss of credibility gave an impetus to the Congress factions opposed to Rao to reposition themselves for a possible change in the leadership. All of this infighting and the loss of cohesiveness in the Congress encouraged the BJP to launch a Rao-hatao (Remove Rao) campaign.

To make matters worse, the Bofors scandal, believed to involve a $200 million payoff to Rajiv Gandhi's coterie, resurfaced in late 1993 when the Geneva Cantonal Court decided to release certain code-named bank accounts to Indian authorities. This in itself did not provide concrete proof of any wrongdoing, but the opposition made capital of the two scandals and introduced a no-confidence motion in Parliament. Rao, with 251 seats in a House of 533, barely managed to scrape through with a 265–251 vote. Rumors later suggested that he had given massive bribes to several MPs for their support.

The Emergence of Caste Politics. Politics became further complicated when Rao undertook the sensitive task of implementing the Mandal recommendations in the form approved by the Supreme Court. In 1992, the Supreme Court had stipulated that the advanced sections of the Backward Castes, "the creamy layer," were not entitled to reservation quotas, nor were the poor among the "forward" castes, as had been recommended by Rao; that the Backward Castes were to be divided into Backward Castes (already well represented in government services) and More Backward Castes, and that only the latter should receive Mandal benefits; that the quotas should apply at the time of appointment (certain categories of skilled jobs, such as medicine and engineering, were excluded from the list); and that promotions should be based on merit only. The Mandal reforms, along with reservations already in place for Scheduled Castes and Scheduled Tribes, raised the total percentage of reservations to 49.5 percent. This large-scale affirmative action plan had the potential of fracturing society even further because it politicized the lower castes and prompted them to strengthen their separate caste identities. Of course, upper-caste Hindus, about to lose their privileged status because of Mandal, found these developments distasteful.

But the Mandal reforms were the logical product of the directive principles of the Constitution and the evolving democratic system that had already witnessed a growing self-assertion of the Backward and Untouchable Castes (the Scheduled Castes) that had given themselves a new name, Dalit (Oppressed).

Rao tried to tone down the immediate impact of this complicated issue by establishing a National Commission for the Backward Classes to oversee the reforms and handle complaints. However, since V.P. Singh and his Janata Dal had taken the lead in representing the cause of the lower castes in the Hindi heartland (which contains a third of India's population), the Congress had to scramble to regain support in this crucial area. The anti-Congress Yadav Backward Caste had already captured power in Bihar and Uttar Pradesh, and the new reservation system gave the Yadavs additional facility to advance their position through official patronage. The Congress's attempt to exploit the frustration of the "creamy layer" of the Backward Castes in these states proved of little tactical value.

The November 1993 State Elections and Their Impact

When Rao called the elections in the four northern states where the BJP governments had been dismissed (Uttar Pradesh, Madhya Pradesh, Himachal Pradesh, and Rajasthan) and in the Metropolitan Council of Delhi in November 1993, he hoped to see his policies, particularly his attack on the BJP for having created the Ayodhya crisis, succeed in regaining ground for the Congress.

The elections brought mixed results. The Congress won in Madhya Pradesh and Himachal Pradesh; since the latter is a very small state, success there provided some psychological satisfaction, but no real national gain. In the larger state of Madhya Pradesh, the Congress victory was truly impressive: the Congress tripled its pre-election assembly strength and the BJP lost over 50 percent of its seats. The Congress came to power in Madhya Pradesh with a clear majority. However, in two other states, Delhi and Rajasthan, the BJP succeeded in forming governments. The Janata Dal did poorly in all these states.

Uttar Pradesh, the home of the Temple-Mosque conflict, provided a real shock to the BJP, the Congress, and the Janata Dal. The BJP lost 34 seats, which reduced its strength from 211 seats to 177 (total assembly seats: 425); the Congress was humiliated, its strength reduced from 46 seats to 28; but it was V.P. Singh's Janata Dal that was totally disgraced, for its representation fell from 91 to 27. The shock was that Mulayam Singh Yadav's Samajwadi Party (SP) (representing the Backward Castes), in alliance with the Bahujan Samaj Party (BSP) (representing the

Dalits) and with the backing of the Muslim voters, gained a combined total of 176 seats, up from 42 in the previous assembly. Though the BJP had still emerged as the biggest party, it could not form a government because none of the smaller parties were ready to support it. Mulayam Singh Yadav, heading the SP-BSP alliance supported by the minor parties and the Congress, became the chief minister. Caste politics had reached an unanticipated height.

The BJP defeats gave heart to the Congress Party, but as India entered 1994 it became abundantly clear that Indian politics had advanced to a new stage. First, though the BJP and the Janata Dal (heading the National Front–Left Front coalition of centrist and left-oriented parties) had suffered setbacks, they remained viable parties and serious contenders for national power; this was particularly true of the BJP. Second, the era of Congress single-party domination of Indian politics was over. Third, the BJP's well-defined platform of *Hindutva*, and the National Front–Left Front (NF-LF) program for "social justice for the backward and downtrodden in the country," meant that the Congress could no longer afford to be an umbrella organization that promised all things to all peoples and that it must have an issue-based program of its own. Fourth, and most important, neither the Congress nor the BJP could ignore the emergence of Backward Caste and Lower Caste politics. In 1994, Kanshi Ram, the dynamic leader of the Bahujan Samaj Party, traveled from state to state to create a national consciousness among the Dalits and spread the BSP network; his efforts met with considerable success.

The elections also should have brought home to Rao that the Congress organization needed strong state leaders who had a healthy relationship with the electorate. The Madhya Pradesh success was entirely due to the hard electioneering work done by outstanding Congress personalities, such as Arjun Singh and Madhavrao Scindia; by the same token, the debacle in Uttar Pradesh was due to the downgrading of that state's leadership. The elections also made it obvious that the Congress would have to work harder to regain the Muslim and Dalit votes. The most important lesson, no doubt, should have been that the electorate was more worried about corruption and accountability than about economic achievements.

Rao was not unaware of the fact that the Congress was riven by dissension, factionalism, and corruption. In fact, two committees set up to investigate the poor party performance in the state elections had named names and placed the blame on the ubiquitous corruption in the organization that had allowed "antisocial" elements to gain tickets for the elections. "The Congress (I)," said the report of one of the committees, "will suffer again if we do not come to grips with the issue of *criminalization in political life*" (emphasis added).[28] But Rao, though authorized to do so, could not afford to revamp the Congress by getting rid of the undesirable regional or state leaders, who were locally popular and could deliver the votes. His inaction was to prove costly to the party. Some political analysts have suggested that Rao, anxious to bolster his position by strengthening his base in the south, had intentionally neglected Uttar Pradesh and Bihar, the old stronghold of the northern prime ministers, by making "the party electorally irrelevant" in these states.[29]

Though he did little to revitalize the Congress, Rao did change his approach toward the Dalits and the Muslims. To regain the votes of the lower castes, Rao quite unabashedly began the process of manipulating the Mandal award. The non-Congress state governments also were abusing the reservation system, but Rao as the prime minister of India should have checked the abuses rather than added to them. The appointment of twenty-five ministers from the Scheduled Castes, Scheduled Tribes, and Backward Castes to the Madhya Pradesh Congress Cabinet of thirty-six (in 1993) may not fall in the category of abuse—it was more a blatant case of wooing the lower castes—but the state's change in admissions regulations in engineering and medical colleges, which allowed reserved candidates to be admitted without qualifying marks in the admissions examinations, surely was abuse.[30] So also was the act of amending the Constitution to permit Tamil Nadu and Karnataka to increase reservation quotas from the legal 50 percent limit to 69 and 73 percent respectively.

The Congress governments in Andhra Pradesh and Karnataka added some of the politically influential more advanced Backward Castes to the reserved list, as did the BJP government in Rajasthan. The non-Congress Tamil Nadu government doubled the number of Other Backward Castes from 150 in the 1970 list to 310 in 1994, while the governments in Uttar Pradesh and Bihar, run by the Backward Class Yadavs, used the Mandal award to increase the allotment of school and civil service jobs to Scheduled Castes and Scheduled Tribes and appoint members of their own caste to key police and civil posts.[31] In anticipation of the November 1994 state elections, the Congress governments in Andhra Pradesh (the prime minister's home state) and Karnataka appointed "forward Shudra caste [that is, Scheduled Caste] politicos as chief ministers."[32]

These actions of the Congress and the other parties not only made a mockery of the original goal of uplifting the bottommost layer but also placed at risk educational standards in the critical areas of science and technology.

As far as the Muslim vote was concerned, the situation was significantly different for the three parties. The Janata Dal expected to gain the support of the Muslims automatically because of its party plank; the Congress, anxious to regain the Muslim vote, had to woo them; and the BJP, eager, at this stage, to legitimize itself as a party of the Hindus, showed limited interest in pursuing the Muslim vote.

Rao as prime minister had one great advantage: he could use government authority to help gain Muslim goodwill for the Congress. In 1992, in a move intended to conciliate the considerable Muslim populations in the areas of Delhi, West Bengal, Bihar, Uttar Pradesh, and Andhra Pradesh, Rao ordered Doordarshan, the state-controlled television network, to telecast Urdu news bulletins from Delhi, Calcutta, Patna, Lucknow, and Hyderabad* because the Muslims considered Urdu to be their language and felt that it needed to be granted greater recognition.

Karnataka, the state in which elections were scheduled for November 1994,

---

*The last four are state capitals of West Bengal, Bihar, Uttar Pradesh, and Andhra Pradesh.

also had Urdu-speaking Muslims who constituted about 10 percent of the state's population,[33] but Rao had so far ignored them because they had good relations with the Hindus historically and, unlike their co-religionists in the other states, had never entered into a violent confrontation with the government over the status of Urdu. However, when the BJP, which was weak in Karnataka, made a clumsy attempt in 1994 to stir up a communal crisis in the state, Rao saw it as an opportunity to win over the Muslims. He decided, in October of that year, to introduce an Urdu news bulletin in the Karnataka Doordarshan programs telecast from Bangalore, but the endeavor backfired. Promoters of Kannada (the language of the state), provoked by the political move, launched a violent agitation, and communal riots spread through the state. The government was forced to postpone a decision on the matter of the Urdu bulletin, but Rao's politically motivated move had handed the BJP an advantage it had not been able to gain on its own.

In the larger context, Rao never seemed to have understood the simple truth that all his manipulative caste and language strategies meant little to a voting public that was getting increasingly disgusted with corruption in politics. While scandal followed scandal, Rao kept his position secure by increasing his hold over power and authority. He did not realize, apparently, that such a personalized style of government meant that the public would blame him personally for anything that went wrong.

In mid-1994, the country was rocked by the "great sugar scandal" that had been created by the government's procrastination in importing sugar. All concerned knew that sugar had to be imported to offset a massive sugar shortage and that if this were not done promptly, sugar prices would skyrocket and lead to hoarding, profiteering, black marketeering, and inflation. The delay in imports gave an opportunity to the producers and retailers to make huge profits, while the government lost 650 million rupees (about $20 million) because of increased subsidies to fixed-price ration shops and the rise in world prices. The sugar scandal outraged the public, which was convinced that politicians and officials had made money out of the crisis.

The government was still struggling to provide an explanation for the sugar crisis when the 1992 securities scandal resurfaced to plague Rao. Rao's government, after a two-year delay, had finally tabled a report in Parliament detailing the action taken on the Joint Parliamentary Committee's report on the securities scam, which had cost the taxpayers 50 billion rupees, but the report was such an obvious attempt to cover up corruption in high places (two of Rao's cabinet members were known to have received bribes) that it unified the opposition and gave it a popular election issue.

Even before the securities scandal had moved from the front pages of the newspapers, the public was appalled to learn that Sharad Pawar, the Congress chief minister of Maharashtra, allegedly had connections with the Bombay underworld don, Dawood Ibrahim, a Muslim who was the prime suspect in the Bombay blasts of 1993, and with other underworld figures who had "terrorized a vast semi-urban and rural area bordering Bombay through their armed goons."[34]

Then, just before the state elections in November 1994, a plaguelike epidemic*
struck Surat in Gujarat and spread to other parts of India as terrified people fled the
area. The epidemic was brought under control within months but not before India's
image had been damaged in the eyes of the world and Rao's image tarnished further within the country. As *India Today* commented in its vividly florid language:
"The plague that is coursing through a limb of western India . . . [is] a reminder of
how cumulative neglect exacerbates . . . the aftereffects of elemental paroxysms.
Shortage of funds is no excuse either. The money has flowed in from Five Year
Plans and international agencies. But between venal politicians and bureaucrats
and the depredation of contractors, this nation has created not underground sewage lines and toilet facilities and waste treatment plants and incinerators and waste
disposal schemes, but rather monuments to excrescence."[35]

As if to prove how correct the *India Today* indictment was, Indians soon learned
that as stocks of tetracycline (the most effective medication for pneumonic plague)
fell, manufacturers lowered the quantity of the active ingredient in their tetracycline capsules; worse, vast quantities of spurious tetracycline capsules, filled with
charcoal, chalk, and sand, had appeared in the market.[36] A poll of the voters in
Andhra Pradesh and Karnataka, on the eve of the elections in these states, revealed
that the highest percentage of voters believed that "removal of corruption" was
"the most important issue facing the country."[37]

The Year-End State Elections, 1994

The November-December 1994 elections in the four states of Andhra Pradesh,
Karnataka, Goa, and Sikkim showed how much the mood of the country had swung
against the Congress. In Andhra Pradesh, the prime minister's home state, the
Congress was thrown out of power, having suffered a most humiliating defeat: its
position in the state assembly (total seats: 294) was reduced from 183 seats to 26.
N. T. Rama Rao's Telugu Desam Party swept the polls, raising its strength from 93
seats to 253. Though Rama Rao had campaigned on a populist program that promised to help the poor by drastically reducing prices of staple commodities, his
victory was largely due to the Congress having lost credibility in the state.

The Congress suffered a similar reverse in Karnataka, where its strength was
reduced from 176 seats to 35 (total seats in assembly: 224). To everyone's surprise, the victor in Karnataka was the Janata Dal, which had raised its strength
from 24 seats to 116. The BJP also made significant gains, winning 40 seats against
the 5 it held in the pre-election assembly. The BJP's status in Karnataka had been
enhanced to such a degree that it now became the main opposition party in the
state assembly.

In Sikkim, too, the Congress did poorly. A year-old party, the Sikkim Demo-

---

*It was immediately analyzed as "pneumonic plague," but by the end of the year scien-
tists doubted the finding.

cratic Front, won 19 of the 32 seats in the state assembly, gaining the right to form a government. Of the remaining 13 seats, the Sikkim Sangram Parishad won 10. The only election where the Congress saved face somewhat was in Goa: it won 18 seats in a 40–member house and formed a minority government. Even in Goa, the BJP with its 4 seats fared well, given that it had never had a presence in Goa before 1994.

The results of the elections again confirmed the view that unless the Congress revitalized the party and improved its image, its future was bleak. The elections demonstrated that the BJP was, indeed, a major second party, though they also forced the BJP to realize that the Ram and the Temple-Mosque cards perhaps were losing some of their popular value and that the issues of corruption and clean, stable government could be made important parts of its platform. The Janata Dal's surprising election success confirmed that that party still had a future and that its call of "justice for the suppressed" was not misplaced.

The Congress debacle in the 1994 elections exploded the myth that Rao had a hold over the south and made the prime minister more vulnerable to attack by the anti-Rao elements in the Congress. Arjun Singh, the minister of human resources and development, a contender for Rao's position as head of the party and his long-standing opponent, was most outspoken in his criticism. He blamed Rao for the electoral losses and declared that Rao's policies over the last four years had created the popular impression that the Congress had fostered corruption by not taking more resolute action in the Joint Parliamentary Committee's report on the 1992 securities scam and by allowing the Bofors scandal to fester. According to Singh, Rao's policies had also alienated the Muslims ("Minorities hold us responsible for the destruction of the Babri Masjid," said Singh), split the party with a "north-south syndrome," and estranged the Rajiv loyalists by deviating from the pro-poor policies established by the Nehru dynasty and by not pursuing Rajiv's assassination probe with vigor. The Congress had become disunited and lost its course.

Singh's highly publicized attack, followed by his resignation from the cabinet, fractured the party even further. Rao expelled Singh from the party on February 6, 1995, and got a number of regional and central Congress leaders to condemn Singh for conspiring to weaken the party. Rao also sought to deflate the sensitive Rajiv issue by inducting some Rajiv loyalists into the cabinet and by paying an official visit to Sonia Gandhi—Sonia was still a person of importance in Congress politics. He also tackled the pro-poor issue by presenting the country with a budget with a human face, which gave tax breaks to the poor, introduced new rural loan programs, and increased subsidies for fertilizers. But none of this helped Rao or the Congress in facing the next set of state elections that were scheduled to be held in Maharashtra and Gujarat, the most industrialized states in the country, and the poorer, but no less important, states of Bihar and Orissa in February–March 1995.

The February–March 1995 State Elections and the Congress Rout

The reverses for the Congress in these elections were even more humiliating than in the November–December 1994 state elections. In Maharashtra, where the Congress had been in power ever since the creation of this linguistic state in 1960, its strength in an assembly of 288 seats was reduced from 141 to 80. The victor was the BJP–Shiv Sena (SS) alliance that captured 138 seats, improving its previous position by 44 seats; the Janata Dal and its allies lost 50 percent of their pre-1995 strength. The BJP-SS alliance proved that, despite the harsh face of the extremist militant Shiv Sena (it had had a hand in fomenting the Bombay riots in December 1992), the platform of clean government attracted the support of an anti-establishment populace, sickened by corruption in Congress politics.

The BJP-SS alliance had made the U.S. Enron Corporation's $2.8 billion power project in Maharashtra central to its election campaign in the state, alleging that corruption had been involved in the making of the deal. The alliance demanded that the project be scrapped because it was too costly and the electricity tariff, to which the Central and Maharashtra governments had committed themselves, was too high. The BJP also raised fears that multinationals were undermining India's national industries and its self-reliant approach to economic development.

The BJP success in Gujarat was far more definitive because here it had no allies: The BJP won 121 seats in an assembly of 182 (raising its strength by 54 seats); the next strongest party was the Congress, which captured 45 seats (12 over the number in the previous assembly). Though both parties made gains at the expense of the Janata Dal, which lost all its 70 pre-1995 seats, the BJP proved that it was, indeed, a party with national stature, a legitimate contender for power at the center. Once again, corruption in the Congress and reports of widespread links between Gujarat Congress ministers, even chief ministers, and underworld criminal elements had shattered the confidence of the common man in the party that had once been identified with the hallowed son of Gujarat, Mahatma Gandhi.[38]

In Bihar, the Janata Dal, led by the incumbent chief minister, Laloo Prasad Yadav, continued in power, having raised its assembly strength from 120 to 160 seats, in a house of 324. The next biggest party, the BJP, won 40 seats, an increase of 1 seat over its previous representation; and the Congress went down in shambles from 72 seats to 29. The Janata Dal had no real reason to be heartened by its success in Bihar because it was not the JD but the dynamic Laloo Prasad Yadav who had, apart from using some strong-arm methods, exploited the Backward Caste, lower caste, and minority (Muslim) politics to the best advantage.

In Orissa, the fourth state holding elections, the JD did as badly as it had done in Maharashtra and Gujarat. The JD was the governing party in Orissa, but it lost 76 of its 122 seats (total house strength: 147) and became the opposition party, handing over the government to the Congress, that had raised its strength from 10 to 80 seats. Surprisingly, the BJP did not even figure in the Orissa elections.

Rao made the Orissa victory a personal triumph—he had electioneered extensively in the state—but in view of the losses in Maharashtra, Gujarat, and Bihar, it was a piffling victory.

The Congress Party's Last Year in Power, April 1995–May 1996

The badly bruised Congress Party was further fractured when, immediately following the elections, Rao's enemies, led by Arjun Singh, convened a rump meeting of the dissidents where Rao was replaced by the Uttar Pradesh party chief, Tiwari, as president of the party. Rao, exercising his legitimate authority as president of the Congress, expelled Tiwari from the party and exploited the situation to increase his control by demanding that Congress members of Parliament sign affidavits of loyalty. Fortuitously for Rao but not the Congress Party, the Congress defeat in Maharashtra had dealt a serious blow to Chief Minister Sharad Pawar's aspirations for national leadership; Pawar's political stature had once been as high as that of Arjun Singh. With the elimination of Arjun Singh, Tiwari, and Pawar, Rao had managed to centralize authority in his hands even more than Indira Gandhi, and he used it for patronage appointments within the government and party, as had Indira. With his one-man rule reinforced, Rao did not bother to hold even one meeting of the All-India Congress Committee during the whole of 1995.

Before the year ended the dissidents decided to split from the Congress under Rao and establish a party of their own, which they named All-India Indira Congress (AIIC). The AIIC did not manage to capture the imagination of the voters, though it did draw Sonia Gandhi into the political arena by harping on Rao's failure to carry on the Rajiv legacy. For the first time in four years, Sonia broke her silence to urge Rao to reinstate Arjun Singh and Tiwari and let them administer the 1996 elections. She also expressed unhappiness over the time taken to complete Rajiv's assassination enquiry. Once again, Rao managed to deflect the incipient threat to his position by reshuffling the Cabinet and coopting two Sonia loyalists. Still, when the elections came, the feeble AIIC did undermine the Congress by splitting the vote.

Unfortunately for Rao, his wily political triumphs were lost in the unending storms created by corruption scandals. In July 1995, news that a former Congress youth leader had murdered his wife and tried to destroy the body by stuffing it into a *tandoor* (oven) created a furor in Parliament and demands that the government release the Vohra Committee Report (named after the home secretary, N. N. Vohra, who had drafted the report) on the nexus between crime and politics; the report had been prepared nearly two years earlier, following the Bombay bomb blasts. The brief, twelve-page Vohra report was placed before Parliament in August 1995. Although the report mentioned the names of only the criminal elements, it stated that crime syndicates with international drug and espionage linkages, and with the protection of Indian politicians who had been bought out with black (i.e., unreported) money, had become a law unto themselves; it further alleged that a politician-criminal nexus was "virtually running a parallel government, pushing the state apparatus into irrelevance."[39] The report also maintained that "some political leaders become the leaders of these [criminal] gangs/armed *senas* (forces) and, over the years, get themselves elected to local bodies, state assemblies and the national parliament. . . . These syndicates have acquired substantial financial and muscle power and social respectability and have successfully corrupted the government machinery at all levels and make the task of investigating and prosecuting agencies extremely difficult; even the members of the judicial system have not escaped the embrace of the mafia."[40]

Following the Vohra report, investigative reports brought to national attention frightful details of how in every state of the union principles were being sacrificed for power. Several leaders candidly admitted that no party was free from the rot that was running deep in the national polity. Only the BJP tried to project itself as a clean party and, indeed, none of its major leaders had been tainted by corruption so far.

Rao's torments were, however, far from over. In late August, Pilot, the internal security minister, embarrassed Rao by ordering the arrest of Rao's friend and consultant, the politically powerful godman,* Chandraswami, who had been under investigation for years for his links with organized crime, including to Dawood, the underworld don of Bombay, and who was reported to have been the conduit of large sums of black money to various political leaders. Among the many scams with which Chandraswami was connected, one concerned an industrialist, S. K. Jain, who was also under investigation by the CBI. Jain allegedly had used *hawala* (illegal foreign exchange) money to bribe many prominent persons; the list included ministers in Rao's government and Chandraswami. According to Jain, Chandraswami had taken Jain to Rao's residence where Rao had spoken to Jain privately and asked for a 25 million rupee (about $800,000) contribution to the Congress Party and 5 million rupees for himself.[41] Chandraswami managed to avoid indictment because the charges against him could not be immediately proved, but the Jain *hawala* case would explode within a few months into the biggest corruption crisis the Congress, or the country, had ever faced.

In the same month of August, the chief minister of Punjab was assassinated by Sikh terrorists who had planted a bomb in his bulletproof car. This lapse of security raised fears that Rao's achievement of peace in Punjab might unravel and return insurgency to the state. The fears proved to be unfounded when a new chief minister took over and life in Punjab retained its normalcy.

By the end of the year, the insurgency in Kashmir gained an international dimension when a new, so far unknown terrorist group called Al-Faran,** composed of non-Indian and non-Kashmiri, pan-Islamic militants from Pakistan, Afghanistan, and other Islamic countries, kidnapped five foreign tourists, two British, a

---

*India has a number of nationally recognized, and worshipped, *godmen* (a uniquely Indian term for a uniquely Indian phenomenon), persons who have attained spiritual godhood and can perform miracles of all kinds. These godmen have millions of followers, among whom one can count ministers of government, prime ministers, politicians, officials, industrialists, and professionals.

**It was later discovered that Al-Faran was affiliated with the Pakistan-based Harkut-ul-Ansar terriorist organization.

German, an American, and a Norwegian. The captors demanded the release of fifteen jailed militants, ten of whom were terrorists from foreign Muslim states. To prove that their threat was serious, Al-Faran beheaded the Norwegian and left his decapitated body lying on a well-traveled road. The government opened negotiations with the captors but refused to release the jailed terrorists. A stalemate followed, and to date (January 2000) there is still no concrete news of what Al-Faran has done with the hostages; it is feared that they are all dead by now. The tragic hostage crisis, nevertheless, did prove that Pakistan was party to the Kashmir insurgency, and the government's firm action did demonstrate to other terrorist groups the futility of using hostages to gain their ends.

Before 1995 ended, the upheaval in Kashmir had claimed nearly 20,000 lives, and Rao raised the possibility of applying the Punjab model in the state by holding elections and setting up a civil government.[42] The election commissioner, however, ruled out the proposal because of unsettled conditions in the state, and the Kashmiri militant groups vowed in any case to sabotage the elections through increased violence.

Foreign Affairs

By 1991, when Rao assumed office, the collapse of the Soviet Union had changed the international environment in South Asia. The withdrawal of the Soviets from Afghanistan had meant the end of U.S. interest in Pakistan as a front-line state, and in 1990, pursuant to the Pressler Amendment,* Washington had even stopped military aid to Islamabad. This gave hope to New Delhi that it could now improve relations with the United States. India needed the United States and the West not only because the newly established state of Russia could not sustain the pre-1990 rupee-based trade with India or maintain the continuity of the supply of high-tech weapons in the immediate future but also because Rao's economic reforms demanded a closer integration with Western economies.

The shift of national attention to economic growth and the reduction in defense spending also motivated New Delhi to improve relations with China; military tensions and the maintenance of troops along the high-altitude Himalayan borders were a costly business. Rao welcomed Premier Li Peng to New Delhi in 1991 and then himself visited Beijing in 1993. These exchanges led to agreements that helped the two countries to set aside border disputes, reduce troops on both sides of the de facto line of control, and establish regular contacts between border commanders. The friendly environment created by Rao's visit was strengthened by the visits of the Chinese defense minister in 1994 and of the chairman of the Standing Com-

---

*The Pressler Amendment to America's foreign aid program, passed by the U.S. Congress, demanded that Washington suspend all military aid and transfer of weapons to Pakistan unless the president of the United States could certify that Pakistan was not developing nuclear weaponry. President Bush could not make such a certification because American intelligence had evidence that Pakistan was assembling a nuclear trigger.

mittee of the National People's Congress in 1995. China, though a supplier of arms to Pakistan, no longer took its side over Kashmir.

Rao's economic rather than security-centered approach had many ramifications. Apart from reaching out to the United States, Western Europe, and Japan, India established a bridgehead with the Association of South-East Asian Nations (ASEAN) and applied for membership in Asia-Pacific Economic Cooperation. By the end of 1994, after Rao and Singapore's prime minister had exchanged state visits, Singapore committed itself to several joint ventures in India. In 1994, seeing that the Russian government was now more settled, Rao also visited Moscow and reactivated India's trade relations with Russia; India needed to update its aging Soviet-made weapons, and Russia needed hard currency and a market for its military hardware.

However, the deplorable relations between India and Pakistan did not change for the better. The 1992 Ayodhya incident was a godsend for Pakistan, and Islamabad used it to try and win over other Islamic states to its view that Muslims everywhere should join to stop Hindu India from "butchering" its Muslim citizens. In 1993, Pakistan took another anti-Indian step in internationalizing the Kashmir issue by raising it at the World Human Rights Conference in Vienna. Benazir Bhutto, who led the Pakistan delegation, gave a graphic picture of a "brutal campaign of repression and slaughter" in Kashmir, but on a point of order, the leader of the Indian delegation condemned Bhutto for breaching the "spirit of solidarity of the conference by referring to a bilateral issue."[43] The speaker was referring to the Shimla agreement between Prime Minister Z. A. Bhutto, Benazir's father, and Prime Minister Indira Gandhi, in which they had decided to treat Kashmir as a bilateral issue. Other Indian speakers mentioned Pakistan's role in fomenting trouble in Kashmir by infiltrating terrorists into the valley. India's stand was helped by the United States, which at the time was threatening to place Pakistan on the list of states supporting terrorism unless Pakistan cut its ties with terrorist groups.[44]

Benazir had been snubbed but not silenced. She once again took up the Kashmir issue at the U.N. Human Rights Commission meeting at Geneva in March 1994, this time in the form of a resolution that condemned India for human rights violations in Kashmir. India sent a high-powered delegation that included Farooq Abdullah, head of the Kashmir National Conference, BJP leader Vajpayee, Finance Minister Manmohan Singh, and Minister of State for Foreign Affairs Salman Khursheed. Abdullah and Khursheed, both articulate, progressive Muslims, led the counterattack. India won a great victory when, pressured by Iran and other Islamic countries, Pakistan was forced to withdraw its resolution. India brought to world notice the fact that Pakistan was supplying the terrorists in Kashmir with highly sophisticated arms, ranging from air-to-ground rockets, automatic grenade launchers, disposable rocket launchers, 107mm shells, 60mm mortars, and solar paneled wireless communication sets (which even the Indian troops did not possess); the Indian security forces had captured "enough weapons to equip an infantry division."[45]

In 1994, amid accusations and counteraccusations alleging the involvement of diplomats in espionage, Pakistan closed down its consulate in Bombay and ordered the reduction of staff in India's consulate in Karachi. In the same year, Pakistan's former prime minister, Nawaz Sharif, aggravated the situation further by announcing that Pakistan was in possession of nuclear bombs. In his August 15, 1994, Independence Day speech, Rao responded to Pakistan's belligerent attitude by declaring that the only unfinished business in Kashmir was the liberation of Pakistan-held Kashmir territory.

Early in 1995, President Clinton made reference to possible abuses of human rights by the Indian government in its efforts to put down rebellion in Kashmir. This troubled Indian leaders because it gave the impression that Clinton was deliberately overlooking Pakistan-controlled terrorism in the valley and human rights abuses by the terrorists. But any comfort that this may have brought Pakistan was offset when two U.S. consular officials in Karachi were killed by local terrorists and Bhutto appealed to the United States to help Pakistan "shut down terrorist training camps, religious schools, and other places used as terrorist fronts" that contributed to "militancy and terrorism."[46]

In August 1995, tensions worsened when five Western tourists were kidnapped in Kashmir (see above), and India blamed Pakistan for the incident. The allegations against Pakistan gained credibility in September, when two Afghan infiltrators surrendered to the Kashmir authorities and provided detailed insight into the manner in which the Pakistan Inter-Services Intelligence wing (ISI) trained them, gave them weapons, and helped them infiltrate Kashmir.[47] In 1996, after Rao had concluded his tenure as prime minister, civil government was restored in Kashmir (discussed in the following chapter), but the troubles between India and Pakistan did not ease.

India-Pakistan tensions, rooted in the Kashmir issue, naturally contributed to the security concerns of the two countries. Consequently, the arms race between India and Pakistan continued unabated. Neither country renounced the nuclear option, and if India had developed its own missiles, Pakistan had followed suit by buying them surreptitiously from China and getting Chinese help to manufacture them indigenously. Despite repeated attempts, Washington failed to get India to sign the Nuclear Nonproliferation Treaty or accept the denuclearization of South Asia. In December 1995, India refused even to support the Comprehensive Test Ban Treaty, which it had cosponsored with the United States in 1993, on the grounds that it did not "reflect the overwhelming world view that there should be an elimination of [all] nuclear weapons *in a given time frame*" (emphasis added).[48] Unless that was done, Indian leaders believed that their country would continue to face a possible nuclear threat not only from Pakistan, but also from China, from the Central Asian republics that had inherited nuclear weapons left behind by the USSR, and from Middle Eastern countries.

India's adamant stand on the nuclear and missile issues was the cause of considerable friction with the United States. In 1992, the United States exasperated

India by refusing to sell to the Indian Institute of Science a supercomputer (similar to the one it had sold to China) and by stopping Russia from supplying a cryogenic space rocket engine to the Indian Space Research Organization—both on grounds that they could be diverted to military use. In 1993, the United States broke its twenty-year agreement with India and withheld the export of uranium fuel for use in the Tarapur nuclear plant, which provides electricity to Bombay, unless India allowed the monitoring of its entire nuclear industry. These pressures were perceived by India as an infringement of its sovereignty and an arbitrary obstacle to its scientific development. Other than annoying India and delaying its timetable, Washington's actions proved wholly futile; India had enough technological knowhow to produce its own satellites, rockets to launch those satellites, surface-to-surface and ballistic missiles, and supercomputers.

By the end of 1994, the United States had quietly reduced its overt involvement with South Asian security issues, although it could not avoid being occasionally criticized as anti-India or anti-Pakistan. In 1993, when Washington debated the proposal to add Pakistan to the list of terrorist nations, Islamabad feared that the United States was tilting toward India. A decision to include Pakistan would have elated India, but in the end it was not added to the list. In 1994, Washington decided to provide Pakistan, as a one-time exception to the Pressler Amendment, with $370 million in arms. This so disturbed the opposition in India that Rao was advised to defer his state visit to the United States, advice which Rao very wisely rejected. In any event, the arms were never delivered. In 1995, India was deeply perturbed by the ill-considered remark of Assistant Secretary of State Robin Raphel that questioned Kashmir's accession to India. It was obvious that Washington had yet to clearly define its policy focus toward the subcontinent.

Despite these periodic ups and downs, India's overall relations with America were primarily guided by economic interests and continued to improve (see section on economic development, above), particularly after Rao's visit to the United States in May 1994. In keeping with the spirit of the agreement between the two heads of state that "the pace and scope of high-level exchanges" would be expanded, Energy Secretary Hazel O'Leary visited India in mid-1994 and again in February 1995; Defense Secretary William Perry and Commerce Secretary Ron Brown visited in January 1995; and Treasury Secretary Robert Rubin came in April 1995. First Lady Hillary Rodham Clinton's visit in March 1995 was personal but nevertheless politically important. As U.S.-Indian commercial relations improved, irritants such as human rights and copyrights issues were gradually given lesser importance by American official visitors. By the end of 1995, the United States had emerged as India's biggest trading partner and the source of 40 percent of foreign investment in the country.

The 1996 General Elections: A Silent Revolution

The general elections of 1996 for the eleventh Lok Sabha were announced in March. Polling was staggered over several days—April 27, May 2, 7, and 21—so that 1.5

million police and paramilitary forces could be deployed to maintain security at the 800,000 polling stations and 1,650 observers could be moved around to ensure that the elections, involving 590 million eligible voters, were fair. Rao's government also decided that elections for the six parliamentary seats from Kashmir would be held; the last set of elections in that state were to conclude on May 26.

The elections were, indeed, peaceful and fair, but they were held under the shadow cast by the Jain *hawala* scandal (see above) that blew up in January. Unprecedented in their scope, the revelations of corruption rocked the entire political establishment of India because several leaders from all the major parties and high officials of the government were involved. Between 1989 and 1991, Jain, a steel and power industrialist, had paid $33 million in bribes to politicians in return for favors. But even more damaging to national integrity, Jain, protected by his relations with powerful political figures had also channelled *hawala* money to Kashmiri Muslim guerrillas.

The CBI, restrained by political considerations, carried on a desultory enquiry into the Jain bribery case, but, admonished by the Supreme Court, it was forced to accelerate its enquiry. (It is worth noting that the action taken by the Supreme Court was in response to a public-interest suit filed by two journalists.) The first list released by the CBI indicted ten politicians, among whom were three members of Rao's cabinet; Advani, the head of the BJP who had made corruption the theme of his election drive; Arjun Singh, who had been dismissed from Congress and formed his own party; Devi Lal, who had been deputy prime minister in the 1989 Janata government; and Sharad Yadav, the Janata Dal parliamentary party leader. The Jain diaries, from which the list was drawn, contained the names of 115 politicians and officials, including former Prime Minister Rajiv Gandhi, who had allegedly accepted bribes.

Advani denied the charges and said that the courts would clear his name, but at the same time he resigned from his position in the BJP to protect the party's image; the moderate and more secular A. B. Vajpayee, who had been the foreign minister in a former Janata government, replaced Advani. The three Congress ministers also resigned from government; later exposures forced several more to leave the cabinet. The scandal may have left Rao feeling that he had emerged with his hands clean and that the opposition parties could no longer use the corruption issue to attack the Congress. But Rao could not escape being splattered by the muck that was being raked by the CBI. Based on Jain's alleged "confession," but not on the written evidence in his diaries, the BJP attacked Rao for receiving 30 million rupees ($1 million) from *hawala* money in 1995. To a public fed up with corruption scandals, it mattered little whether the charges were alleged or true; Rao was not a clean politician.

Apart from Vajpayee, the only politician of national standing and high visibility who still had a clean image was V. P. Singh, the Janata Dal leader. But even his task of forging a National Front alliance out of a motley collection of small opposition parties was made more onerous because of the corruption scandals that had tainted the reputation of many in the JD and other parties. Just weeks before the elections, the dark shadow of corruption fell on Laloo PrasadYadav, the Janata Dal chief minister of Bihar, when the Patna High Court ordered the CBI and Income Tax Department to inquire into a $200 million embezzlement case involving the Animal Husbandry Department; the Animal Husbandry Department had drawn these monies from 1977 on for the maintenance and improvement of cattle stock that existed mostly on paper! In Uttar Pradesh, India's largest state, 180 of the 425 legislators had criminal records.

Ironically, though fortunately for the country, such a dismal political setting produced two positive developments that to a degree counterbalanced the crisis in governance, strengthened democratic institutions, and renewed public faith in the machinery of the state. These developments—one associated with the Supreme Court and the other with the chief election commissioner—were directly related to the decline of the Congress as the dominant party and the decline in the ability of the Congress prime minister to exercise absolute power.

The Supreme Court

Rao, who headed a weak parliamentary party, found it increasingly difficult to intimidate the judicial system or the chief election commissioner, as Indira Gandhi or Rajiv had done. This change in the balance of power permitted the emergence of the Supreme Court as a corrective agency. As it became obvious that the executive had lost its capacity to eradicate corruption, the Supreme Court took on a uniquely new role: it began to exert pressure on the CBI, indeed to order that powerful body, to bring charges against persons involved in corruption cases, regardless of how highly placed these accused were. The Supreme Court's instrument to achieve this end was public-interest litigation, a mechanism created after Indira Gandhi's emergency rule to ensure justice for the underprivileged.

Thus, apart from the infamous Jain *hawala* case, which had captured the national imagination, the Supreme Court used public-interest litigation in several other important areas, such as ordering political parties to file income tax returns that indicated the source of their funds (which made it impossible for them to hide illegal contributions); opening the corruption-ridden tender and licensing operations to court scrutiny; and forcing factories to introduce pollution controls. The Supreme Court even ordered many ex-ministers and high officials to vacate the official residences that had been allotted to them when they were in office but which they had continued to occupy illegally for years after their retirement.

Although some legal experts expressed their apprehension that the Supreme Court actions could be construed as going beyond the limits of its constitutional prerogative, the public was happy to see an activist judiciary attack the assumption that politicians and high officials were above the law. The Supreme Court was lauded for tackling the issue of corruption by compelling the government and the investigating agencies to perform their duties "by the book."

The Chief Election Commissioner

During the last years of Rao's government, the Election Commission, under the chief election commissioner, T. N. Seshan, emerged as a spectacularly outstanding institution. Seshan had to organize and oversee the massive 1996 election exercise and ensure its fairness. His was a difficult, if not an impossible job, but he carried it out with aplomb. Seshan had to work out the election schedule; arrange for the polling booths; deploy the security forces to prevent booth capturing or harassment of voters; prevent candidates from exceeding campaign finance limits; stop the parties from polluting the environment by plastering the walls with posters (millions were normally put up but none taken down after an election), exploiting religion in their campaigns, or from carrying on noisy rallies after 10:30 p.m.; and conduct fresh polls if votes were tampered with in any area.

Practically since 1950, when the Constitution was introduced, and increasingly so thereafter, elections came to be corrupted by bribery, intimidation, and booth capturing. To everyone's surprise, however, the 1996 general elections were the most free, fair, and orderly of all the eleven parliamentary elections. As one foreign newspaper reporter put it, "Mr. Seshan has declared war on what he calls 'the 3 M's—money, muscle, and minister power' that he, like many Indians, believes have dictated the course of past elections. . . . He has sent out word that politicians who try to outwit him risk losing their seats, if elected, and probably facing prosecution, too."[49] Another reporter commented that "Seshan's zeal haunts politicians," but "his crusade for clean elections" has earned him "kudos from many Indians fed up with corruption and political dirty tricks."[50] Seshan retired a few years after the 1996 elections, but the standards he had set were zealously maintained by his successors.

Election Manifestos

The 1996 election manifestos of the major parties reflected the differences in their ideologies, but except for the CPI(M), the three national parties—the Congress, the BJP, and the Janata Dal (the main party of the National Front–Left Front alliance)—accepted, with slight variations, the need for the continuation of Rao's economic reform programs and foreign investment. All manifestos also reflected the need to woo the lower castes that had emerged as a new factor in Indian politics during the preceding five years.

The Congress manifesto promised, among other things, a stable government based on democracy and secularism; a vibrant economy that would achieve 8 to 9 percent annual growth in the GDP; an independent judiciary with simplified procedures for a quick disposal of all pending cases; anti-corruption measures; special help for the minorities; emancipation of the poor and their early entry into the middle and higher classes of society; near full employment by the year 2002; cheaper food grains and housing; and improved health and education facilities for the nation. The manifesto did not mention socialism and was silent on the Ayodhya issue.

The BJP manifesto promised a leaner government and projected a four-point goal that aimed at bringing security, probity in public life, self-reliance in the economy, and social harmony to the country. The manifesto also gave a detailed economic program that would reduce government involvement with commercial activities and promote the private sector; encourage capital creation; create a supportive financial mechanism; invite foreign capital to invest primarily in the improvement of the infrastructure, in high technology, and in the export-oriented sector; and help the backward sections of society by maintaining fertilizer subsidies, spending 6 percent of the GNP on education, and allocating 60 percent of the plan funds for the improvement of the agricultural and rural sectors. The BJP emphasized *Hindutva* as a means to "re-energize the soul of India" and reiterated the party's desire to build the temple at Ayodhya. The party proposed to abrogate Article 370 of the Constitution, which gave special status to the state of Kashmir; amend Article 30, which permitted the minorities to run separate educational and cultural organizations; ban cow slaughter; and introduce a uniform civil code. The BJP manifesto was not overtly anti-Muslim and pledged that all minorities would be guaranteed equal treatment.

The Janata Dal in its manifesto still insisted on retaining a strong public sector but also committed the party to the deregulation of the economy so that the country could develop entrepreneurial skills and minimize corruption. The party maintained that the state, not the private sector or the multinational corporations, should develop Indian economic infrastructure, and that the state should insulate sensitive financial services like insurance and capital markets from foreign financial cartels. Even so, it accepted the need for foreign capital in certain sectors. The party promised to make the right to work a fundamental right and protect labor from exploitation; use the industrial infrastructure to produce mass consumption goods; subsidize fertilizers and other agricultural inputs; extend job reservations to the private sector; provide social security to labor; and increase investment in education to 6 percent of GNP.

The Communist Party of India (Marxist) manifesto promised to reverse the policies of economic liberalization by stopping the privatization of the public and financial sectors and revising other reform policies; reduce prices of fourteen essential commodities by 50 percent; make the right to work fundamental; provide free, compulsory education to age fourteen and increase allocations for education to 10 percent of the national budget and 30 percent of the state budget; protect rights of agricultural workers and introduce crop insurance schemes. The CPI(M) would give no licenses to foreign companies for joint ventures or allow foreign ownership of the print media.

All the manifestos promised much to the poor of India, but none indicated where the money for their programs was going to come from.

Election Results

Even before the elections were announced, the major national parties began to forge alliances with regional parties. The Congress joined hands with three re-

The Election Results		
Party	1991 (544 total seats)	1996 (543 total seats)
Congress	253	140 (Congress + allies: **143**)
BJP	119	161 (BJP + allies: **195**)
NF-LF	(JD: 55)	**113** (JD:44)

gional parties that included the Tamil Nadu ruling AIADMK Party. (This proved to be a very unwise decision on Rao's part, for it led to the defection of several Congressmen to an anti-Rao Congress faction; furthermore, the elections did not return a single Congress or AIADMK candidate to the parliament from Tamil Nadu). The BJP found allies in the Shiv Sena, a local Haryana party, and the Akali Dal party in Punjab. The National Front-Left Front (NF-LF) was already an alliance of several small regional parties.

The pre-election polls indicated that the results would bring a hung parliament and that the Congress and its allies were likely to outperform the BJP and the NF-LF. The polls were right on the first count but wholly wrong on the second: the election outcome finally confirmed the decline of the Congress Party.

Of the several surprises produced by the elections, one pleasant one was that, after six years of hiatus, elections were held in the troubled state of Kashmir. The militant groups had threatened that elections would increase violence, and Farooq Abdullah's National Conference had refused to participate in the elections unless the government agreed to restore the pre-1953 status that limited the center's powers in Kashmir. The 110 candidates, most of them independents, who entered the contest for the six parliamentary seats indicated that there were still many people who were ready to respond to the call of democracy. Though the polling booths were heavily guarded and the voters were escorted to the booths, the turnout belied those who alleged that people had been coerced to vote. This strengthened the view that state elections could be held later in the year to bring back normalcy to the region.

At the national level, the results of the 1996 parliamentary elections (see box) created a confusing situation because no single party or alliance of parties commanded a clear parliamentary majority. Under the Constitution, the president was supposed to invite the head of the party with the largest number of seats to form a government, but only if the president was assured that the party could form a stable government—the invited party would have to prove this by winning a vote of confidence in parliament within weeks of taking over.

Although the BJP, it along with its allies, had emerged as the biggest single bloc with 195 seats, it had little chance of winning the confidence vote because all the other parties had declared that they would not support it; the BJP still carried the stigma of being a *communal* party. As an alternative, the Congress, controlling the second largest number of seats (143), could be invited if it could assure the president that it had the backing of the NF-LF, which it could not do because the NF-LF leaders had ambitions of their own.

As far as the NF-LF was concerned, it had yet to work out a common minimum program that could both unify the disparate group of parties (with contradictory platforms) that formed the alliance and attractive other parties to its fold. To achieve this end, the NF-LF renamed itself the United Front (UF). The UF, after much horse trading, comprised thirteen parties—including the Janata Dal, the Tamil Nadu DMK Party, the Communist parties, the Samajwadi Party, and the Asom Gana Parishad—that represented twenty-five states of the union. The United Front now controlled 180 seats in the Parliament but had no leader of stature other than V. P. Singh. But Singh, who was ailing, declined to head the alliance and serve as prime minister. Efforts to get Jyoti Basu, the eighty-one-year-old Communist chief minister of West Bengal, as prime ministerial candidate also failed. Ultimately, an unknown politician, Deve Gowda, the Backward Caste chief minister of Karnataka, was elected leader of the alliance. Still, the United Front, when it was formed on May 15, needed the support of Congress to win a confidence vote. Meantime, the BJP formally named A. B. Vajpayee, who had liberal, Muslim-friendly credentials, to lead the BJP parliamentary party, in the hope that if the party were invited to form the government, Vajpayee would lure many independent members of parliament to the BJP camp.

On May 16, 1996, India's forty-eight-year tradition of Congress-style secular governments was broken. Faced with a choice between the bungling United Front, which still lacked a credible plan for government, and the BJP, which was bound to lose the confidence vote, the president of India invited the latter to form the next government. This was a great triumph for a party that twelve years earlier had won only two parliamentary seats. The big question that remained, however, was how long the isolated BJP government could last. As prime minister, Vajpayee tried to reassure the Muslims (the first cabinet member to be sworn in after Vajpayee was a Muslim) and other minorities (a lower-caste Hindu and a Tribal were included in the cabinet), but otherwise could hardly tone down the hard-line policies enunciated in the BJP manifesto, including the building of the temple.

The BJP failed to lure support from even a single member in the vast opposition of diverse groups that were unified in their view that the BJP was illiberal, nonsecular, and exclusionist. On its thirteenth day in office, minutes before the confidence vote in Parliament was to be taken, the Vajpayee government resigned.

The president of India, informed in writing that the Congress would support a United Front government, then appointed Deve Gowda as prime minister. This, as we shall discuss in the next chapter, changed the nature of the Indian polity.

Notes

1. *India Today,* November 15, 1985, p. 8.
2. *India Today,* January 15, 1986, p. 54.
3. *India Today* (International Edition), June 15, 1986 p. 18.

4. *India Today*, February 15, 1987, p. 17.

5. *India Today*, August 31, 1987, p. 17.

6. *India Abroad*, January 19, 1996, p. 3.

7. See *India Today*, July 31, 1987, p. 17.

8. Bharat Wariavwalla, "Drift, Disarray, or Pattern," *Asian Survey*, 29, no. 2 (February 1989), p. 194.

9. Richard Sisson, "India in 1989," *Asian Survey*, 30, no. 2, (February 1990), p. 117.

10. M.J. Akbar, *Kashmir: Behind the Vale* (New Delhi: Viking Penguin India, 1991), p. 213.

11. *Asia 1990 Yearbook*, p. 134.

12. *India Today*, September 15, 1989, p. 42.

13. Sarvepalli Gopal, *Jawaharlal Nehru: A Biography* (Cambridge: Harvard University Press, 1984), Vol. III, p. 284.

14. S.K. Ghosh, *Muslim Politics in India* (New Delhi: Ashish Publishing House, 1987), p. 21.

15. Sri Ram Sharma, *The Religious Policy of the Mughal Emperors* (Delhi: Munshiram Manoharlal Publishers, 1940), p. 131.

16. See "The Rubaiya Sayeed Bungle," in *India Today*, December 15, 1995.

17. Sumit Ganguly and Kanti Bajpai, "India and the Crisis in Kashmir," *Asian Survey*, 5 (May 1994), p. 405.

18. See *India Today*, July 15, 1991, p. 40.

19. For the data see *Asia 1993 Yearbook, Asia 1994 Yearbook,* and *Asia 1995 Yearbook* (Hong Kong: Review Publishing Company, 1993, 1994, and 1995).

20. "India Is Elbowing into China's Limelight," *Wall Street Journal*, January 12, 1995, p. A14.

21. "Bengal Communists Woo Private Capital," Reuter News Agency, quoted in *India News Network Digest*, II, September 7, 1995.

22. *Business World*, December 27, 1995/January 9, 1996, pp. 42–57.

23. *The Economist*, April 13–19, 1996, p. 30.

24. See, for example, Khushwant Singh, "India: The Hindu State," *New York Times*, August 3, 1993, p. A17.

25. Ramesh Thakur, "Ayodhya and the Politics of India's Secularism: A Double Standards Discourse," *Asian Survey*, 33, no. 7 (July 1993), p. 661.

26. Zafar Agha, "A Symbol of Identity," *India Today*, December 31, 1992, p. 48.

27. See the nationwide opinion poll published in *India Today*, January 15, 1993, pp. 14–20.

28. See *India Today*, March 31, 1994, p. 14.

29. See *India Today*, November 15, 1994, p. 20.

30. Manoj Mitra, "Racketeering in Quotas," *India Today*, November 15, 1994, pp. 36–38.

31. Ibid.

32. *Asia 1995 Yearbook* (Hong Kong: Review Publishing Company, 1995), p. 128.

33. Paul R. Brass, *The Politics of India Since Independence* (New York: Cambridge University Press, 1994), p. 180.

34. "Another Finger Points at Pawar," *India Today*, September 15, 1994, p. 42.

35. *India Today*, October 15, 1994, p. 3.

36. See *India Today*, October 31, 1994, p. 23.

37. *India Today*, December 15, 1994, p. 24.

38. See Uday Mahurkar, "Cashing In on Corruption," *India Today*, March 31, 1995, pp. 46–48.

39. See *India Today*, August 31, 1995, p. 27.

40. See *India Abroad*, August 11, 1995, p. 4.

41. Zafar Agha and Avirook Sen, "Above the Law," *India Today*, October 15, 1995, pp. 98–107.

42. Sumit Sharma, "India must win hearts before Kashmir polls," Reuter news release, October 12, 1995.

43. *The Times of India,* June 17, 1993, p. 10.

44. *The New York Times International,* April 25, 1993, p. 7.

45. "Kashmir: Militancy Fueled by Sophisticated Weaponry," *India News,* April 15, 1994, p. 7.

46. *The New York Times International,* March 22, 1995, p. A8.

47. S. Ramani, "Pakistan Behind Civil War in Afghanistan and Pushing Afghans into Kashmir," *India News Network Digest* on World Wide Web, September 5, 1995.

48. See report on Foreign Minister Mukherjee's press conference in *Delhi Business Standard,* December 27, 1995.

49. John F. Burns, "For Indians, An Election Is Honest But Boring," *The New York Times International,* May 7, 1996, p. A9.

50. Jonathan Karp, "Do Not Disturb: Strict Rules Take the Fun Out of Election Campaigns," *Far Eastern Economic Review,* May 2, 1996, p. 21.

10

The Rise of the BJP, 1996–2000

Toward a New Polity

The 1996 general elections brought to a head political trends—not all of them necessarily negative—that had become increasingly visible since the 1980s: a drift towards the fragmentation of national politics, marked by instability, institutional decay, and the escalation of a states-oriented polity; the seemingly unstoppable decline of the discredited Congress party; the improving position of the BJP and its emergence as a first-ranking political party, a phenomenon that confounded the projections of many Westernized middle-class intellectuals; the increasing importance of the lower and backward castes and classes in local and national politics; and the advent of what may be termed the coalition government syndrome.

The results of the 1996 elections (see last chapter) compelled the country to rethink its polity because the withering away of the Congress party marked the end of one-party dominance of Indian politics. The BJP, despite its gains, did not have the puissance once enjoyed by the Congress and there was no other party that could step into the vacuum.

It took three years for the country to evolve a radically new polity that appears to augur well for future stability and growth. However, these years were some of the most troubling in post-independent India. Internally, the country was racked by roller-coaster politics, witnessing, partly because of the Congress's desperate attempt to keep the BJP out of power, the rise and fall of three governments in quick succession and two costly and exhausting parliamentary elections.

Contrary to the Congress's hopes and calculations, the popularity and electoral strength of the BJP increased with every election, while those of the Congress declined precipitately. Though the Congress tactics, and the short-lived governments they engendered, were counterproductive and distressful to the country, they produced two important results: they proved that though coalition governments, depending heavily on state-level parties, were the path of the future, they would gain stability only by coalescing around a strong national-level party; and

---

Some Important Dates and Events, 1996–2000

1996	*Eleventh elections for Lok Sabha*
May 1996	**Prime minister, A. B. Vajpayee (BJP),** Government lasts thirteen days
June 1996–March 1997	**Prime minister, Deve Gouda (United Front)**
April 1997–Nov. 1997	**Prime minister, I. K. Gujral (United Front)**
Nov. 1997–March 1988	Gujral heads a caretaker government
1998	*Twelfth elections for Lok Sabha*
March 1998–April 1999	**Prime minister, A. B. Vajpayee (BJP)**
May 1998	India carries out nuclear tests
Feb. 1999	Vajpayee pays a state visit to Pakistan
April–Sept. 1999	Vajpayee heads a caretaker government
May–July 1999	India-Pakistan war over Kargil
1999	*Thirteenth elections for Lok Sabha*
October 1999–	**Prime minister, A. B. Vajpayee (NDA)**

---

they gave the BJP, yet unseasoned in national politics, time to fully appreciate the importance of the emerging coalition government syndrome and to accept it as the path to follow.

After two troubled stretches in power, Vajpayee—who had emerged as a popular leader of national stature—established the National Democratic Alliance (NDA) to fight the 1999 general elections. Its broad-based agenda (it did not include the controversial political program of the BJP) made the NDA attractive to a host of regional parties representing the complex caste and class politics of the country. And it was the NDA, a stable alliance of twenty-four parties, that won a resounding victory in the 1999 general elections, the third in three years. The NDA success ended the three trying years and brought back political stability to the country, because it meant that the new government would have no difficulty in completing a full five-year term.

The economy continued to do well during the period 1996–1999; it did become sluggish in 1998 but rebounded with great vigor in 1999. As India entered the year 2000, there was widespread optimism that the NDA's market-friendly reform policies had finally put India on the path of dependable growth and development.

In external affairs, foreign relations during the years 1996 to mid-1998, except for the continuing troubles with Pakistan, remained on an even keel. The established pattern of foreign relations was sharply upset in May 1998 when the Vajpayee government carried out a series of five nuclear tests: Pakistan responded by testing six nuclear devices of its own and further raised cross-border tensions by launching a limited war in Kashmir in June 1999 within months of Vajpayee's goodwill visit to Pakistan; there was worldwide criticism of India's tests though only the United States, Japan, Canada, and the Scandinavian countries imposed sanctions on India; and India's relations with some countries, particularly China, suffered a temporary setback. India, at the time of this writing (January 2000), has been actively trying to restore its international standing. Its efforts have brought some significant successes, and even relations with the United States, which had led the chorus of condemnation against New Delhi, have improved to the extent that President Bill Clinton has decided to pay a state visit to India in March 2000.

The Two United Front Governments: 1996–1998

The Deve Gowda Government: June 1996–March 1997

As we noted in the last chapter, the 1996 elections did not bring to power either of the two major *national* parties—the Congress and the BJP: the BJP as the largest single party did form a government but it lasted only thirteen days. The impasse was finally settled by the appointment of Deve Gowda of the United Front as prime minister; he formed a minority government with the explicit support of the Congress.

Gowda had the daunting task of preparing a Common Minimum Program (CMP) that would satisfy the thirteen disparate United Front parties and the Congress and of making appointments to the cabinet that would placate the alliance groups. He carried out this phase of his task with amazing confidence.

The Common Minimum Program unveiled by Gowda on June 5, 1996, was an ambitious new model for development and growth that aspired to reconcile secularism, federalism, social justice, and modernization within the framework of, as the document puts it, an "Indian synthesis."

According to this program, the United Front (UF) aimed to strengthen federalism through a devolution of central political, administrative, and economic powers; confront communal forces that had eroded the multiethnic, multireligious, and multilinguist character of the nation; improve the economic and social status of Dalits, Scheduled Tribes, Other Backward Castes, and women; guarantee a minimum wage to agricultural workers and subsidies for fertilizers and essential commodities; make education a fundamental right; abolish poverty and illiteracy by the year 2005; and fight corruption in high places by introducing the Freedom of Information Bill, which would bring greater transparency to official conduct. The UF also committed itself to upholding Article 370, which offered the maximum degree of autonomy to the people of Kashmir, hoping, no doubt, that this would facilitate the return of civil government to that state.

This was a commendable wish-list, but Deve Gowda, even if he had been able to pull together the thirteen parties in the alliance, could not be sure that his government would last long enough to launch even the most modest of his programs. After all, he was holding office at the mercy of the Congress Party, which, as it turned out, did withdraw its support and bring down the Gowda government before it had barely completed ten months in office.

The Congress, which had had a hand in the communalization of Indian politics, justified support of the UF coalition (which included several sectarian parties) in the name of so-called *secularism*, though its real aim was to keep the BJP out of office and to use the respite offered by the UF government to strengthen and expand its organization for the next general elections. The BJP, too, waited on the sidelines for the unstable UF coalition government to collapse. The BJP's approach to the inevitable next Lok Sabha elections, however, was different from that of the Congress. The BJP, though with some hesitation, accepted the notion that the trend toward coalition governments was unavoidable for the foreseeable future—or, looking at it another way, that the days of single-party governments were over for the moment—and began to hunt for support from smaller regional parties.

Deve Gowda's short-lived government did make some significant breaks with the past: it replaced the hold of the upper castes over national politics and tilted the balance of power from the center to the states. Gowda, unlike the eleven upper-caste prime ministers who preceded him, hailed from a low peasant caste. He spoke Kannada (his mother tongue), halting English, and no Hindi, and he was a regional leader with no experience in how the central government worked. His cabinet, too, gave primacy to the lower castes and regional leaders, with or without governmental experience: of the first batch of twenty-one ministers sworn in, fifteen belonged to the Backward Castes, Other Backward Castes, and the Scheduled Castes; ten of the twenty-one had never served in any government, and of the remaining eleven, seven had experience only in state-level governments.[1]

Gowda's government, deriving its strength from regional parties, also made a positive move toward a greater sharing of central power with the states, "a process which revolutionized Indian politics in 1996."[2] Many political thinkers had for years suggested that greater federalism and decentralization of power would not only strengthen democracy, providing greater political voice to the dispossessed lower classes, but hasten economic growth. As one political analyst put it, "The Indian society is pluralistic in character and, therefore, its perennial quest has been unity in diversity. . . . Decentralisation [with a loose federation] should, therefore, be the keynote of our federalism."[3] Gowda's image of a prime minister out to lessen the overbearing power of the center was strengthened when, immediately after his taking over, he decided to hold elections in Kashmir. These elections, for parliamentary seats, were followed, later in the year, by elections to the state legislature. Even though the turnout was not significantly high, the elections, after a six-year hiatus, brought back some sense of normalcy to the insurgency-troubled state; Dr. Farooq Abdullah, head of the victorious National Conference party, became chief minister.

In the field of economic development, Deve Gowda showed remarkable sagacity. Since, back in his own state, Gowda had helped to develop Bangalore as India's Silicon Valley, he appreciated the necessity for carrying on Rao's economic reform programs and making India more attractive to foreign investment; this was signaled by the appointment of Chidambaram, a former minister in Rao's government and an advocate of the free-market approach, as finance minister. The United Front government gained the respect of the nation for its supportive efforts to buoy the market and boost economic growth. Despite the slowness with which the acute problems of infrastructure were being tackled, the government's economic liberalization policies and quick approval of projects involving foreign investment succeeded in nearly doubling the flow of foreign direct investment in 1996–1997 (the financial year begins on April 1).[4] The nation's GDP grew by about 7 percent in the fiscal year 1996–1997 and inflation went down by a point to 6.6 percent.

Initially, the United Front government was not troubled by any overt interference in its work by the Congress party (on whose support the UF was wholly dependent) because the elections had weakened the prestige of the Congress and the charges of corruption against Rao had weakened its president. But once the accumulating corruption charges forced Rao to resign in September 1996 and hand over the presidency to a seventy-seven-year-old party colleague, Sitaram Kesri, the situation changed radically. The impression that the United Front government under Deve Gowda was settling down quite well disturbed the new Congress president, who was also unhappy with Gowda for his not letting up on the corruption cases against Congress leaders. Suddenly, in March 1997, without any warning and without any regard to the damage the action might cause to the national economy, Kesri withdrew his party's support from the Gowda government and threw Indian politics into turmoil. Kesri's charge was that "the United Front government headed by Mr H.D. Deve Gowda are determined to marginalize the Congress and to allow urgent national issues to take a back seat."[5]

However, Kesri's calculation that the fall of the Gowda cabinet would give the Congress a chance to form the next government, supposedly with the outside support of the UF, was wholly unrealistic. And since the Congress could not form a government of its own and was not ready to go to the polls, it had no alternative but to continue its support of the United Front—albeit under a new prime minister, Inder Kumar Gujral, who had held the foreign-affairs portfolio under Gowda. Kesri's blundering action had only further tarnished the Congress's public image; there were no changes in the United Front that would ensure that the Congress would not continue to be "marginalized."

The I.K. Gujral Government: April–November 1997 (–March 1998)

The mild, soft-spoken Gujral, who assumed office at the end of April 1997, retained practically the whole of the Gowda cabinet. Gujral, too, like Gowda, declared his commitment to the eradication of corruption; in his Independence Day address to the nation on August 15, he reaffirmed that this was "my first duty and a promise to the nation." But Gujral, heading a troublesome, fractious coalition, could do precious little to push his agenda. One of his most troublesome allies was the corrupt, idiosyncratic Laloo Prasad Yadav, chief minister of Bihar, whose state was in such a condition of disorderliness that there was pressure on Gujral to dismiss Yadav's government and impose President's Rule in Bihar. Yadav threatened to withdraw from the UF and pull down the national government. Gujral had no recourse but to refrain from taking any action on Bihar. Within a few months, the Central Bureau of Investigation (CBI) filed charges against Laloo Prasad and fifty-five other Bihar officials for their involvement in a $270 million fodder scandal—funds meant for fodder had been embezzled while fraudulent bookkeeping showed disbursals for nonexisting cattle. Thereupon, the maverick Laloo Prasad broke away from the Janata Dal, established his own backward-caste-based party, Rashtriya Janata Dal, and installed his semieducated wife as chief minister, before surrendering to the CBI court. There were similar troubles in Uttar Pradesh, where political power had shifted into the hands of the Dalits and other backward castes.

In any event, Gujral's biggest trouble came from the Congress. In early November 1997, leaked information from a report prepared by the Jain Commission (which had been set up in 1991 to enquire into Rajiv Gandhi's assassination that year) revealed that the Tamil Nadu Dravida Munnetra Kazhagam (DMK) party had had a hand in Rajiv's assassination. The Congress faction headed by Sonia Gandhi wanted Gujral to drop the DMK ministers from the UF government or face withdrawal of the Congress support. Sitaram Kesri, knowing that that would lead to a general election (for which the Congress was ill-prepared), tried to delay putting pressure on Gujral. Sonia won, Gujral resigned on November 28, and the second UF government concluded its rule of eight months. The president, thereupon, called for fresh elections—to be held in February–March 1998—and asked Gujral to stay on till then as the head of a caretaker government.

By bringing down two cabinets within one year (1996 and 1997), the Congress appeared to have added a new dimension to the field of political chicanery and corruption and, more importantly, placed the massive burden of a general election, the second in two years, on a poor nation. The year 1997 marked the fiftieth anniversary of India's independence, but the country found itself in no mood for celebration.

Prime Minister Gujral will be remembered for his success, however limited, in fostering better ties with neighbouring Nepal, Bangladesh, and Sri Lanka, and for his initiatives that helped to improve relations with China and the United States. Unfortunately, his laudable efforts to revitalize relations with Pakistan—he had several, apparently very cordial, meetings with Prime Minister Nawaz Sharif at international summits—failed because of the contentious Kashmir issue (see Chapter 9).

Beyond South Asia, India was anxious to be recognized as a major regional, if not a global, player. New Delhi would have liked the world powers to appreciate that India's refusal to give up either the nuclear option or its missile development had more to do with its perception of threat from other states than from the over-militarized, politically unstable Pakistan. However, Cold War politics and Paki-stan's self-perception committed Islamabad to match India missile for missile (India's June 1997 test-firing of the Prithvi missile was immediately followed by Pakistan's test-firing of its Korean/Chinese-made Haft-III missile that had a longer range than the Prithvi) and, if necessary, nuclear weapon for nuclear weapon. In-dia was therefore denied that international recognition.

The political upheavals of 1997 did cast a shadow over the market, but thanks to the creative policies of Finance Minister P. Chidambaram, who held office un-der both the UF governments, the national economy, hemmed in by the anti-re-form bias of the leftist parties in the UF and obstructionist Congress moves, managed to do better than expected, though growth did slow down under Gujral.

The Twelfth General Elections

Immediately following the fall of the Gujral government, all the political parties began feverishly to mobilize for the twelfth general elections scheduled to be held in February–March 1998. Of the two major parties involved, the Congress was in worse shape than the BJP. Sitaram Kesri, president of Congress, lacked the cha-risma and the vision to pacify the factions in the party and lead a unified Congress into the electoral fray. While bickering and infighting made it difficult for the Congress high command to work out a contention-free campaign agenda, several disgruntled and frustrated leaders started abandoning the party. Mamata Banerjee, the fiery Congresswoman from West Bengal, provides a good example of this situation. She was so openly critical of the party's vacillating policies that she was expelled from the Congress on December 22, 1997. Mamata promptly established her own party, the Trinamool Congress, and on December 28—exactly a month after Gujral resigned—two more West Bengal Congress leaders quit the party and joined the Trinamool Congress.

The Congress had no clear-cut election issue and no leader with a national image. At this point, on December 29, Sonia Gandhi, encouraged by her coterie of loyalists, decided to step out of seclusion to "save the party." The disoriented Con-gress leaders heaved a sigh of relief: Sonia, a nationally recognized "face" that could draw crowds, had filled the leadership vacuum. And there was also no longer any need to agonize over the framing of election issues: the election campaign could be centered on Sonia, the widow of Rajiv Gandhi, the daughter-in-law of Indira Gandhi, and a worthy member of the Nehru dynasty. One of the popular Congress-inspired ditties summed it up rather well:

> Ab to Sonia Gandhi aayi
> Jeet Gayi ab Congress(I)

> (Sonia Gandhi has arrived;
> now Congress(I) is bound to win.)

The BJP, on the other hand, was far better prepared than the Congress to fight the elections. In mid-April 1997, two days after the fall of the Deve Gowda government, Atal Bihari Vajpayee announced that the BJP would put aside its contentious parochial issues and initiate alliances with various regional parties to work for the establishment of a national democratic front government. Vajpayee's move was more than a strategy to win the elections; it revealed his visionary approach to the distressing and knotty political situation that India was facing. To get rid of the impression that the BJP was a sectarian Hindu party, Vajpayee distanced himself from the hard core of the extremist Hindu organizations and commenced to openly court the minorities and lower castes. Asked by an interviewer whether there wasn't a danger that the BJP was coming to resemble the Congress, Vajpayee replied: "We are a middle-of-the-road party. Occupying the ground being vacated by the Congress doesn't mean embracing Congressism."[6] With Vajpayee's new approach and his language of conciliation and compromise, the BJP did manage to establish alliances with several important regional parties, such as the "socialist" George Fernandes's Samata Party in Bihar, the Akali Dal party in Punjab, the Haryana Vikas party, Biju Janata Dal in Orissa, Lok Shakti in Karnataka, Trinamool Congress in West Bengal, and the All-India Anna Dravida Munnetra Kazhagam (AIADMK) party in Tamil Nadu.

The canvassing for the 1998 general elections was vigorous. Sonia Gandhi, who had entered the fray only a month and a half before the elections, carried out a blitzkrieg campaign, traveling over 37,000 miles in thirty-four days and addressing over 130 rallies. Sonia may not have wholly succeeded in reviving the mystique of the Nehru dynasty (though she never lost an opportunity to mention the dynasty's great sacrifices and contribution to India or her own place in the family and identification with the nation), but she certainly brought a touch of charisma to the party and did manage to raise the morale of the party members. Even before the elections were over, it had become evident that Sonia Gandhi had emerged as the supreme leader of the Congress, and the party officially confirmed her new position by unanimously electing her party president. She also assumed the office of chairperson of the Congress parliamentary committee. This gave her the authority to centralize power in her person and establish an Indira Gandhi-style of leadership.

The twelfth general elections, like the previous three, resulted in a hung parliament, but with two noteworthy differences.

First, while the Congress did no better than in 1996 (140 seats in both elections), the BJP emerged as the single largest party with 177 seats, 16 more than in 1996 (delayed results later increased the figure to 178 and the gains to 17). The BJP's new alliance partners also did much better than the old ones had: they won 73 seats, 47 more seats than in 1996. The BJP could now be considered much more of a "national" party than it had been earlier: it had become a prominent player in south and east India, where it hardly had any presence earlier; and it had done significantly better than the Congress in both the rural and urban constituencies and among the

---

Results of the 1998 General Elections*

Party

BJP   177   (BJP + allies: **250**)

Congress   140   (Congress + allies: **166**)

United Front   **98**   (Janata Dal: 6)

*For details of the 534 seats declared, see *India Today,* March 16, 1998.

---

upper and Other Backward castes (the Congress did garner more Scheduled Tribes and Muslim votes than the BJP). Unfortunately, despite its broader base and the fact that the BJP-led alliance included several so-called secular parties, erstwhile allies of the Congress, and, indeed, parties that had been established by dissident Congress leaders, the BJP continued to be attacked as a communal party.

Second, though the United Front had been shattered, it in no way meant that the role of the regional parties in national politics had been lessened.

The BJP Government: March 1998–April 1999

As could be expected, the BJP ranks were euphoric when Vajpayee was called upon to form a government. In fact, Vajpayee faced a practically impossible task: the alliance fell short of a majority in the Lok Sabha by a slight margin and in the Rajya Sabha by a significant one; the 1998 BJP alliance strategy had moved the coalition party syndrome a step further but the new BJP coalition government was not unified by a common ideology; and, lastly, the opposition parties, headed by the Congress, were clamoring to keep the BJP out at all costs.

As a consequence, the BJP's success was grievously marred: not only did the party have insufficient latitude to push its own agenda, it could not even fashion a common program that had the unquestioning support of all the parties in the coalition. The most troublesome of the alliance partners was, no doubt, the mercurial J. Jayalalitha, the head of AIADMK, who had half a dozen corruption cases pending against her in Chennai courts. From day one she used the leverage provided by her eighteen MPs to repeatedly hold the government to ransom. To add to Vajpayee's woes, the Congress, not for any ideological reason but just to prove that the BJP was incompetent and ineffective, exhibited a penchant for blocking legislative bills. For example, the Congress contributed in the stalling of the Insurance Regulatory Authority (IRA) Bill, a much-needed reform measure which had earlier been moved in parliament by the Congress itself, when it was in power.

Opposition, merely for the sake of creating hindrances, made the Congress appear more interested in political gain than in upholding its ideological commitments. The high point of this cynical approach was reached when Sonia Gandhi, taking advantage of the predicament created by Jayalalitha's withdrawal from the BJP coalition, brought down the fourteen-month-old Vajpayee government in April

1999. There appears to be little doubt that Sonia believed that this move would bring her to power. We shall discuss this development a little later.

Although the aggravations created by Jayalalitha and the Congress were significant, it was factionalism within the BJP, infighting among the parties in the BJP alliance, and BJP's poor floor-management of parliamentary proceedings that appeared to justify the opposition's criticism that the BJP was inept and unfit to govern. Within weeks of the BJP government's coming to power, the view began to surface that Vajpayee was a weak leader incapable of taking decisive action to control the fractious coalition.

Whether to consolidate its position to counter the United States' pro-China tilt (U.S. President Bill Clinton was scheduled to visit China in June), or fulfill the BJP's election agenda, Vajpayee's government took a major decision, indeed a historic decision, to conduct five nuclear tests in May 1998; the first three were simultaneously carried out on May 11, the remaining two on the 13th. India's strategic position in the world had been changed irrevocably.

The detonations brought a sense of great pride to the nation as a whole and temporarily silenced the leaders of the Congress and other Opposition parties who, too, had all along kept open India's nuclear option and who were all committed to not signing the Nuclear Nonproliferation Treaty. The tests consummated the long-standing desire of all those who had wanted India to possess the means to exercise an autonomous foreign policy befitting a nation that formed one-sixth of humanity. Even the repercussions of these tests—Pakistan's six nuclear tests (May 28 and 30); the massive condemnation by Western nations; the chilling of relations with China (that had a nuclear arsenal and had helped to convert Pakistan into a nuclear state); and the imposition of sanctions by the United States and other powers—were taken in its stride by the country.

Unfortunately, the nuclear tests did not long help the BJP to improve its image of a bumbling government, and, even though the 5 percent economic growth rate in 1998 was not unimpressive, the year-end state elections in Delhi, Rajasthan, Madhya Pradesh, and Mizoram reflected the widespread disillusionment with the party. In Delhi, Rajasthan, and Madhya Pradesh the main contest was between the BJP and the Congress; the former two states had BJP governments while the Congress was the ruling party in Madhya Pradesh. The BJP was totally routed in its home states and could not exploit the anti-incumbency factor to oust the Congress government in Madhya Pradesh. These victories, naturally, raised the spirits of the Congress party members, further boosted Sonia Gandhi's prestige, and consolidated her dominant leadership position.

1999: Atal Bihari Vajpayee Emerges as a National Leader

The reverses in the state elections brought home a much-needed awareness to the BJP that it could not continue to live off its parliamentary election success and that it needed to make a far greater effort at internal cohesiveness and unity to retain popular endorsement. One healthy consequence of this setback was that the party factions, realizing the importance of Vajpayee's role as the final arbitrator, strengthened his authority. Vajpayee used his new status to nudge the party to accept his more moderate, centrist policies, to project with greater effect his governance plank into the national agenda, and to fulfill more of his economic liberalization programs. Vajpayee showed skill in outmaneuvering the extremist Hindu organization such as the Shiv Sena and the RSS (witness the appointment of Jaswant Singh, who was opposed by RSS, as foreign minister in December 1998) and in demonstrating that non-BJP parties in the alliance could be depended on to help in the realization of the national agenda (e.g., the importance given to George Fernandes of the Samata Party).

The most important factor that affects any government in power is the economic health of the nation, and there is no denying that in this arena Vajpayee's government confounded the skeptics. Vajpayee was late in getting directly involved with the issues of economic development but, once he did, he and his team, headed by Union Finance Minister Yashwant Sinha, displayed commendable resolve. By mid-1999, there were some convincing signs that the BJP government's reform policies had led to the resurgence of a long-depressed economy: the inflation rate had hit a twenty-year low of 1.83 percent; fiscal revenues and exports were rising; in the April–June quarter 1999, the profits of 105 companies increased by 27 percent and the Bombay Stock Exchange Sensitivity Index (Sensex) had touched an all-time high of 4810; and there were projections that the country was set to achieve a 6.8 percent growth in 1999–2000—well above that projected for China and Southeast Asia.[7] The BJP government was voted out of office on April 17, 1999, but, to the joy of the commercial world, its 1999–2000 union budget was passed, without a change, on April 19.

Even the manner in which the BJP-led government was ousted from power brought greater respect for Vajpayee than for Sonia Gandhi because of the dignified fashion in which the former handled the nefarious affair. From mid-March 1999, on completing her first year in office as president of the Congress, Sonia Gandhi surprised the country by adopting an explicitly forward policy and making it known that the Congress was ready to replace the BJP government. She even went so far as to predict that this switch would take place "in a month's time" (that is, some time in April). It seemed that Sonia Gandhi could not afford to let the BJP, which had, at last, got into the governance mode, strike roots and gain popularity.

Ironically, events did take a turn that appeared to favor the fulfillment of Sonia Gandhi's prediction. In mid-April 1999, the capricious Jayalalitha caused a "political earthquake" by withdrawing support from the government on the grounds that Vajpayee had refused to accede to her unacceptable demand that George Fernandes be removed from the defence portfolio for his role in dismissing the chief of naval staff, Admiral Vishnu Bhagwat, a matter which Bhagwat had taken up in court. Having weakened the shaky BJP alliance, Jayalalitha then brazenly shifted her allegiance to Sonia Gandhi. This was a godsent opportunity and opposition politicians of every hue, encouraged by the Congress, began to scurry around to unite the non-BJP-alliance parties and bring down the government. Whether or not the Congress had actually taken the first step in this conspiracy was irrelevant because the popular impression was that it had indeed been the prime mover.

To cut the sordid story short, Vajpayee, forced by the president to prove that he still had a working majority, asked for a vote of confidence in the Lok Sabha on April 17. He lost by one vote when Mayawati, the leader of the Bahujan Samaj Party (BSP), after having publicly declared that her party's five MPs would abstain from voting, stunned parliament by voting against the Vajpayee government (so much for political ethics). The BJP government resigned on the following day.

A few days later, a jubilant, arrogantly self-confident Sonia Gandhi met the president and announced that a minority Congress government would be in place within forty-eight hours with the backing of 272 MPs (the Congress MPs included), one more than the simple required majority of 271. Two days later, despite all the horse trading and unethical commitments, a very different, crest-fallen, and humiliated Sonia Gandhi had to inform the president and the nation that the support for the Congress was limited to 233 MPs. Sonia Gandhi's first major, desperate gamble for power had failed and as a consequence the president had to order fresh elections to the Lok Sabha in September 1999. Meanwhile, he requested Vajpayee to continue as caretaker prime minister.

Whether Gandhi had been misguided by her loyal advisers or driven by her personal yearning for power or her immature understanding of politics to take the action she took, it was the country that suffered—for the third time in a little over three years, the nation had to bear the enormous burden of another round of general elections.

This was the first time that Sonia Gandhi, in her role as the Congress head, had participated in the game of high politics and, because she failed, this was also the first time that her Italian origin became an issue within the Congress party and questions were raised about the feasibility of having a "foreign" prime minister. A month or so later, this issue split the Congress party, and Sharad Pawar (a very senior Congress member), leading the group of Sonia Gandhi's critics, broke away to form the Nationalist Congress Party.

The malicious anti-BJP propaganda that had preceded the fall of the Vajpayee government, coupled with the public display of unprincipled political tactics by the opposition parties, brought a wave of sympathy for Vajpayee, who, by contrast to Sonia Gandhi and her allies, emerged as a leader of integrity. What was *secular* about the Congress and the parties it was wooing? And what was *democratic* about their stratagems? These two words, that had been tossed around with abandon by the opposition, lost whatever little meaning they may have had.

The sympathy that Vajpayee won from the common man for the appalling treatment he had been subjected to might not have lasted long had it not been for the developments in external affairs that got blended with internal politics.

The 1998 nuclear tests had provoked harsh international criticism and isolated

India, but Vajpayee had handled foreign affairs with such tact and diplomacy that, by 1999, relations with China (Beijing had been angered by India's position that the tests had been undertaken partly to counter potential threat from China) were, more or less, back to normal; and those with the major Western powers, particularly with the United States, vastly improved. By employing the strategy of sending both government and nongovernment envoys to foreign capitals and establishing two-way dialogues at high diplomatic levels, New Delhi had managed to promote a better international understanding of India's strategic interests. By the time the government fell, Jaswant Singh, Vajpayee's special envoy, had held eight meetings with U.S. Secretary of State Strobe Talbott; the talks were confidential but it was widely known that Singh had established a good rapport with Talbott and that the talks had brought the two countries closer on a number of strategic and economic issues. Some sanctions were eased and foreign investors began to return to India with a greater confidence in the country's future growth.

Pakistan: Friend or Foe?

Bus Diplomacy. Vajpayee succeeded in stilling Pakistan's fears to such an extent that Nawaz Sharif invited him to take the inaugural Delhi-Lahore bus (introduced in February 1999 to ease travel between the two countries) and pay a state visit to Pakistan. The trip, another historic first, was undertaken by Vajpayee to confirm, once and for all, that India had accepted the two-nation theory that gave birth to Pakistan and to lay to rest apprehensions that India was obsessed with a desire to reestablish *akhand Bharat* (a reunified India). Foreign Minister Jaswant Singh was quoted as saying that "like Richard Nixon's visit to China it was a kind of gesture only a leader with strong conservative credentials could get away with at home." The meetings between the two leaders were suffused with goodwill and the summit concluded with the Lahore Declaration, which held promise that the deadlock of fifty years was going to be replaced with a new era of peace and harmony, drawing together the two peoples in the cultural and commercial fields.

Kargil Crisis. But all hopes of a genuine reconciliation evaporated within three months of the Lahore accord. In May 1999, India discovered to its shock and dismay that Pakistani troops and Pakistani-armed Islamic militants had surreptitiously crossed into the India side of the Line-of-Control (LoC) in Kashmir and occupied some of the commanding heights in Drass and Kargil, from which they began to rain down heavy artillery fire on the strategic Srinagar-Leh highway. India was, indeed, caught by surprise, but what did Pakistan hope to gain from this dangerous venture? Sharif, like every Pakistani prime minister before him, could not be seen to be sacrificing the "Kashmir cause" for peace with India. It appears that according to the calculation of his top generals, Indian politics was in such disarray (Vajpayee's government had fallen a few weeks earlier and was now administering the country in a caretaker mode) and Indian troops in Kargil were so unprepared that, by the time the armed forces could be mobilized, the Pakistanis would have severed Leh and Ladakh from the rest of the state of Jammu and Kashmir. This would be a great victory for Pakistan, which had never won a war with India so far. Besides, by maintaining the myth that the successful operation was carried out by Kashmiri mujahideen,* Pakistan would breathe new life into the Kashmir secessionist movement. Finally, the resulting Kashmir crisis would, willy-nilly, attract foreign involvement and internationalize the Kashmir case, which India had, so far, refused to allow.

India's immediate response was limited and tardy, resulting in heavy losses of men and materials. In the early weeks of the war, and war it surely was, Pakistanis even had the temerity to use hand-held surface-to-air missiles to bring down two Indian air force planes. However, the government of India quickly realized the full gravity of the situation and, supported by an angered nation, mobilized its awesome military power to evict the enemy. And even though the Indian army was not prepared for a high-altitude war, which the enemy was, the courage and resolve shown by its officers and men soon demoralized the enemy.

Once the Indian armed forces began operations in earnest, Sharif realized that all his calculations had proven wrong. Instead of the local success that he had hoped for, Sharif was faced with the possibility of a full-fledged war. Pleading that India had sinister intentions, Sharif scurried to Beijing, Washington, and London, among other foreign capitals, to internationalize the Kashmir issue and gain the backing of Pakistan's erstwhile "friends." Sharif, in a manner of speaking, did internationalize the issue but not to Pakistan's advantage. China, which shares borders with Kashmir and Pakistan and had reasons to believe that Muslim fundamentalists (trained in Pakistan) were also targeting its own Muslim-majority province of Xinjiang, offered no support. U.S. President Bill Clinton was far more forthright in demanding that Pakistan withdraw its forces from the India side of the LoC and then restart the Lahore dialogue. Prime Minister Nawaz Sharif, who had sought the short-notice meeting with Clinton, was constrained to agree to Clinton's demand, which was repeated by some of the other Western powers. And though Sharif insisted that no Pakistani troops were involved and that, therefore, he could only "request" the mujahideen militants to withdraw, his "request" produced surprisingly quick results. Sharif met Clinton on July 4, and the withdrawal was more or less completed by July 18. The swift denouement of the conflict was only possible because, as pointed out by the *Washington Post*, "This time around in often-contested Kashmir, the Pakistanis are plainly to blame for having started the fighting,"[8] and Sharif could order home the intruders because most of them were Pakistani soldiers in disguise. Of course, India's nonstop bombardment of the Pakistani posts and the hand-to-hand fighting that resulted in the high casualties of the Pakistani forces, many more than on the Indian side, had also been a major factor in Sharif's decision.

---

*Mujahideen are Muslim fundamentalists who dedicate themselves to fighting a holy war against infidels.

Why did the United States, and the Western bloc it leads, come out in support of India, a country that had not received very high respect from them earlier? Among the reasons put forth by analysts were the following: first, with the end of the Cold War, the United States no longer needed Pakistan to fight its proxy war in Afghanistan; second, the United States was getting wary of the growth of international terrorism fostered by the Taliban—Islamic fundamentalists who govern Afghanistan—and the Taliban-style religious fanatics trained in seminaries in Pakistan* and supported by the Pakistan government (Sharif had nearly succeeded in amending the country's constitution and introducing the Islamic-Shariat-law; third, the Islamization of the Pakistani army and its close links with Islamic fundamentalist groups raised grave fears that nuclear weapons could fall into the hands of extremists/terrorists; fourth, the United States noted, in the Kargil context, the contrast between the irresponsible Pakistani statements regarding the first.use of nuclear weapons and the restraint shown by Vajpayee, who announced that the Indian army would not cross the LoC, even in hot pursuit; and fifth, the United States, apprehensive that China (then under a cloud for having stolen nuclear and missile technology from the United States and for its saber-rattling in the Taiwan Straits) might fill the vacuum created in central and south Asia by the collapse of the Soviet Union, perhaps also felt the need to reappraise India's strategic position in the region.

The Kargil conflict had hardly quieted down when militant groups began to infiltrate the Kashmir valley and massacre innocent men, women, and children. Vajpayee announced that India would not restart any talks with Pakistan till Islamabad put a halt to the infiltration of terrorists.

During the two months of conflict, which officially ended in late July, a wave of nationalism swept through the country: for the first time since independence, the peoples of India felt like a nation. Television and the print media brought Kargil into the homes of all the communities across India. Images of exhausted but determined Indian soldiers and officers, fighting in an inhospitable region, often wounded but always cheerfully confident; images of dead heroes, wrapped in the national flag, being returned to their grieving families by military honour guards; the pride and tears of the bereaved; and the stirring details of the valiant last moments of the fallen warriors touched the hearts of millions of viewers.

The point was not lost on the audience that those who had made the highest sacrifice hailed from every state—from Kashmir to Tamil Nadu and from Nagaland to Gujarat—and from every religion and community. And the people of the country too disregarded their religion and caste distinctions to donate their blood and make cash contributions, often from their very meager salaries (nearly two billion rupees were collected by the end of July 1999), in the great Kargil cause. Most

---

*In 1997, Washington had branded the Pakistan-based Harkat-ul-Ansar—the group responsible for abducting and killing five Western tourists in Kashmir—as a terrorist organization.

importantly, the Kargil crisis revealed not only that Muslim young men were fighting and dying for their motherland but that the Muslim community, as a whole, had not been found wanting in patriotism: it had severely condemned Pakistan for dishonoring Islam by exporting religious fanaticism and using it to destabilize India. The war was costly and debates rage as to who was responsible for it, but the legacy of a heightened sense of nationalism was worth the price. When India achieved independence, even educated Indians had only limited understanding of the peoples and territories that constituted the country. In 1947, to most northerners all those residing in the south were "Madrasis," and few even knew the distinction between the south Indian languages, Tamil, Telugu, Kannada, and Malayalam. In 1962, most southerners were hardly moved by the Indo-China war. Kargil has done more for nation building than many of the political strategies employed by nationalist politicians in the last fifty years. Many hoped that self-centered and cynical political parties, out to denounce each other, would not destroy the spark of idealism that had quickened the pulse of India.

However, as India turned its attention to the ensuing Lok Sabha elections, it became apparent that this hope was misplaced. The Congress leaders and other opponents of Vajpayee, fearing that the prestige he had gained by his handling of the Kashmir crisis would influence the voters, launched an undignified vilification campaign. The Congress praised the armed forces for their triumphant operation (in the face of the national mood it could hardly have done otherwise) but asserted that the costly war could have been avoided if Vajpayee's government had been more alert and had given timely consideration to military intelligence (a post-Kargil commission of enquiry found that military intelligence had failed); the Congress even hinted that the Kargil blowup was artificially created to give the BJP an advantage in the elections! The Congress's bid to separate government action from military accomplishment may have cheapened the Kargil victory, but it did not help the Congress in its electoral campaign.

The Thirteenth General Elections

As the months of mutual, highly acrimonious attacks rolled by, it became abundantly clear that the September 1999 general elections would be won or lost not on the basis of the Congress's or the BJP's ideologies but on the ability these two most important political parties to win allies from among the scores of smaller parties regardless of whether these parties were secular or sectarian (communal). In any case, ideologies had come to mean very little to a harried electorate whose five decades of experience had taught it to dismiss the promises in party manifestos as empty gestures. The overwhelming demand of the common citizenry was good governance and an incorrupt political system that would provide all inhabitants (most of whom lived in the countryside) with basic amenities, such as safe drinking water, electricity, medical clinics, schools, decent road connections, and employment. The urban commercial interests were looking forward to an era of political stability and economic reforms, and it augured well for these interests that both the Congress and the BJP-centered National Democratic Alliance (NDA) had about the same positive approach to issues of economic policy.

The Congress, however, differed from the BJP over the question of coalitions. In September 1998, at the Congress session at Pachmarhi, Sonia Gandhi had decided, as a matter of policy, that the Congress would work to return to power on its own (form a single-party government), and, though it might seek outside support of like-minded parties and make electoral adjustments with them, it would not form a coalition government. Sonia had displayed a similarly rigid stand in April 1999 when, at the fall of the BJP government, she spoke of forming an exclusively Congress administration. Though that had not worked out, the Congress went into the September elections with the optimistic view that it would emerge as the single largest party. The Congress, however, did adopt the strategy of seeking allies for electoral seat adjustments to minimize the splitting of votes. In striking contrast to the Congress approach, the BJP, which had already had the experience of running a coalition government, prepared itself for the forthcoming elections by going a step further and hammering out the twenty-four-party National Democratic Alliance (NDA).

The Congress election campaign focused on Sonia Gandhi, identifying her as a worthy scion of the Nehru dynasty and the only national leader who could lead the tried and trusted grand old party, the only party that *knew how to govern*, to victory. This was the positive side of the campaign; on the negative side, the campaign was designed to demolish Vajpayee's image of a successful prime minister by denouncing his bus ride to Lahore as immature diplomacy, attacking him for his "failure" in Kargil, and accusing him of various treacherous actions, including collaboration with the British before independence.

At a more practical level, the Congress's efforts to enter into an electoral understanding with regional and minor parties undermined its moral high ground and its "clean" image because several of these parties held political views that were antithetical to the Congress ideology and some of them were led by politicians whose unprincipled and corrupt behavior was well known. Among the parties Sonia Gandhi teamed up with were the AIADMK, headed by J. Jayalalitha, who, until April, had been a partner in the BJP ruling alliance and was facing several massive corruption cases; the caste-based Rashtriya Janata Dal, whose boss, Laloo Prasad Yadav, had bankrupted Bihar and was currently on bail for his involvement in the infamous fodder scam (see above); the Prakash Ambedkar faction of the caste-based Republican Party of India (it was said that Ambedkar had shifted to the Congress after failing to woo the BJP and Pawar's Nationalist Congress Party); and the Indian Union Muslim League, an obviously sectarian, religion-based Muslim party. These moves of Sonia Gandhi made a mockery of the Congress's high moral stand and its much-touted secular ideology. Incidentally, Laloo Prasad Yadav, a Congress ally, provided an interesting definition of secularism by declaring that "[The BJP] wants to destroy secular forces, but we will invoke Durga's blessing to destroy these demons."[9] The avowedly secular were invoking a Hindu goddess to defeat the "Hindu" BJP at the hustings!

On the other side, the BJP put aside the contentious issues of the Ayodhya temple, the uniform civil code, and Article 370 of the Constitution, and decided that the National Democratic Alliance would fight the elections on the basis of a common National Agenda for Governance. The BJP thus pushed the coalition government syndrome to a new stage because, though the NDA was not a party, for purposes of the elections, it could act as one. And by embracing parties that represented a wide spectrum of regional, ethnic, and backward castes' interests— interests once accommodated under the umbrella of the Congress party—the BJP had, both spatially and socially, taken on the image of the old Congress and acquired a secular look.

In this context it is worth mentioning that the newly created Janata Dal (United) (JD[U])— a breakaway segment of the once-very-"secular"-and-anti-BJP Janata Dal—also joined the NDA. Sharad Yadav, the leader of JD(U), when asked whether, by doing so, his party would forfeit the immense Muslim support it had always enjoyed, said: "I am confident that we will be able to convince [the Muslims] that we have chosen the best path in the circumstances."[10] The BJP's new image and appeal were also helped by Arun Nehru, once a close associate of Rajiv Gandhi, who chose to join the BJP.

Having discarded its identifying ideology, the BJP mobilized its entire energy to the task of winning the elections. Like the Congress's stress on Sonia Gandhi, the BJP focused its election campaign on Vajpayee. Atal Bihari Vajpayee was portrayed as a wise, experienced national leader who embodied the spirit of the National Democratic Alliance; a nationalist, patriotic leader who, though just thrown out of office, had risen above petty politics to bring victory at Kargil; and an international figure who had managed to win the goodwill of the world through his sophisticated diplomacy—in short, a leader who knew how to *govern* and could be trusted to lead the country successfully into the twenty-first century. Not surprisingly, the NDA manifesto devoted several pages to photographs of Vajpayee (no other leader was portrayed); the rest of the document provided a centrist agenda for tackling the economic and social problems of the country. The one significantly new element was a promise to change the Constitution to ensure a fixed five-year term for the Lok Sabha and the state assemblies; this debatable measure was, ostensibly, meant to guarantee future political stability.

All parties vigorously carried out the election campaigns, though the media, as was to be expected, centered much of their attention on Vajpayee and Sonia. The picture that emerged, of mutual mudslinging and low-level attacks, was reprehensible: the Congress outdid the NDA in this odious competition. Some of Sonia's speeches made her appear to be a mean-spirited person who did not hesitate to make base, unfounded allegations against Vajpayee and his government. Although some people in the NDA, too, stooped so low as to malign Sonia for her foreign birth and

Results of the 1999 General Elections		
Party	1999 (total Lok Sabha seats: 545)	1996 (543)
BJP	182 (NDA: **304**)	177 (+ allies: **253**)
Congress	112 (+ allies: **134**)	140 (+ allies: **166**)
Others	**107**	

her family background—one remarked that Sonia's only contribution to India was two children in a population of one billion—Vajpayee assiduously kept himself above the shameful fray and his speeches were always highly balanced, dignified and prime-ministerial. He also admonished his colleagues to keep the election clean.

The thirteenth general election was staggered over five phases and lasted the whole month of September 1999. Considering the size of the exercise (620 million voters and 4,648 candidates for 543 seats), the elections went off peacefully though violence did mar polling in Bihar, Kashmir, and the northeast. Also, because of the militants' boycott of elections and their threats, polling at some places in Kashmir was extremely light.

Elections Results

Because it was the third election in three years and because ideologies were no longer a major issue, many urbanites, weary of chaotic politics, voted for the party they thought would bring stability and efficiency to the government. In the rural constituencies, the voters were largely indifferent to national issues and, keeping in mind local problems such as the shortage of potable water, electricity, schools, and good roads, voted for candidates and parties who were most likely to focus their attention on these issues.

When the results of the elections were declared, the nation heaved a sigh of relief because the National Democratic Alliance had won a majority of the seats, which meant that the new BJP-led government would no longer be an unstable minority government. The National Democratic Alliance's impressive victory—it had gained 304 of the 545 parliamentary seats—spelled the end of four years of political instability and the promise of a full five-year term for the new government. Although the BJP's tally had improved only by 3 seats, from 179 to 182, there was no doubt that it was the BJP chief, Vajpayee, who had carried the NDA allies to victory. After an unbroken parliamentary career of more than four decades, Atal Bihari Vajpayee had, at last, earned his rightful place in post-independence India as a distinguished national leader.

The biggest shock of the elections was the debacle suffered by the Congress: it won only 112 seats, 28 less than its 1998 strength. In the soul-searching that followed the election, Congress leaders, privately or publicly, expressed a variety of opinions: that the "dynasty factor" had been overplayed and proven counterproductive; that Sonia's meeting with Jayalalitha in April had created a widespread impression that she had plotted the downfall of the Vajpayee government (to paraphrase one Congress leader: "Vajpayee went into the election with the halo of a statesman who had been gratuitously humiliated by a power-hungry party"); that Sonia did not have the political experience and the statesman-like qualities to win the respect of the populace; that the Congress decision not to form a coalition government had been unwise; and that the Congress's undemocratic feudal style had corroded the party's internal democracy and dynamism.

As for the Third Front, the elections reduced its size from 143 to 107 seats. The Third Front lost its erstwhile leverage at the center, although the Samajwadi Party and the Bahujan Samaj Party had done surprisingly well.

The 1999 elections had, once again, confirmed the political sagacity of the so-called common voter. Despite all their populist policies, parties ruling states such as Bihar, Punjab, and Orissa were punished by the electorate for bad governance. By the same token, N. C. Naidu (leader of the Telugu Desam Party), chief minister of the state of Andhra Pradesh, who had taken several unpopular measures, such as stopping the sale of highly subsidized cheap rice, gained an overwhelming vote of confidence for his good governance and farsighted economic reforms. In Tamil Nadu, an anticorruption sentiment saw Jayalalitha's Lok Sabha seats drop from 18 to 10.

The BJP Government: A New Beginning

Internal Affairs. The Vajpayee government was sworn in on October 13, 1999. At this writing (January 2000), the transition from caretaker government to legitimate government has been smooth. There was some tussle over cabinet berths but, between the declaration of the election results on October 8 and the swearing-in on the 13th, the entire sixty-nine–member Council of Ministers was in place. Immediately after taking over, a very self-confident Prime Minister Vajpayee, who had retained all his key ministers in their earlier posts, hastened to put his stamp on the country's future development. In the larger, long-term context, the government's reform programs were outlined in the President's Address to the opening session of the thirteenth Lok Sabha (October 25, 1999). The government promised to make a bold departure from past policies and practices in order to tackle the endemic issues of poverty, health, education, unemployment, and gender/caste discrimination. It would do so by providing a strong regulatory leadership, strengthening local democratic institutions, and enlivening the private sector. More specifically, the reforms would curtail public expenditures, lower government stakes in public sector undertakings, upgrade the country's economic infrastructure, and eliminate corruption. The government also declared its intention to introduce an electoral reform bill and amend the Constitution to provide fixed terms to Parliament and state assemblies.

Whether the government would be able to fulfill all these promises only time will tell, but that it was serious about resuming stalled economic reforms became amply evident from the record of the NDA government's first hundred days in office. Within days of coming to power, it moved the Parliament to clear a host of long-pending measures of far-reaching importance. These measures, such as the Insurance Regulatory Bill, the Foreign Exchange Management Act, the Securities Contract Regulation Bill, and the institution of the Foreign Investment Implementation Authority, were intended to speed up India's economic development and facilitate foreign direct investment and joint enterprises.

These bold moves were welcomed by the Indian and foreign business communities. Industrial growth showed immediate signs of an upswing, the rupee stayed stable, inflation hovered around 3 percent, prices of most consumer goods remained steady, and stock indices rose significantly. The country will get a better picture of future reforms when the 2000–2001 budget is presented in March 2000; the budget will indicate how the government intends to rein in the ever-mounting fiscal deficit, reduce subsidies, privatize the loss-producing public sector units, and find moneys to improve the infrastructure and upgrade education and health care, particularly in village India.

In the political sphere, the government's success, so far, has been qualified. It has yet to work out an integrated plan to contain Pakistan-inspired terrorism in Kashmir and other parts of India that is undermining the internal security of the country. And it has yet to confirm that the BJP leaders have, indeed, distanced themselves from the extremist Hindu movements represented by organizations such as the Rashtriy Swayamsevak Sangh and discarded the narrowly Hindu-based ideology of *Hindutva* for the secular pluralism rooted in the Hindu ethos. If it is unsuccessful in the latter endeavor, the NDA will not only fail to carry the country with it, but also lose the support of its coalition partners; India will then face another period of political instability. If it succeeds, it may initiate an era of stable coalition governments that, through their "unity in diversity," will bring unity to the multifaceted pluralism that characterizes the country.

Foreign Relations. India's foreign image got an unexpected boost from developments in Pakistan. The day before Vajpayee's cabinet was sworn in, Pakistan's army chief, General Pervez Musharraf (who had directed the Kargil operation), ousted Prime Minister Nawaz Sharif and imposed a military government in Pakistan. This, in itself, was a disturbing development, but while the Musharraf coup was internationally condemned, India received high praise for its commitment to democracy.

However, India-Pakistan relations, already strained since the Kargil crisis, now deteriorated further and touched their lowest point since the Bangladesh war. The back-channel (Track Two) diplomacy that kept the two sides talking was scuttled by Musharraf, who not only redefined terrorism to exclude *jehad* in Kashmir but asserted that Pakistan, indeed all Muslims, had a moral obligation to come to the aid of the so-called "freedom fighters" in Kashmir. After Musharraf's coup, there was an upsurge of terrorist violence in Kashmir, and the 2,000 foreign mercenaries in Kashmir armed by Pakistan's Inter-Services Intelligence (ISI) with high-caliber rocket launchers, mortars, and antitank missiles amended their tactics to include direct attacks on Indian military and police headquarters. The ISI also infiltrated Northeast India and other parts of the subcontinent to abet insurgency movements and destabilize the Indian economy by smuggling huge amounts of counterfeit currency bills.

In late December 1999, five armed Islamic terrorists, later found to have Pakistani connections, hijacked an Indian Airlines plane soon after its departure from Kathmandu and, after touching down in Amritsar, Lahore, and Dubai, forced it to land in Kandahar. At the end of six terrifying days, during which the hijackers killed one of the 178 passengers and injured several others, the ordeal for the passengers and crew ended when New Delhi agreed to release three Islamic militants jailed in India who were associated with Pakistan-backed Islamic fundamentalist terrorist organizations, such as the Harkat-ul-Ansar.

This book has placed a special emphasis on the role of Kashmir in India-Pakistan relations because the Kashmir issue has pushed the politics of India and Pakistan into a cul-de-sac and made their positions intractable. While Pakistan's declared intention is to "free" Kashmir, even if—in the words of Prime Minister Benazir Bhutto—"it takes a thousand years," Delhi's most recent response was that India would not hold any talks with Pakistan till Pakistan vacates the Kashmir territory it occupies and—in the words of Vajpayee—"gives up [all] its claims on Jammu and Kashmir."[11]

Kashmir represents the continuation of the problems created by partition. Pakistan—the "K" in the name stands for Kashmir—sees Kashmir as integral to its Islamic identity and a part of the Muslim homeland. India, as a secular state in which Muslims constitute nearly 12 percent of the population, cannot allow Kashmir to secede just because it is a Muslim-majority area. All parties, from the Congress to the BJP, have expressed fears that the secession of Kashmiri Muslims would undermine the notion of constitutive secular nationalism and raise the question of loyalty to the union. The transference of the valley to Pakistan not only raises the horrendous specter of another partition; it also prompts several questions that have serious ramifications for the Indian state. If Kashmiri Muslims are allowed to secede because of their religion, then what right has the state to keep any other religious or ethnic community, like the Sikhs in Punjab or the Nagas in Assam, from doing the same? If Kashmiri Muslims, just because they are Muslims, cannot stay within the union, what right have the other Muslims to stay on in the country? Would their loyalty not be suspect? Would not such a secession strengthen the militant right-wing Hindu forces and enkindle anti-Muslim hostility in the hearts of all Hindus?

The tremendous price that India has paid, and is paying, to keep Kashmir within the union is a reflection of the fact that the problems created by partition have not yet been settled, that India and Pakistan have yet to respect each other's territorial integrity, and that neither country has succeeded in creating a national identity that makes local loyalties to religion, caste, language, and culture subservient to the greater loyalty to the state.

The United States, aware of the activities in India of Pakistan-based terrorists, was as helpful as it could possibly be during the hijacking, but it stopped short of declaring Pakistan a state sponsor of terrorism, as India would have liked it to do. Washington's concern was that the isolation of Pakistan could further radicalize the forces of fundamentalism and terrorism in that country. In any case, Washington felt that the issue of Pakistan should not keep India and the United States from improving their relations. Officially, Washington continued to call for an end to India's nuclear weapons and missile programs and to demand that India sign the Comprehensive Test Ban Treaty (CTBT) and take other antiproliferation measures before sanctions could be lifted and relations normalized. But behind the scenes, Foreign Minister Jaswant Singh's confidential talks with Deputy Secretary of State Strobe Talbott provided Washington with a more realistic understanding of India's constraints.* It appeared that India was close to signing the CTBT in return for bilateral economic and technological cooperation. Whether or not the U.S. Senate's rejection of the CTBT in October 1999 weakened Washington's case had yet to be seen, because the two countries had not, at the time of this writing, spelled out the contents of their newly evolving relationship.

As the United States and India entered the twenty-first century, relations between them *had* improved. Washington had started discussions on the need for the United States and India to cooperate on issues ranging from cross-border terrorism, drug trafficking, and regional security to information technology. The softening of Washington's stand was reflected in President Clinton's waiver of some of the sanctions and his decision to visit India for five days in late March 2000. A resolution, passed unanimously by the House of Representatives International Relations Panel, even urged President Clinton to "broaden our special relationship with India into a strategic relationship."

The pressure on Clinton also came from the American corporate world, which perceived India as the new place for foreign investment. For example, Enron, the huge American energy company, which had had a few rough years setting up its $2 billion power plant in India, now declared its readiness to participate in various projects worth $10 billion.[12] Stanley Weiss, chairman of Business Executives for National Security, advised Clinton to "stop thinking of India and Pakistan as Siamese twins," because "Pakistan has become a basket case" while "the World Bank and the International Monetary Fund estimate that India will be the world's fourth largest economy in [the twenty-first] century. It has the second biggest pool of English-speaking scientific manpower after the United States. Its software exports should increase from $4 billion today to $50 billion by 2008, revolutionizing India's balance of payment position and allowing an even more liberal attitude towards trade."[13] India was being made out to be a "natural ally" of America.

---

*The talks began in June 1998, immediately following the nuclear tests, and have continued into 2000.

The warming relationship between Washington and New Delhi is not likely to affect India's quite stable ties with Russia; the ties are primarily economic since the collapse of the USSR. But the evolving U.S.-India links are likely to disturb China, whose relations with India touched a low point after the 1998 nuclear tests (India had asserted that the tests were in response to the threat posed by China). Although many in India believed that China was trying to contain India by taking a hard line on India's tests while openly supporting Pakistan and maintaining very close and friendly relations with Islamabad, Indian Foreign Minister Jaswant Singh did go to Beijing to ease tensions. However, his efforts were undermined when General Musharraf visited China (January 17, 2000) and was welcomed by President Jiang Zemin and Premier Zhu Rongji with unequivocal expressions of friendship, solidarity, and support. At this time the West was worried by developments in Pakistan, and India was pushing for international isolation of Islamabad because ISI had increased its terrorist activities in Kashmir and was believed to have masterminded the hijacking of the Indian Airlines plane. It is possible that Beijing used Musharraf's visit to send a message to the West about China's role in south Asia or to put pressure on India to tread carefully on the issue of the 14-year-old Karmapa Lama; to the embarrassment of China, Karmapa, the second most powerful spiritual leader after the Dalai Lama, had fled Tibet and taken refuge in India on January 5. Beijing did not want India to grant Karmapa political asylum and use him to inflame anti-Chinese sentiment in Tibet.

Analysts in India believe that once China realizes that India has limited nuclear ambition and that economically bankrupt Pakistan has limited utility as a counterweight to India, China will give up its confrontational stance and return to its earlier, more realistic and flexible policy toward India.

During the Cold War, India's relations with Japan were primarily economic in nature; by the 1990s, Japan had emerged as the largest donor of bilateral economic aid. The end of the Cold War opened the way for better political and security cooperation with Japan, but, before India could make much headway in that direction, the 1998 nuclear tests resulted in a strong condemnation by Japan and Tokyo's decision to impose sanctions against New Delhi. Indo-Japan relations entered a short period of deep freeze. It took over a year for relations to improve and, once again, it was Foreign Minister Jaswant Singh who, during his visit to Japan in November 1999, managed to explain to Tokyo's satisfaction India's compulsion for undertaking the tests. In January 2000, Defence Minister George Fernandes visited Japan and, after a series of high-level discussions, announced that "after fifty years of aloofness . . . India and Japan have decided on a security and defence-related dialogue on a regular basis."[14] The Japanese have not yet withdrawn the sanctions, but relations between the two countries have become warmer and smoother.

India's relations with other Asian states and Europe have remained on an even keel.

A Summing-Up

As India celebrates, on the 26th of January 2000, its 50th anniversary as a republic,* it has much to be proud of and much to worry about.

India can rightfully be proud of the fact that, despite being a poor Third World country burdened with enormous problems linked with poverty and the bewildering array of diverse castes, ethnic groups, languages, and religions, it has managed to establish a democratic system ("the world's largest democracy"), which few of its neighbors have been able to achieve.

There have been several occasions during the last fifty-three years when regional linguistic controversies, secessionist movements, and political excesses of the center brought the country to the verge of collapse, but on each occasion the political system displayed a remarkable resilience, and the "self-correcting mechanism of Indian democracy," as Ashutosh Varshney has called it, brought balance back to the structure.[15]

The new activism of the Election Commissioner and the Supreme Court and the emergence of a relatively stable coalition government can be viewed as the latest examples of such corrective mechanisms because these institutional changes have the potential of reversing several destructive trends that emerged in the 1980s and the early 1990s. They hold the promise of reducing the overcentralization and personalization of power at the center, providing a cleaner government, improving center-state relations, strengthening democratic institutions, empowering the socially downtrodden and, most importantly, continuing economic reform programs. Unfortunately, the expectation engendered by the successful reintroduction of electoral politics in Kashmir in 1996, which reflected the people's "desire for peace and rejection of guns,"[16] was thwarted by the Kargil war and the subsequent heightening of ISI activities in that state.

Kashmir, it appears, will remain a troubled region till India and Pakistan accept the LoC as the international border and normalize relations so that they can coexist as good neighbors.

In the larger national framework, despite the fall of three governments in three years, the silent revolution that surfaced with the Gowda government has gathered strength and the National Democratic Alliance can be said to be its current, not necessarily its final, product. The 1996, 1998, and 1999 elections gave abundant proof of the vitality and acumen of an electorate that turned its anger against political corruption and bad governance. It is equally remarkable that all the political parties and the peoples of the country without question accepted the verdict of the electorate and that the transition of power has invariably been smooth and peaceful. The quick changes in government caused no shock or panic and, by and large,

---

*India gained independence on August 15, 1947, but its Constitution came into force only on January 26, 1950.

the business community felt that there was no reason to lose confidence in the center's will to continue on the path of economic reforms. The country has evolved remarkably well since 1947. As *Newsweek* pointed out on the eve of the 1999 elections, "The political parties need to disagree on *something*. . . . But on the fundamental question of how best to win prosperity for India's one billion people, there is wide agreement that the country is finally on the right path."[17]

India is also maturing as a civil society. Innumerable citizens' associations all over the country have initiated movements to fight the state over issues such as civil rights, human rights, pollution, environmental degradation, corruption, and women's rights. The country can also be proud of its impressive advances in the agricultural and industrial fields. Famine has become a thing of the past. The percentage of the poor who live below the poverty line has gone down significantly. And though the liberalization of the economy came late, it has led to an explosion of entrepreneurial endeavors that has changed the face of the nation. India has a vast pool of indigenously trained engineers and scientists, and it can effectively service the growing commercial and defense demands of the nation, from television sets and automobiles to supercomputers, rockets, and satellites. To take just one example from the modern sector: India exported about $1.5 billion worth of electronics and computer software in 1996,[18] $2.6 billion in 1998, and predictions are that software exports will touch $12 billion[19] (and become the country's biggest foreign-exchange earner) by 2003 and $50 billion by 2008.[20] Such developments are very encouraging, but of course much remains to be done. Apart from having to grapple with the problems of economic growth and modernization, any future government of India will have to deal with the endemic problems of poverty, unemployment, disease, and illiteracy with much greater vigor.

While these are long-term problems, the most important immediate concern is the future of the party system. It is obvious that the Congress single party dominance system, which in any case outlasted its original utility, is dead and that for some considerable time to come neither the BJP nor the Congress is likely to emerge with the kind of strength that will make a conventional two-party system feasible. Until that time, the center will be run by coalition governments. It is too early to tell, but all the signs are there that, as the BJP has shown, coalition governments need not be unstable and a host of disparate parties can work effectively toward a common end. If the Congress, too, accepts this thesis, then it is possible that a Congress-led left-of-center coalition and the more centrist BJP-led NDA can alternately share power at the center and establish a novel kind of "two party/alliance" system. The personalized, populist ruling style of the Congress might then be replaced by a system that, perforce, has to stress policy and programs.

However, there is also the possibility that the revitalization of the Congress may take a much longer time than envisaged by its current leaders and that the BJP will come to replace the Congress as the dominant party of the country. This possibility, however remote, raises fears in the minds of many people, especially the Westernized, liberal Indian intellectuals, because the BJP is viewed as a militant communal Hindu party that may lead the country to a civil war. These fears are understandable because the BJP rose to power in the wake of the traumatic Ayodhya incident, and its *Hindutva* vision explicitly appealed to Hindu nationalism. The BJP has also had close relations with extremist Hindu organizations, such as the Rashtriya Swayamsewak Sangh (RSS), the Hindu Mahasabha, and the Bajrang Dal—the so-called Saffron Brotherhood (saffron being the holy color of Hinduism). And, of course, the Saffron Brotherhood's boast that a vertical divide between the Hindus and the minority groups is already in the making is most troubling.

These concerns would be relevant if the BJP truly were capable of creating a monolithic Hindu cultural bloc. But a thoughtful person who has given some consideration to India's tradition and its history would reject the BJP quest as visionary and unachievable. The experience of the last several years has brought home to many in the BJP that if they want to succeed as a political party, the *Hindutva* approach needs to be modified. By generating communal tensions over Ayodhya, the Saffron Brotherhood did manage to excite Hindu passions that conveyed a certain sense of Hindu unity, but that emotional response was temporary. The communal violence that followed the Ayodhya Incident embarrassed and appalled most Hindus.

While the BJP is not incorrect in its view that the Indian ethos is basically a Hindu ethos, it misunderstood the nature of India's traditional socioreligious society, and therefore its early attempt to build a national identity around this ethos was flawed. India's socioreligious tradition, which divides society into so many autonomous parts, is too strong to be reshaped by a top-down approach, a lesson that Nehru and the Congress learned the hard way. In the socioreligious society of traditional India, a multitude of caste groups,* living in autonomous worlds of their own, showed tolerance toward each other by following their own separate caste *dharma*. The relationship between the groups was well defined: all groups were a part of the sacred whole and as long as each part accepted its role in the whole, there was harmony. The self-contained Hindu social units worshipped different deities and followed disparate rituals, but were linked with each other by sociospiritual notions of rebirth, *karma, dharma*, and *moksha*, by cautionary myths, legends, and stories from the *Mahabharata* and the *Ramayana*, by the centers of pilgrimage, and by the universal acceptance of commonly recognized saints and sages. It is this overarching unity that produced the Hindu ethos, transformed the subcontinent into a sacred space, and provided unity in diversity and a unique sense of secularity.

In this Hindu India, the political state played a very small residual role as a supervisory agency. Even an incipient nationalism that is tied to the notion of a territorially defined political state had no place in the scheme of things. States could multiply or decline or disappear, but Hindu India carried on forever. There were no adversarial

---

*According to the Anthropological Survey of India, there are some 4,599 separate communities in India who speak 325 languages and dialects in twelve distinct language families and have some twenty-four separate scripts.

relations between religion and state; the king, too, followed his *dharma* in the framework of the Hindu ethos—one of his functions was to honor all religions and sects (following the practice established by Emperor Ashoka in the third century B.C.E.). This environment gave birth to Indian pluralism.

Within this Hindu ethos all religious groups were treated with tolerance as long as they lived their separate lives in their own communities. The Islamic invasions, followed by the establishment of an Islamic state in India, created problems, but as long as the Muslim rulers left the Hindus to carry on their personal and social lives in the manner to which they were accustomed, even Islam made no dent in the Hindu socioreligious system.

The British brought a radical change to the subcontinent by making the state more important and intrusive than it had ever been, and they created modern communalism by encouraging Muslim separatism. The British also did everything possible to retard the growth of Indian nationalism or an Indian national identity while establishing a communal, constitutional polity. However, nothing that the British did changed the traditional pattern of group life.

The Congress, during the last four decades of its struggle against British domination, rarely used the term *secularism*, emphasizing nationalism instead as an antithesis of the British-promoted communalism. By propagating the view that Indian nationalism was rooted in the tradition of tolerance, pluralism, and syncretism, the Congress hoped to unify the people in their fight against British imperialism. However, the Hindu-Muslim discord of the 1930s and 1940s, and the establishment of Pakistan in 1947, diminished if not destroyed the relevancy of this thesis.

After independence, when communalism continued to grow unhindered, the Congress leaders chose to retain their pre-1947 version of the national cultural identity, and by substituting secularism for nationalism, they made secularism the antithesis of post-1947 communalism. However, the presumption that secularism (based on the old tolerance-pluralism-syncretism *mantra*) would destroy the forces of communalism proved as fruitless as the expectations of nationalism in prepartition India. In the final analysis, the Congress not only failed to create an integral nationalism but actually contributed to the rise of large-scale communalism.

The Congress failure can be partly traced to the contradictions inherent in the Constitution. For instance, the Constitution directs the state to promote the welfare of the Scheduled Castes and Scheduled Tribes (SCs and STs). This Directive Principle, without doubt, was sincerely motivated, but it had one very negative connotation: since these communities belonged to the Hindu caste system and since the Constitution denied similar welfare to the suffering poor of the other religious communities (a destitute Untouchable converted to Christianity was exploited by society in the same way as a Hindu Untouchable but could not seek assistance from the state),* the Constitution displayed a nonsecular, pro-Hindu bias.

---

*The laws were changed in the 1990s to include the depressed sections of Christian, Muslim, and other minority communities.

Nehru's expectations that the basically secular Constitution and the democratic institutions would help to create a secular citizenry were also undermined by another factor. The Congress had inherited a strong state-centered political system, and the Constitution made the state even more fundamental to Indian life. However, the power vested in the state for the purposes of social engineering and the protection of religious minorities was used in strangely undemocratic ways by the post-Nehru Congress, ways that bolstered communalism.

For example, in the Shah Bano case, the Congress passed a bill that for all future time (or until the bill is rescinded) denies a divorced Muslim woman, a free citizen of India, the right to bring an alimony case to the secular courts of the land and forces her to depend wholly on a communal group (the Muslim group to which she belongs) for her support. Thus, it has come about that non-Hindus (the Hindus are governed by the Hindu code bills) "can equally exercise the right to belong to a religious community but not hold equal right, based on the Constitution, to divorce, adopt, or inherit, due to the claims of their separate communities."[21] Similarly, the state's reservation policies by promoting welfare of Scheduled Castes, Scheduled Tribes, and Other Backward Castes by categories has undermined the sanctity of the legal status of the individual in the democratic republican system: instead of applying affirmative action to individuals, the state turned the notion of democratic egalitarianism on its head by emphasizing caste and community groups at the expense of the individual, thereby advancing group, not individual, rights. The reservations were supposed to end within ten years of the promulgation of the Constitution. Instead, they have grown in numbers, cover many more castes and groups than they did in 1950, and are likely to be in use for decades to come.

The weak secular consensus molded by Nehru was demolished further by his daughter and grandson, who shifted to communal themes in order to woo Hindu and Muslim vote banks. As critical observers have pointed out, in the 1980s "themes of Hindu hegemony that would appeal to India's Hindi heartland, gained currency in Indira's political speeches."[22] And it was, after all, Rajiv who used his parliamentary majority to overrule the Supreme Court's decision on the Shah Bano case and pass a bill that made Muslim personal law a part of the secular legal structure of the nation, thereby undermining secularism and impeding the possibility of a uniform civil code. It was also Rajiv who opened the locked doors of the Ram Temple in Ayodhya to the Hindu public, an action that ultimately led to the Ayodhya incident. Actions such as these destroyed the credibility of Congress as a secular organization.

Apart from all this, Nehru, who never fully appreciated the role that Hinduism played in Indian life, or that "the secular" in India "is encompassed by the sacred,"[23] gained few true adherents. In contrast, most Indians were readily drawn to Mahatma Gandhi's religion-tinctured political ethos; Gandhi had no faith "in the ultimate worth of any purely secular end."[24] As Norman Brown puts it, Gandhi could not fortify "mass support without being religious, [and] he could not be religious without being Hindu."[25]

Post-Nehru Congress leaders, without discussing the matter publicly, allowed the all-pervading Hindu ethos to quietly infiltrate the secular domain (today the BJP merely does the same a little more openly). After the 1979 elections, Indira Gandhi, for example, postponed the forming of her government by eight days:

> She refused to be sworn in until January 14th, a very auspicious day according to the Hindu calendar, and therefore much recommended by her astrologers. This curious behavior was entirely characteristic of Indira . . . her reliance on astrologers, soothsayers and holy men was well known. . . . So superstitious had she become that "priests specially invited from the holy city of Varanasi conducted purifying rituals for eight days" before she moved house again to 1, Safdarjung Lane [the prime minister's residence], which had been her home from the time of her father's death in 1964 until her defeat in the General Election in 1977.[26]

As Malhotra, author of the above quote, points out, "With the passage of time, the view that Indira was acquiring . . . more of a 'Hindu' role was steadily to gain ground."[27] Similarly, in his 1985 election campaign, Rajiv Gandhi "highlighted Indian unity with implicit, but discernible, reference to Hinduism."[28] The last Congress prime minister, Narasimha Rao, with his Hindu godman adviser and visits to Tirupati Temple, quite overtly followed the path of his predecessors. By 1996, the Hindu cultural (religious?) idiom had come to mark the political life of India.

As a consequence, under the Congress, equality before the law and casteless citizenship became meaningless terms, and secularism was an ideal that had little to do with reality. Ironically, the Congress policies managed to alienate both Hindus and Muslims.

The humiliating failure of the Congress in the 1999 elections provoked several Muslim intellectuals to probe the nature of Congress "secularism." One telling comment was the following:

> The danger [to secularism] arose when the dominant political party, the Congress, fell back on an incantation of "secularism" as a means of keeping in its fold the substantial [Muslim] minority vote bank, raising images of a pampered minority and thereby inviting a Hindu backlash. The consequence of these convulsions was that the Congress *kept the communal agenda centrestage*, even while *screaming "secularism."* The BJP, in other words, was to a large extent a *beneficiary of communalized politics sustained by the Congress over a long period of time* (emphasis added).[29]

As another columnist pointed out,

> The Congress pretence to secularism has been exposed as never before. Muslims have now realized the significance of the fact that communal violence took place only in Congress-ruled states. . . . Muslims now know how to remain secure. If we just keep the Congress out of power security is guaranteed.[30]

In a much briefer time frame than the Congress faced, the BJP too has had to confront the social and political realities that confounded the Congress. Although, unlike the Congress, the BJP started off with the stigma that it was a *Hindu party* (implying that it did not represent the multiple interests that constituted the nation), it, so far, has shown a far more flexible and creative approach to the business of governance than the Congress. The BJP learned one very important lesson quite early: that, unlike the other nonpolitical Hindu organizations in the Saffron Brotherhood, the BJP was a *political party* and, as such, could not afford to indulge in irresponsible extremism. The first signs of change in the BJP outlook became visible in 1995 when the BJP formed state governments in Gujarat, Maharashtra, Bihar, and Karnataka and softened its *Hindutva* plank. The BJP's performance in these states, as compared to the previous Congress governments, was spectacular. The BJP leadership was obviously talented and able and not yet tainted with corruption scandals. In 1996, the BJP, knowing that it did not have numerical strength, still chose to form its thirteen-day government in order to present its agenda and demonstrate its secular credentials by appointing a Muslim and a low-caste Hindu as ministers in the cabinet. It is worth noting that the public at large was not perturbed by the BJP agenda; more importantly, it came to view the BJP as a victim, hounded out of office by a disparate opposition united only in its desire to get rid of the BJP. In a public opinion poll carried out at the time, an "enormous sympathy wave for the BJP . . . [and] a phenomenal support for its leader Atal Bihari Vajpayee" was reported. And in answer to the question, "Is the BJP a communal body?" 56 percent of the respondents answered no; only 33 percent said yes.[31] This view was strengthened in 1998, by which time the BJP had taken another important step: it sought allies from among a disparate group of parties representing various parochial interests. The BJP's most convincing and persuasive shift of policy came in 1999 when it put aside the more obviously contentious elements in its agenda and formed the National Democratic Alliance, which included a host of so-called secular parties. The nation responded by giving the BJP-led NDA a five-year mandate to rule the country.

The basic question whether the BJP is a religious party still needs to be addressed. According to the eminent political scientist Paul Brass, whatever the BJP's rhetoric,

> It's mistaken to consider the BJP a "fundamentalist" religious party. Hindu religious beliefs and symbols serve the BJP as a focus for creating a national identity, but the party's goals are secular: to transform India into a modern, industrial, military power with a united nation and a disciplined work force. The party favors the dismantling of India's public sector industries and bureaucratic controls and the transformation of the economy into one based on the market and private enterprise. Its second rank of leaders comes from the most modern sectors of society and the economy.[32]

Hinduism, as we have emphasized in this work, is not a religion in the recognized sense of the term; it is not revealed, it has no one religious book, no prophet, and no church. It is far more a *culture,* a culture of tolerance and universalism to which all Indians can belong. The BJP's initial image suffered because it had a relatively rigid agenda and was primarily a party of high castes and could be attacked for not being *inclusive*. The party has tried to modify that image by launching a drive to win over the lower castes and the minorities and by assiduously wooing smaller parties of various hues.

Though the doom-oriented political analysts have, so far, been proven wrong about the BJP, the danger still exists that the party, after Vajpayee leaves the helm, may give in to the fanaticism of the lunatic fringe elements and change its broadly liberal and consultative policies. Hopefully, that will not happen because many in the BJP have realized that, though the composite Indian culture does have Hindu roots, it would be a grave mistake to overlook the logic of Indian pluralism; the presence of a Hindu ethos does not in any way support the notion that India can be turned into some kind of a Hindu state. On the other hand, in the period of transition to modernity, the unique sense of secularism embedded in the Hindu ethos can safeguard Indian pluralism by protecting the core religion-oriented identities of the differing caste, tribal, and ethnic communities. As modern educational, social, and economic forces impact on the newly politicized backward castes and tribes, those identities will evolve, acquiring a shared *national identity* that will create the sought-after modern nation state. These backward sections of society, with local variations, can be expected to take the same path the upper-caste ruling elite has followed during the last fifty years: because of education, political participation, and economic opportunity, the elite dropped their traditional ritual status and roles to adopt a modern national outlook.

Since the nature of *secularism* has been an important theme of this book, it would be proper to conclude this brief discussion with Vajpayee's recent view on the subject:

> I would like to assert that we believe in the principle of *Sava Panth Samabhav*, equal respect for all faiths. This is the cornerstone of our view of secularism and the secular state. The state will protect all its citizens, irrespective of their caste, creed, gender or religion.[33]

To conclude, it can be said that Prime Minister Atal Bihari Vajpayee's BJP-centered NDA has made a good start, but the tasks that face the new government are daunting. The problems crying for attention—and they range from ineffective governance and corruption to massive poverty, illiteracy, and unemployment—are well recognized by both the NDA and the populace and need no repetition. The country has high expectations of the NDA, and the NDA has made many promises. How the future unfolds is a matter for conjecture, but one thing is sure: India is entering the twenty-first century as a dynamic, creative country with a palpable spirit of change in the air, a sense of confidence, and no shortage of intellectually gifted people who have the ability, given a supportive environment, to remake every aspect of the country. Perhaps V.S. Naipaul has expressed it best:

The idea of freedom has gone everywhere in India. Independence was worked for by people more or less at the top; the freedom it brought has worked its way down. People everywhere have ideas now of who they are and what they owe themselves. . . . The liberation of spirit that has come to India could not come as release alone. In India, with its layer below layer of distress and cruelty, it had to come as disturbance. It had to come as rage and revolt. India was now a country of a million little mutinies. . . . [Indians now had] a central will, a central intellect, a national idea. . . . What the mutinies were also helping to define was the strength of the general intellectual life, and the wholeness and humanism of the values to which all Indians now felt they could appeal.[34]

Notes

1. See Inderjit Badhwar, "Pitfalls and Promises," *India Today*, June 30, 1996, pp. 20–26.

2. *Asia 1998 Yearbook* (Hong Kong: Review Publishing Company, 1998), p. 120.

3. Iqbal Narain, "Amending the Indian Constitution: Some Macro Considerations," in S. C. Kashyap, ed., *Reforming the Constitution* (New Delhi: UBSPB, 1992), p. 359.

4. See Figure 1 in Lawrence Sáez, "India's Economic Liberalization, Interjurisdictional Competition and Development," *Contemporary South Asia*, vol. 8, no. 3, November 1999, p. 325.

5. For Sitaram Kesri's letter to the president of India withdrawing support from the United Front Government, see http://www.rediff.com/news/mar/30cong4.htm.

6. See "'I Will Be a Decisive Prime Minister: Bajpai,'" *India Today*, December 29, 1997.

7. For further details, based on Deutsche Bank and JP Morgan assessments, see George Mathew, "At Last Spring Is in the Air," *Indian Express*, July 26, 1999, p. 11. See also "The Bulls Return," *India Today*, May 14, 1999, p. 14.

8. "War or Peace in South Asia?" *Washington Post*, June 28, 1999, p. A20.

9. See interview with Laloo Prasad Yadav in *India Today*, October 5, 1998, p. 20.

10. See "Interview of the Week," in *The Indian Express*, July 25, 1999, p. 8.

11. See *The Indian Express*, February 7, 2000, p. 1.

12. See *Newsweek*, September 27, 1999, p. 37.

13. See Stanley A. Weiss, "Develop Separate Policies for India and Pakistan," *International Herald Tribune*, January 28, 2000.

14. "India, Japan Will Have Closer Defence Ties: Fernandes," The Times of India News Service, January 16, 2000.

15. Ashutosh Varshney, "The Self-Correcting Mechanism of Indian Democracy," *Seminar 425: India 1994*, January 1995, p. 38.

16. See *India Today*, June 30, 1996, p. 14.

17. "India Growing Smartly," *Newsweek*, September 27, 1999, p. 36.

18. See *India News*, April 1, 1996, p. 7.

19. See *Newsweek*, September 27, 1999, p. 37.

20. Weiss, "Develop Separate Policies for India and Pakistan."

21. William J. Everett, "Religion and Federal Republicanism: Cases from India's Struggle," *Journal of Church and State*, vol. 37 (1995): 22.

22. Atul Kohli, *Democracy and Discontent* (Cambridge: Cambridge University Press, 1990), p. 310.

23. T. N. Madan, "Secularism in Its Place," in T. N. Madan, ed., *Religion in India* (Delhi: Oxford University Press, 1991), p. 402.

24. W. Norman Brown, *The United States, India and Pakistan* (Cambridge: Harvard University Press, 1963), p. 104.

25. Ibid.

26. Inder Malhotra, *Indira Gandhi: A Personal and Political Biography* (London: Hodder & Stoughton, 1989), p. 217.

27. Ibid, p. 231.

28. K. Chakravarty, "Toward a Genesis of the Recent Upsurge in Communalism," *Communalism in India: Challenge and Response* (New Delhi: Manohar, 1994), p. 17.

29. Saeed Naqvi, "Why Vajpayee Occupied the Middle Ground: Doing a Congress on the BJP," *The Indian Express*, August 13, 1999, p. 8.

30. Sultan Shahin, "Muslim Politics: Beyond the Secular-Communal Divide," *The Times of India*, August 25, 1999, p. 14.

31. See *India Today*, June 30, 1996, pp. 30–31.

32. Paul R. Brass, *The Politics of India Since Independence*, (Cambridge: Cambridge University Press, 1994), p. 88.

33. *Newsweek*, October 18, 1999, p. 17.

34. V.S. Naipaul, *India: A Million Mutinies Now* (New York: Viking Penguin, 1991), pp. 517–518.

Index

Ranbir Vohra was born in pre-partition Punjab and grew up in a political environment. His maternal grandfather was a well-known member of the Indian National Congress, who spent years in jail for his involvement in Mahatma Gandhi's pacifist freedom movement. One of his uncles was a socialist revolutionary hero who, at the age of twenty-four, was hanged by the British in the infamous Punjab Conspiracy Case in 1931. When India was partitioned in 1947, Mr. Vohra's family was forced to flee their home in Lahore and seek refuge in India.

After graduating in 1946 from Government College in Lahore, Mr. Vohra joined the government-run All India Radio (AIR) as a program officer. In 1956, the Indian government sent him to study at Beijing University; on his return in 1959, he took charge of the Chinese Broadcasting Unit of AIR. During his eighteen years with AIR, Mr. Vohra was in a unique position to observe first-hand the reshaping of the Indian polity, and his stay in China helped to sharpen his understanding of the reasons why India's path to modernization would always be different from that of China. Mr. Vohra left AIR in 1964 to enter Harvard Graduate School, where he received his Ph.D. in East Asian Studies in 1969.

From 1969 to 1997 Mr. Vohra taught a variety of courses dealing with this history and politics of China, Japan, and India at a number of institutions of higher learning in the United States, including Harvard University. He is currently Charles A. Dana Professor of Political Science (Emeritus) at Trinity College in Hartford, Connecticut. Mr. Vohra has published widely and is the author of *Lao She and the Chinese Revolution* (1974), *China's Path to Modernization* (3rd ed., 1999), *China: The Search for Social Justice and Democracy* (1991), and *China and India: Two Paths to Modernization* (forthcoming).